Rugby League Back o' t'
The history of Sharlston Rovers

Sharlston Rovers 1945-46: Back row: J. Robinson, W. Wood, H. Booth, G. Green, G. Lingard, J. Dooler, D. Bradley, H. Cleveley, T. Chalkley; Front row: P. Golding, L. Bailey, A. Cardall, W. Booth, H. Dooler, B. Lingard, F. Dooler, D. Chalkley, D. Ward; front: M. Scott, E. Hudson.

Graham Chalkley

LONDON LEAGUE PUBLICATIONS Ltd

Rugby League Back o' t' wall
The history of Sharlston Rovers ARLFC

© Copyright Graham Chalkley
Forewords © Neil Fox and Peter Fox. Preface © David Hobbs, Introduction © Maurice Oldroyd.

The moral right of Graham Chalkley to be identified as the author has been asserted.

Cover design © Stephen McCarthy. Photographs © the photographer or contributor of the photograph. No copyright has been intentionally infringed.

Front cover photo: The 2005 Sharlston Rovers players celebrate winning the Yorkshire Cup (photo: Alan Grimshaw); Jonty Parkin and Carl Dooler (with cap) (photos: courtesy Robert Gate). Back cover: Top: The 1923-24 Sharlston Rovers team: (players) Back: E. Smith, C. Stevenson, G. Green, J. Dooler, E. Cowey, W. Shaw, S. Handley; Middle: P. Gill, H. Goodfellow, W. Howcroft, E. Hepworth (captain), J. Allen, M. Jarvis, R. Dexter; Front: R. Cowey, F. Patrick, R. Cowey (mascot), L. Nixon, W. Chalkley.
Bottom: The Fox brothers in 1966 when they were all playing for Wakefield Trinity (photo: Photo Makeovers).

This book is copyright under the Berne Convention. All rights are reserved. It is sold subject to the condition that it shall not, by way of trade or otherwise, be lent, resold, hired out or otherwise circulated without the publisher's prior consent in any form of binding or cover other than that in which it is published and without a similar condition being imposed on the subsequent purchaser.

A CIP catalogue record for this book is available from the British Library.

First published in Great Britain in November 2006 by:
London League Publications Ltd, P.O. Box 10441, London E14 8WR

ISBN (10):	1-903659-28-0
ISBN: (13)	978-1903659-28-1
Cover design by:	Stephen McCarthy Graphic Design
	46, Clarence Road, London N15 5BB
Editorial & Layout:	Peter Lush
Printed and bound by:	CPI Antony Rowe
	Eastbourne, Great Britain

Foreword

Two of the most distinguished people from Sharlston involved in rugby league have written forewords for this book.

I was delighted when Graham asked me to write the foreword to his history of Sharlston Rovers Football Club. It is one of the oldest amateur clubs in the country, is steeped in rugby league history and down the years has produced players of exceptional ability and is a well known breeding ground for good rugby players.

I was born in Sharlston - and proud of it - in 1939 just across the road from the Back o' t' wall ground and my first recollection of rugby was as a six year old watching my father, Tom, who was captain of the Rovers, in a match that really put them on the map. It was against professional club Workington Town in the first round first leg of the Rugby League Challenge Cup and the Rovers gained a sensational 12-7 victory. It didn't matter that they went to Workington, lost the second leg 16-2 and were out of the cup on aggregate. They had their moment of glory and it would be talked about for years to come. I can't say I remember much about the game - I was only six - but I was there.

In those days Sharlston was a close knit mining community and the pit dominated their lives. Rugby was its life blood and they talked of nothing else. Jonty Parkin and Herbert Goodfellow, who had a big influence on my career, worked at the pit as did many others, too numerous to mention here, who went on the find fame on the rugby field.

I count myself lucky to have been born into a rugby family for my mother, a Sharlston girl born and bred, was also a staunch supporter, her father played for Normanton and brother for Sharlston. All the Fox boys attended the local council school and it was there that I was given every encouragement to play rugby by the sports master, later headmaster, Joby Musgrave and his wife Betty, who gave up a lot of her time to look after the boys. They put me on the first rung of the ladder in a career which brought me enormous enjoyment and every honour in the game. There are only two regrets in my career, not playing for Sharlston Rovers - I signed for Trinity at 16½ - and missing the chance to go to Australia to play for Parramatta.

I have fond memories of the Back o' t' wall ground. I trained there most nights with Peter and Don practicing kicking and catching and it was a good grounding for me.

I still keep in touch with Rovers, reading the match reports and it's good to see that the club is booming and playing a high standard of rugby.

Graham has had a huge task researching the club's history and I think every rugby league enthusiast will enjoy reading it. My father used to talk to me a lot about Rovers and it will be a pleasure to rekindle those memories.

I have a lot to thank the village of Sharlston for and I wish the club the best of luck for the future.

Neil Fox MBE

Neil Fox won every honour in the game, including being a member of the Rugby League Hall of Fame, and is the game's world record points scorer.

I was born at Sharlston in 1933 at Westfield Terrace, which was demolished many years ago, and attended the local council junior school where I was first introduced to rugby league. My father made me my first pair of rugby boots from an old pair of boots, stuck on another sole and knocked in some studs.

I remember as a lad the 1946 Workington Town cup tie at Sharlston when my father was captain. I was on the touchline, inside the ropes, when Billy Ivison was injured and went to sit on the Workington bench. He sent me to Ramsden's shop for a packet of 10 Capstan cigarettes. Billy became a brilliant loose-forward and we often talked about that Sharlston cup tie in later years. In those days we used to sit on the wall waiting for a taxi to turn up at Herbert Goodfellow's house. If he came out we knew he was playing for Trinity and used to walk to Belle Vue to watch him. He was the best uncapped player I have ever seen.

At 15 years of age in 1948 I represented Yorkshire in the first schoolboy county match after the War, against Lancashire and scored the only Yorkshire try in a 24-3 defeat.

My first introduction into the Sharlston Rovers first team came in the same year, 1948, and I played in the second-row alongside George Green for a few games. Playing for Sharlston in the late 1940s and early 1950s was tough and very hard as the Rovers had a reputation to uphold and they had good players. My first regular position was full-back but I later moved to loose-forward. I was very proud every time I wore the blue and white Sharlston jersey.

In October 1952 I signed professional forms for Featherstone Rovers from the famous Sharlston Rovers. The hard times of playing for Sharlston on a strange shaped field stood me in good stead for my professional career. Sharlston is where I learned my rugby. What a fantastic rugby village. I am still very interested in the progress of Sharlston Rovers because of their reputation over the years and I would go as far as to say that three of the best scrum-halves in the world have been Sharlston born lads: Jonty Parkin, Herbert Goodfellow and my brother Don. Can any other village boast that?

I was also born into coaching but that's another story. Enjoy reading the book and the best of luck to the club for the future.

Peter Fox

Peter Fox played for Featherstone Rovers, Batley, Hull Kingston Rovers and Wakefield Trinity but it was his coaching skills at the highest level that earned him lasting fame. At various times he was in charge of Yorkshire, England and Great Britain and at club level Featherstone Rovers, Bradford Northern, Bramley, Leeds and Wakefield Trinity.
Photo: Peter in 1948 when selected for Yorkshire.

Preface

How do you create a talking point within a small community? Easy, just write a book about the history of its amateur rugby league club.

On opening this book, there will be an almost overwhelming temptation to flick to the pages that cover your particular era, however, when you decide to relent and turn back to the very beginning, you will quickly start to uncover the true meaning of community life and become immersed in the spirit that was common amongst all mining villages.

Reading about such a close community should not leave you surprised when suddenly you come across a familiar name; surely that can't be my Grandfather and is that my uncle Albert? You will then embark on a fascinating journey through the years at Sharlston Rovers and will be amazed at its content, bringing back to you so many memories of people that you may have played rugby with, or grew up with in the community and if you were a supporter, all your favourite players are there.

You may also be interested to find out how many players went on to join professional clubs. Whilst the mining communities supplied their fair share of players to the professional ranks, it's fair to say that Sharlston per head of population would be up there with the best. I came through a similar system down the road at Featherstone and remember watching games at Back o' t' wall with my dad and listening to the banter between the supporters of each team.

Credit must be given to Graham, he has truly left no stone unturned in order to deliver such a factual encounter, of each year, through the ages and thanks to his determination and dedication to Sharlston Rovers, has created a most compelling read for all. To collate such a wealth of material is testimony to him. Whether you enjoy rugby league or not, it cannot be denied that it has played a dramatic part in the life and times of Sharlston and one man's passion for his club and community has brought a lasting memory to everyone's fingertips.

David Hobbs

David Hobbs played for Featherstone Rovers, Oldham, Bradford Northern and Wakefield Trinity. He won the Lance Todd Trophy in 1983 when Featherstone beat Hull 14-12 in the Challenge Cup Final. He won 12 Great Britain caps, and was a Lions tourist in 1984. He also played for England and Yorkshire. He was Wakefield Trinity's coach from 1994 to 1995, and is currently coach at Featherstone Rovers.
Photo: David Hobbs in 2006 at Featherstone (David Williams - rlphotos.com)

Introduction

I was delighted when I was invited to write a contribution to Graham Chalkley's history of Sharlston Rovers. Sharlston is a former mining village with a population of about 2,500 which makes nearby neighbours Featherstone look like a major metropolis and Wakefield the capital of the universe.

What a boost it will give to every amateur club to see the story of Sharlston published and what an example that story gives to the rugby league game and to the sporting world as a whole. Everyone should be grateful to Graham for his diligent, in-depth research during the last five years. However, it was in the local pub that a couple of old codgers – Graham's terminology, not mine – gave him the original idea and impetus.

I am sure that much will be made in the book of Sharlston's distinguished history, with three Lance Todd winners, Neil Fox, Don Fox and Carl Dooler, originating from the village and even more impressively, two members of the Rugby League Hall of Fame in local boys Neil Fox and Jonty Parkin. All amateur players aspire to play for their teams against professionals in the game's oldest competition, the Rugby League Challenge Cup. Few ever finish on the winning side but Sharlston have performed this giant-killing act twice – in 1946 beating Workington Town 12-7 in a first round, first leg tie and repeating the feat in 2004, when they beat Dewsbury 30-28.

Amateur rugby league has always been a passionate, community-based sport with great rivalries between clubs. Rovers epitomise all that is best about amateur rugby. Indeed government policy via Sport England over recent years has based its strategy on the fundamental principles of encouraging community amateur sports clubs (CASCs), which are the bedrock of all grass roots sport in England. Such organisations as Sharlston Rovers depend almost entirely on the input of volunteers, a point emphasised by Sebastian Coe in his preamble to clinching the 2012 Olympics for Britain.

In the dim and distant past as an amateur scrum-half, I played for Moldgreen and Underbank Rangers. I never, to the best of my recollection, ever played against Sharlston. However, my family's own club Elland has in recent years had many highly competitive and exciting games against Rovers and, dare I say it, a great bond has been forged between the clubs. One of my proudest days might have been one of Sharlston's darkest, when Elland beat Rovers in the Yorkshire Cup final of 2001 at Headingley. Adam, my son, another scrum-half, scored the winning try. Indeed, it was an emotional occasion as my wife Mary, a stalwart worker at the club, had died suddenly just weeks before the final and the members at Elland termed it "Mary's Final" and the lads duly delivered the goods against an outstanding Sharlston team. Where I live some people believe that Sharlston have moved into the Pennine League just to get their own back. The league games between these two regional giants are matches to be savoured.

My friend Geoff Lofthouse, Lord Lofthouse of Pontefract, is another life-long amateur enthusiast. Geoff, Chair of the All Party Parliamentary Rugby League Group at Westminster, as well as being President of BARLA, often happily relates to me his pleasure in playing for Willow Park against the Rovers at Back o' t' wall.

Sharlston has a record that compares well with any amateur club of any sport but it is the future that now counts and I have no doubt that Sharlston will continue to set an example to all and will be among the sport's pace-makers for many years to come.

Maurice Oldroyd
Maurice Oldroyd was one of the founders of BARLA, and became its chief executive and then chairman. He has given a lifetime's service to amateur rugby league.

About the author

Graham Chalkley is Sharlston born and proud of it. Like most of the lads from this rugby mad village he was brought up with the oval ball with one goal in mind, to play for t' Rovers. In 1966 he followed the Chalkley tradition - father, brother and countless relatives have played for the club - and pulled on a Rovers jersey and quickly made his mark in the forwards. He played for the Wakefield District team and soon caught the eye of the Yorkshire selectors, playing several times for the County before receiving the highest honour for an amateur player when he was selected to play for his country against France at Bordeaux in 1969. My career at Sharlston spanned the same period as Graham's, we had played together for the Wakefield District and County teams and when he was selected for his country again in 1970 against France at Salford, I joined him in the England pack. It was a proud moment for us.

He had trials with Wakefield Trinity, but in 1970 followed Sharlston legend Don Fox to Batley and began his professional career. Graham will tell you that the pinnacle of his career was playing alongside Don Fox whom he describes as "an amazing player and a wonderful man off the field." In 1973 he left the Gallant Youths and joined rivals Dewsbury, playing in a good side with players like Nigel Stephenson, Mike 'Stevo' Stephenson, John and Alan Bates, Alan Agar and Jeff Grayson. He ended his professional career there in 1976 and had a season with Sharlston in 1977 before retiring.

I would like to pay tribute to Graham as a player and a friend. About 15 years ago I was asked to pick a team of Sharlston Rovers all-time greats that I had played with and seen. Graham is one of three players from that team who would be in my present day Sharlston greats. Without doubt he is the best player I have ever played with.

I am a few years older than Graham but I still look up to him as a great friend and he is my rugby hero. He is now a Rovers committee man, popular and respected by players and supporters alike.

There is no more passionate supporter of Sharlston Rovers than Graham Chalkley and it is his love for the club that the idea for this book was born. It has taken him five years to research and he says it has been a long but enjoyable journey. It is a book that will appeal to all ages and will bring back a flood of memories to everyone who has followed the club. Long may Sharlston Rovers prosper.

Billy Wood

Photo: Graham Chalkley (Peter Lush)

Acknowledgements and thanks

Most of the information in this book has come from studying the files of the *Wakefield Express* at the Local Studies Department, Balne Lane Libraries, Wakefield, and I would like to extend my thanks and appreciation to the Express and to the staff at Balne Lane for their help at all times. Photographs used are courtesy of The *Wakefield Express*, David Williams and Sig Kasatkin of rlphotos.com, Robert Gate, Alan Grimshaw, Alpha Photography and Peter Lush.

I must also thank many individuals who have contributed to the compilation of this book and without their help it would not have been possible. These include my friend, Malcolm Abbott, who without his advice and help it would have taken me a lot longer to complete; also Mrs Lingard, Mr and Mrs Goldie, Ralph and Joan Hobbs, Harold and Betty Ward, Doug Greaves, Jimmy Goodfellow, Mrs R. Fisher, Eddie Dyson, Doreen Lockwood, Rose Foley, Jack Goodfellow, Wick and Elsie Riley, Billy Wood, Trevor Bailey, Terry and Denise Mullaney, Doreen Green, Gilbert Mosley, Mr and Mrs Harper, Mrs B. Dooler, Ron Ramsden, Denis Chalkley, Mrs E. Baxter, Joyce Schofield, Zoe Palmer, Bill Paver, David Siddans, David Hobbs, Paul Coventry and Jayne Chalkley. They were only too pleased to share their memories with me. If there is anyone I have forgotten to mention please accept my apologies and thanks.

A special thank you is due to Neil Fox, Peter Fox, Maurice Oldroyd, Joe Mullaney, Tommy Smales, Vaughan Thomas, Keith Bridges and Ivor Lingard for their valued contributions.

I would also like to thank all my family and friends who share my love for Sharlston and in particular my brother, Barry, who read the manuscript and supported me all the way. Finally I owe a huge debt of gratitude to my wife Linda - my rock - for her wonderful support and patience during the five years of writing this book.

Thanks as well to Peter Lush of London League Publications Ltd for his editorial and layout work and with Dave Farrar for agreeing to publish the book, to Steve McCarthy for designing the cover and the staff of Biddles Ltd for printing the book.

Graham Chalkley
Sharlston, September 2006

Photographs

Some of the photographs used in this book are quite old, or were not taken in good light. Therefore they are not always as good a quality as we would like. However, we felt that it was better to use them so that the Sharlston Rovers story could be told as fully as possible. This does not imply any criticism of any photographer.

Left: Sharlston's primary school where many famous players first played rugby league.
Right: The Sharlston, formerly The Sharlston Hotel – next to the club's ground.
(Photos: Peter Lush)

Contents

1. The 1800s - rugby union — 1
2. Into the Northern Union — 11
3. The 1920s - The Yorkshire Senior Competition — 27
4. The 1930s - The All Blacks — 45
5. The 1940s - Workington Town — 63
6. The 1950s - The Yorkshire Cup — 75
7. The 1960s - Revival — 93
8. The 1970s - Consolidation — 105
9. The 1980s - Progress and Parramatta — 125
10. The 1990s - The Rovers return — 147
11. Into the new Millennium — 175

Appendices:

1. Professional players from Sharlston — 217
2. Club honours — 219

Sharlston Colliery 1865 – 1993
In memory of the mineworkers who worked at the colliery
(Photo: Peter Lush)

Wembley Memories

Three Lance Todd trophy winners from Sharlston: Neil Fox (1962), Carl Dooler (1967) and Don Fox (1968).

Steven Mullaney leads out the Wakefield under-11 team at Wembley in 1986. Steven was killed in a car accident in 1987, and the trophy the under-11 teams play for at the Challenge Cup Final was named after him. In 2006, the 20th anniversary of his Wembley appearance, his sister Lauren presented the trophy at the final at Twickenham and the BBC showed his winning try from the 1986 match.

1. The 1800s – rugby union

Sharlston is an old mining village, dating back certainly to the fourteenth century or even earlier. A monk at the nearby Nostell Priory recorded digging for coal in the area, and Sharlston is mentioned in the Coroners' Rolls of 1342. The *Oxford Dictionary of British Place Names* dates the village from 1180.

Sharlston was mainly agricultural until the 1860s, and there are still five local farms today. In the middle ages most homes were on The Green, by Sharlston Hall. Maybe, as in other towns and villages, the villagers played folk football on holidays and festivals. In 1837 there were 243 residents. The Earl of Westmorland owned most of the land and was Lord of the Manor.

A new colliery was built in 1865. From this date there was a large influx of people looking for jobs down in the mine and the district was transformed from quiet country life to the hustle and bustle of industry. In 1871 the population was 800, 10 years later it had grown to 2,000. By 1888, there were three schools, with the colliery one having 600 students. In 1929, Sharlston became a Parish. St Luke's Church opened in 1887.

The colliery ceased production in 1993, and was the last working mine in the Wakefield area. 535 jobs were lost, despite it being one of the most profitable pits in Yorkshire, producing a million tonnes of coal a year. The mine had employed over 2,000 miners at its peak. In the 1984-85 miners strike, 1,000 miners were on strike in the village, and most stayed out for the full 12 months of the strike.

The village is situated between the rugby league strongholds of Wakefield, Castleford and Featherstone in West Yorkshire. Sharlston Parish is made up of three villages; Old Sharlston, New Sharlston and Sharlston Common. The population in 2001 was 2,756.

Rugby has been played on the same piece of land at Sharlston for well over 100 years. In the late 1880s it was described in an old map of the village as Jubilee Recreation Ground, but was famously (or infamously!) known for miles around as Back o' t' wall. It was a curiously shaped field and the local lads were cheered on by their sometimes aggressive supporters to "get ower t' nob", meaning the high ground in the centre of the field. It was rough land, mainly stubble and bore no resemblance to the ground and facilities the club enjoys nowadays. Alas, the wall is no longer there, but will be long remembered by the villagers.

The ground is now enclosed, with a modern clubhouse, and is still home to Sharlston Rovers ARLFC. It is now called The Councillor G. H. Green Memorial Playing Fields after a man who, apart from his contribution to village life as a councillor and NUM activist, played a prominent part as a young forward in February 1946 in the club's famous 12-7 victory over professional club Workington Town in the first round, first leg of the Rugby League Challenge Cup. This was a memorable triumph and historic occasion for the club and village. Workington Town won the second leg in Cumberland and progressed through to Round Two.

George Green subsequently signed for Halifax RLFC along with the team's full-back Denis Chalkley. Denis went on to play for Halifax against Bradford Northern in the Challenge Cup Final at Wembley in 1949.

The actual date and circumstances of the birth of the Sharlston club are lost in the midst of time and it will never be known when rugby was first played in the village, despite long and careful search through newspapers from the 1870s. As well as the rugby club, there was a literary institute in 1873, and a cricket club in 1874, both supported by the colliery owners.

In 1939 Mr W. H. Ward, the club secretary said that "rugby football at Sharlston covered a period of 65 years", from 1874. An old villager, Joe Mosley supported this also in 1939 when he said he had been connected with rugby in Sharlston as a player, official and bag carrier for over 60 years. Rugby was being played in surrounding villages in the 1870s - clubs were formed at Ackworth in 1875 and Normanton four years later, so it is not unreasonable to assume that Sharlston did have a team in this period though they were 'small fry' compared to clubs such as Wakefield Trinity.

There is no doubt that Sharlston is one of the oldest rugby clubs in existence and early records documented both fierce and controversial encounters with opposing teams, which led eventually to Sharlston being banned sine-die from rugby union.

The Rugby Football Union had been formed in 1871, and as organised rugby spread to the industrial north, West Yorkshire was one of the key areas for the code. Yorkshire played Lancashire in 1870, and soon a Yorkshire County Committee was formed. Clubs were developing from the mid 1860s in the major cities, such as Hull, Bradford and Leeds. Wakefield Trinity were formed in 1873.

Early matches

The first report of a Sharlston match in the *Wakefield Express* was in October 1881. Outwood won easily at Sharlston, scoring three goals, eight tries and 15 minor points to nil. In December 1881 Sharlston played Wakefield Christ Church at home. Again, the visitors won easily by two goals, five tries and 14 minor points to nil. Matches in these days were 'friendlies' as there were no league competitions at this time.

The next appearance of the Sharlston club in the local press is in January 1885. This time Sharlston won, beating Featherstone, with two goals, three tries and six minor points to nil. The next month, it was reported that Old Sharlston played Featherstone and Purston United's second team at Featherstone, scoring two goals, five tries and 10 minor points to one minor point.

In October 1885 Warmfield were hosts to Sharlston Common United. Warmfield scored two tries, from A. Auty and C. Paver, six minor points to one minor point by the Sharlston side. The same month, Sharlston played Featherstone & Purston's second team again, winning at home by one goal, by G. Smith from a free kick, a try by W. Hunter and six minor points to two minor points.

In November, Sharlston travelled to play Horbury Zingari's second team, narrowly winning by a try from J. Rudge and one minor point to two minor points. Sharlston's second team played Featherstone Trinity at home, winning by two tries from Allen and Baddeley and three minor points to five minor points.

The next month, Sharlston visited Glasshoughton Colliery with A. Lamb scoring a try for the visitors, to three minor points by the Colliery. Warmfield & Sharlston United played Warmfield's second team at Normanton. A. Anson kicked a goal for the United side, who also scored one minor point to two minor points by Warmfield. Normanton Shamrocks played New Sharlston in Sharlston. Anson kicked two goals for the home side, who also scored a try and four minors to a goal and two minors for the visitors.

There were various teams based around Sharlston at this time. The next reports are from 1887. In October, Sharlston & Warmfield United played Normanton St John's at Normanton Common. United won with a try by Nicholson and three minors to one minor.

In December 1887, New Sharlston travelled to Wakefield to play Wakefield St Johns' second team. Sharlston scored a goal, dropped by Anson, and two minors to St Johns' five minors. Later that month, Streethouse beat the same Sharlston side at Sharlston with a try from A. Faulkner and five minors to three minors. Sharlston visited Normanton United, narrowly losing through Davies's try. Both sides scored three minors.

Streethouse won again at Sharlston, scoring a try by Blackburn and three minors, and kept New Sharlston scoreless. In the new year, Normanton Parish Church visited Sharlston and lost to a goal dropped by Anson, and a try from C. Bettney and two minors to one. In March 1888, Lee Brigg Rovers came to Sharlston and went home defeated by two tries and four minors to a try and a minor.

The 1890s

The next report of rugby in Sharlston is from October 1891. By now rugby union in Yorkshire was more organised, with a league competition for senior clubs, and the Yorkshire Cup competition a regular highlight.

Sharlston visited Kinsley and won 5-2. Sharlston scored a goal from a try by A. Ramsden to Kinsley's try. The *Wakefield Express* reported that Ramsden played well. The club had "hopeful" prospects and was run by Mr H. S. L. Wilson as president, Reverend A. Middleton as vice-president and others. The captain was A. Ward and the vice-captain H. Earnshaw. The committee's "energetic" secretary was Mr W. E. Sparham.

Also in October, Sharlston won "capitally" against Outwood Church's second team. Ramsden scored the only major, which was "the result of a fine bit of play". Sharlston showed marked improvement and the local paper expected to see them "in higher company" as they were "holding their own" at a lower level. Later that month, Heath visited Sharlston. This match resulted in an easy win for the homesters. Sharlston had a goal dropped by G. Ward and a try by A. Ward, resulting in a 6-0 victory.

In November, Sharlston played Normanton St John's 'A' team at home. Sharlston's backs were described as "a very capable set". Ward, the captain, was "in fine form", scored a try and "had a hand in pretty nearly every other point scored. He kicked two goals from places and passed so accurately that his three-quarters dropped another couple." Lackenby also showed "grand football," running threequarters of the length of the ground to score under the posts. Sharlston won by four goals, one try and five minors to St John's three minors. Chalkley and G. Ward dropped one goal each and A. Ward converted two goals. The tries came from Newsome, Lackenby and A. Ward.

In February 1892, Sharlston easily defeated Ackworth, making them touch down by no fewer than 12 times. The Earnshaw brothers and W. Spiers "were always to the front with grand footwork and the backs played an excellent game, especially A. Ward, who dropped a goal, kicked one from a fair catch and obtained a try." Newsome and Ramsden also scored tries, and Sharlston won with two goals, three tries and 12 minors. Ackworth failed to score.

The next month, Sharlston beat the visiting Thornes United in "a very hard struggle". The visitors were beaten in the forwards, and were unable to stop the rushes of Smith and Earnshaw. A. Ward and Taylor played well at half-back, and A. Ramsden stood out at centre three-quarter. W. Newsome scored a try which A. Ward converted. A. Ramsden also scored. The final result was Sharlston one goal, one try and five minors. The visitors did not score.

1892-93

In September 1892, it was reported that the Sharlston Football Club had a "capital" list of fixtures arranged by their secretary, Mr W. E. Sparham. Mr Wilson was still president.

The club was looking forward to a successful season.

The first reported match was against Kinsley, from Hemsworth. Sharlston won through good back play, notably by Taylor, Ward and Ramsden, "whose passing was quite a feature." The forwards also played well.

The *Wakefield Express* was now speculating that "Sharlston Football Club will soon be providing some recruits for Wakefield Trinity or possibly some candidates for County honours". They easily beat Royston Trinity, mainly due to "the grand footwork of the forwards" with the backs playing a safe game. Sharlston lost A. Ward, one of their half-backs, early in the first half but the remaining XIV won by two goals and three tries to one try. Smith, with two, Howell, Earnshaw and Ramsden got the tries and W. Taylor converted two of them.

The team's success continued in October. Newmillerdam were beaten with Sharlston scoring two goals and four tries, and kept their opponents scoreless. Ramsden, Ward, Spiers and Lackenby scored tries, one of which was converted by Ward. Ramsden also dropped a goal. Royston also failed to score a point against Sharlston, losing by three tries and four goals to nil. Howell, Ward and Ramsden obtained the tries, Ward kicked the goals. Ramsden also dropped a goal.

On Feast Monday (St Luke's Day – the nearest Monday to 18 October), Sharlston easily defeated Streethouse. Sharlston's forwards "were in grand form, their dribbling being a marvel to witness. The halves too played a grand game while the three quarters fairly nonplussed those of their opponents." Ward, Nicholson and Ramsden all played well for Sharlston, who lost one of their best forwards early in the second half and had to play with XIV men to the finish. The local paper said that "Sharlston are now taking a lot of beating". Sharlston won by a try and a goal to nil, Nicholson scoring the try and Ward converting. H. Hayley was the referee.

1893-94

The next reports of Sharlston's matches came in October 1893, with Sharlston United playing a fixture at Altofts Parish Church. Pickin kicked off for Altofts, the visitors replying back to Sykes who dropped at goal, the United full-back kicking dead. After the drop out Altofts' A. Chell and L. Brown dribbled "in fine style" to the line and Brown scored but failed to convert a goal. At half time, Altofts led 3-0. Play then was very even with only two minors scored in 25 minutes. The game ended in a 3-0 win for Altofts.

In November, Sharlston St Luke's visited Eastmoor in the second round of the Charlesworth Challenge Cup Competition, and lost 9-3. The home team played with a strong wind in the first half. Parkinson with a huge kick caused the visitors to be pressed until the Sharlston forwards, headed by Smith, rushed to the home team's 25. Morgan relieved but soon afterwards the visitors' forwards rushed over the line. Ward gained a try which was not converted. Then Morgan got possession and scored a try for Eastmoor, Parkinson missing the conversion. Eastmoor continued to press and after a pretty bout of passing by the home forwards, Parkinson ran over the line, but lost possession and Archer scored the try. Parkinson missed the conversion. Archer then scored his second try, Parkinson again missing with the kick. Eastmoor led 9-3 at half-time, and a scoreless second period saw Sharlston eliminated from the cup.

Then Sharlston visited Normanton White Rose in front of 500 spectators. The visitors were outplayed from beginning to end and lost 7-0. The club's development was shown in January 1894 when J. Lee and A. Earnshaw signed for Wakefield Trinity.

There was no competitive rugby for junior clubs in those days; clubs were left to arrange fixtures on a friendly basis. For the senior clubs, the Yorkshire Senior Competition had been set up in 1892, and soon the junior clubs wished to follow this example. In April 1894 Mr George Stubbs, Featherstone's secretary, sent a letter to the Yorkshire County Rugby Union committee: "I am instructed to lay before your committee a proposed competition in this district. We have already had two meetings and the general feelings are that unless something is done to stimulate the junior clubs they must die away altogether as almost every club is in debt."

Wakefield and District League

Thus the West Riding Competition was formed in 1894 but did not include Sharlston who did not have a team in 1894-5; they had their first taste of competitive rugby a season later, in 1895-6 when they joined the newly formed Wakefield and District League with fixtures against Half Acres Trinity (Castleford), Gawthorpe OB, Castleford United, Stanley St Peter's, West Ardsley, Bottomboat Trinity, Alverthorpe Church Youths, Normanton Rangers, Healey (Ossett), Calder Vale Rovers and Wrenthorpe St Anne's.

On 29 August 1895, 22 clubs from Yorkshire and Lancashire met at the George Hotel in Huddersfield and formed the Northern Union, breaking away from the Rugby Football Union. The Sharlston club, along with other junior clubs, stayed with the RFU.

Sharlston's first match - a 19-0 victory - was against Normanton Rangers on 21 September 1895. They could not have got off to a better start and the fine form was continued throughout the season with only two defeats from 20 league fixtures and they were crowned league champions.

In the Wakefield District Cup, Sharlston faced Castleford Half Acres Trinity. The final was replayed at Stanley following a dispute when the final was played on Easter Saturday at Normanton. Sharlston had the best of the game and won 9-0, scoring three tries. The tries came from D. Howell, A. Ward and T. Lackenby. The *Wakefield Express* reported that "Castleford acknowledged they were fairly beaten on Easter Saturday at Normanton but the game was replayed as stated above over a dispute. On Monday the Sharlston club drove round the district in a wagonette."

To celebrate, a concert was held in Old Sharlston, with the players having the medals presented to them in the Old Sharlston School. The presentation was made by Mrs Wilson, wife of Mr H. S. L. Wilson JP, of Crofton Hall. The local paper reported that she said she has been a spectator at several matches in which the football team of one of the public schools in the North of England had taken part and she had watched the game with great interest from a mother's point of view. On one occasion one of the players got his finger dislocated and another hurt his knee and to her football seemed to be a sort of miniature battle.

In 1896-97 Sharlston again won the Championship and as champions comfortably defeated a Rest of the League team in the traditional end of season fixture on a Tuesday afternoon at Sharlston. The teams were:

Sharlston: Taylor; Goodfellow, Ramsden, Ward (captain), Lackenby; Lunn, Spawforth; M. Wood, Earnshaw, Howell, Green, Froggatt, Dooler, Bailey, Allen.

The Rest: H. Carter (Normanton Rangers); Rev. W. P. Kingston (captain, Stanley St Peter's), J. Wilkinson (Wakefield St Michael's), J. Tilson (Normanton Rangers), A. Longley (Wakefield St Michael's), W. Tansley (Normanton Rangers) J. Garrity (Sharlston - as substitute); F. Smales, Rogers (Stanley St Peter's); H. Harrison, H. Hawthorne (both Normanton Rangers), J. W. Blayden, B. Wilkinson, E. Wroe and E. Puliston (all St Michael's).

Lofthouse, Carlton and Whitwood had been unable to send players and as

Bottomboat Trinity and Outwood Wanderers are suspended for non-payment of fines, their players were also not available for selection. The team was still a strong one. Sharlston were without G. Wood and Skitt, but Bailey and Allen were good replacements.

In the first half Sharlston played with the slope, but The Rest held their own. Close to half-time Goodfellow, took a pass from Ramsden near the half-way line, made a strong run and scored in the corner. Taylor missed the conversion, so at the interval Sharlston led 3-0.

The Rest expected that playing downhill they would gain the upper hand but were disappointed. Sharlston played with such determination that only twice were the visitors able to get past the half-way and then only briefly. They had to defend throughout and were completely overcome by the homesters. After 10 minutes Lackenby scored, Taylor converting. Goodfellow punted towards the line, and Carter, the visitor's full-back, missed the ball, Bailey scoring. Ward converted and Sharlston won 13-0. The *Wakefield Express* said that "They fully deserved their success and ought indeed to have run up a much larger score in the second half. The medals were not ready for presentation on Tuesday but they will be handed to the players at a concert which will be held shortly."

1897-98

The next season saw Sharlston competing in the Barnsley Beckett Competition, a small league of only nine teams: Sharlston, Purston, Kinsley, Thornhill Lees Trinity, Pontefract, Doncaster, Kippax, Knottingley and Carlton.

Kinsley, Purston and Sharlston were in contention for the title all season, which was not decided until Sharlston's last match victory against Thornhill Lees Trinity.

There was a good attendance at Purston in November when Sharlston were the visitors, Purston just getting home 6-5. In the first half Purston pressed almost continuously and Smales, from a pass by Jones, scored and the same player afterwards had another try disallowed. Some fine defensive work was done by Ward, Garrity and Taylor for Sharlston and at half-time Purston were leading 3-0. Sharlston started better after crossing over. Ward just missed with a drop at goal, but Blackburn, Jones and Bolton passed well, with Bolton scoring an unconverted try. Sharlston strove hard to break through the home defence and Garrity scored, Howell converting. In March Sharlston gained an easy victory against Methley, the home team winning 13-5, scoring from Green, Bramham, and Garrity with Bramham dropping a goal from a mark.

After the second try things were going so smoothly for Sharlston that for kicks at goal the players were saying "my kick next". Barrett, Howell and Bramham all played well.

The club was given permission to present extra medals to D. Taylor and H. Schofield who had helped to win the Barnsley Competition, subject to Taylor appearing before the County committee in respect to a charge made against him.

In March, Sharlston made their first appearance in the Yorkshire Challenge Cup, 'T' owd Tin Pot' as it was popularly called. It was a tough baptism against Alverthorpe who had just won the Yorkshire No 2 Competition.

The *Wakefield Express* reported that "All sorts and conditions of persons wended their way to Sharlston to witness the struggle between the team of that name and Alverthorpe... That one cannot put old heads on young shoulders was once more proved and the Alverthorpe men, or several of them – Tommy Harnell especially - were too old fashioned for the home team, who were not prepared for the tricks which Alverthorpe had up their sleeves."

The visitors' forwards were superior to Sharlston's, and Sharlston's backs had few chances. When they did get possession however they indulged in some "pretty passing" but the Alverthorpe threequarters marked them tightly.

Goodfellow, Sharlston's county threequarter, was injured early in the game. In the first half Bastow scored following confusion between two Sharlston players. Goodyear missed the goal. However, he then scored for the visitors, but again the conversion was missed. At half-time, Alverthorpe led 6-0. They continued to dominate and Scraton, intercepted a pass and scored under the posts. He kicked the goal. Near the end Sharlston scored a try, but missed the goal. Alverthorpe won 11-3. The *Wakefield Express* concluded that "Some of the scrimmages were warm ones and no doubt there would be many sore shins knocking about long before the match had run its course."

The season was a success, but was not without incident. In November J. Green was suspended until the end of the season for kicking a Kinsley player and faced another charge of striking the Kinsley touch judge. In January 1898 a Kippax touch judge was reported for striking a Sharlston player and was suspended for the rest of the season.

At the end of the season the Barnsley Beckett Competition disbanded and the following season, 1898-99, Sharlston joined the Yorkshire Rugby Union No. 2 Competition (Castleford Group), comprising Bottomboat Trinity, Knottingley, Doncaster, Sharlston, Fairburn, Brotherton, Kippax and Hemsworth.

Before the season opened they lost players to clubs in the Northern Union. Fred Goodfellow, Wood and Garrity signed for Holbeck and Ward and Taylor went to Featherstone. Nevertheless they had a good captain in Froggatt and a lot of promising recruits with ambitions to develop the club further.

In September before the league programme started they played a home friendly against Stanley and crossed their opponents' line on 14 occasions, winning 50-0. This was a club record. Burrows, Green, Chalkley, Froggatt and Southeran all played well. Hemsworth should have opened the season at Sharlston but didn't turn up and Mr A. A. Abbott, the Sharlston secretary, received as an excuse that "the conveyance was not to be got and that the defaulter would play instead on 18 February and pay 10 shillings towards the loss which will prevent litigation".

There was much interest in the game with Bottomboat Trinity in October as Bottomboat had not lost a match until then. On this occasion, however, they played a poor game and Sharlston won 20-0. The visitors were well beaten and all Sharlston's threequarters scored. Froggatt, the club captain dropped a penalty goal and scored a try. J. Doo1er got two tries and J. Green scored one. The Burrows brothers played well at half-back.

Early season end

But the 1898-99 season ended early for Shar1ston in regrettable circumstances. On Christmas Eve 1898, in the home game against Kippax, fighting broke out between the players, spectators joined in and ugly scenes followed. The Kippax club made a charge of 'rowdyism' against the Sharlston club. The Yorkshire Rugby Union investigated the game and their findings were reported as follows:

"Sharlston Club Suspended Sine Die"

The Yorkshire Rugby Union Committee investigated a charge of rowdyism by the Kippax Club against the Sharlston Club. Mr Bennett, secretary, and Mr Green, captain, represented the Kippax club and Sharlston were represented by Mr Kistell and Mr Gill.

The referee, Mr J. W. Roberts, was present. The Kippax representatives said that during the match at Sharlston on 24 December, about 10 minutes before the end of play, one of the Kippax players was kicked in the stomach by a Sharlston player. The referee intervened and a general melee ensued. Spectators came onto the field and joined in the fighting. The Kippax players had to be taken by the police from the field. Some could not get dressed and two had to run two miles to escape their assailants.

Mr Bennett claimed that the Sharlston players "played skittles" with the Kippax team and that spectators assisted them. One player, because of the treatment he received, had to remain in bed a week. The referee had to "take his hook" with the Kippax players. Mr Green said it was "a shameful do". The Sharlston men went for them with their fists and felled all they could reach. Sharlston played all right until they saw they were a beaten team.

For Sharlston, Mr Kistell admitted that the charge against his club was true and said he had nothing to say except that he wished to exempt D. Howell, H. Southeran, A. Abbott, L. Crossland, B. Bailey and S. and J. Burrows from complicity in the fray. These players had gathered round the referee to protect him. One of the players, whom he named, ought to be debarred from playing football altogether.

Mr Roberts, the referee, gave his version of the case and said there was nothing in the play to object to until the first kicking incident mentioned. He was about to take the man's name when the Sharlston men began fighting and the Kippax players hurried away, leaving the match unfinished. The Kippax players did not ask him before leaving the field. He was in no personal danger at all. Mr E. Gill, one of the Kippax players, said he was knocked insensible and a colleague shared the same fate.

Mr Kistell denied this player's statement, and said that some Sharlston players said they were simply "paying off old debts" as they had been badly treated at Kippax before.

The President said that the committee felt that it was the most disgraceful case they had ever had before them. They had decided to suspend the Sharlston club, ground and players *sine die* with the exception of Southeran. Howell and Abbott, who were suspended for the rest of the season.

The committee hoped that if a club was again formed at Sharlston it would be run in a proper spirit and that the players would protect their opponents and not assault them or look on quietly and see them assaulted as had been done by some of the players in this instance.

Mr Kistell said that he would have nothing further to do with them. A *Free Press* reporter spoke to Sharlston secretary. It seemed that bad feeling had existed between the two clubs following a match played between Kippax and Sharlston in 1897-98, when, it was alleged, a Sharlston player was both kicked by both a Kippax player and their touch judge.

The paper was also told by a Sharlston player that the referee approached A. Abbott for the name of a player which he refused to give on the grounds that he had spotted the wrong player. While they were talking the players on both sides had a proper "set to" which lasted for about a minute. The Kippax players then left the field quickly. The spectators did not enter the field but it is true that they struck some players as they left the field.

This player also said that Mr Bennett's assertion was wrong about the referee having to be guarded off the field, as that gentleman, along with Mr Abbott, were the last to leave. The police were not on the field but one was in the dressing room. The only bother in that room was between George Wood and Mr Bennett, when the latter had twitted Wood about one of the Kippax players not being present and saying that it was better for him that he (the absent player) was not there. Mr Wood then said that if he was off the field he was not out of Sharlston and then a fight followed. The *Wakefield Free Press* concluded that "With respect to the decision some of the Sharlston people expected the result while others are of the opinion that it a trifle too 'stiff'."

This suspension of the club ended their rugby union days but most of the clubs in the area were now going with the tide of joining the Northern Union and by 1900 there were very few local teams playing under the Rugby Football Union's control.

In those pioneer years it is impossible to name all those who wore a Sharlston jersey between 1880 and 1900, but they included: Abbott, Allen, Anson, Baddeley, Bailey, Barrett, Bramham, Bettney, S. & J. Burrows, W. & J. Chalkley, Crossland, J. Dooler, H. & A. Earnshaw, Ellis, Froggatt, Garrity, Goodfellow, Green, Hunter, Howell, Lamb, Lackenby, Lee, Lunn, Newsome, Nicholson, Ramsden, Riley, Rudge, Russell, Skitt, N. Smith, Spiers, Southeran, Spawforth, Schofield, Taylor, A. & G. Ward, Wood, M. Wildman, Willis and Woolley.

Sharlston's first star

Frederick Goodfellow was Sharlston's first rugby star and legend. He was an outstanding young player and a great honour was bestowed on the Sharlston Club when in 1897 at the age of 17 he was selected for the Yorkshire county side. He attracted many press reports for his play.

On 13 November 1897 Yorkshire played Northumberland in Newcastle: "F. Goodfellow (Sharlston) had very few chances to distinguish himself." The next week, the county played Lancashire at Dewsbury: "Goodfellow, the young man from Sharlston, gave a very satisfactory account of himself", and "...making a good opening for Goodfellow, the speedy Sharlston youth sprinted over and scored."

He played several times for Yorkshire in 1897 and 1898 and had he not turned professional and joined Holbeck in 1898, there were high hopes he would play for the England Rugby Union team. The *Wakefield & West Riding Herald* said in December 1897: "Supporters of football in the colliery village of Sharlston have a hero in F. Goodfellow, the promising county three-quarter. Indeed aspirations are so high that in the villagers' estimation it is thought he will soon be an international."

He was a fine threequarter and goal-kicker and later captained Dewsbury in 1906, playing for Yorkshire in his time there, after playing for Holbeck and Hull. At Holbeck in December 1901 he was suspended sine die by the Northern Union for breach of professional laws and was not reinstated until March 1903.

At the end of his professional days he returned to play for his village team - he also had spells with the Normanton club - and in 1920 Sharlston arranged a benefit match for him against a team captained by Billy Batten. He kept very fit and was still playing for Sharlston in the 1921-22 season when they were in the Yorkshire Senior Competition but he was injured against Selby in November 1921 and that was to be his last season. He was then 41 years old.

Fred died in 1925, without seeing his son, Herbert, become one of the greatest scrum-halves of the 1930s and 1940s. A product of the Sharlston Council School, he played for Yorkshire Schoolboys, but did not play any intermediate level rugby before he signed for Wakefield Trinity in 1932. He made his first team debut in 1933 aged just 16, and made the scrum-half berth his own for almost 20 years. His partnership with loose-forward Len Bratley was one of the most successful in the game. He finished his career with Oldham, having asked Trinity for a transfer in 1951. He made 434 appearances for

Trinity and a further 23 for Oldham. Many people feel that he never got the recognition he deserved. He played for Yorkshire five times, but only got one international cap, for England against Wales at Odsal in 1939. He was considered by many to be a certainty for the 1946 British Lions tour to Australia and New Zealand, but was overlooked.

Fred and Herbert Goodfellow

Left: Fred Goodfellow

Right: Herbert Goodfellow

Below: Sharlston Council School team 1930. Back: R. Cowie, Harry Speight, Harry Arnold, Arthur Whittaker; Middle: Tommy Clarke, Joe Margrave, Herbert Goodfellow, Stanley Carter, Ernest Westmorland; Front: Kirton, Albert Bailey.

2. Into the Northern Union

Following their suspension in 1899 from the Rugby Football Union, there is no record of Sharlston playing rugby in a league again until 1901-02 when they joined the Castleford & District League. They were then called Sharlston Rovers and this was their first season under Northern Union (later to become The Rugby Football League) control. Players suspended by the Rugby Football Union were reinstated by the Northern Union. It was a season of promise and they could take satisfaction from finishing in fourth place.

Castleford & District League 1901-2

	P	W	D	L	Pts
Half Acres Trinity	16	15	0	1	30
Bowers Allerton	16	13	0	3	26
Grovetown Juniors	16	10	0	6	20
Sharlston Rovers	16	7	2	7	16
Pontefract Clarence	16	6	0	10	12
Brotherton	16	6	0	10	12
Castleford Paddock Rangers	16	4	1	11	9
Streethouse	16	3	1	12	7
Lock Lane	16	3	0	13	6

When the league committee issued the final table, they said the following: "It will be seen from the above table that Half Acres Trinity FC have again won the medals, this being the third year in succession. In order to give some other team a chance it has been decided not to allow them to take part in next season's contest."

Sharlston also took part in the Wakefield Wellington Cup Competition (named after the Wellington Hotel in Kirkgate, Wakefield) defeating Whitwood Colliery and Normanton Nonconformists in the earlier rounds and Streethouse 8-0 in the semi-final at Horbury. The other semi-final between Methley and Lofthouse Gate went to a replay and in the course of a very rough game five players were sent off and the referee stopped the game 20 minutes before time. Mr L. Walton, the donor of the cup, without consulting the Committee decided to expel Lofthouse Gate from the competition for playing 'wrong men' and said publicly that if they had been in the final he would have withdrawn the cup altogether.

The final between Methley and Sharlston was played on the Castleford ground witnessed by about 3,000 keen spectators. The match was well contested with Methley ultimately running out winners 7-0. Mr T. Atkinson of the Allerton Bywater club presented the cup and said "the game had been a very good one and although defeated the Sharlston team had certainly not been disgraced (hear! hear!) and he hoped they would have better luck next time".

Although Methley won and were presented with the cup, for some unrecorded reason the final was replayed at Castleford, Methley again proved their superiority and won 7-3.

There were many objections in the competition, at one meeting the committee spent 2½ hours discussing objections against teams playing ineligible players. New Scarborough lodged an objection against Streethouse for playing Charlie Morris who had played for Sharlston in the Castleford and District League. Streethouse said Sharlston had no authority to register him and Morris had written a letter saying he preferred to play for Streethouse. It was agreed that he could play for them.

1902-03

The 1902-03 season saw Sharlston in the Wakefield & District League, but the opposition was weak. After defeating East Ardsley at Sharlston 33-0, the *Wakefield Express* said: "The score did not represent the true state of the game and if Sharlston had exerted themselves they could have doubled it. With teams like Sharlston pitted against juniors, the league, I fear, will be a thing of the past."

The club's season was kept alive by playing in cup competitions. Alverthorpe, who were in the Yorkshire Senior Competition, thought they would have little difficulty in winning when they visited Sharlston in the first round of the Charlesworth Clayton Hospital Cup, but the home side played an outstandingly good game and at the interval the score was 5-5. In the second half Sharlston shocked the visitors. Abbott scored two tries and Bailey one, Sharlston winning 14-5. They failed to get the better of Pontefract in the second round but put up a splendid performance, losing 8-2. Pontefract were champions of the Yorkshire Senior Competition, winning all their matches and conceding only 38 points all season. They went on to win the cup.

Sharlston again reached the final of the Wellington Cup, but were defeated again, this time by Castleford Half Acres Trinity. After playing a pointless game, the teams met again at Normanton before a fairly good crowd. In the first half Castleford's Smalley scored a try which was not converted. In the second half the Sharlston men tried to get on even terms without success and the game ended in a 3-0 win for Castleford.

Sharlston outplayed Dewsbury Mashers, 17-2, in the Heavy Woollen District Cup, then withdrew from the competition. The Dewsbury side, at a meeting of the Committee of the Heavy Woollen District Challenge Cup Competition, objected to Sharlston playing C. King, who they said was not a *bona fide* member of the club, that C. Russell was not registered and they also objected to Hammerton, Goodfellow and Bull. Mr Howell, on behalf of the Sharlston club, argued that his club had played *bona fide* men and that Goodfellow did not play in the match. The objection was sustained on the ground that Russell was not registered and the committee ordered the game to be replayed at Ravensthorpe. Mr Howell, however, stated that his club would not replay the game, and thus they withdrew from the cup.

1903-04

The club joined the Yorkshire Senior Competition in 1903-04, a season which saw the introduction by the Northern Union of XII-a-side play as an experiment for amateur clubs, with six forwards, two half-backs, three three-quarters and a full-back. This lasted for just one season, although further changes were to come.

The season opened in September with a narrow 5-0 defeat at Outwood - a rough affair and Sharlston had to wait until March for their solitary away victory at Alverthorpe.

Sharlston went to Ossett in October on the back of two convincing wins, against Alverthorpe, 30-6, and Ravensthorpe Nelson 21-0, but were narrowly defeated, 10-7. It was reported that: "Good play was seen on both sides... had the Sharlston backs been as clever at handling the ball as the home backs were they would probably have won. The threequarters were much swifter than the home trio and they followed up remarkably well but apart from their speed they did not display great capacity for football.

...The Sharlston touch judge who, as a sort of sideshow, created a considerable amount of interest and amusement. The Sharlston Committee would be well advised however, if in future they appoint to this position a man who has some knowledge of the game and some idea of what the duties of a touch judge are as the individual in question seemed to have the impression that he was there to instruct the referee."

When Ossett came to Sharlston for the return match, before the largest crowd of the season, rough play characterised the game and four players were sent off. The *Ossett Observer* commented after an Ossett player was injured: "This man was attacked by four Sharlston men in the most deliberate fashion and the players were assisted in their work by the touch judge who used his flag with great effect. And yet only one of the homesters was given marching orders and he refused to leave at once but stayed to argue the point with the referee. With only a minute or two left for play the referee gave a free kick against a Sharlston player for obstruction. The position was fairly favourable and Aldred placed the ball for a shot at goal. One of the Sharlston players refused to take up his position at the point where the penalty was awarded and upon requested by the referee to do so defied the official and deliberately kicked the ball over, thus refusing Aldred the kick. The referee then blew his whistle to signal that the game was closed. The Sharlston people were somewhat agitated by his decision and the referee had to be escorted from the field by a couple of constables."

The match came before the Senior Competition committee for decision and they ordered it to be replayed. Ossett objected and appealed to the Northern Union Committee who awarded them the match. On the Sharlston spectators, the *Observer* said: "In the use of vicious and threatening expressions the women – and there are a large proportion of women at football matches in this salubrious Colliery village - were equally as bad as men. 'Pawse 'is 'eead off' was an expression that was frequently used by those gentle amazons. Still the crowd was not without its humorous side for those who could detect the unconscious humour. If anyone happened to say to a Sharlston spectator in the usual casual manner that the home team were playing rather roughly and were using a little too much brute force he was always certain to receive the reply 'What did Gath do to so and so at Ossett. The man had to have five stitches put into his eye and he has not worked since.'

This became quite monotonous and it was quite a relief to hear an Ossett man replying on one occasion with the remark 'but he is not dead is he'. But the humorous part of the affair was that while the spectators desired the players to pay Gath out for this alleged - and perfectly groundless charge - they did not know which of the six forwards Gath was and they went for some other man on each occasion. This was rather rough on the others but it would at the same time been unreasonable to have asked Gath to show himself in order that he might have his head well punched." Reports in the *Ossett Observer* were always written in the same stirring, impartial manner.

Sharlston's home form was good. Only Ossett, who were destined to become the champions, won at Back o' t' wall. The *Wakefield and West Riding Herald* said that "the motto to visiting teams entering [Sharlston's] enclosure is 'All hope abandoned by those who enter here'."

Sharlston's final league placing was fifth, but they were badly beaten at Thrum Hall in the last match of the season by 65-0, a club record defeat.

There were problems on and off the field and following the match at Cleckheaton both clubs were instructed to post warning notices regarding the conduct of their spectators; the Sharlston touch judge, W. Sparham, was also suspended from officiating in future Senior Competition matches.

John Garrity and Albert Green, two Sharlston players, were each summoned and found guilty of assaulting the landlord of the Commercial Hotel, Cleckheaton, and of being disorderly and refusing to leave the hotel. They were sentenced to a term of imprisonment and suspended sine die by the Northern Union.

Sharlston's involvement in the NU Cup was not prolonged. Outwood came to Sharlston in the second qualifying round and scored a try immediately after the start and it was not until well into the second half that Abbott got over for Sharlston to force a replay at Outwood. However, the conduct of Sharlston at Outwood came to the attention of the Cup Committee at Manchester. The match had been in progress for 20 minutes and Outwood had scored two tries when Sharlston left the field and refused to continue. The Committee awarded the match to Outwood and suspended Willis, the Sharlston captain until 27 February."

At the end of the season Sharlston, Outwood Church, Birstall and Otley were suspended from the Senior Competition for not paying fines for broken engagements.

1904-05

In September 1904, Sharlston decided to "pay up" and so were re-instated, but decided to go back to the Wakefield & District Junior League which comprised Whitwood Colliery, Streethouse, Knottingley, Loscoe, South Kirkby and Ryhill. The local press did not show much interest in this league and information is in short supply, but Sharlston reached the Intermediate Round of the NU Challenge Cup for the first time visiting old foes Ossett. It was a very keen game but Sharlston returned home defeated 5-0.

The *Ossett Observer* said that "Sharlston must be feeling mad. But such are the ups and downs of a football career. If they had been good enough to beat Ossett last Saturday... they would have been appearing on the Leeds ground next Saturday. But they were a long way from that. Although the score indicates that Ossett were only five points better than their opponents... points do not represent play... Sharlston should have scored for they had a penalty kick in a ridiculously easy position but they failed."

Any hopes of winning the Yorkshire Junior Cup were dispelled when they were eliminated by Knottingley.

1905-06

Warmfield and Crofton joined the league for 1905-06 and, with the abandonment of the Yorkshire Senior Competition, Castleford Half Acres, Outwood Church and Wakefield Trinity Reserves joined, but Whitwood Colliery, Loscoe and South Kirkby dropped out.

Sharlston started the season in brilliant fashion and after nine games had only lost once, against Castleford Half Acres in November. They did not concede a point in seven of their games. They were so impressive that the *Wakefield Express* said: "Sharlston Rovers are determined to carry off the championship of the Wakefield and District League and it seems almost certain that they will be successful, whilst they have also got their 'peepers' on the Charlesworth or Clayton Hospital Challenge Cup.

Their performance in the league is certainly a most creditable one and up to the present they have won eight matches out of nine... They have scored 160 points and only five have been obtained against them... Much of their success is undoubtedly due to a fine set of forwards, who have proved too strong for the majority of their opponents. One of their most prominent men is undoubtedly Garrity who, seeing that he has already played for such clubs as Wakefield Trinity, Broughton Rangers and York, should have gained plenty of experience. He is extremely useful in the loose and is just the man to bring out of the pack when the occasion arises. Green and Bruce are the half backs and they are a most energetic pair, the former being very dangerous when near the line. The penultimate line is perhaps the weakest but the men in this important department are not made the best use of, and probably it would be well if the Rovers did not depend too much on their willing forwards but tried back play."

Rovers were drawn to play at Warmfield, in the first round of the Yorkshire Junior Cup, but Warmfield, were unable to raise a team of men on their register, and awarded Sharlston the match. The teams did play a 'friendly'. Garrity played amongst the threequarters for the Rovers. Sharlston won 10-5. Lackenby and Maurice Wood each obtained a try and the former kicked two goals, one from a mark.

Sharlston had a comfortable victory over Wakefield Trinity Reserves at Belle Vue in September, 13-0, and the return encounter on 23 December was much awaited but the outcome was unusual. To this point, Rovers had only lost one match during the season.

At the kick-off the home forwards were off-side and a scrimmage was formed at the centre. The visitors' forwards got the ball out and eventually a minor was forced. On the drop-out Rovers attacked and Nicholson came close to scoring. Green also made great efforts to force his way through but was stopped. Lackenby missed from a free kick.

Slater then scored a drop-goal for Trinity. The game was keenly contested and Willis of Sharlston was sent off for "some informality in the scrimmage," according to the local paper. Wakefield conceded a minor. The drop-out was ordered to be re-taken, but then the Wakefield captain took his players off the field. The referee, Mr Jackson, said that he had no complaints of undue roughness and awarded the match to Sharlston.

However, the match was ordered to be replayed on the Outwood ground, Trinity Reserves gaining a narrow 5-0 victory. The referee sent off three Sharlston players and complained to the League of the bad language used by the Sharlston players.

Sharlston travelled to Outwood in January 1906 for the league fixture and won by a try to nil. The home touch judge pulled up the corner flag alleging that Riley the Sharlston player had knocked it down in attempting to score. The referee, however, had seen the deception and awarded the try to Sharlston.

There followed correspondence in the *Wakefield Express* between Mr O. B. Milnes, a Sharlston schoolmaster, and the secretary of the Outwood Club, Mr Robinson, which shows the ill feeling between the two clubs.

An allegation against Outwood Church FC

Mr Milnes described the incident with the touch judge and added "To-day (Monday) I was waited upon by several of the Sharlston players who showed me the terrible bruises they had received during the match." He said the bruises were shocking and could not have been caused accidentally. The injured players missed work due to the brutal treatment by the Outwood team.

He added that when the match was over the victors were stoned from the field and had to drive to Wakefield to dress. He concluded that "the present conditions of playing football in the Wakefield and District League should be radically altered or the game will simply degenerate into brutal contests. I cannot but think that refereeing is not carried out as it should be in the true interests of the game."

The next week, Mr Robinson responded. He denied that the Outwood touch judge pulled the corner flag up when one of the Sharlston players was scoring a try. He disputed the injuries received by the Sharlston players, and denied that stones were thrown at them.

He also said that the Sharlston players both washed and dressed and had refreshments at the Outwood Church FC's expense in the dressing room at the British Oak Inn, Outwood Church FC's headquarters.

He went on to say that Outwood Church FC has never had a single man suspended *sine die*, let alone a whole team. It is also very recently that the Wakefield Trinity team came off the field at Sharlston owing to their brutal work.

He concluded: "Why everybody who knows anything about football knows that it has degenerated long ago into brutal contests at Sharlston and as regards the referee I think the referee who conducted the game at Outwood on that day has forgotten more than Mr Milnes knows about football... I hope Mr Milnes will withdraw these allegations..."

The correspondence continued the next week with Mr Milnes' reply. He asked why the touch judge put his flag up? He then confirmed that he and others saw the bruises sustained by the Sharlston players. He also confirmed that stones were thrown at the Sharlston players.

He continued "Sharlston met Outwood in the cup-ties two years ago. The Sharlston players were so roughly handled that they did not consider it worthwhile to run any further risks, so the Sharlston captain took his men off the field. For so doing he was suspended for a month and the match was awarded to Outwood. A decision with which I agree, as the referee alone has the power to stop the match. After the cup-tie contest Outwood had to fulfil a league match at Sharlston but they failed to fulfil their engagement. I may state here that when Outwood met Sharlston at Sharlston on 28th October last the match was splendidly contested and there was an entire absence of foul play. The fact is, the Sharlston players in years gone by have got a bad name in the football world and the result is that to-day under the conditions it is very difficult to get a good one." He also asked why the match with Wakefield Trinity reserves was replayed.

In his reply, Mr Robinson offered to pay £5 to the Clayton Hospital if Mr Milnes would do the same, if he does not prove his allegations. He also recalled the Sharlston club and players being suspended sine die.

Mr Milnes again refuted the points made by Mr Robinson, and was supported by Mr A. A. Abbott of Sharlston Common, the honorary secretary of Sharlston FC in 1898-99, who sent the paper a long letter in which he confirmed most of the statements already made by Mr Milnes. With that, the editor declared the correspondence closed.

There was a sting in the tail for the Outwood secretary. In March Outwood met Wakefield Trinity Reserves in a Charlesworth Cup match at Outwood and resorted to various questionable tactics. This culminated in an assault by a player on one of the touch judges and an assault at the end of the match on the referee. Outwood's captain was charged with inciting the crowd to assault the referee and was suspended until the end of November. The ground was closed until the end of the season

Local derby matches always provided much interest and this season Crofton who had a 'beautifully situated ground' were newcomers to the league but were no match for Rovers. Streethouse provided stiffer opposition but still lost on their own ground. The local paper said: "At the outset two or three players seemed inclined to exhibit too much keenness but after being satisfied that the referee was going to stand no nonsense the game, competitively speaking, was pleasantly contested. Sharlston, thanks to the fine work of their forwards, proved the better team and won by three tries to nil. Bruce played a fine half back game for Sharlston." There had been some difficulty finding a referee, three persons refused the whistle, until Mr Newton of Wakefield agreed.

In the cups, Sharlston were defeated 15-11 by Bradford A in the Junior Cup semi-final at home In the first half, Sharlston kept the ball close in order to check the Bradford backs. The home forwards played a fine game. Astbury, G. Green, and Garrity scored tries for Sharlston. G. Bruce, a young Sharlston recruit, was a great success in the threequarter line. Bradford beat Castleford PC in the final.

Sharlston reached the final of the Charlesworth Cup, but lost 8-2 to Wakefield Trinity Reserves at Belle Vue. The Sharlston forwards were stronger and got possession from the scrummages time after time. Their backs, however, played poorly and kicked on almost every occasion.

Rovers had several opportunities to win in the second half but easy passes were missed. At the close the cup and medals were presented by Miss Leigh, The Chairman of the Hospital Saturday Committee.

1906-07

The Northern Union introduced changes to the game since the 1895 breakaway in the hope of making it more interesting for spectators and in 1906 the decision was taken to reduce the number of players in a team from 15 to 13, and new play-the-ball and ball back rules.

This season saw the amalgamation of the Heavy Woollen League and the Wakefield & District League to form the Dewsbury, Wakefield & District League with the following teams: Sharlston Rovers, Wakefield Trinity 'A', Castleford Half Acres, Knottingley, Felkirk, Woolley Colliery, Pontefract Grovetown, Outwood Church, Horbury Amateurs, Hopetown, Birstall, Ossett Rovers and Castleford Parish Church.

Mr Alma Day was the new league's secretary; he had been secretary of the Heavy Woollen League and also a referee. The Northern Union Committee decided to provide a Challenge cup for junior and 'A' teams within 12 miles from Dewsbury Town Hall and 12 miles from Wakefield Cathedral.

The season was remembered for two unfortunate incidents in October which were to overshadow Sharlston's achievement in becoming the league's first champions, winning 21 out of 24 games.

"A disgrace to civilisation" was how Mr Percy Tew described the conduct of the Sharlston spectators in fining one of them £2/17/9 (£2.89) for assaulting the referee in the Sharlston and Woolley Colliery match. Neither a player nor official of the club attempted to protect him. Proceedings were ordered to be taken by the Dewsbury, Wakefield & District League, who wanted to stop such conduct. The following week, on 20 October, in the match against Wakefield Trinity Reserves which became known as 'The Belle Vue Riot', the Sharlston club was severely censured, two players were suspended sine die and the baggage man and touch judge prohibited from taking any further part in matches in connection with the Dewsbury, Wakefield & District League. The match was ordered to be replayed.

The *Yorkshire Post* reported the events as follows: "An unprecedented and indescribable scene occurred at Belle Vue... From the beginning it was noticeable that the game was going to be of a more than keen description and the cries of the Sharlston spectators to "knock 'em sick" did not help to improve matters. The first part of the game was very even, but "shady" tactics on each side were noticeable. The Sharlston players however resorted to open-hand roughness with the result that early in the second half 'Ginger' Dooler was ordered off the field for kicking Dawson, the half-back of the Wakefield team, after he had parted with the ball. Sharlston took the lead about 20 minutes off time with a penalty goal, the score then being 6-5. Sidwell then got away, and came into contact with a Sharlston player. The referee observed something wrong and brought both players out to take their names. No sooner had he done so than the

Sharlston man Howell - it is alleged - struck Sidwell a violent blow on the jaw. McDonald, a Wakefield player, intervened, whereupon another Sharlston player joined in. The melee amongst the players then became general, and the 1,200 spectators, who had been worked up to fever heat, swarmed on to the ground.

The Sharlston players then came in for a deal of rough usage and two policemen - nothing of the kind being anticipated - were unable to stem the torrent. A couple of city policemen went to the assistance of their West Riding brethren but the players were not got off before they had been seriously maltreated. Dawson, the Wakefield half-back, was struck on the head with a heavy stick and rendered partially unconscious. A Sharlston player chivalrously assisted him off the field. Taylor, another Wakefielder, was damaged by having his hand bitten, whilst the Sharlston baggage man who interfered, came in for perhaps the worst treatment of all As the Sharlston players left in a wagonette, they commenced hurling derisive remarks, whereupon they were assailed with a shower of stones which caused them to take refuge by lying as close as they could on the bottom of the wagonette."

The paper said that nothing like it before had been seen at Belle Vue. Sharlston were found guilty of riotous conduct, but a motion at the League's committee meeting to expel them was lost 7-6, and they were severely censured. However, Sharlston players J. Dooler and J. Howell were suspended *sine die*. Also, A. Abbott, the Sharlston baggage man and J. Froggatt, the Sharlston touch judge, were suspended from taking any further part in matches connected with the League.

Following this decision, Trinity's Dr Hein resigned from his position as vice-president and the Wakefield team said they would withdraw from the League. The disciplinary decisions were subsequently confirmed by a Yorkshire County Committee meeting. They also said that "the Sharlston club be notified that in the event of an occurrence of a similar kind in the future by the Sharlston players or spectators the Committee will take extreme action."

However, Wakefield Trinity reserves did not leave the league. Following the trouble, Hopetown at first refused to meet Sharlston home and away but later reconsidered their decision and fulfilled the fixtures, one of which they lost 57-0.

Meanwhile, on the pitch, the opening match of the season for Sharlston was against Birstall. There was a large crowd to examine the affect of the new rules. In general, supporters felt that the game was more interesting to watch. The ball was constantly on the move. The visitors were outclassed as tries were scored by A Howell, with two, T. Bruce, G. Abbott and B. Green.

Rovers were the first team to defeat Wakefield Trinity reserves at Belle Vue, winning 5-0 in February. There was some anxiety about the nature of the game following the earlier clash at Belle Vue and though it was a hard fought game there were no unsavoury incidents.

There was a big attendance, probably 1,500 or 1,600. The game was splendidly contested and the players did not resort to any rough play. The Trinitarians had strong forwards but the Sharlston men were their masters. In the scrums they packed well and worked desperately hard and if they had lost no blame could have been attributed to them. They got possession on many more occasions than the Wakefield men and when the latter did get hold the ball came out of the scrimmage so slowly that the Wakefield halves had not much opportunity of getting away.

For Trinity, Land threw away a glorious chance to score. He broke away and on approaching the full-back he had Jack Walton and two other players alongside him. Instead of passing however he preferred to kick and only a minor resulted.

Sharlston then attacked and their efforts were rewarded. The *Wakefield Express* said that "Bruce got hold and threaded his way through his opponents in fine style; and when he placed the ball over the line the supporters of each team loudly applauded him. The goal was kicked and nothing further being scored, Sharlston won 5-0."

The paper concluded that "On the day's play Sharlston were certainly the better team and no one should begrudge them their victory. Strong forward play was supported by safety and coolness on the part of their backs who made no mistakes when the pressure was severe but the feature of their back play was the accuracy and coolness with which they caught the ball... All the players on their side did well, but a special word of praise is due to Piper, their full-back, who played a clever game. Morton was a weak spot in Wakefield's back department, and he was not a success either at centre three-quarter or full-back. Slater worked like a Trojan at half-back but there was a lack of combination amongst the three-quarters and individual efforts proved unavailing. The Rovers supporters were naturally pleased with their performance and this is the first time this season the Trinity Reserves have been defeated at Belle Vue. They have now suffered three defeats and Sharlston have been responsible for two of these. No wonder there is joy in the Rovers camp."

The first of Sharlston's three defeats in the league came on Christmas Day at Castleford Half Acres when the home team's Bedworth and Sharlston's A. Howell were sent off. Sharlston objected to the result claiming that spectators had encroached on to the field and assaulted a touch judge. However, their objection was not upheld.

In the cup competitions, Sharlston had mixed fortunes. In the Junior Cup, a preliminary round defeat at New Blackpool soon put paid to any hopes the Rovers had of a good cup run.

In the Northern Union Challenge Cup, following victories over Outwood and Woolley Colliery, 53-5 with six tries from F. Dooler and seven goals from T. Bruce, Sharlston confidently travelled to Brighouse St. James. But there was a rude awakening in store. The home team were "an old fashioned lot" with players who had played for the Huddersfield club and the defunct Brighouse Rangers. About 1,500 saw the match, which was very fast and open with an absence of the roughness often associated with cup-ties. However, Brighouse St. James won 15-0.

Success came in the Dewsbury, Wakefield & District Cup. A first round bye and victories against Felkirk, Ackworth and Outwood saw Sharlston through to the final of this new competition to meet Castleford Half Acres at Belle Vue.

Sharlston Rovers won 8-5, with two tries and a goal, Castleford Half Acres scoring a try and a goal. Sharlston were defending at first, Castleford attacking strongly but then the game evened out. Then a Sharlston player was sent off for kicking. Castleford narrowly failed to score with a penalty, the ball only missing the cross-bar by inches. Then Harris broke away to put Warner in to score for Castleford. The conversion put them 5-0 up. There was no further score up to half time

Shortly after the break, Howell scored for Sharlston, with the try being converted by Bruce. Dooler put Sharlston ahead by scoring the winning try, which Bruce failed to convert.

Mr W. Newsome, the League's president, complimented Sharlston on their splendid victory. Mrs Newsome then handed the cup to W. Blacker, the Sharlston captain, and the medals to the players, wishing them every success and hoping they would occupy the same position next time.

Intermediates

Rovers formed an intermediate team this season, playing in the Wakefield & District Intermediate league.

The *Wakefield Express* reported that "Sharlston have got together a very enthusiastic team captained by J. Bruce, one of last year's members of the Normanton Juniors team. Evidence is forthcoming from the practices held during the past few weeks that they will be a hard nut for opponents to crack".

In their first match, on 8 September they scored 73 points against Ossett Shamrocks at Sharlston, then won five of their first six matches, only Horbury PC beating them.

Their final league position was third, winning 12 of their 16 matches. They were well served by Bruce in the centre, Haycock and Jones on the wings, Griffiths and Buckley at half-back, Nicholson at full-back and the forwards were ably led by Cowey.

They rose to the occasion in the J. B. Cooke Shield Competition, which they won after defeating Outwood Old Boys in the semi-final 8-5, when "Buckley of Sharlston, a boy of diminutive stature who nevertheless played a rattling good game throughout at half-back". Featherstone provided the opposition in the final at Mopsey Garth, although the match started late because the secretary forgot to bring the ball.

The first half consisted mainly of kicking exchanges, several marks being made. Each side had a chance to score from penalties but none were scored. In the first half Arnold Jones scored a try for Sharlston but Gorman's conversion failed.

At the start of the second half, Sharlston were awarded a penalty nearly from half-way and Bruce scored. Shortly afterwards, Featherstone's Hamer hit the post from a penalty. Towards the finish Fellows kicked a drop-goal for Featherstone which were the only points they were able to obtain, the game concluding with a 5-2 victory for Sharlston.

During the match Featherstone objected to Bruce, who they alleged was over age, and Sharlston were disappointed that the presentation of the cup, which was to have been done by Mr Tinley Smith of Featherstone, could not take place. The objection was to have been heard on Monday night, but then Featherstone withdrew it.

Dual celebration

At the end of the season, both Sharlston teams celebrated at the Sharlston Hotel. Medals were presented for winning the Dewsbury, Wakefield & District League and Cup. The cup, adorned with blue and white, the club's colours, was on view, together with the J. B. Cooke Shield, which had been won by Sharlston Juniors.

The presentation was made by Mr Alma Day, the league's energetic secretary. Everyone enjoyed a musical evening. Mr D. Butterfield played a selection on the piano, and the songs were ably rendered by Piper, Lomas, A. Green, J. Tunnicliffe, Owen and G. Lomas.

Mr Day praised Rovers' play and said they had won both the League and the Cup by pure, honest and fair football. They had created a record by carrying off the double. Thirteen medals were presented for the League and thirteen for the Cup. Additional medals would be presented later to reserve players. Mr T. Bettley, Sharlston's secretary moved a vote of thanks to Mr Day for presiding.

The 1906-07 Sharlston Intermediate team (Photo: *Wakefield Express*)

1907-08

Batley Reserves and Normanton joined the Dewsbury, Wakefield & District League in 1907-08 but several clubs were missing when the season opened and the league comprised just nine teams. This gave cause for concern and advertisements were put in the *Wakefield Express* and *Dewsbury Reporter* asking for new clubs to join. In August Sharlston informed the league that they were withdrawing, having declined to continue playing, but in September Mr Kistell attended a meeting of the Dewsbury, Wakefield & District League as Sharlston's representative with an application that the club be re-admitted to the league. The Committee decided that if they reported satisfactorily as to the management as soon as possible, they would be accepted.

The committee expressed no confidence in the old management and preferred that the club be an entirely new one. It was agreed that Sharlston be re-admitted.

Two players left the club for the professional game at the beginning of the season, Piper to Wakefield Trinity and Howell to Leeds, although he returned to Sharlston later in the season. Player permits were confirmed for F. Green, I. Brear, H. Price and J. Price to play for the club.

The team started the season in great style, their first defeat was at Knottingley on Christmas Day, but fell away in the second half of the season losing four of their last six matches. Third position in the league was secured behind Knottingley and Wakefield Trinity Reserves, but it was a disappointing end to the season which promised so much.

The season was not without its interesting moments. There was no love lost between Sharlston and Castleford Half Acres as a result of incidents in the previous season's cup final and the league match at Castleford on Christmas Day 1906. Sharlston had not appeared this season at Castleford and the latter refused to play at Sharlston, the league arranged for the fixtures to be played at Mopsey Garth, Normanton. Knottingley had refused use of their ground strongly objecting to them being allowed to play on a neutral ground. They did threaten to withdraw from the league but as they were top of the league at the time and went on to become champions, nothing came of it.

When the two sides met in the first fixture in February 1908 there was a large crowd and a posse of policemen, but they were only called upon once when a gatekeeper complained that a spectator had got in without paying. Rovers lost both league fixtures and the second round cup-tie. At first Sharlston, who had been drawn at home, agreed to play at Featherstone but changed their mind and claimed ground advantage. The league ordered Castleford to play at Sharlston, which they did, or forfeit the match.

Both matches were won against Normanton, but it was a narrow victory by one point at Mopsey Garth. Bruce came close to scoring early on, but was frustrated by R. Ward pushing him into touch. Normanton attacked and some clever play by Dooler, Howell, Ward and Scamens kept Sharlston busy defending. However, Sharlston took the lead with a penalty from a mark by Bruce.

Shortly afterwards Brown's attempt at goal hit the upright for Normanton. At half-time, Sharlston were 2-0 ahead. Normanton were now playing uphill and the opening stages after the interval were in their favour, Ward's cross-kicking helping them to gain ground. However, from one of these, Bailey got possession and by kicking and following up, received a pass from Bruce, and scored under the posts. Bruce's kick went in off the post. Ward scored from a scramble for Normanton, but Brown's kick missed. Then Scamens scored Normanton's second try. Johnson needed to convert to put Normanton ahead, but he missed. Sharlston won 7-6.

The fixtures with Wakefield Trinity Reserves were always keen affairs and Sharlston gained a narrow 13-12 victory at home but lost 5-3 at Belle Vue. The *Wakefield Express* said that "shady tactics were indulged in - tripping being very frequent - but the worst of all was when the Sharlston full-back foully charged Simpson after he had kicked the ball. The referee... awarded Wakefield a penalty but not a word did he say to the offending player. It was during Simpson's absence that Sharlston scored their try. The game was principally of a forward character and in this kind of play Sharlston were the masters."

Sharlston players G. Bruce and F. Dyer were chosen for the Wakefield & District Intermediate team to play the Hull & District League. There was a considerable discussion about the remuneration for players selected. Castleford Half Acres said their players would not play unless they received a certain sum as they could not afford to miss work. It was understood that if anything was made out of the match the players would receive some remuneration over and above their railway fare and 1/- (5p) for tea.

Dewsbury, Wakefield & District League 1907-08

	P	W	D	L	Pts
Knottingley	16	14	1	1	29
Wakefield Trinity Res	18	12	3	3	27
Sharlston Rovers	16	11	0	5	22
Castleford Half Acres	14	10	1	3	21
Normanton	18	8	2	8	18
Felkirk	15	6	0	9	12
Woolley Colliery	12	3	1	8	7
Batley Reserves	15	3	1	11	7
Outwood Church	10	2	1	7	5
Ackworth United	16	1	0	15	2

The 1907-08 New Sharlston School team: Back: Mr Denham, Len Thomas, Joe Nightingale, Arthur Holland, Mr Day. Standing: Horace Sandham, G. Wilkinson, Percy Armitage, George Bastow, Bailey. Sitting: Ernest Bruce, Osbert Bettice, G. Fox (captain), Henry Earnshaw, Jonty Parkin. Kneeling: P. Crowther, M. Jarvis, P. Chalkley, Sam Stead.

There was no intermediate team this season, but Jonty Parkin was making his mark in schools rugby. When New Sharlston School played High Street Boys at Streethouse "... from a cross kick Crowther scored another try and he added two more tries after clever play by Reeves and Parkin. Parkin dropped a goal and New Sharlston won 14-2". Against Normanton Woodhouse he scored three tries.

In July 1908 at the annual meeting of the Dewsbury, Wakefield & District League the secretary reported that during the past season 494 players had been registered. Only 22 players had been sent off the field for misconduct, which was considered satisfactory. About £6 had been lost on the year's working. The following resolution was passed: "That any Northern League Club signing on a player from a junior club pay such Club the sum of £1 on securing his signature and a further £4 after playing him in six matches, with either first or second teams, the six matches to be completed in three months otherwise the players shall revert to the junior club and the £1 paid be forfeited."

1909-10

Sharlston withdrew from the league for the 1908-09 season but were back in 1909-10. The league had increased to 15 clubs and Sharlston finished in the top half of the table. However, the final placings were of little importance as some clubs made no effort to complete their fixtures, claiming that the league was too big and cup matches ruined the league programme. It was suggested that no champions be declared and the top four play-offs be abandoned, but they went ahead without Wakefield Trinity Reserves who withdrew from the contest.

Pontefract Victoria visited Sharlston for the opening match of the season, with Rovers running up a cricket score, finally winning 44-8. In the first half the home backs made several good passing movements and Pontefract men were outclassed. Astbury and G. Bruce both scored two tries, with J. Bruce, J. Nicholson and T. Bruce also scoring, with the latter converting five goals and his brother, George, one. The visitors scored twice, with one conversion. In the second half, J. Nicholson with two and Astbury scored for Sharlston, while T. Bruce dropped a goal just on time.

The season's first defeat came against Purston White Horse, but Sharlston objected, believing that Purston had played an ineligible man, G. Savage. They later withdrew the objection when it transpired that there were two players of the same name, one registered with Purston and the other with Knottingley.

"One of the finest exhibitions of Northern Union football seen at Mopsey Garth for many a long day" was the gist of remarks heard after the Normanton versus Sharlston match. The game was full of exciting incidents and interest was sustained right up to the finish. It was reported that "Thanks to the firmness of the referee, Mr F. Renton, all elements of roughness were speedily checked." Normanton won 14-8.

It was a different story when the two met at Mopsey Garth in the replayed qualifying round of the NU Cup. The tie was not finished the previous week due to the late arrival of the referee and the match could not be concluded on account of darkness with 12 minutes left for play and Normanton leading 3-2. The rearranged match was described thus: "A disgraceful exhibition took place at Mopsey Garth on Saturday, where Normanton and Sharlston met again to replay the NU cup tie... Normanton were much superior in the first half." Warner scored a try which Haycock improved and soon after Bob Ward completely beat the opposition and scored, the conversion being missed. T Bruce kicked a penalty goal for Sharlston and the half-time score was 8-2.

On resuming Sharlston played strongly and a break away by the home forwards resulted in another try. Sharlston players now started abusing the referee who sent off Tom Bruce. The player was not happy, but Mr Smith stopped the game and Bruce reluctantly left. After this the game was "a disgrace to sport and civilisation." Ellis, a forward, picked out 'Ponk' Walker and struck him violently. The home man retaliated and both were sent off.

Until the end of the game the Normanton players were kicked regularly. The referee sent man after man off, all Sharlston players, but to no purpose. Smith, one of the home forwards, was carried off unconscious and remained so for three hours. The home men took their treatment 'lying down' and one had to wonder what would have happened had they retaliated. The visitors finished with four men, three or four having left the field on their own account. This disgraceful affair was reported to the Cup Committee. The referee reported that after Normanton scored the Sharlston team played brutal football, which resulted in the sending off of Tom Bruce, F. Bruce, Ellis, Fletcher and Russell of Sharlston and Walker of Normanton. The Committee suspended the five Sharlston players to the end of the season and Walker of Normanton for one match. David Taylor of Sharlston Rovers was charged with using filthy language to the referee after the match and was suspended to the end of the season.

The festive season was miserable for Rovers. Netherton United were the visitors on Christmas Day and went away with the points, winning 16-3, and Featherstone Rovers won the Boxing Day fixture 14-5 and trounced Rovers 37-0 in the season's last match.

Sharlston's final league placing was seventh, winning 10 out of 23 matches. Once again the team disappointed in the latter part of the season and all was not well with the club. In January 1910, T. Bruce and Fred Goodfellow joined Normanton and J. Nicholson and A. Taylor went to Hull KR. These departures seriously weakened the team.

In November 1909, future Rugby League Hall of Fame member Jonty Parkin registered with Sharlston Rovers as a player.

Sharlston also featured in some of the league's meetings. E. Willis of Sharlston was reported for deliberately kicking in a Hemsworth and Sharlston match. Willis wrote to the Committee saying it was accidental and he would try to do better in future. However, he was suspended for three matches.

A warning was issued to players regarding the indiscriminate signing of registration forms after J. Jukes, who was registered with the Leeds club, was reported for having signed two forms, one for Featherstone Rovers and another for Sharlston Rovers. He admitted signing for the clubs and said he would have signed for another two if he had been asked.

Streethouse, who were playing competitive rugby before Sharlston in the 1890s reported that their players refused to play any further matches away from home and withdrew from the league.

A referee reported himself for being very late for a match at Purston. He had evidently had a very exciting time of it and said in four closely written pages, that he would have to study timetables more carefully in future.

J. Froggatt of Sharlston who was one of the touch judges in the Belle Vue riot nearly three years ago, and who was suspended along with players, was reinstated.

However, local rugby enthusiasts' worst fears were realised when Sharlston withdrew from the Dewsbury, Wakefield & District League before the start of the 1910-11 season and did not appear again until 1913-14, and then only for a short period. There was an Intermediate team, Sharlston Red Rose in 1912-13, who finished in the top four of their league, and were defeated by a strong North Featherstone side in the play offs, 24-0. They also reached the final of the Cooke Shield.

One player stood head and shoulders above the rest for North Featherstone, Sharlston born Jonty (Jonathan) Parkin who had signed for Wakefield Trinity in March 1913 but was allowed to play out the season with the Featherstone side who won the league and cup. He was 16 years old.

1913-14

Rovers were back in business in 1913-14 in the Leeds & District League, the Dewsbury, Wakefield & District League having disbanded, however they were no longer a force to be reckoned with and it was no surprise when they ceased activities with only two victories from eight league matches.

The crushing blow came when they were dumped out of the NU Challenge Cup at the qualifying stage by the newly formed Harrogate Club 45-0.

It was a different story for the Junior (Intermediate) side. They had a splendid season, losing only two games and finishing second in the Wakefield league although they were defeated by Belle Vue 8-0 in the championship final at Wakefield Trinity's Belle Vue.

The game was well fought and the result in doubt almost to the end. At half time neither side had scored. Well on in the second half Miller picked up the ball near the line and scored for Belle Vue. This roused the Sharlston lads and when they attacked, one of their players foolishly dropped at goal when two or three of his side had a clear field. Sharlston still kept attacking. Eventually Miller again got the ball and after dodging several opponents scored under the posts, this being a particularly fine effort, which the spectators greatly appreciated. Pollard kicked the goal.

The local paper said that "Although the Sharlston lads were defeated, they put up a splendid fight and the exhibition given by both teams would have done credit to any senior team... Sharlston were quicker with their passing and the tackling of the backs on both sides was fine. For the winners Miller, Pollard, England and Faux shone most amongst the backs whilst on the Sharlston side Reeves, Sandham and Walton were probably the pick."

In August 1914 Norman Reeves signed for Featherstone Rovers. He was regarded as the best amateur in the district in the centre position, and scored 44 tries in the 1919-20 season. He was Featherstone's captain in their first match when they became professional in 1921-2, but then broke a wrist and only played four games that season.

It was 1919 before open age rugby was played in the village again due to the outbreak of the First World War.

The First World War

When Britain went to war with Germany in August 1914 there was great expectation that it would be all over by Christmas that year but it was four and a quarter years later on 11 November 1918 before peace returned. During this time some professional rugby league clubs managed to keep going, the Football Association decided to carry on but the Rugby Football Union closed down for the duration. After June 1915 rugby league continued on an amateur basis, playing friendly matches, no club being allowed to make payment to players except for tea money of 2/6 (12½p).

Competitive rugby league, except for schoolboys and intermediates under 20 years old, was suspended during the war and by 1918 the game was virtually shut down.

The open-age junior teams in the Wakefield area ceased activities but intermediate teams (under-18 and -16) Sharlston Rovers, Wakefield Juniors, Thornes United, Streethouse, Eastmoor, Normanton, Primrose Hill, Portobello, Alverthorpe, J. Rhodes & Sons, Outwood, Cradock & Sons, Loscoe, kept the game alive in 1916-17 and 1917-18.

In spite of the war conditions Sharlston competed in the final of the intermediate Challenge Cup in 1916-17 at Belle Vue losing 3-2 against Thornes United. Bettridge scored for Sharlston. Silcock, Henderson and Bettridge stood out for Sharlston.

In the same cup final in 1917-18 at Belle Vue Sharlston lost 6-0 against Alverthorpe. Also that season, Sharlston competed in the final for the Cooke Shield losing 16-0 against Outwood, tackling well, but were unable to score. There was no reward for them in any of the finals but they performed creditably in all three matches.

3. The 1920s - The Yorkshire Senior Competition

With the end of hostilities, rugby league resumed full scale activities in 1919. The Leeds & District and Wakefield & District Leagues were revived for the 1919-20 season, and included Sharlston Rovers in the latter. Sharlston's programme opened with a narrow defeat at Dewsbury but they had a good season, finishing third in the Wakefield & District League, behind Featherstone and Normanton with a visit to Mopsey Garth in the play-offs. Normanton had defeated Sharlston in the league fixtures but this time before a big crowd, Rovers won 10-0 and the scene was set for a showdown with Featherstone at Belle Vue in the final.

Featherstone were in a class of their own amongst the junior sides and had won the league matches against Sharlston, but both were keenly contested and Sharlston were unlucky not to win at Featherstone when Patrick scored a try and Goodfellow missed an easy goal to win the match. The teams lined up at Belle Vue as follows:

Featherstone Rovers: Anderson; Denton, Reeves, Seymour, Stott; Chapman, Williams; Williams, Walker, White, Baggott, Haigh, Barraclough.
Sharlston Rovers: Hardwick; Taylor, Bloomfield, F. Goodfellow, H. Sandham; G. Bruce, Patrick Dooler; Hepworth, Harrison, Cowey, Jones, Holland.
Referee: Revd Frank Chambers

An interesting player in the Sharlston pack was Fred Harrison. He made his debut for Leeds in 1906. After making 10 first team appearances he was advised to rejoin his original club, Streethouse, for a short spell, but he was back for the start of the 1907-8 season and soon became one of the mainstays of the Leeds team, making 280 appearances. In the Featherstone threequarters was Reeves who was an outstanding member of the Sharlston Intermediate team before the War.

The Championship trophy went to Featherstone with an 18-0 victory but was not as one-sided as the score suggests. The Sharlston team came to Belle Vue an unknown quantity and played very well. Fred Goodfellow had a remarkably good game considering the number of years he had been playing. Taylor played a useful game in the threequarters and Patrick at half-back was very nippy. In the forwards Fred Harrison and Dooler were often prominent.

Three days later the teams met again at Sharlston, before a crowd of 2,000, in the Wakefield & District League Cup semi-final and once again Featherstone won, but narrowly, 7-5.

Sharlston played brilliantly and for much of the game were the superior side, but luck was against them and they had to concede the match to Featherstone through a try awarded against them for obstruction. Bruce kicked a penalty for Sharlston, soon equalised by Williams; then Sharlston were penalised under their own posts and Clements put Featherstone ahead with the penalty. Williams was obstructed in diving for the line and the referee had to award a try. Dooler scored a try for Sharlston and two minutes from time G. Bruce failed to take the ball with the line at his mercy.

The Final did not take place. Hemsworth refused to play on any other day but Saturday, but Featherstone could not play on Saturdays due to league commitments. The League fixed the match for a Monday, 3 May, at Normanton and a big crowd gathered but Hemsworth failed to appear and the cup and medals went to Featherstone.

Sharlston's progress in the Junior Cup came to a halt against Hull BOCM at the semi-final stage in Hull.

The Intermediate side had a good season but it ended disappointingly when they were easily defeated by Westgate in the Championship Final.

Sharlston could look back on the first season after the War with a great deal of satisfaction. Before the War one factor emerged clear and unarguable, they had a powerful set of forwards with moderate backs. Now they had put together a good all round team. Their players were being noticed by senior clubs and in January 1920 Frank Astbury and Baddeley signed for York. Astbury, a scrum-half, had been playing regularly behind the Sharlston pack in co-operation with Luke Nixon, stand-off, whom York had recently signed. Rugby was flourishing on the village for as well as having teams in the open age and intermediate leagues, the council and national schools were represented in the Featherstone & District Schools' League.

1920-21

If Featherstone Rovers had entered the ranks of senior rugby league one season earlier, the 1920-21 season could have been a very good one for the Sharlston club. As it was Featherstone defeated them in four competitions and the final Sharlston won, the Leeds & District Cup, Featherstone withdrew from owing to other commitments.

There was no doubt that Featherstone were the undisputed champions of junior football and a class above the rest. In six meetings, Sharlston did win the league match at Back o' t' wall in November. Many felt that Featherstone did not accept this in a sporting manner and the comments made by the Featherstone president after the match caused bad feeling between the clubs.

Nixon had forced his way over for a try to win the match for Sharlston, but Featherstone protested that he had not grounded the ball, but the referee ruled otherwise. Reports appeared in the press alleging rough play on the part of Sharlston and after the match Councillor Johnson, the Featherstone president, spoke out strongly about alleged foul tactics by some of the Sharlston players and said they would not arrange future fixtures with Sharlston.

At the request of the Sharlston Committee the club secretary, Mr E. Jones, wrote to the *Wakefield Express*. He rejected the allegations of rough play and pointed out that Mr C. Peel of Bradford, a well known NU referee, was in charge and had not cautioned any players for rough play. He continued: "It appears that if a team beats the high and mighty Featherstone Rovers at football they call a special meeting and declare that under no circumstances will they arrange fixtures with them again. So look out Wakefield 'A', Leeds 'A', Hull 'A' and others."

He also denied that the Sharlston team was composed of old players, and the team that played Featherstone averaged 23½ years. He asked for an enquiry by the NU Council into the allegations and for the postponement of the return league match at Featherstone on New Year's Day until an apology was forthcoming.

The League committee enquired thoroughly into the match and a long letter was read from the referee, who said that during the whole game he had not cautioned a single player. Mainly due to this report the allegations were rejected.

This was not the end of the matter. The biggest crowd of the season gathered for the return fixture at Post Office Road, the gate receipts of nearly £100 being a record for any league match at Featherstone. Arriving at the Rovers' headquarters 30 minutes late minus some of their regular players, Sharlston refused to take the field unless Johnson apologised. He considered the record crowd present and after an impromptu meeting including the referee, Mr Swift of Wakefield, he apologised.

The 1920-21 Sharlston School team. Jim Chalkley is the captain.

Sharlston were forced to play a few 'good old has beens' and the Featherstone fans were anticipating a runaway victory. But Sharlston played excellently and for the first 20 minutes were continuously in the Featherstone half. There was a cup-tie doggedness which upset Featherstone's calculations. Sharlston scored first when Seymour and another Featherstone back bungled about 18 yards from the line and Ward scored.

Sharlston played well to the end but Featherstone scored tries through Haigh and Hirst, F. Williams adding the goal to the latter's try to make the final score 8-3.

In April Sharlston had to play two vital home games in the space of three days. On Monday they were defeated 3-2 by Castleford Rovers in the third round of the Leeds & District Cup. In a keenly contested game, one player was sent off and others cautioned. It was alleged by Sharlston that the visitors had brought over a team of 'first class footballers' including some, though they played under assumed names, were easily recognisable by the crowd and club officials. Sharlston entered an objection to four players on the grounds that they were ineligible to play for the Castleford club.

Two days later they were defeated 7-0 by Normanton in the semi-final of the Wakefield & District League. They were forced to field a weakened team as a result of the casualties suffered on the Monday. Taylor, Millard, Cowey and A. Holland were all missing. The objection against Castleford was upheld and the match was ordered to be replayed at Featherstone and this time Sharlston won 11-7. Castleford then appealed, alleging that three Sharlston players were ineligible. The Leeds District Committee decided that the evidence was not clear and they appealed to the Yorkshire County Committee to have the case reheard. The latter decided that the Leeds & District Committee should again investigate the matter and then the match was awarded to Sharlston. They were through to the final against Knottingley at Headingley.

Knottingley were decisively beaten by 11-0 in the final. It was a great game and those present claimed it was the finest game Sharlston had ever played. A brilliant try was scored by Horace Goodfellow after a sprint of 75 yards. He also scored another try and a third came from Fred Goodfellow. Charlie Fellows dropped a goal in the last two minutes. The Sharlston players received the cup and gold medals.

In the Yorkshire Cup, there was a record crowd for the season of 5,000 or so at Post Office Road for the second round tie against Sharlston. Closely contested in the first half, Featherstone led 3-0 at the interval. The second half saw Featherstone at their best and there was no doubt about the home team's superiority. Goodfellow had a kick charged down by Blakey who walked over for a try. Sharlston were well beaten. The teams were:
Featherstone Rovers: Burridge, Stott, Hirst, Seymour, Denton, Howarth, J. Williams, Blakey, Harrison, Baggot, Haigh, Walker, W. Williams,
Sharlston: F. Goodfellow; Bloomfield, Taylor H. Goodfellow, Astbury; Patrick, Nixon; J. Holland, A. Holland, Cowey, Hepworth, Jarvis, Dooler.

The Leeds & District Championship Colliers 'derby' Final was played at Headingley between Featherstone and Sharlston and resulted in a 10-5 win for Featherstone. The teams were level at the interval, Williams dropped a goal for Featherstone, and Denton scored a try. Holland obtained Sharlston's try, Fellows adding the goal. The game was close until the last few minutes before Denton sealed it with a try, Williams converting.

Featherstone also won the Wakefield & District League semi-final at Post Office Road by 25-0. The local paper said that "Sharlston were decisively beaten as ever they have been in their career. They were not as smart as they were earlier in the season."

G. Bruce, a half-back, who formerly played with Dewsbury and assisted Hull during the war, forward James Harrop and threequarter William Howcroft, joined Wakefield Trinity. The latter played for Trinity until 1929-30, but only made 15 appearances.

Sharlston fulfilled the promise of last season, performing consistently in both leagues and while the cups had disappointments, on each occasion they were beaten by the best junior team in the country.

The Yorkshire Senior Competition 1921-2 and 1922-3

In April 1921 the question of a Yorkshire Senior Competition was discussed by the County Committee and started from the beginning of the 1921-2 season. The League comprised the 'A' teams of the senior Yorkshire clubs: Dewsbury, Featherstone Rovers, Halifax, Huddersfield, Hull, Hull KR, Hunslet, Keighley, Leeds, Wakefield Trinity and York together with the better class junior clubs: Castleford, Elland, Sharlston Rovers, Normanton, Wyke, Selby and Knottingley.

Before the start of the season a smoking concert was held at the Sharlston Hotel to bring together the club's players and supporters. Guests included John Wilson (secretary of the NU) Mr S. Foster (manager of the NU team to Australia) and Mr F. Hoyle (chairman of the Yorkshire Senior Competition).

Sharlston did not win anything this season but this was probably their best ever season. They were on the fringe of senior football and competing against clubs fielding some players with senior rugby experience and others on the verge of making the first team in the professional game. They didn't get off to a good start, losing at York in the opener, but then had a succession of victories against Huddersfield - home and away, Wakefield Trinity, Normanton, Batley, Selby, and Keighley - home and away, before succumbing to Halifax. By the end of November they were leading the table and the giant Senior Competition flag, 12 feet by six feet, was flown across the main road against the field for as long as they retained the leadership. They secured a notable double with victory over Leeds at Headingley and surprised the Leeds reserves with their clever play. The match was regarded as the best seen on the ground for a very long time. Horace Goodfellow intercepted a pass and scored a try after running half the length of the field. Although they won matches in the New Year, their play was not up to their earlier high standard owing to injuries and their half-back, Henderson, who had been playing brilliantly, signing for Wakefield Trinity. In February Halifax became the only team to win at Sharlston this season. The final table was:

	P	W	D	L	Pts
Leeds 'A'	33	26	1	6	53
Halifax 'A'	34	24	2	8	50
Hull 'A'	34	24	0	10	48
Sharlston	32	22	2	8	46
Wakefield T 'A'	34	21	3	10	45
York 'A'	34	21	2	11	44
Elland	34	19	2	13	40
Hull KR 'A'	30	17	2	11	36
Castleford	33	15	3	15	33
Normanton	34	14	0	20	28
Hunslet 'A'	34	10	5	19	25
Dewsbury 'A'	34	11	2	21	24
Wyke	33	10	4	19	24
Knottingley	31	9	4	18	22
Huddersfield 'A'	33	11	0	22	22
Keighley 'A'	33	10	1	22	21
Batley 'A'	30	8	1	21	17
Selby	34	7	2	25	16

Some of the season's highlights included:

Wakefield Trinity 'A' 6 Sharlston Rovers 15
In September 1921, Sharlston Rovers "very clever and enterprising team," fully deserved this victory. Sharlston's half-backs, Patrick and Henderson, had a far better understanding than Quinn and Moore, the Wakefield halves, and provided their backs with plenty of opportunities. Goodfellow, played a smart game on the wing, and scored two of his side's tries. The Sharlston backs' cohesion was better than that shown by the Trinitarians. At full-back, Hardwick played "a rattling good game" for Rovers, "he kicked well and his following up caused his opponents much anxiety."

Sharlston Rovers 22 Selby 3
In October, Selby's team included players well known in top flight Northern Union rugby, including Scamans, Ford, Todd and Gawthorpe (Leeds), Benns and McMichaels (Bradford) and Midwood (York). Sharlston played well as a team and it was the "intelligent understanding" among their players that gave them victory. Rovers won with two goals and six tries to Selby's one try. Hardwick played well at full-back. Sharlston's tries were scored by A. Holland with three, C. Fellows, C. Scott and H. Goodfellow, the goals came from J. McGee and Fellows.

Huddersfield 'A' 5 Sharlston Rovers 11
The same month, Rovers' excellent form continued with victory at Fartown. Rovers scored a goal and three tries against the home side's single goal and one try. Sharlston were congratulated on their performance by the Huddersfield players and some of their supporters. The game was a fast one. The Sharlston players tackled well, and "had their opponents down before they had time to think." Rovers combined well and all played well. Henderson and Patrick, the half-backs, combined well and their understanding was a valuable asset to the team. The forwards packed solidly and in addition to scrimmaging well, were effective in the open and tackled strongly. Rovers' tries came from H. Goodfellow, Mortimer and Henderson, with J. McGee adding the goal.

Sharlston Rovers 11 Hull 'A' 0
In December, Hull's 'A' team were beaten, despite including several players who had played in the first team; Milner and Gwynne at half-back, and Garratt, Taylor and Mason in the pack. Sharlston played well together, outclassed the men from the Boulevard and by "clever combination" they penetrated their opponents' defence. H. Henderson, C. Scott, C. Fellows, and H. Goodfellow all played splendidly. Tries were scored by H. Goodfellow, C. Scott and C. Fellows. J. Hardwick kicked the goal.

Sharlston Rovers 5 Normanton 0
Challenge Cup 3rd qualifying round
A record crowd attended this match in February. The local paper said that "A great amount of keenness was manifested in the game but this was only to be expected and on the whole the match was pleasantly contested." The referee handled the game well. Rovers played in "wholehearted fashion" although they were the lighter side. From a scrum the ball was kicked well up, Baddeley took the ball on the bounce and scored a try, which Hardwick converted. This was the only score. Rovers tackling and the pack, led by McGee, won them the match. The best man on the visitors' side was Haycock.

Elland knocked Sharlston out of the Cup in the fourth qualifying round. Hardwick was injured after 25 minutes and took no further part in the match. This was a severe blow to the Rovers who became disorganised and Elland took full advantage of this.

Sharlston Rovers 0 Halifax 'A' 4
Later in February, Rovers' ground was covered in snow and although it was snowing at kick-off, the match went ahead and produced Sharlston's first home defeat this season.

Rovers were handicapped by the absence of prominent players such as Fellows, Patrick - owing to illness - and C. Scott - due to suspension. They were replaced by W. Hepworth and F. Stott at half-back - the former being a forward, and A. Holland, at centre, who was also a forward. There was a poor gate. Those present saw a well-fought game, despite the wintry conditions. Halifax took the lead through a Kitson penalty. Rovers attacked in the second half but Kitson, the visitors' full-back, kept them out. Kitson added a second penalty to win the game.

Sharlston Rovers 7 Leeds 'A' 5
The next month Rovers defeated the league leaders through "splendid" defence. In the first half, Leeds only scored a penalty by Davidge. Near the interval Hardwick kicked a goal for the Rovers. In the second half Sharlston attacked in "wholehearted fashion although they were outweighed in all departments". The game was the best seen on this ground for years.

From a scrum in the visitors 25, Scott scored a try which Hardwick converted. Soon afterwards Leeds scored, but failed to convert. Special mention must be made of the tackling of the Sharlston players who, following the ball, were on their opponents quickly All the Sharlston team played well. The Leeds team included players such as Short, Hook, Lyons, Graham, Walker, Brown (a Yorkshire half-back), Goodward, Davidge, Thomas and W. Ward.

Rovers finished fourth in the league, scoring 308 points and conceding 208, but lost to Leeds in the semi-final play-off 7-3. The form book didn't work out; Sharlston had done the double over Leeds 'A' in the league and Halifax performed the same feat over Sharlston, but Leeds 'A' easily defeated Halifax 20-5 in the final.

The under-19 intermediate side were defeated 12-7 by Lofthouse, at Belle Vue in the Wakefield & District League final. The Sharlston team was: Chalkley, Lunn, Wooton, Dooler, Allen, Stott, Goodfellow, Bailey, Wilkinson, Stead, Burrows, Schofield, Smith. On the day, Stott, Wooton and Chalkley were Sharlston's best players.

Sharlston and Salem Intermediates met in the Final of the Cooke Shield. However, the game was a farce as Sharlston commenced with nine players, then a tenth arrived and finally the complement increased to 11. The result was a 36-5 defeat.

At the end of the season a benefit match was arranged at Belle Vue when a team got together by Jonathan Parkin played Sharlston Rovers, the proceeds of the match being given to Taylor, a winger, who broke his leg in the league match at Halifax.

1922-23

This season was disappointing for Sharlston. They had been in the top four of the league throughout the previous season but failed this season to find the same consistency. Despite winning four of the first five matches, they only managed another three wins in the rest of the season, finishing 11th position in the 14 team league.

However, there were some interesting league encounters:

Sharlston Rovers 6 Wakefield Trinity 'A' 16
After 20 minutes Sharlston lost Nixon with a twisted knee. There were some 'incidents' which were not in the rules. Moran, a Wakefield forward, and a Sharlston man were sent off but the local paper said that their deeds were not as bad as two more actions which were not punished. In both cases Wakefield men were deliberately struck by Sharlston men and the referee administered a caution to one player but the other incident was not detected by the officials.

For Sharlston, Hardwick played well at full-back, and his kicking was powerful and well directed. Stott was the best threequarter, while Patrick worked hard at stand-off.

Normanton 0 Sharlston Rovers 8
The heavy ground conditions made handling difficult, but Sharlston at times took the ball cleanly. Neither side was at full strength and some intermediate players were included.

Sharlston had about six intermediates playing because some of their players "are dubious of turning out away from home." Rovers opened the scoring after 30 minutes. Howcroft, a former Wakefield Trinity winger, scored. Hardwick missed the conversion. Play was "too keen at times" and the referee sent off Green of Sharlston and later Normanton's Blakemore. Then Sharlston added to their lead. They were pressing on the Normanton line when the ball went to Howcroft who scored his second try. Hardwick was successful with the kick.

Hunslet 'A' 5 Sharlston Rovers 3
Nearly 2,000 spectators saw a good match. Sharlston started well and Patrick was prominent with some good kicking. Howcroft received the ball on the right, beat a number of opponents and raced for the line. He kicked past the Hunslet full-back, and won the race for the ball to score. Patrick missed the conversion. In the second half Rovers put up a good fight but eventually Howarth scored a try for Hunslet and Mason added the goal.

Hull K R 'A' 3 Sharlston Rovers 0
The visitors' play surprised the home club's supporters who had expected a comfortable victory, especially as they had fielded a strong side. The Sharlston players "worked like Trojans". There was some good hooking by J. Hall, and Hardwick, the Sharlston skipper and full-back played a great game. Barker scored the only try for Hull. A draw would probably have been a fair reflection of the game.

The newly formed Sheffield Hornets team which included Wrigley, the former Huddersfield player and other men formerly prominent in the Northern Union started their home programme at Darnall and Sharlston were their first opponents. Sharlston won 6-0 and the play of the Rovers gave a very good impression to the spectators who seemed to enjoy the game.

Sharlston scored 169 points in the league, but conceded 261. The final table was:

	P	W	D	L	Pts
Hull 'A'	26	21	2	3	44
Leeds 'A'	26	19	0	7	38
Hull KR 'A'	26	17	1	8	35
Castleford	26	15	2	9	32
Elland	26	16	0	10	32
Wakefield T 'A'	24	15	1	8	31
York 'A'	22	13	1	8	27
Hunslet 'A'	26	11	0	15	22
Halifax 'A'	26	12	0	14	22 (2pts deducted for ineligible player)
Keighley 'A'	26	9	2	15	20
Sharlston	24	8	0	16	16
Featherstone 'A'	26	7	1	18	15
Wyke	26	6	1	19	13
Sheffield H	26	2	3	21	7

Sharlston had been drawn at home in the first round of the Yorkshire Cup, but by arrangement the match was played at Batley with a crowd of 2,000. The experience and superior class of the Batley 'A' backs was more than the Sharlston defence could handle and Batley scored five tries in the first half and went on to an easy 32-11 victory. In the closing stages Green and Fellows were sent off. Rovers' team was: Hardwick; Sandham, Fellows, Bloomfield, Stott; Howarth, E. Hepworth; Cowey, Hall, Green, Baddeley, W. Hepworth, Holland.

Sharlston travelled to Castleford in the third qualifying round of the Challenge Cup, gave a very disappointing display and lost 23-0. Rovers protested that Castleford played two players who were on Bramley's books. Castleford produced correspondence with Bramley giving them permission to play the men but on the grounds that they had not actually been struck off the Bramley register the league ordered the match to be replayed and as it was a technical breach of the rules gave Castleford the choice of ground. Castleford won the replay 6-0 at home. The replay attracted double the attendance of the original match and there were above 2,000 fans present. Rovers made changes to their side and put up a much better performance. Jolly played at full-back for Hardwick, Howarth played half-back in place of Broadbent and Willis and Morgan were brought into the forwards.

In the first half it was a typical cup-tie game, strenuously fought and both sides put in some excellent play. Castleford scored two tries, the second of which came 10 minutes from time when Sharlston were a man short.

The Intermediates (under-21s), reached the final of the Fotherby Cup at Belle Vue, losing 5-2 to Normanton. Sharlston missed chances through poor handling, and their only score came from a penalty by Chalkley. After the match, Sharlston objected to a Normanton player, which necessitated withholding the medals. The objection was considered frivolous by the Wakefield Committee, but Sharlston appealed to a higher authority. The County Committee heard the case, which was that J. Wilson, one of the Normanton players was suspended. However, the Wakefield Committee had reconsidered their original decision and reduced the suspension therefore making Wilson eligible for the match. The Wakefield representative said that they were in order to reduce the suspension. The County Committee however, decided that the player's appeal against the suspension ought to have been made to the County Committee and that the Wakefield League had no power to reduce it. They allowed Sharlston's objection and ordered the match to be replayed.

Normanton 3 Sharlston Rovers 0 (replay at Belle Vue)
Both teams had a large number of fans. One in the pavilion was so noisy that the police told him to stop his racket. Normanton's try came in the second half. Chalkley and Dexter played well for Sharlston, and G. Dooler, Sharlston's full-back, played a safe game and was the best man on the field.

Normanton 13 Sharlston Rovers 0
Wakefield & District League Intermediates Final (under-21)

Normanton won their third cup, scoring two goals and three tries to defeat Sharlston at Belle Vue. For Sharlston Morley and Hepworth were sent off in the second half.

At the end of the 1922-3 season, Wakefield, Dewsbury, Batley, Featherstone, Sharlston and Normanton withdrew from the Yorkshire Senior Competition for financial reasons. The Trinity Committee said it had proved too expensive and it was their view that there would be more interest in a local league. They also felt that unless they kept the game alive in the Wakefield and District, association football would get the upper hand. The above mentioned teams joined West Ardsley, Dewsbury Celtic, Bruntcliffe, Birstall Old Boys and Bottomboat in the Wakefield, Dewsbury & District League.

1923-24

This season Sharlston had some silverware to show for their efforts. The Yorkshire Junior Cup was won for the first time and also the Wakefield, Dewsbury & District cup, which they first won in 1906-7, when it was introduced.

On their journey to the Yorkshire Cup Final they eased past Bottomboat, Featherstone British Legion and Bruntcliffe but in the fourth round Featherstone Rovers

'A' provided stiffer opposition. Sharlston won 10-7, but the Featherstone correspondent of the *Wakefield Express* was not very generous with his comments: "Sharlston deserved their victory although they have not much to write home about as to the quality of their play". Sharlston overcame Rastrick in the semi-final and went on to meet Hull BOCM in the Final at Belle Vue.

Sharlston Rovers 14 Hull BOCM 5
Yorkshire Junior Cup Final

Sharlston were worthy winners, and were far too strong for the Hull combination. There was a large and enthusiastic following from Sharlston. The local paper said that one supporter who was in the press box "must be a big asset to his side, for his 'loudspeaker' of 'Now, Sharlston' must have been heard all round the enclosure." The teams were:
Sharlston Rovers: W. Chalkley; M. Freeman, H. Goodfellow, E. Hepworth, J. Allen; F. Patrick, L. Nixon; E. Cowey, J. Dooler, G. Green, M. Jarvis, C. Baddeley, E. Smith.
Hull BOCM: W. Sowerby; J. Tomlinson, D. Cooper, A. East, E. Lowther; J. Winship, J. Rayner; K. Harrison F. Stephenson, H. Dixon, E. Bartle, J. Burnell, H. Rimble.

The Sharlston pack was too strong for their opponents and they got the ball five times out of six. The backs, in particular Patrick, kicked too much. However, he scored the first try, Chalkley missing the conversion. Sharlston did not lead for long as from the kick-off Chalkley made a mess of the kick and Dixon scored, with the goal added. Sharlston attacked and Patrick passed to Goodfellow who broke through to score. Chalkley again missed the goal, but Sharlston had the lead. In the second half, Sharlston attacked and Cowey got over for Chalkley to convert. Nixon added a fourth try.

In the pack, Dooler was following in his father's footsteps who played for the club some years before. In the second half E. Smith was withdrawn from the forwards to help the backs and even with only five forwards the ball still came out the right side. Sharlston's hardest working man was Patrick, while Nixon, who had played for York, was strong at stand-off. Goodfellow was an effective attacking centre, while Hepworth, the captain, worked hard. At full-back, Chalkley started poorly, but improved.

Four days later Sharlston met Normanton in the semi-final of the Wakefield, Dewsbury & District League Cup and earned the right to play Batley 'A' in the final by defeating the home side 14-0. Sharlston deserved their success although Normanton were handicapped much of the game through losing the services of their captain and centre, Cusworth, who accidentally broke his leg in the first half after falling awkwardly.

Sharlston Rovers 5 Batley 'A' 0
Wakefield, Dewsbury & District League Cup Final

The match was disappointing with little exciting play. It was spoilt by the dismissal of three players, two from Sharlston and one from Batley. The teams were:
Sharlston Rovers: W. Chalkley; Freeman, Dexter, Goodfellow, E. Hepworth; Patrick, Nixon; E. Cowey, Green, Dooler, Jarvis, P. Gill, E. Smith.
Batley 'A': Ineson; Kirby, Scholes, Morton, Stephenson; Brannan, Thackray; Griffiths, Demaine, Macreth, Crabtree, MacAvoy, Buckley.

The first score came after 20 minutes when Chalkley landed a penalty. After cautioning one or two Sharlston players, the referee, Mr A. Brown, sent off Jarvis for something which occurred when his side were attacking on the Batley line. Sharlston started the second-half 2-0 ahead and with only 11 men, Gill being absent "owing to some slight illness." He was only away for a few minutes, however but during that time Sharlston scored. The ball went to the wing where Green scored. The conversion was missed and Sharlston were 5-0 ahead. In the second half, Batley lost Demaine, who was carried off with concussion, and both sides were further depleted when Dooler and Thackray were sent off for rough play.

For Sharlston, Chalkley played "a brilliant game. He took the ball well and kicked with good length and excellent judgment. Another prominent feature in the play of the winners was the keen and sure tackling of Goodfellow."

Castleford, who were in the Senior Competition, visited Sharlston in the final qualifying round of the Challenge Cup. Rovers were up against an experienced side but made a good sporting fight of it, but lost 16-0. Sharlston objected to Castleford playing three ineligible men. The protest failed, but the club's deposited fee was returned although they had to pay the expenses of the Castleford representatives at the hearing.

Sharlston won seven of their 13 league matches and were not involved in the play-offs. They did well in their engagements with Wakefield Trinity 'A'. After drawing at Sharlston they took both points in the return at Belle Vue. Wakefield Trinity 'A' had a splendid record in this local league, of which they were easy leaders and it was no mean performance on Sharlston's part to secure three out of the possible four points especially when one takes into consideration the fact that they were not at full strength owing to their important cup final with Batley 'A' the next evening.

Presentation to Jonty Parkin

The *Wakefield Express* reported that the residents of Sharlston took great interest in the rise to fame of Jonty Parkin, the Wakefield Trinity and international half-back who was from the village and had played for the local intermediate team. It was decided to give him a small token of their appreciation of his selection again, and captaincy, of the team to tour Australia

This took place at the Sharlston Hotel. Mr Jones presided and Mr Fairclough handed Jonty a handsome gold wristwatch. In accepting the gift Jonty said that "he appreciated the kindness (Courtesy Robert Gate) and feeling, which had prompted it and any help which he could render the Sharlston football club he would only be too pleased to give."

Speeches were also made by C. Varley, E. Jones, T. Bruce and F. Willis and an appeal was made for the Rovers to be better supported in their efforts to provide the town with good football. Mr C Lumb presided at the piano and the evening's harmony was contributed to by Jonty Parkin, A. Taylor (Outwood), F. Mappin, J. Howden, W. Hollin, J. Dodd, T. Bartley, G. Lomas, F. Brayford and H. Bailey. At the end of the proceedings the members of the company carried their guest downstairs to a waiting motor car.

Jonty wrote to Tom Bruce from Brisbane on 4 July about the tour, saying that the team were getting ready for the third test, and that they had been unlucky with injuries, with 11 players out. But they had won the Ashes, "so we have also done what the boys wished me when you made me the presentation at the Sharlston Hotel. I do hope we win on Saturday, which I think we shall, as we shall have a much stronger team out than for the two previous Tests. I not only want to break the record for my own sake, but to uphold the traditions of my native village." Sadly, Great Britain lost the third test.

It came as no surprise when all the 'A' teams who had withdrawn from the Yorkshire Senior Competition last season decided to rejoin it in 1924-5. Wakefield Trinity said it was neither good for the club or the game that their reserves should have to play some very weak teams in the Wakefield, Dewsbury & District League. This left the League with just six clubs, as Bruntcliffe and West Ardsley had joined the Leeds & District League. They were: Alverthorpe, Bottomboat, Cliffe Athletic (Crigglestone), Dewsbury Celtic, Sharlston and Yorkshire Main.

Before the start of the 1924-5 season a meeting of supporters and players was held at the Sharlston Hotel, with the Secretary of the Wakefield, Dewsbury & District League and President of the Wakefield & District Intermediate League, as speakers, to discuss junior club finances.

An appeal was made for the speakers as members of the League Management Committee to endeavour to get junior clubs a grant from the proper quarters because it was essential that something must be done if the game has to make progress. Sharlston were in debt by £50 and had done everything they could to reduce this amount.

Sharlston should have been in a more competitive league than the Wakefield, Dewsbury & District League but their finances did not allow it. They were not well supported by the villagers. It was inevitable that they would be league champions in 1924-25, Cliffe Athletic were defeated in the final by 42-0, and they had to look to the Qualifying Rounds of the Challenge Cup and the Yorkshire Junior Cup for any competitive rugby.

In their first league match they received a visit from Yorkshire Main, Edlington, who before this season had played rugby union. Sharlston won 28-10. The visitors, who were unfamiliar with the rules, tried hard but were outclassed by Rovers. Sharlston went on to be undefeated in the league. Alverthorpe were comfortably defeated in the semi-final play-off and on they went to face Cliffe Athletic in the league final.

Sharlston Rovers 42 Cliffe Athletic 0
Wakefield, Dewsbury & District League Final.

Sharlston soon took the lead at Belle Vue. At half-time they were ahead 19-0, with two tries from Riley and one from Shaw. Chalkley converted twice, dropped a goal and also kicked three penalties. In the second half, further tries were added by Shaw with three, Patrick with two, Wood, Dexter and Stott, with four more goals by Chalkley.

The Sharlston pack was far too strong for the Cliffe forwards and thus Sharlston's backs were constantly in possession. At stand-off Patrick broke through repeatedly and his passes were well timed. Wood, in the centre, played unselfishly and gave Shaw at least three tries that he could have scored himself. Stott and Dexter also played well and at full-back Chalkley kicked nine goals, including two from the touchline.

The Challenge Cup qualifying rounds provided incidents, excitement and objections. The earlier rounds resulted in comfortable victories for the Rovers, but the fourth round brought the smart Leeds outfit Spring Gardens to Sharlston.

Sharlston Rovers 8 Spring Gardens 5

A crowd of about 1,000 included a good following from Leeds. Stubborn defence – 'real Sharlston tackling' - kept the visitors out at first, but after 15 minutes they went ahead from a penalty goal.

Then there was an 'ugly scene.' The *Wakefield Express* said that "The referee, Mr Holliday, found it necessary to speak to Gill, a Sharlston forward. It is alleged that Gill struck the referee and ugly things followed. Followers of both teams encroached on the field and there were many fights. The referee stopped the game but some 10 minutes later peace was restored and play was resumed, Sharlston losing Gill's services."

It was 2-0 to the 'Gardeners' at the break, but early in the second half Sharlston went ahead, Shaw scoring after a great passing move with Patrick and Wood. The latter missed the conversion, but shortly afterwards put Sharlston further ahead with a penalty. Then the visitors scored a try, making the score 5-5. Sharlston won with a try from Hepworth from the best move in the game. Sharlston hung on although about five minutes from the finish Hepworth received his marching orders.

Spring Gardens put in an objection, which was sustained and the match was ordered to be replayed, at Sharlston

Sharlston Rovers 3 Spring Gardens 0

Mr E. Ward of Batley, a well known referee, was in charge and there were none of the unpleasant incidents which marked the first meeting. The game was keenly but cleanly fought and was excellently controlled. About 1,200 spectators, many of whom were supporting the visitors, saw a typical cup tie.

The winners would be at home to Castleford in the last qualifying round, the winners of which would go through to the first round proper.

Sharlston were beaten for possession in the forwards. In the backs, Patrick, who played a great game at half-back, Dexter, Wood, and Shaw outclassed the visitors.

Sharlston went ahead when Shaw scored a try in the corner. The conversion was missed. In the second half there was no further scoring so Sharlston earned the right to entertain Castleford, and "should reap much needed financial benefit therefrom."

Sharlston Rovers 5 Castleford 7

Sharlston could not be persuaded to switch the tie to Castleford, so a crowd of 2,000 came to Sharlston, including many visiting fans. For the visitors, Sherwood had to come off in the first half with an injured ankle and so they did well to win. Sharlston were without Patrick and Dexter. Wood missed a penalty for Sharlston from a good position. Hargreaves kicked a penalty for the visitors. Then following forward pressure, Riley scored for Sharlston. Chalkley had kicked a penalty goal, but he failed to convert the try and Sharlston thus were ahead 5-2.

Before the break Hargreaves kicked another penalty and at half-time Sharlston were leading by one point. With only five minutes left, Castleford got in front when Nash scrambled over for an unconverted try.

Rovers played a very creditable game and it was disappointing for their supporters that they were deprived of victory so near the finish. Stott was their outstanding player.

Sharlston protested to the League Committee to the result on the grounds that L. Farrar and B. Booth were not *bona fide* members of the Castleford club. The protest was dismissed and £2 of the Sharlston deposit was forfeited as the Committee considered the protest was frivolous.

Sharlston, holders of the Yorkshire Junior Cup, had to visit Normanton in the third round this season and the tie was decided on penalty goals, Normanton winning 4-2. With a nice day and no local counter attractions a good crowd was present. Both sides fielded their strongest teams:

Normanton: Wilson; Walker, Stephenson, Arthurs, Harper; Carswell, Parkin; McGuire, Duran, Loxton, Welsby, Handley, Hepworth.

Sharlston Rovers: Chalkley; Shaw, Dexter, Wood, Goodfellow; Patrick, Stott; Green, Hepworth, Baddeley, Riley, Mortimer, F. Stott.

Normanton played down the slope in the first half and led at the half-time by two penalty goals from Wilson. Sharlston's supporters were ultimately disappointed, for, although Chalkley managed to reduce the deficit to two points from a penalty, Normanton lasted the better in the second half. Normanton were penalised during one of the visitors' attacks and Chalkley tried to level the game. The position was rather far out, however, and his well directed kick fell short. Normanton deserved their victory, although Sharlston were far from disgraced. For the visitors, Patrick was "a box of tricks". At full-back Chalkley, fielded the ball and kicked well.

Sharlston entered for the first time, and won, the Castleford & District Cup, defeating Normanton at Featherstone's Post Office Road ground in the final. It was the last match of the season, and Sharlston won by the only score of the game - a try, about half way through the second half. The pitch was very heavy and made good football difficult, and play was rather scrappy.

1925-26

The 1924-25 season was followed by two quiet seasons with very little to shout about. Rovers joined the Castleford & District League in 1925-26 when the Wakefield & District League disbanded. No trophies were won; Castleford 'A' in the Yorkshire Junior Cup and Normanton in the Challenge Cup were responsible for Sharlston's cup exits. Rovers performed well to keep in contention for the League Championship, but their progress was halted by Knottingley in the play-off semi-final.

Normanton 6 Sharlston Rovers 2
Rugby League Challenge Cup First Qualifying Round

The teams were:
Normanton: Walker; Harper, Reeves, Hepworth, Kielty; Goodyear, W. Hepworth, Loxton, Lee, Morley, Baddeley, Yates, Handley.
Sharlston Rovers: Dexter; F. Hepworth, Owen, Chalkley, Handley; Patrick, F. Stott; T. Chalkley, Gill, Stevenson, Riley, Schofield, F. Stott.

A try in each half by Harper, the Normanton winger, sealed Sharlston's fate. For long periods in the first half Sharlston attacked but met a solid defence. Only one point separated the sides at half-time, Patrick having kicked a penalty for Sharlston. Early in the second half Harper scored his second try and the Normanton defence held out. Near the end, Sharlston's Schofield was sent off.

In the Yorkshire Junior Cup, Sharlston lost 28-0 at Castleford. Sharlston arrived late with a weakened team. Castleford scored eight tries to go through.

The League play-off semi-final was closer, Knottingley Rovers beating Sharlston 6-3. The scores were level at half-time, both teams having scored a try, Barrett for Knottingley and Stott for Sharlston. However, Sharlston's G. Green was sent off for disputing a referee's decision. In the second half Sharlston tackled well but with a man short they were unable to keep their opponents out, and after several scrums conceded a try and for the remainder of the game were on the defensive.

1926 was a terrible year for the working class generally and the miners in particular. In coal-mining there was a background of wage cuts, dismissals and falling living standards. On 3 May the TUC called a General Strike, then suddenly nine days later called it off. But the miners struggled on for six months before being forced to go back to work, accepting longer hours and lower wages.

Many years later Alan Schofield, a Sharlston forward in the 1920s, told a rather pathetic story from the 1926 strike, when things in the area were as hard as they have ever been. A playing colleague sold him his Yorkshire Junior Cup gold medal for 2s 6d (12.5p) but he later became desperate for money and pawned it for 3s 6d (17.5p).

1926-27

Sharlston were now back in the revived Wakefield & District Junior League. However, the most notable feature of this season was the number of players sent off the field. No fewer than eight players: Schofield, Jukes, A. Dooler, J. Dooler, T. Chalkley, E. Cowey, E. Baddeley and G. Green - received suspensions ranging from two to six matches. The club was going through a mediocre period. Many players left the club, mostly to join Normanton - there had always been 'comings and goings' between the two clubs - but a promising young full-back called Chalkley joined Batley.

Sharlston had to travel to Windhill in the qualifying round of the Challenge Cup and were beaten by the only try of the game. In the league, they lost the play-off semi-final to Stanley Rovers.

1927-28

Sharlston had more to show in honours this season, winning the League Championship and Knock-Out Cup competitions, but they were no longer serious contenders for the Yorkshire Junior Cup, losing in the second round, or in the Challenge Cup, being defeated in the third qualifying round.

Sharlston Rovers 21 Stanley Rovers 2
Wakefield & District Junior League championship Final

Sharlston were the heavier and more experienced side at Belle Vue and although Stanley Rovers fought hard, in the second half they lost Bramner through injury. Chalkley opened the scoring for Sharlston with a penalty, and then Hudson got an unconverted try. Edwards kicked a penalty for the Rovers. In the second half, Stanley defended well for a time but eventually Sharlston got the upper hand and added another 16 points, including four tries.

Wakefield & District Junior League Cup, Sharlston beat Lofthouse Colliery 22-4 in the final at Featherstone. On the way to the final they had a real tussle with Stanley Rovers in the second round, the match going to a replay.

In the Challenge Cup, Sharlston played Castleford Recreation in the third qualifying round and lost. As happened so often when Sharlston faced a Castleford team, a protest was made. Sharlston objected to Castleford playing W. Sherwood, alleging that he was not eligible to play. They claimed that Sherwood had been suspended for eight matches by the Yorkshire County Committee and had not completed the suspension. Castleford Recreation submitted a list of matches which they said they had played but this was challenged by Sharlston's officials. The protest was not upheld. Interestingly at the same meeting Kirk Sandall protested against the result of their match with Askern Welfare on the ground that W. Batten, the former international, was not a *bona fide* member of the Askern team. Kirk Sandall claimed that Batten only joined the club a week before the cup match, his first for Askern. The protest was upheld and the Committee ordered the match to be replayed at Askern, the home club to play without Batten.

In the league, Sharlston played 22 matches and lost only three. They finished top of the table, one point ahead of Stanley Rovers.

1928-29

This was a satisfactory campaign by Sharlston, but apart from finishing the season as league leaders - they headed the table throughout – and losing only one match out of 24, there were no trophies to show for it. Rovers finished six points clear of the second team, Sutcliffe's, and lost the championship final to third- placed Stanley Rovers. In November Hepworth, Loxton, Hudson and Howcroft were suspended until the end of the season.

Stanley Rovers 10 Sharlston Rovers 7
Wakefield & District League championship final

The teams were selected from:
Sharlston Rovers: W. Chalkley, P. Owen, E. Richardson, J. Chalkley, M. Freeman, C. Owen, W. Westwood, J. McGee, H. Jukes, C. Baddeley, E. Brooks, Riley, W. Hepworth, E. Cowey.
Stanley Rovers: A. Burton, C. Taylor, H. Browning, R. Burton, H. Dennison, J. Kirby, Stead, J. Smales, E. Robinson, Capes. W. Morley, A. Greenwood, S. Dickinson, W. Clegg, H. Guest, W. Kale, A. Yates.

Although both teams were capable of playing a passing game, there was too much kicking in the final at Belle Vue. Stanley produced the first score. Browning scored a try, and Smales converted. William Chalkley then kicked a penalty for Sharlston and later had a great chance to score a drop-goal, but the ball went wide. Sharlston applied pressure and Richardson went over for a try, which was converted by William Chalkley. Stanley now attacked strongly, and Burton kicked a drop goal to make the half-time score 7-7.

C. Taylor scored the winning try for Stanley in the second half. Sharlston attacked for all their worth, but the Stanley defence held out, giving them victory.

Sharlston were favourites to retain the Wakefield & District Knock-Out Cup when they met Sutcliffe's in the Final. But Sutcliffe's had finished second in the league and put Sharlston out of the Challenge Cup in the qualifying rounds. Nevertheless Sharlston had comfortable victories against them in the league and victory was expected. There was much disappointment when Sharlston lost their second final of the season.

Sharlston Rovers 0 Sutcliffe's Works 8
Wakefield & District Cup Final

There was a very good attendance at Featherstone and more enthusiasm than at any Featherstone senior game this season. Ladies were very prominent in the crowd and they must have been intensely disappointed with the result. The teams were:
Sharlston Rovers: W. Chalkley; Freeman, J. Chalkley, Richardson, T. Hepworth; W. Hepworth, Westwood; McGee, Cowey, Brooks, Baddeley, Ramsden, Riley.
Sutcliffe's Works: Walker; Adams, Oakes, Lawley, Schofield; Dobson, Scott; Wood, Hardcastle, Todd, Noble, Frisby, Pybus.

From the start there was little open play and too much kicking. Sutcliffe's' forwards beat Sharlston for possession from the scrums and their scrum-half worked hard.

Adams, gave Sutcliffe's the lead before the interval. The game got tougher after the interval, with Sharlston the worst sufferers, at one time only having 11 players on the field. Walker increased Sutcliffe's lead with a drop-goal from a penalty, preferring to drop than kick in the usual way. Adams put the issue beyond doubt with his second try,

The cup was presented by Mrs Hudson, the League President's wife.

1929-30

The 1929-30 Wakefield & District League season opened without Ackworth, Hall Green and Altofts, who dropped out and were replaced by Normanton, Thornhill and West Riding Auto Co. The teams in the league were Hemsworth Colliery, Hopetown, Horbury, Kinsley, Kirkhamgate, Lofthouse, Normanton, Sharlston, Stanley, South Elmsall, Sutcliffe's, Thornhill and West Riding Auto Co.

Sharlston got off to a flyer with wins over Kirkhamgate, Hopetown, Sutcliffe's and South Elmsall, but their run of success came to a halt at the hands of an old enemy, but newcomers to the league, Normanton, who achieved their first victory of the season. However, Rovers went straight back to winning ways and by Christmas were top of the league. They had two real battles with Hemsworth Colliery in January, getting full points at home before playing a 0-0 away game.

Even in the lower scores of these times, a 0-0 draw was rare. In the first half the Colliery team played uphill with the wind at their backs. Play was fairly even for the first 15 minutes and from a scrum on the Hemsworth '25', Stott broke through and passed to Morgan who beat all the opposition except the Sharlston full-back, but due to a broken bone in his left hand, he was unable to pass to Gill and what ought to have been a certain try was missed. Hemsworth pressed for some time and there was some good kicking and relieving by Warrington, the home full-back. The home side won a penalty, but J. Hall missed. Sharlston were also unsuccessful with a penalty from an easy position. In the second half play was keenly contested. Owen accepted a pass from Stott and rushed towards the Sharlston line, but was pushed into touch by J. Chalkley.

Sharlston and Stanley Rovers had been the more dominant teams in the league since it was revived in 1926-27, but this season Stanley had the better team, winning both league fixtures and the League Cup semi-final.

In the Challenge Cup, Sharlston reached the fifth qualifying round by defeating Brotherton St James 4-3. Having beaten Lindley in an earlier round, Brotherton St James expected to beat Sharlston. According to the *Wakefield Express's* Brotherton correspondent, "Luck was against them. They had a bad off day and Sharlston were never really dangerous". Sharlston lost to South Elmsall in the next round. In the Yorkshire Junior Cup, Sharlston lost to Castleford BL, and in the league, the club did not reach the semi-final play-offs. In September 1929, William Chalkley, a former full-back for Sharlston and Batley, passed his referee's examination. Once again, the club were in trouble with the game's authorities, and for playing W. Shaw and A. Grandidge, who were ineligible, at Hopetown, Sharlston were fined 5s (25p) and 5s for playing M. Freeman at Stanley.

Two teams from the 1920s and 1930s

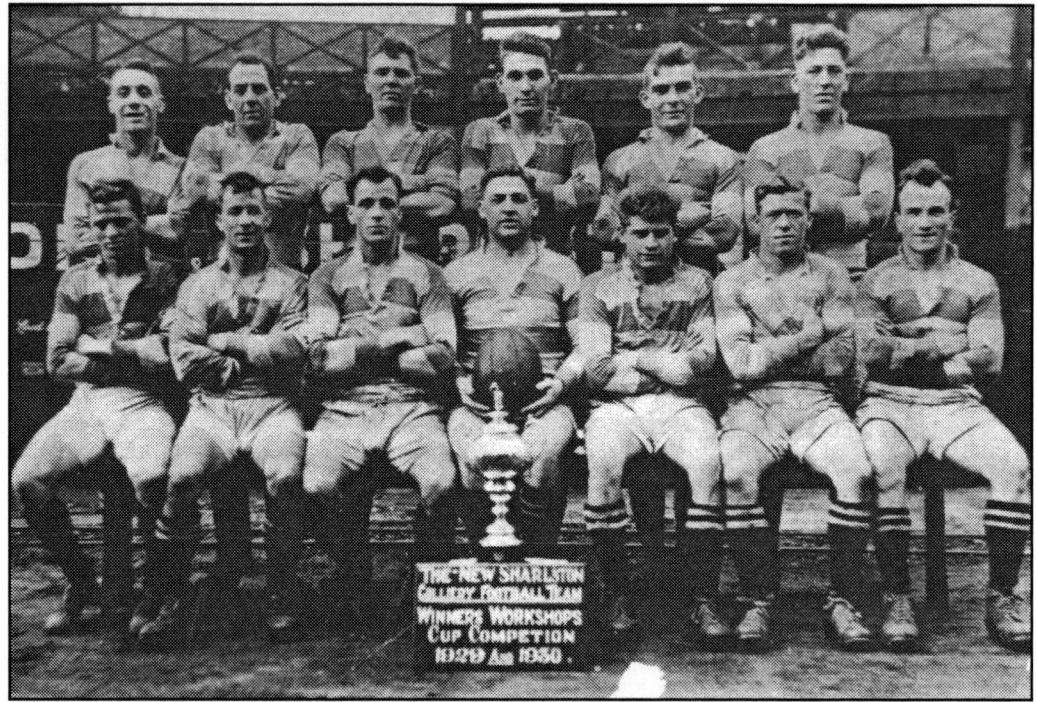

The New Sharlston Colliery team – winners of the Workshops Cup Competition in 1929 and 1930. Most of the players played for Sharlston Rovers. Back: Bag Shaw, Ned Westwood, Arthur Loxton, Albert Musgrave, Albert Riley, Jim Chalkley; front: Josh Ward, Cocky Crummack, Walt Hepworth, Billy Chalkley (captain), Bill Wood (?), H. Dodger Hudson, Fred Hepworth.

The 1932-33 Sharlston All Blacks team: Players: back: L. Wain, J. Wildman, J. Bruce, H. Smith, N. Westwood, W. Wildman, T. Ackroyd; Sitting: M. Hargreaves, T. Bowers, M. Greatorex, J. Pollitt, B. Lingard, B. Wood, B. Reynolds. Kneeling: A. Green, A. Wilson.

4. The 1930s - The All Blacks

The 1920s had seen very hard times for the village and all those connected with the club deserve praise for keeping going. At times they were seriously in debt, although there had been success on the pitch. The 1930s would see further development of rugby league in Sharlston

1930-31

Batley Celtic were admitted to the Wakefield & District League, but Featherstone's application to join was refused because in the previous season they had been members of the Castleford and District League.

Sharlston saw some tangible reward for their labours this season, winning the league championship, but they lost in the Yorkshire Junior Cup Final and just failed to reach the Challenge Cup first round proper, surprisingly losing at Featherstone Juniors in the final qualifying round. There was a lot of interest in the match and the gate receipts were about £25. The Sharlston forwards controlled the pack and their half backs had abundant possession. However, the backs kicked too much. Sharlston took the lead when Ward kicked a penalty. Early in the second half Sharlston were penalised and with a magnificent kick from near touch Johnson equalised. The try which settled the match came from a passing movement in which Fisher kicked smartly over the line and Joe Evans touched down, so Featherstone won 5-2.

It was thought that this was the first time in the history of rugby league that an intermediate team had reached the first round of the Challenge Cup. Featherstone were members of the Wakefield and District Intermediate League which meant that no player in the team was over the age of 21 at the start of the season. In the first round they travelled to Wigan Highfield and lost 41-3.

There was no easy passage for Sharlston in the earlier rounds of the Yorkshire Junior Cup before they beat Hull St Mary's 9-8 in the semi-final and earned the right to play the strong Lindley side in the Final at Huddersfield. Lindley had a great season, won every amateur competition they entered, as well as qualifying for the Challenge Cup first round proper, losing 13-2 to Rochdale Hornets.

Lindley 13 Sharlston Rovers 5
Yorkshire Junior Cup Final

The first half was played in a 'vigorous' fashion, and the referee called both teams together to caution them. Owen scored for Sharlston after a great run in which he beat Lindley's full-back, Sowden, with ease. Losing at half-time, Lindley were quick to score when Sowden kicked a penalty. They finally took the lead when excellent passing left Morgan with a clear run to the line. Sharlston went on the attack and equalised when Grandidge dropped a goal. Then came the best try of the game. Lindley's Nestor collected a deep kick, accelerated towards the left corner and scored. Sharlston went further behind when Jones scored under the posts leaving Sowden an easy conversion.

In the League Cup, Sharlston were defeated by Normanton. However, Rovers were worthy League Champions. They were top or thereabouts all season, winning 15 of their 20 matches, drawing one. They were edged off top spot by Normanton in the closing matches and the two met in the championship final at Featherstone.

Sharlston Rovers 8 Normanton 4
Wakefield & District League championship final

Featherstone Rovers were great supporters of amateur rugby league and local people respond well to an admission price of 6d or 8d, maybe reflecting the hard times in this mining village. There was an excellent attendance when Sharlston Rovers and Normanton met in the Wakefield and District Junior League final.

The ground was in splendid condition, but the two teams were so keen to win that they forgot the finer points of the game while preventing the other team from scoring.

Patrick played well for Sharlston, but was sent off in the second half by the referee, Mr Parkinson of Wakefield. Sharlston took an early lead with an excellent goal by Chalkley from near halfway. As the first half went on, Normanton came more into the picture. Before the interval another passing movement by Sharlston, ended in a try by Gaskell, but Chalkley missed the goal.

Sharlston's lead was reduced early in the second half by a penalty from Plant. The Normanton full-back and Sharlston's Stott were off the field for a time through injury, but before they went Gaskell had scored his second try - an individual effort. When Patrick was sent off Sharlston were badly handicapped. Eventually Stott resumed and the Normanton full-back also returned but was not much use. With 13 players to 12, Normanton had most of the play, but their passing was poor. The only other score was a second penalty by Normanton and Sharlston's victory was well deserved.

The cup was presented by Mrs Reyner, wife of the League secretary and there were medals for the members of both teams.

Sharlston players, Jim Chalkley and Owen were signed by Wakefield Trinity and Leeds respectively, and the secretary of the Wakefield and District League was asked to write to these clubs about the non-payment of signing-on fees. The opinion was expressed that clubs ought not to be allowed to sign any player until the £2 signing on fee had been paid.

1931-32

The Wakefield & District League was reduced to 10 teams, from 14, but it was good to see Streethouse back in the fold, though Sharlston would be well aware of their presence before the end of the season. In both the League play-off semi-final and the League Cup Final, Streethouse got the better of Rovers.

The League was a very poor one, Normanton, Streethouse and Sharlston drawing well clear of the pack. Goodfellow, Hepworth and Howcroft left the club, the first two joining Askern and the latter going to Streethouse. It was the performance of the intermediate team which delighted the villagers this season, winning the Fotherby Cup and becoming League Champions

The Fotherby Cup

Sharlston and Featherstone's junior teams drew in the final at Belle Vue, and Sharlston won the replay. The teams lined up as follows:
Featherstone Juniors: Greenfield; Brogden, Johnson, Plenderleith, Jones; Carey, Taylor; Wood, Nash, Keeble, Bingley, W. Johnson, S. Taylor.
Sharlston Rovers: Pollitt; Smith, Speight, Lingard, F. Bowers; Quinn, Garrity; Mosley, Simpson, Gough, Pearson, Fisher, Hargreaves.

The referee was Mr L. Thorpe from Wakefield. Poor weather restricted the crowd, and there was a heavy ground and difficult ball to handle.

Featherstone had the heavier pack, but the light Sharlston forwards packed solidly and in spite of the weight against them they secured the ball quite often. As the second half progressed, their efforts waned and they appeared to be drained. Territorially the game was Sharlston's for they applied pressure for considerable periods without being able to find a way through to the line. Neither side gave anything away and the game ended in a pointless draw without extra time being played. On a wind and rain swept ground the pace maintained was a fine testimony to the fitness of the players.

The replay: Sharlston Rovers 2 Featherstone Juniors 0

This time the weather conditions were ideal. Taking Saturday's encounter as a guide, Sharlston were favourites. However, the interval arrived with neither side having registered a point.

The second half opened at a fast pace. There was a melee near Featherstone's posts and careless kicking proved to be their undoing. Strong forward rushes and kicks sent the ball cleanly into Speight's hands, who dropped a goal 10 minutes from the end. Then Keeble of Featherstone and Sharlston's Gough commenced 'all-in' wrestling and ended up with a fight. The referee gave both players their marching orders. As they were leaving the pitch, Hargreaves struck at Gough and he too was sent off. After this incident Featherstone tried to break through the Sharlston ranks but failed and victory went to the better team. The cup was presented by Mr Hudson, the League president. He was introduced by Mr Tony Bland, the League secretary.

Sharlston Rovers 5 Featherstone Juniors 0
Wakefield & District Intermediate League Championship final

Sharlston and Featherstone met again, before a large crowd, on the Featherstone Rovers ground in the League final. Featherstone were weakened by Brogden's absence, their centre, who had joined Wakefield Trinity and were missing other players. Sharlston had a big following, including hundreds of women and girls, who saw them win their second trophy of the season.

The game was keenly contested and in the second half one player from each side was dismissed. The forwards were evenly matched but with the exception of their scrum-half, the Featherstone backs were very disappointing.

Featherstone's defence was at fault when Sharlston scored the only try of the match, which was converted, and at half-time Sharlston led 5-0.

Featherstone did more attacking in the second half but could not finish. Some fierce scrums were fought out near the Sharlston line, but the defence prevailed and Sharlston proved worthy 5-0 winners. The cup and medals were distributed by Mr Graham Woodhead, a member of the Wakefield Trinity Committee.

What a great season for the Intermediate side. They were top of the League, winning 12 of their 14 matches, losing one and drawing one, and collected two trophies.

1932-33

In August 1932 the organiser of the Wakefield & District League announced that following a meeting of the league it was decided that it should be disbanded. The reason given was that "the higher authorities have encouraged teams to leave the league and also refused permission to other clubs who wished to join". They later changed their minds and a league was formed but with only six clubs in it: Crigglestone, Jackson's Sports, Kinsley, Normanton, Sharlston Rovers and Streethouse. Jackson's Sports later withdrew. The league was farcical and there was very little interest in it. With so few teams in the league it was decided that the League Cup should be thrown open to any club, but it was decided that no player on the professional register of any league club would be eligible to play.

Lindley defeated Sharlston in the second preliminary round of the Challenge Cup, and Normanton saw them off in the second round of the League Cup. And there was no joy for them in the Junior Cup.

The remarkable achievements of the Intermediate side, known locally as the All Blacks, made them the pride of Sharlston. Playing in the Wakefield & District Intermediate League of 11 teams, their final league record was 20 victories from 20 games, scoring 603 points and conceding 58.

They were also the Champions of Yorkshire, defeating Hull 14-3 in the County Final at Dewsbury; and won the Fotherby Cup. Three trophies won for the village - a wonderful season.

Sharlston Rovers 7 Featherstone Juniors 3
Fotherby Cup Final at Belle Vue

Featherstone's Asquith scored first, but failed to add the conversion. Shortly after this Pollitt kicked a penalty for Sharlston and with only one point separating the teams the game was continued with much excitement. Both teams played vigorously, but there was no addition to the score before the interval.

There was some fast play after the break. Green got the ball from the pack and after a splendid movement in which he was assisted by Wilson, Bowers and Lingard, the latter scored a try and from an easy position Pollitt converted.

Mr T. Bland, the League secretary, formally introduced Mr W. E. Dey, who presented the cup and shaving sets to the winners, and wrist watches to the runners-up. Mr Dey, as head of the Sharlston Council School, knew all the Sharlston players from their school days.

Sharlston 5 Normanton Garth House 0
Wakefield & District Intermediate League Championship final

There was a large crowd to see the final at Belle Vue, with gate receipts of £29. The teams were:
Sharlston Rovers: J. Pollitt (capt.); T. Bowers, E. Garrity, C. Reynolds, B. Lingard; G. A. Green, A. Wilson; E. Westwood, T. Wildman, J. Bruce, L. Hargreaves, H. Smith, T. Ackroyd.
Normanton Garth House: A. Brighton; W. Bryant, T. Price, A. Hall, J. Cairns; J. Hilton, J. R. Maddock; G. Poundall, W. Milner, J. Crossley, J. Dyson, A. Fisher (capt), G. Brighton.

Rovers were keeping the ball tight and their forwards did some effective dribbling, reminiscent of the rushes of by gone days. After 17 minutes, Normanton were penalised for obstruction and from a distance of 40 yards Pollitt kicked the penalty. At the break, Sharlston led 2-0.

In the second half, Sharlston wore down their opponents and there were some very keen scrums on the Normanton line. Five minutes from the end there was the first passing move by the Sharlston backs. Lingard scored, but Pollitt missed the conversion.

From a spectators' point of view the game was disappointing with too much individual play or the ball was left to the forwards, or the backs did too much kicking. Passing movements were rare. For Sharlston, Eddie Garrity, the son of Jack Garrity, the old Sharlston, Dewsbury and Wakefield full-back, and Benny Lingard were the pick of the threequarters, and Arthur Green worked hard at half-back.

The cup was presented to John Pollitt, the Sharlston captain by Mr Lazenby from Normanton. Mr Tony Bland, the organiser of the Intermediate league, who was doing a great deal for junior rugby, said that match finished a brilliant season in connection with the Intermediate section, for Sharlston had carried off three trophies and had won the Championship of Yorkshire, a performance they were proud of. Sharlston have followed in the footsteps of other clubs who have brought honour to the league. There were some players on the field who would have to say goodbye to intermediate league football, but he hoped they would go higher to play with prominent clubs.

Mr Lazenby said he was pleased that Sharlston had won the cup, and that they were turning out good footballers today, just as they had done in times gone by.

It is not clear where the Intermediates played or why they were called the Sharlston All Blacks when their proper name was Sharlston Rovers. The obvious explanation for the latter is that it was a nickname given to them by the villagers because they played in an all black strip, but it was suggested many years later that they got the name from coming out of the pit with black faces - no pithead baths in those days - throwing on a rugby shirt and going straight on to the field. A good story, but not be taken seriously.

Where the team played is more difficult to resolve. Older villagers say that they played at the bottom of the brick yard after it had been levelled from being a quarry; one remembers his father cutting down nettles so they could play.

The Sharlston All Blacks included Jack Wildman, Fred Astbury, Les Wain, Les Westwood, Wilf Wildman, Tom Ackroyd, Len Hargreaves, Tommy Bowers, Joe Bruce, John Pollitt, Benny Lingard, Bill Wood, Butch Reynolds, Tubby Wilson, Arthur Green, Eddie Garrity and Harry Smith. The latter turned professional with Featherstone Rovers and made his first team debut in 1933. He played until 1938 when he retired through knee problems and was honoured in 2006 as Featherstone's oldest past player.

Benny Lingard and John Pollitt were selected to play for Yorkshire against Lancashire at Oldham. According to reports, Pollitt had an outstanding game, and was soon attracting scouts from the professional game. He joined Castleford, and was one of the most promising players in intermediate rugby. When he signed he was 20 years old, 5 feet 9½ inches and 12 stones. He belonged to Wakefield and he came into prominence when he kicked 121 goals and scored 13 tries for Sharlston Rovers.

Swinton, Rochdale Hornets, Oldham, St Helens, Warrington and other clubs in Yorkshire were interested in signing him. However, he came under the intermediate rules, which kept a player to a limited area until he became 21. This meant he could only join Wakefield Trinity, Featherstone Rovers or Castleford. He came from a well-known Castleford family. His father had lived at Ryebread. He made 31 first team appearances for Castleford between 1933 and 1937, scoring one try and 58 goals. He played for Castleford in their first match against the Australians in 1933. The tourists won 39-6.

1933-34

Sharlston withdrew from the Open Age League before the start of this season. Mr Johnson, the Featherstone representative on the Wakefield & District League Committee, made a special visit to the club to try and get them into the League but to no avail.

The intermediate side played in the Intermediate League but most of last season's successful team had moved to other clubs and they were a much weakened force. They resigned from the League in March having won six of their 15 matches. It had been a struggle to keep going for so long. As well as Pollitt, three other players joined the professional ranks. Benny Lingard had joined Featherstone, Les Westwood had gone to Wakefield Trinity and Fred Astbury joined Castleford.

1934-35

They were down and out in 1933-34, but the Rovers were back in the open age with a vengeance in 1934-35. Unbeaten and top of the League at Christmas they stayed there for the rest of the season and won the League Championship. In 11 league games, they won 10, drew one and scored 180 points to 25, their line having been crossed only once.

The mainstay of the team was George Goldie, the former Featherstone, Leeds and Batley player who was a tower of strength all season. But the icing on the cake for any junior club is to win through to the first round proper of the Challenge Cup and the possibility of David slaying Goliath. This season after beating Brotherton St John's and Buslingthorpe Vale - conceding ground advantage in each case - Sharlston were in the first round by defeating Bagley's Recreation, 11-2, in the final qualifying round. They were now looking forward to the draw and sent officials to Manchester to witness it. Of the four amateur clubs taking part Sharlston was the only one drawn away, with a long trip to Barrow, although two others, Astley & Tyldesley Collieries and Barrow Marsh Hornets, both switched their games to their professional opponents' grounds.

Barrow were not having a particularly good season, and finished 20th in the League table, with 31 points from 38 matches.

Sharlston had a good blend of youth and experience for as well as Goldie they had Wood, formerly with Batley and Bramley, Newitt, who had played for Dewsbury, Lister, formerly of Featherstone and Lingard, who had played with Wakefield Trinity. Although there was little likelihood of them becoming giantkillers, they were expected to give a good account of themselves.

Barrow 28 Sharlston Rovers 3

According to the *Wakefield Express*, Sharlston played a "very plucky" game and "stuck to their guns right to the end." They had more of the game than the score indicated. However, Little, the Cumberland county half-back, and Gummer, Barrow's young Welsh centre played prominent roles for Barrow. Barrow scored six tries before the interval and two more afterwards.

Sharlston's forwards had pressed Barrow back early on, and had chances in the first half. Hudson was tackled near the Barrow line. At half-time Barrow were 20-0 ahead.

Sharlston exerted pressure in the Barrow '25' but they only scored once, shortly after half time when Lister took a pass and scored a try. Sharlston had played better in the second half, but could not match their professional opponents. Dooler and Goldie both missed with penalties for Sharlston in the second half. The teams were:

Barrow: Bennett; Johnson, Barton, Gummer, Harris; Maddock, Little; Yarr, McKeating, Skelly, Troup, Ayres, Griffin.
Sharlston Rovers: Dooler, Hudson, Goldie, Speight, Lingard, Wilson, Wood, Simpson, Wildman, Lister, Schofield, Newitt, Bailey.

Right: The Sharlston teamsheet for the Barrow match. The team had to leave at 7.30am for the train trip to Barrow.

The gate receipts were £197/19/7. Once expenses were deducted, including £4/5/0 for teas, Sharlston's share was £68/12/8 plus £9/15/0 for the train fares.

Yorkshire Junior Cup

In the Yorkshire Junior Cup Sharlston survived a second round replay against Streethouse to progress to the semi-final and a meeting with Normanton - the holders - in a tie they lost, again after a replay, by one point.

Normanton were fortunate that Goldie, the Sharlston full-back, who throughout the match gave a flawless display, was in poor goal-kicking form. He had 12 shots at goal, none from a difficult angle, yet he was successful only twice.

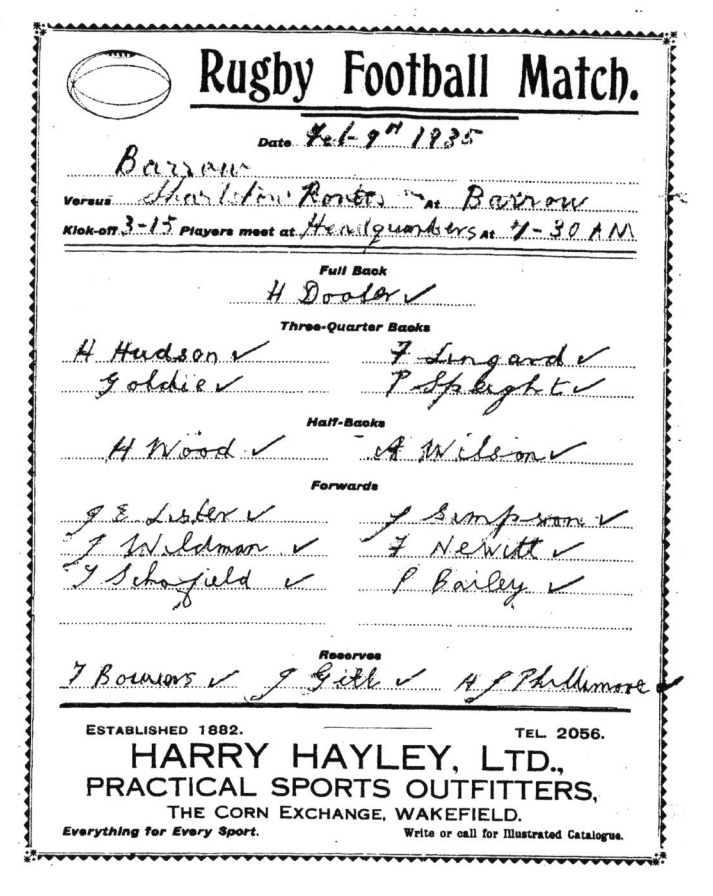

The first match was a 0-0 draw. The replay was seen by 1,300 spectators, paying £17, and was "a grim fight so typical of the long standing rivalry between the two clubs." Normanton made two changes from their usual side, but Sharlston were at full strength.

Normanton took the lead Owen charged down a kick on the wing, gathered the bouncing ball, and ran over unopposed, although Plant missed the kick. After 15 minutes of the second half, Sharlston were in front, Goldie converting two penalties under the Normanton posts.

Sharlston appeared well set for the final, but as in the first half, they came up against a solid defence and they were unable to add to their lead. With 15 minutes left, Normanton took the lead again when Plant landed a great penalty almost from the halfway line. Before the end, however, Sharlston missed several good chances. Dooler ran into a tackle when four Sharlston players were awaiting a pass which would have resulted in a try. Twice in the closing minutes Goldie missed penalties from simple positions. Normanton won by one point, 5-4.

It was a good comeback season for Sharlston. Last season they had a break and the village went over to association football, they came back and once again upheld their proud rugby league reputation. They did not compete in the Intermediate League.

1935-36

Sharlston joined the Leeds & District League, a lower standard league than a few years before. It included Eastmoor, Buslingthorpe, Burley Vale, Leeds Corporation CD, Gawthorpe, Lindley, Normanton, Lee Moor, Castleford, Stansfield Rovers and Streethouse. The intermediate team was back in action in the Wakefield & District League and did very well, winning the League play-offs and the Fotherby Cup.

The Challenge Cup

Once again the open age team reached the final qualifying round of the Challenge Cup. Given a scare by Streethouse Intermediates in the first preliminary round, scraping through by the odd point, the following rounds brought easier victories, the most surprising being against Normanton, who were defeated 30-7 in the fourth qualifying round. The gate receipts were £14, showing the interest in matches between these bitter rivals.

After an early Sharlston onslaught, Normanton rallied to within three points in the first half. But in the second period, Rovers ran riot and their 30-7 victory was a surprise to their own followers. Normanton's collapse was mainly due to poor play in the scrums and unimpressive work by their backs. The Sharlston backs handled the ball much quicker. Sharlston's tries included a hat-trick by Dooler, with others from Worth, Ward and H. Wood. Crummack kicked six goals.

Rovers had the luck against them in the draw for the final qualifying round, having to make the long journey to Seaton, near Workington, but were confident of victory. This was not to be and after a plucky fight they were defeated 7-2. The team was selected from: Crummack, A. Wood, Worth, Dooler, Wilson, Ward, H. Wood, Hale, Simpson, Lister, Wildman, Bucknall, Gidman, Oldroyd, Fox.

The Challenge Cup Competition was the highlight of the season. They were knocked out of the Leeds & District Cup by Leeds Corporation DC and did not progress beyond round two of the junior cup. After finishing fourth in the league, they were defeated in the semi-final play-off by Eastmoor 7-0. Prior to the play-off Eastmoor had visited Sharlston in an important league fixture, but to the surprise of the Eastmoor team and supporters, Sharlston refused to turn out The explanation of some of the Sharlston people was that it was a club matter, a domestic affair. Some of their supporters had gone to Belle Vue to witness the Fotherby Cup Final between Sharlston Intermediates and Streethouse Intermediates, but this was not given as the reason.

Eastmoor had only lost one game all season and the only team to lower the Eastmoor colours were Sharlston Rovers. The semi-final play off was the only match this season in which Sharlston had not scored.

The Intermediate team was involved in four semi-finals, the All Yorkshire County Intermediate Cup, losing to Rastrick, the Wakefield & District Intermediate Cup, the Fotherby Cup and the League championship. The team won the last three semi-finals and were successful in the finals.

Sharlston Rovers 5 Streethouse 3
Fotherby Cup Final

About 1,000 supporters were present at Belle Vue for this local derby between Sharlston and Streethouse. Streethouse reached the final by beating Lupset and Sandal and

Sharlston defeated Balne Lane and West Ardsley. The teams were:
Streethouse: G. Wilson; C. Hollis, J. Rooney, J. Hale, R. Bulmer; T. Johnson, J. Ackroyd; H. Nickolson, C. Jones, H. Lyman, E. Adams, A. Farley, J. Riley.
Sharlston Rovers: H. Lockett; J. Bailey, R. Turton, B. Harper, J. Hunter; W. Allen, R. Speight; D. Bradley, K. Bloomfield, J. Goulding, D. Davies, E. Allen, S. Speight.
The referee was Mr F. Chappell of Ossett.

Sam Speight missed an early penalty for Sharlston. The Sharlston pack was more lively in the loose and from a quick break from a scrum they forced Wilson, the Streethouse captain, to touch down behind his own line.

Then Sam Speight missed another penalty kick for Sharlston from the '25' yard line and another Sharlston attack was repulsed by Wilson with a well judged kick.

The opening try came when Bloomfield secured possession for Sharlston from a scrum, and R. Speight passed to Harper, who beat his man and outpaced Wilson to touch down. From near the posts Sam Speight was inches wide with the conversion.

Half time arrived with the score 3-0 in Sharlston's favour. Throughout the first half Sharlston displayed better understanding than Streethouse, who were lucky to be only three points in arrears.

In the second half Sharlston's superiority was more marked and their star was definitely Johnny Bailey, who landed a good goal from 40 yards out for a penalty for offside. Streethouse replied immediately, and Ackroyd scored a try just wide of the posts. Farley's kick hit the post, which was the difference between defeat and victory.

The trophy was presented by Mr C. Shayler, the manager of the Wakefield Playhouse, who introduced Mr T. Bland the competition secretary. He said that they had seen a fine match between two clever teams and his only grumble was that there were not more people present.

Sharlston 8 Streethouse 3
Wakefield & District Intermediate Cup final replay

Both the final and the replay were played at Featherstone Rovers ground. The first match was a brilliant exposition of the handling code, with scarcely a dull moment. The game was well refereed by Mr Raynor from Eastmoor.

After Sam Speight and Bailey missed penalties, W. Allen finished a great passing movement with a try to give Sharlston the lead after 30 minutes, Speight converting. Within five minutes, Streethouse reduced the lead when Barraclough scored, but Wilson missed the conversion. Turton sent Sharlston further ahead with a brilliant try, following excellent play by backs, Speight converted to give Sharlston a 10-3 lead which did not reflect the run of play. After the interval Streethouse played inspired football and Sharlston defended desperately, Johnson was unsuccessful with a drop at goal and Barraclough and Johnson nearly scored tries. A penalty in the Sharlston '25' area saw Farley score.

Streethouse heightened their efforts and Wilson grounded for Farley to add the goal. With the scores level both teams went all out for a winning score, a Sharlston player was sent off, but when W. Allen scored a try, Streethouse seemed to be finished. However, Bulmer snatched a try but Farley missed the kick and this game finished 13-13.

The replay was three days later. Rain fell steadily during the second half, so that the ground was slippery, and handling of the ball was difficult. The teams had met four times and the honours were even, Streethouse the league leaders had not lost a game, had beaten Sharlston both at home and away, but were beaten by Sharlston in the final for the Fotherby cup and the Yorkshire Challenge cup.

Both clubs made team changes for the replay, which were:
Streethouse: Wilson (capt.), Hollis, Bulmer, Barraclough, Marsh, Johnson, Ackroyd, Nicholson, Rooney, Farley, Riley, Adams, Hale
Sharlston Rovers: Lockett (capt.) Hunter, Harper, Dooler, Turton, R. Speight, W. Allen, Goulding, Bloomfield, Bradley, Davies, E. Allen, S. Speight.

Sharlston quickly attacked following a serious bungle by the opposing backs and Streethouse had to defend strenuously but Wilson cleared. Lockett found touch and Sharlston charged forward enabling W. Allen to scramble over and give them a three point lead after 10 minutes. Sam Speight missed the goal. Farley then missed a penalty for Streethouse.

Streethouse had a great opportunity to level the scores after 35 minutes. Barraclough drew the opposition and passed to Marsh. The latter beat his man and had only to touch down, but he seemed intent on grounding near the posts and when challenged slipped and dropped the ball. Streethouse improved in the second half and appeared the more robust side but Sharlston were more cohesive and handled more neatly.

Then Sam Speight kicked a penalty to put Sharlston further ahead. Soon afterwards Marsh scored a well earned try for Streethouse from an opening by Bulmer, Farley missed the conversion. In the last 10 minutes, Turton ran round the scrum to score for Sharlston, but Speight missed the goal, Sharlston finished worthy winners. Both teams received gold medals which were presented by the League President, Mr W. Britton.

Sharlston 20 J. & J. Charlesworth's 3
Wakefield & District Rugby League Workshops Competition

The final was played at Belle Vue. In the semi-finals Sharlston defeated Eastmoor and J & J Charlesworth's beat Nostell. There was a gate of nearly 2,000 with receipts of £15.

From the start the Sharlston pack were on top. 'J and J's' or 'Market', as the colliery team's supporters called their favourites, were weak in defence and allowed their opponents too much space. But Sharlston were not very convincing, but did back up well. A gap in Market's defence provided Sharlston with their first try, Hale sprinted over almost unchallenged. Pollitt kicked the goal. Soon afterwards Charlesworth's scored when Shirley engineered an opening and put in a short kick and Burton followed up to score. Ward failed with the conversion. Pollitt increased Sharlston's lead to 7-3 with a drop-goal before half-time. In the second half, Sharlston asserted their superiority and further tries came from Wood, Turton and Bulmer. Pollitt landed two goals.

The mayor of Wakefield, Alderman A. Charlesworth presented the cup and awards. As winners, each member of the Sharlston team received a clock and the runners-up got a case of cutlery each. Alderman Charlesworth congratulated both teams and said that much credit was due to the players many of whom had done a hard day's work before playing football.

He was disappointed at not being able to attend the Workshop Competition before that night, for he said the players were always triers and that was something they did not always find in the best of clubs. In some Northern Rugby League clubs there were a number of shirkers but they were not to be found in workshop competition matches. He wished the competition every success and mentioned that part of the gate money was to be sent to Clayton Hospital.

1936-37

The 1936-37 and 1937-38 seasons were not memorable for the seniors in the Open Age League. In April 1937 they were suspended from the Leeds & District League for non-payment of fines and did not appear again until 1938-39.

They started promisingly enough in 1936 defeating Wakefield Trinity 'A' in a friendly at Belle Vue, but there was very little to enthuse about after that. They were knocked out of the Challenge Cup by Buslingthorpe Vale, the Yorkshire Junior Cup by Goole and the Leeds & District Cup by York Clarence, all at the second round stage.

Undoubtedly their best performance of the season was against Buslingthorpe Vale in the league game at Sharlston. Farley opened the scoring with a penalty for Sharlston and shortly afterwards Hibbert equalised. Two minutes later, Allen cut through to score a brilliant try and from a difficult position, Farley converted.

Following a move by the home threequarters, Owen scored in the corner and Farley kicked the goal. Just before the break Hibbert kicked another penalty, so Sharlston led 12-4 at half-time. In the second half the Rovers controlled play and scored tries by Quinn and Wildman; Farley and Barraclough kicking the goals. Hibbert added a try for the visitors; the final result was 22-7.

The intermediate team kept up their trophy-winning habits, retaining the Fotherby Cup. They were defeated by the Hull Champions, St Mary's, in the semi-final of the Yorkshire Intermediate County Challenge Cup at Featherstone and by Sandal in the League Final. An interesting name in the Sharlston pack was Len Marson, who went on the make 305 appearances for Wakefield Trinity, scoring 32 tries. He also played regularly for Yorkshire and once for England. He was unlucky not to be selected for the 1950 Australian Lions tour. He joined Hunslet in 1952.

Sharlston 8 Hull St Mary's 13
Yorkshire County Intermediate Cup semi-final

This semi-final was at Featherstone Rovers ground for the right to meet Hunslet Carr in the Final. The teams were:
Sharlston Rovers: W. Allen; R. Green J. White, B. Harper, J. Hunter; R. Speight, W. Berry; D. Bradley; K. Bloomfield, L. Marson, E. Allen, J. Riley, S. Speight.
Hull St Mary's: T. Hastings; J. Wells, H. Brown, W. Ness, S. McLaughlan; Lawrence, R. Mills; J. Sharpe, F. Noble, E. King, M. Wells, R. Swift, H. Morgan.
Referee: Mr W. P. Thompson (Knottingley)

Hull began strongly, but Sharlston's pack fought their way downfield and Berry, White and Harper set up Harper to score, but he tripped when racing for the line.

Sharlston were well placed when Hull were penalised but R. Green failed badly with the penalty. Another good move initiated by the Sharlston full-back W. Allen saw Hunter, Harper and White in full flight for the line, but Hastings retrieved the ball and turned the tables. Sharlston dominated the scrums and only keen tackling kept them from scoring. They did take the lead after 15 minutes when Sam Speight landed a penalty.

Then Sharlston were penalised in their own '25' and Brown equalised for Hull. Sharlston were still the stronger side and handling well forced their way to the Hull line, where from an opening by R. Speight, E. Allen touched down, Sam Speight failed with the conversion; the interval arrived with Sharlston 5-2 ahead.

The second half was hotly contested with two penalties bringing Sharlston an advantage. Harper dodged several opponents to score in the corner, with Sam Speight again failing to convert, so Sharlston led 8-2. But Hull's threequarters beat the opposition for Wells to score in the corner. Brown missed the conversion.

In the ensuing play E. Allen made a mistake by running inside when he had three colleagues unmarked on the outside.

At this stage Hull were playing as if inspired, heeled the ball out beautifully and time and again beat Sharlston with swift passing. From one move, Ness passed to Brown who scored. Hull were now on top and Wells touched down for another try to win 13-8.

Sharlston Rovers 0 Sandal 11
Wakefield & District Intermediate League. Championship final

The teams were:
Sandal: G. Ramsden, L. Standaloft, A. Bell, W. Watson, L. Tippin, R. Hamilton, H. Herberts, R. Margreaves, T. Heley, H. Murton, W. Singleton, W. Wood, J. Margreaves.
Sharlston Rovers: W. Berry, J. Hunter, G. White, B. Harper, E. Green, R. Speight, W. Allen, D. Bradley, J. Bloomfield, L. Marson, J. Riley, E. Allen, S. Speight.
Referee: W.L. Wraith

The first half at Belle Vue was disappointing. There was too much kicking and the ball being frequently dropped. Sharlston had one fine chance when Green made for the line, but a splendid tackle sent him into touch.

Sandal also missed a glorious chance when Bell intercepted and ran to the full-back, but the ball was thrown to a player inside who was tackled from behind. There was no score in the first half.

In the second-half, play was more interesting and the Sandal backs were soon in action, the ball went from Herbert to Hamilton and then to Bell who scored.

Immediately afterwards Standaloft raced over in the corner, in each case the goal was missed. With a six point lead it looked as if it was an easy thing for Sandal but Sharlston were by no means done with in spite of being a man short.

Berry came from the full-back position and worked the scrummage, and having a good supply of the ball Sharlston were on the attack for 15 minutes. Watson and Tippin held Hunter twice when he looked like scoring. Sharlston were on top but could not score while Sandal added another five points. Bell intercepted a pass on the Sharlston '25' and raced away to score under the posts, Tipping added the goal. It was a pity that Green had to leave the field as he was Sharlston's best attacking player.

At the conclusion of the game the cup and medals were presented by Mr G. H. Exley, the Wakefield Trinity and Great Britain player.

Sharlston Rovers 9 Thornhill Lees 3
Fotherby Cup Final

There was a good attendance to see the Wakefield and District Intermediate League Fotherby Cup Final at Belle Vue. The ground was slippery, but the weather was ideal. However, bad feeling crept into the game and the referee sent off three players, Riley from Sharlston, who was suspended for two matches, and Holmes and Ellis from Thornhill in the second half. Before the official took this action there were unsavoury episodes in the match.

The cup was presented to Sharlston by the Mayor of Wakefield, Councillor George Hemingway. Watches were given to each player.

1937-38

Without an open age team, it was left to the intermediate side to keep the flag flying this season and this was one of their more disappointing seasons. They did get to the Fotherby Cup Final after losing to Whitwood in the semi-final, but were awarded the match after they objected to Whitwood playing an unregistered player Their opponents in the final were Purston, who won comfortably 14-5; Purston also defeated them in the League semi-final play-off and went on to win the Championship.

The club was well represented in the county trial match at Belle Vue with Stead, Thompson, H. Speight and Roscoe all playing for the 'Probables' side.

1938-39: Sharlston Red Rose

Sharlston were back in the Leeds & District Open Age League as Sharlston Red Rose. This name lasted for only one season; the club reverted to Sharlston Rovers after the Second World War. The other teams in the league were Buslingthorpe Vale, York Clarence, Glasshoughton, Leeds Corporation, Coghlans Sports and Bramley 'A'.

Again, as in 1934-35, it was the Challenge Cup which brought the most excitement. In the first qualifying round Sharlston met Glasshoughton who the season before had reached the first round proper, but on their home ground found Rovers too strong and lost 6-2. Next to fall to Red Rose were Buslingthorpe Vale, quite easily, 21-4. North Bridge (Hull) were their third qualifying round victims but few teams have gone away from Sharlston commanding such respect as the Hull side did. North Bridge fought admirably after the early dismissal of one of their forwards and though for the greater part of the game they were defending their own line they made a spurt after half-time which brought them to within one point of the Sharlston score. Sharlston, encouraged by a constant roar from their supporters fought off this challenge and countless attacks were met by a stern defence. The climax to all the excitement came 10 minutes from time when Frank Dooler, the Sharlston centre, leapt high to intercept a pass one-handed and sprinted the 10 yards to the line unchallenged. Wilson converted and Sharlston won 13-7. The last qualifying round brought Lindley to Sharlston and they were quite comfortably beaten, 17-5.

Sharlston were elated at the result of the first round draw: Bramley at home, the first professional club to visit Back o' t' wall in the Challenge Cup. The 'red letter' day was 4 February. The players assisted in building the banking at the ground to accommodate 4,000 spectators. There were two severe frosts before the game which was in doubt right to a few hours before kick-off. Ten to 15 oil drums were placed on the field with fires in them to thaw out the frozen pitch and all this enabled the match to go ahead.

Sharlston were hard hit by injury of two of their best players, Henry Dooler and Sam Speight. Bramley had in their side the vastly experienced New Zealand half-back Ted Spillane. He was brought to England by Wigan, having twice played for his country. He left Wigan for Keighley and in his time there transformed the Keighley team. His next move was to Bradford Northern before rejoining Keighley in 1937, but this was only for a short spell before signing for Bramley before the start of the 1938-39 season. He played a big part in Sharlston's defeat.

> **OFFICIAL PROGRAMME**
>
> BEFORE AND AFTER THE MATCH, CALL AT THE
> ## SHARLSTON HOTEL
> J. DOOLER, PROPRIETOR
>
> FOR the first time in the history of the Sharlston Club, which covers a period of 65 years of Rugby Football, we have the honour of playing at home in the First Round of the Rugby League Challenge Cup. Our records for a great number of years are very well known throughout Yorkshire, and we trust that, in having Bramley as our visitors (they have carried on for a number of years in spite of great opposition and poor support) we shall have a great game—and may the better team win !
>
> We have been wanting a home draw for long enough, and now we have got it. One word to our local supporters. Please give our visitors a great reception, and show them what great sportsmen we are ! Thankyou !
>
> W. H. WARD, Hon. Sec.
>
> 1st Round Rugby League Challenge Cup   Played at Sharlston, Sat. 4 February 1939
>
> ## SHARLSTON RED ROSE v BRAMLEY
>
> | SHARLSTON RED ROSE | BRAMLEY |
> |---|---|
> | 1. G. WILSON | 1. H. TAYLOR |
> | 2. C. ECCLES | 2. L. BROWN/J. BIRMINGHAM |
> | 3. E. BARRACLOUGH | 3. E. J. MURPHY |
> | 4. F. DOOLER | 4. I. REES *BIRMINGHAM* |
> | 5. J. WORTH | 5. A. HODGKISS |
> | 6. R. SPEIGHT | 6. E. STARLING *REES* |
> | 7. A. WILSON | 7. E. T. SPILLANE (Capt.) |
> | 8. D. BRADLEY | 8. W. GRAHAM |
> | 9. J. SIMPSON | 9. J. SUDDES |
> | 10. E. ADAMS | 10. J. DESBOROUGH |
> | 11. W. GIDMAN | 11. E. WEBB |
> | 12. A. OLDROYD | 12. B. PEARSON |
> | 13. S. ~~SPEIGHT~~ *DAVIES* | 13. G. H. COOPER/E. NORCLIFFE |
>
> REFEREE—   TOUCH JUDGES—
> Mr. G. S. PHILLIPS (Widnes)   H. RICHARDSON, W. RATCLIFFE
>
> BEFORE AND AFTER THE MATCH, CALL AT THE
> ## SHARLSTON HOTEL
> J. DOOLER, PROPRIETOR
>
> Harris Bros., Printers, Featherstone. Tel. 252

The official programme from the match.

Sharlston Red Rose 5 Bramley 23
Challenge Cup First Round

A crowd of 2,500, paying £104, packed into Sharlston's small ground to see the match, one of the most memorable day's in the village's outstanding rugby league history.

The teams were as follows:
Sharlston Red Rose: G. Wilson; C. Eccles, E. Barraclough, F. Dooler, J. Worth; R. Speight, A. Wilson; D. Bradley, J. Simpson, E. Adams, W. Gidman, A. Oldroyd, D. Davies.
Bramley: H. Taylor; L. Brown, E. Murphy, J. Birmingham, A. Hodgkiss; I. Rees, E. Spillane, (capt.); W. Graham, J. Suddes, J. Desborough, E. Webb, B. Pearson, B. Cooper.

Bramley were thrown back on their '25' for at least 20 minutes as Sharlston foraged well and tackled with deadly accuracy.

In spite of all their pressure, Sharlston only once looked like breaking down the Bramley defence, when Gidman was tackled just as he appeared to have got through.

Sharlston could not keep up such a pace. At the first sign of weakness by the home side, Spillane, at the base of a Bramley scrum came into his own, and was not subdued again for the rest of the game. He made several attacks which were only stopped by Sharlston's full-back George Wilson.

Eventually Bramley scored. Cooper went over after the ball had gone through about half a dozen hands. Thereafter Sharlston were a harassed side, Rees scored a try with the defence completely beaten, and then Hodgkiss beat Wilson to touch down. Murphy added a fourth try, which like the others was unconverted.

In the second half, Bramley missed Birmingham who left the pitch just before half-time with a hip injury. Sharlston attacked and after a scrum, A. Wilson intercepted a pass from Spillane, and scored, but the position was too far out for Eccles to convert.

Sharlston added a penalty from George Wilson soon afterwards, but Bramley added three more tries through Pearson, Hodgkiss and Cooper. Taylor improved one, making the final score 23-5. Territorially, Sharlston had slightly more of the game than their visitors and considering their disadvantage in size could justifiably be proud of their performance. Their young second-row Bill Gidman worked particularly hard. The best performance from the backs came from George Wilson, mainly in defence.

In the second round Bramley won 5-0 at Swinton, but then lost 20-0 at Salford.

'Little Sharlston has a big rugby league reputation'

A report published around the time of the Bramley match showed how many rugby league players had come from Sharlston. The writer compared Sharlston to Wales for finding boxers and Yorkshire for finding cricketers.

He mentioned Jonty Parkin and a young centre called Morris, who had just joined Wakefield Trinity, and said that after the cup tie, the village would still be turning out rugby league players. It had produced more players than any other village of its size.

He looked at the old registers in the village school, and said that "From the 20 or 30 names which went to make a class for the past 40 or 50 years there was one which brought back memories... from the stage when they started kicking their cap about, the headmaster has seen them all grow, scores of young fellows". He mentioned Gidman of Hull KR, Henry Dooler of Batley, Horace Crummack of Halifax and Featherstone Rovers, Willie Hughes of Wakefield Trinity and Featherstone Rovers and Frank Marshall of York as a few chosen at random from a list that "goes on and on."

He said that the Sharlston speciality is half backs and centres. The school-master noticed that Sharlston lads "will have nothing to do with the wing positions where there is not enough hard work to go through."

He noticed that the Parkins of the future were up to their 'rugger tricks" in half a dozen corners of the school field. He also met Joe Mosley "who after 60 years as player, official and bag carrier is still doing his bit."

In this school there were Goodfellows, Parkins, Crummacks, Chalkleys, Baileys, Doolers and Lingards, all representatives of Sharlston rugby league families, who were "adding up their sums and dreaming of football fame". He spoke to a "smiling seven year old who told me that his name was Goodfellow and that his football club would be Wakefield Trinity, the place where his uncle Herbert is now a leading light."

Sharlston Rovers 1939.
Back: George Goldie, Bill Gidman, Doug Bradley, Eric Adams, Sam Speight, Johnny Bailey, Alvin Oldroyd, Percy Owen. Front: Bob Mosley (bagman), Tommy Johnson, George Wilson, Jack Simpson, Henry Dooler, Frank Dooler.

Sharlston's Challenge Cup exit was not the end of their season for they had progressed to the Finals of the Yorkshire Junior Cup and the Leeds & District Cup, but it was a case of so near, yet so far, for they lost both to Coghlans' Sports and York Clarence respectively.

In the Yorkshire Junior Cup they got the better of York Clarence, 7-6 in the semi-final and though defeated by Coghlans' by the comfortable margin of 13-4 in the final, Sharlston had the misfortune to lose Johnny Bailey, one of their wingers, who fractured his collarbone in the first half.

The final was played at Featherstone Rovers and Coghlans' were the more balanced team and deserved their victory. Coghlans were ahead 5-2 at half-time, with a powerful wind behind them. When the advantage of the wind went to Sharlston it could not be used because of positional changes caused by Bailey's injury. The outstanding player was Coghlans' centre Kelly, formerly of Featherstone Rovers. He scored all his club's three tries. Fletcher kicked two goals. For Sharlston, Wilson, the full-back kicked two goals. Their best man was Henry Dooler at scrum half.

The cup and medals were presented by Mrs A. Bullock who was accompanied by her husband, Featherstone Rovers' president.

Sharlston and Glasshoughton drew 7-7 in the first round of the Leeds & District Cup at Glasshoughton, but Red Rose took command in the replay and won 33-2. Turton was in brilliant form and scored four tries. His excellent display was watched by representatives of four leading rugby league clubs and he eventually joined Hunslet. York Clarence were the opposition in the final and took revenge for their defeat in the Yorkshire Junior Cup semi-final.

Sharlston Red Rose 0 York Clarence 14
Leeds & District Rugby League Cup Final

Sharlston, were without Gidman and Speight, two of their regular forwards, and fielded a very light pack at Headingley. This, along with the fact that practically the whole team had come straight from work at the pit, may have contributed to a lacklustre display.

The Sharlston team was:

G. Wilson; P. Owen, W. Allen, F. Dooler, J. Bailey; H. Dooler, E. Barraclough; D. Bradley, Golding, Davies, A. Oldroyd, E. Adams, J. Worth.

Sharlston pressed from the start but could not score. A kicking duel between the full backs ended when Wilson put a weak kick into touch. The heavier York pack then began to exert pressure and from a penalty awarded for a scrum infringement the York full-back hit the post.

Unfortunately, Sharlston's clearing kick was caught by the York full-back who dropped a goal to put York Clarence 2-0 ahead. Sharlston returned to the attack and a penalty against the York scrum-half gave Barraclough a chance to equalise, but his shot went outside the post.

The first move of note in the second half was a passing movement by the Sharlston backs, ending in Percy Owen being brought down on the York '25'. After seven minutes, following a scrum on the Sharlston line, York forced their way over to score, but missed the conversion. York attacked strongly and after 24 minutes the Sharlston full-back attempted to field a kick, but allowed the ball to rebound straight to a York player, who crossed the line for a gift try. York's third try soon came after good passing covered threequarters of the field. Sharlston's Worth was sent off. Following a scrum, the York loose-forward forced his way over to secure victory for his team.

The end of season Workshops Competition in aid of funds for the Clayton Hospital provided good entertainment and this season Sharlston were in the final against Walton Colliery (Sharlston West). One professional player was allowed in each side and Pollitt, of Featherstone Rovers, turned out at full-back for Sharlston, and Bratley, the Trinity loose-forward, was in the Walton team. The Red Rose side showed the more polished form. In the first half tries came from Sam Speight, Worth and Ned Westwood with Pollitt kicking two goals for Red Rose to turn round with a 13-0 lead. Freeman, playing for Walton, was injured and had to retire for a period but eventually he resumed. In the second half Sharlston continued to show superiority and Worth scored two tries for the game to end in a convincing 19-0 victory for Sharlston.

During the season, Wakefield Trinity signed 18-year-old Albert Roscoe, who had played with the Sharlston intermediate side. G. Wilson was selected to play for Yorkshire County Amateur team.

The workshops final turned out to be Sharlston's last match for six years due to the outbreak of the Second World War in September 1939. Sharlston, along with many amateur clubs, were compelled to give up the struggle to keep going under war conditions and the amateur game was almost extinct.

Two teams from the 1940s

Sharlston Rovers 1947-48. Back: Henry Dooler, Ray Bennett, Denis Chalkley, Billy Howcroft, F. Goldie, Unknown, B. Bishop, Colin Andrews, J. Smith, Jim Fisher, Les Jones, Wilf Smith, Billy Wood, G. Hawkhead, H. Booth, P. Bailey, G. Green, Charlie Bailey, Albert Gill; Middle Row: Ted Birkitt, Les Bailey, Herbert Moseley, Eric Allan, Alf Cardall, D Barrett; Front: John Willie Booth, T. H. (Dick) Ward, Tubby Wilson, Jack Simpson, Herbert Wood, G. Jukes.

Sharlston Rovers 1948-49. Back: E. Allan, D. Bradley, G. Jackson, G. Hawkhead, T. Foster, L. Jones, G. Green, F. Simpson, T. Bland; Middle: T. Birkett, E. Booth, J. Fisher (captain), A. Cardall, Miller; Kneeling: L. Bailey, J. Goodfellow, M. Cardall, Hellison.

5. The 1940s - Workington Town

There was a lot to celebrate in May 1945. Germany had surrendered, bringing to an end six years of war in Europe. Thirteen men from the village paid the ultimate price. On 8 May there was a national holiday to mark Victory in Europe (VE Day). People left their homes to sing, dance and party together. There was dancing in the streets to celebrate the joy of peace, street parties, little children waved their flags and the pubs and clubs were full. An extensive programme of events had been arranged on the village but had to be curtailed because of bad weather. However, a large crowd assembled at Old Sharlston cricket field to watch the inter-school sports and all the events were completed before it was decided to abandon the meeting.

There were hard times ahead and it would be a long time before things got back to normal. Something was needed to get the villagers buzzing again and the Rovers certainly lifted their spirits with some memorable moments on the rugby field which will never be forgotten.

Sharlston quickly got together a team to play in the Wakefield & District League together with Snapethorpe, Thornhill, Wakefield, Featherstone, Glasshoughton, Salem, Wheldale Colliery, Leeds and Wheldale Miners.

The Challenge Cup had continued through the war, with guest players allowed, but not all clubs taking part. However, for the 1945-46 season the competition was back to full strength, with the final returning to Wembley Stadium. Once again, it was the highlight of Sharlston's season.

To qualify for the first round proper, the renamed Rovers had a walkover in the first qualifying round when a Hunslet team disbanded. In the next round, Batley were beaten 24-9; but an objection was raised by the Batley club and the tie was replayed. Sharlston won again, 12-6. The last qualifying round saw Rovers beat Buslingthorpe Vale 8-2. However, their hooker, Jack Simpson, broke his arm early in the first half.

The first round proper was played over two legs. When the draw was announced, Sharlston were to face Workington Town on 9 February. Workington were newcomers to professional rugby league, and this was their first season.

Featherstone Rovers, who had a home tie with Halifax on the same day, offered Sharlston the use of their ground if the Sharlston versus Workington match was played on 16 February, but the Sharlston committee decided that they could not accept this offer as the match would clash with the Wakefield versus Huddersfield second leg at Belle Vue.

A willing band of volunteer workers improved the dressing rooms and erected fencing and canvas screens around the playing area. Thomas Chalkley, the club secretary, had not been able to obtain a turnstile for the entrance and anticipated a crowd of around 3,000 in spite of the counter attraction at Featherstone. Local housewives banded together to provide food for the teams and officials, 60 of whom had a meal at the Working Men's Club. Whatever happened in the home tie, 60 people booked places on two coaches for the second leg match at Workington.

Mr J. Robinson had been responsible for training the team, all of whom were miners. Although 11 players were under 21 years old, three had experience of senior rugby league. Benny Lingard had played with Batley and Featherstone, Henry Dooler with Batley and Tommy Fox with Featherstone. The leading try scorer prior to the cup-tie was winger Walt Booth, with 11 in league games. He was making his first cup-tie appearance. One forward, George Green, had kicked 10 goals in the qualifying rounds.

Workington Town had exploded onto professional rugby league on 25 August with a stunning 27-5 victory over Broughton Rangers, but as the season wore on it was evident that they lacked experience. In December 1945 they embarked on a recruiting mission. Albert Pepperell, the Huddersfield scrum-half, later to be a Great Britain Test player, and Ned Hodgson, the Broughton Rangers international forward, were signed, followed by Billy Holding, the veteran county full-back. 'Ginger' Hughes, the father of England football captain, Emlyn, was signed from Barrow and they had two youngsters who were destined to go a long way in the game: hooker Alvin Ackerley and centre Billy Ivison. Ackerley's future was with Halifax for whom he played close on 400 games, but Ivison played out his career at Workington. At the time he was described as "big, strong and fast and may be tried out as a loose-forward". He became one of the greatest loose-forwards the game has produced.

The *Yorkshire Evening News* reported there was "cup-tie fever at Sharlston". Their reporter spoke to the team's captain, Tom Fox, who formerly played for Featherstone and is now the steward of the local Working Men's Club, and said: "Though we don't pretend to class ourselves with the best senior clubs, we have a good team and we will give Workington a good game. I think we have a chance of winning."

Jack Simpson, the team's hooker, who had broken his arm in the final qualifying round said: "I don't know if I will be fit in time for the cup-tie or not, but if I can't play I will be very disappointed." The youngest member of the side was Denis Chalkley. His father, Thomas Chalkley, the club secretary, declared to the reporter: "We have a fighting chance".

The report also said that the players and supporters enjoyed a film and a talk, by Jim Brough, a *Yorkshire Evening News* lecturer and former international full-back. He promised to visit Sharlston before the cup-tie and give the players a demonstration of important moves in the game.

Sharlston Rovers 12 Workington Town 7
Challenge Cup First Round first leg

The last amateur club to beat a professional one was Beverley, who beat Ebbw Vale, then members of the Northern Rugby League, 7-2 in 1909.

The game with Workington created a tremendous amount of interest. 1,200 enthusiastic supporters were present, and it felt like every resident of the village had turned out to encourage their young team. Jack Simpson missed the match, and the teams were:
Sharlston Rovers: D. Chalkley; W. Booth, L. Bailey, F. Dooler, B. Lingard; H. Dooler, A. Riley; D. Bradley, E. Golding, T. Fox, G. Green, E. Stott, H. Booth.
Workington Town: B. Holding; W. Askew, J. H. Rodgers, H. Smith [B. Ivison], G. Armstrong; G. Jepson, A. Pepperell; N. Hodgson (capt.), H. Bradshaw, F. Hughes, J. Hayton, J. B. Inglesfield, S. Hayton.

Billy Ivison was on leave from the army, and played this match under the name H. Smith. He was injured after 20 minutes.

Despite a downpour the previous night, the ground was in good condition. The visitors scored first, Billy Holding kicked a penalty after 10 minutes from long range. George Green equalised with a penalty for Sharlston after Workington were penalised for a scrum offence, but then Holding landed another penalty from halfway for Workington, after Dooler was penalised. So Workington led 4-2 at the break. Pepperell and Jepson had led the Workington attacks.

Rovers had the better of the second half, and took the lead when Dooler scored, with Green converting. Green scored a try following good forward play, which he also converted to make the score 12-4. Then Armstrong scored a try for the visitors following a move involving Pepperell, Jepson and Rogers. Holding missed the conversion, so the final score was 12-7.

The *Workington Star's* report claimed that Sharlston's 'spoiling tactics' put Workington off their normal game, and the professional side were drawn into a forward battle. The writer also claimed that the "cramped ground was all against the visitors, who did not properly operate their passing machinery".

In the second half, the heavier Workington pack could not match 'the tenacity and grit of the young Sharlston forwards,' who's marking and tackling upset the visitors' play.

In the *News Chronicle*, Tom Longworth said: "Financially the system of playing the Rugby League Cup-ties on the home and away principle is sound, but it robs matches of much of the traditional element of uncertainty. Providing scoring is kept within limits it is reasonably possible for most 'first leg' visiting teams to wipe out the arrears at the second meeting. For that reason Workington Town will not be unduly worried about this set-back at the hands of Sharlston Rovers, one of the five junior teams competing in the first round ties. It was a surprising result and whatever happens at Workington in the return, the performance of Sharlston Rovers loses none of its glamour."

The *Yorkshire Post* added that "There was no fluke about Sharlston's victory over Workington. Their forwards won a good share of the ball and their teamwork was impressive, with George Green, a 20 year old forward, giving a capital display." The *Manchester Guardian* said that Sharlston's win was "the surprise of the first ties in the Rugby League cup."

In the *Yorkshire Evening News*, Jim Brough wrote: "It was Sharlston's day of days last Saturday and I was glad I went along to see the village club's cup triumph over Workington. Before the match everybody seemed to have turned out to greet the visitors and the scenes in fact reminded me of the rugby league touring team going to a country town in Australia.

Jonty Parkin came back to the scene of his early successes for the match. He was with the boys in spirit and they were imbued with the Parkin 'never say die' spirit all afternoon. The scenes each time the Rovers scored are indescribable. When Workington brought the scores level the spectators were quiet, but sportingly, they did not blame anyone in particular - not even the referee. As the final whistle sounded we had the VE Day scenes all over again.

The crowd were wildly delighted. They shook hands with anyone and everyone but in the midst of their triumph the people of Sharlston did not forget to congratulate their sporting guests.

There was a really homely atmosphere in the evening... I had intended going to see the Dewsbury versus Hunslet match but I am glad I went to Sharlston."

The village's women made and collected food for the party after the game. Points and rations were sacrificed by the villagers as 150 players, officials and supporters dined in the Working Men's Club.

Gracing the centre table was the Fotherby Cup which Sharlston had won a week earlier by beating Glasshoughton at Featherstone.

Mr Meageen congratulated the players on a good, clean game, as did Workington's captain, Ned Hodgson. Jack Wildman, Sharlston's president, reciprocated the compliments. The guests, enjoying the home-made cakes and pastries, agreed that Sharlston's cooks were as good as its footballers.

Jack Simpson and Tommy Fox talking to supporters before the match
at the Sharlston Working Mens Club.

SHARLSTON RUGBY LEAGUE CLUB

1st Round R.L. Cup at Sharlston—Saturday 9 Feb. 1946

SHARLSTON v WORKINGTON

	SHARLSTON		WORKINGTON
1	D. Chalkley	1	Holding
2	W. Booth	2	Askew
3	L. Bailey	3	Carr
4	F. Dooler	4	Division
5	B. Lingard	5	A. N. Other
6	H. Dooler	6	Jepson
7	A. Riley	7	Pepperall
8	D. Bradley	8	Hodgson
9	E. Golding	9	Bradshaw
10	T. Fox	10	Hughes
11	G. Green	11	Hayton
12	E. Stott	12	Kavanagh
13	H. Booth	13	Cunliffe

SHARLSTON HOTEL	SHARLSTON & DISTRICT
(Club Headquarters)	W.M.C.
Proprietor—John Dooler	J. Smith's, Sam Smith's
(President of the Club)	
Beverleys Beers are Best	**ALBION & TOWER ALES**

It is the Sharlston Club's first season since 1939, some of the boys never having previously played Rugby. They won the Wakefield and District K.O. Cup last Saturday. Sharlston have played Rugby for over 60 years and have turned out some very notable players—The late Fred Goodfellow (father of Herbert Goodfellow of Wakefield). Jonty Parkin (three times England Captain in Australia), C. Hepworth, W. Chalkley, G. Goldie (played with Featherstone), and others too numerous to mention. In the last twenty years the club have won 14 cups, and entered the 1st Round of the Rugby League Cup three times—and hope to do so many more times.

Harris Bros. (Gazette) Ltd., Printers, Featherstone.   Tel. 252

WORKINGTON TOWN
RUGBY LEAGUE FOOTBALL CLUB, Ltd.

RUGBY LEAGUE CHALLENGE CUP
FIRST ROUND — 2nd LEG.

Workington Town
versus
SHARLSTON

On Borough Park Ground,
Workington.

SATURDAY, FEBRUARY 16th, 1946

Kick-off at 3-30 p.m.

ADMISSION (including Tax):
GROUND 1/6
GRANDSTAND & ENCLOSURE 2/3

PROGRAMME 3d.

KEEP THIS PROGRAMME
IT MAY BE LUCKY   1243

Upon Production of the Winning Programme the Holder will receive TWO GRANDSTAND TICKETS for the NEXT HOME LEAGUE MATCH

The match programmes
(Workington programme courtesy
Workington Town RLFC)

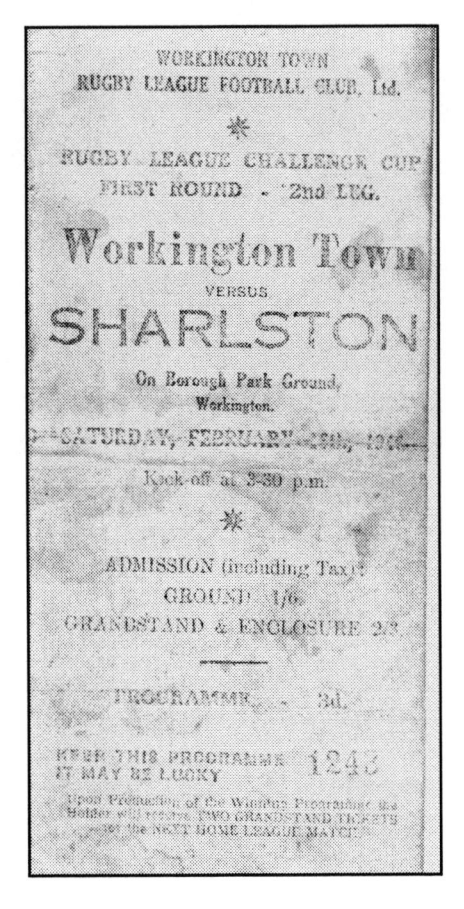

66

The Workington Town match programme for the return leg outlined: "Who are these Sharlston Rovers? Are they a team of Australians or some unknown quantity? Without a doubt they created the greatest surprise of the day last Saturday by defeating our team by 12-7. They will come full of confidence to-day.

What awaits them - victory or defeat? With the exception of about 100 who will be accompanying the village lads, practically every other visitor to Borough Park expects the Town side to have a convincing win. Nothing has been left to chance.

The directors have made drastic changes in the team. Jim Brough came down especially on Thursday to give them an object lesson on how to play the game. He stripped out and for two hours put them 'through it'. He was as fit as any player on the field. He will be there to encourage us on to victory on Saturday. You will see Hughes, the Welsh International, playing at home for the first time since he was transferred from Barrow, also J. B. Carr, the latest capture from the rugby union and Darrell Watson, who created such a good impression in his first match against St Helen's."

Workington Town 16 Sharlston Rovers 2
Challenge Cup First Round second leg

A crowd of between 9,000 and 10,000 saw the return leg. The teams were:
Workington Town: B. Holding; G. Armstrong, J. Carr, D. Watson, J. H. Rodgers; G. Jepson, A. Pepperell; F. Hughes, H. Barker, N. Hodgson, W. D. Cavanagh, C. Hughes, S. Hayton.
Sharlston Rovers: D. Chalkley; B. Lingard, Cardall, L. Bailey W. Booth; H. Dooler, A. Riley; T. Fox, E. Golding, D. Bradley, E. Stott, G. Green, H. Booth.

The referee was Mr W Hemmings of Halifax.

The *Workington Star* said that Sharlston "gave an object lesson in spotting and tackling during the first 40 minutes," and that the visitors could have increased their lead in the first half, when Sharlston were on top. Cardall was penalised for offside in front of the posts and Holding kicked the goal, giving the home side a 2-0 half-time lead, but with Sharlston three points ahead on aggregate.

In the second half, Carr gathered a loose ball on his own '25' and made a swerving run beating three men before passing to Watson, who advanced about 10 yards and passed to Rodgers, who ran along the touchline and beat Chalkley to score. Holding's conversion hit the post. It was now level pegging over the two games and the crowd got behind the home team. Pepperell, from a scrum near the line, side-stepped the Sharlston half-backs and sent Watson over for a try. Holding converted, giving his side a 10 point lead on the day, and five points on aggregate. Jepson then scored, but Holding missed the conversion. Pepperell then put in a short kick past Chalkley and beat him for the touch down. It was too far out for Holding to convert.

Near the end the home side were penalised for a play-the-ball infringement, and George Green kicked the penalty. The final score meant that Sharlston lost 23-14 over the two legs. It was only in the last 15 minutes that Workington had controlled the tie.

The *Wakefield Express* commented: "Although defeated, after their chances at one time looked rather rosy, the Rovers are to be congratulated on their great effort. With all the excitement now at an end for this season, they will be able to look forward to the future with confidence and there is every hope that a village which has produced some famous players and which has now many young players of considerable promise, will next season take an important part in rugby league football."

After all the excitement of the Challenge Cup there was the league programme to complete. Glasshoughton, Wheldale, Featherstone and Sharlston were the top teams in the league. Sharlston finished fourth and lost at Glasshoughton in the play-offs.

Rovers entered an Intermediate team in the Wakefield & District Fotherby Cup. They had been successful in this competition on several occasions before the War and once again victory was gained, albeit by a narrow margin, against Glasshoughton.

Sharlston Rovers 3 Glasshoughton 2
Wakefield & District Fotherby Cup Final

The final had been scheduled for Boxing Day, but was postponed because of fog, and was played at Featherstone on 2 February. Sharlston applied pressure but two free kicks by Glasshoughton brought a scrum on the Sharlston '25' line, where a penalty was awarded. Martindale kicked a penalty for Glasshoughton, but Sharlston replied with a strong attack and were rewarded when a passing movement by Hudson, Cardall, Riley and Bailey resulted in Booth scoring a try, which Green failed to convert. He also missed a penalty in front of goal.

There were no further scores in the second half, so Sharlston won by one point. Mr Rayner, the secretary of the Wakefield & District Rugby League, thanked the spectators and players for their support and congratulated both teams on their performance under unenviable conditions. A small boy presented the cup to the Sharlston captain, A. Green.

And so ended a memorable season for Sharlston Rovers. It was remarkable that despite the period of inactivity during the War, the club could quickly get together such a good team with a number of promising youngsters. It was just what was needed to lift the gloom of the War years. But there would be a price to pay for this success.

Left: Harry Booth, Denis Chalkley and George Green – all selected for Yorkshire against Cumberland at Solway Park, Glasson on 13 April 1946. Right: The Yorkshire team sheet for the match. Porky Hudson was at stand-off for Yorkshire, but is not in the photo.

1946-47

There were mass departures from the club before the start of the 1946-47 season. It is inevitable that when an amateur club has a successful season and promising young players come to the fore that senior clubs will sit up and take notice. That is what happened at Sharlston. Denis Chalkley, George Green and Walt Booth went to Halifax and 'Porky' Hudson and J. Derry to Keighley and Dewsbury respectively. But the hammer blow came when seven players joined the revived Normanton club who were in the much more competitive Yorkshire Senior Competition.

Rovers were hard pressed to field a team and it was not until October before they finally rejoined the Wakefield & District (Open Age) League, a woefully weak competition. The League had been advertising for teams to join it more than a month after the season had started and had to settle for just seven teams - Earlsheaton, East Hunslet LC, Nelson Rangers, Hartley Bank Colliery, Fitzwilliam, Sharlston and Glasshoughton. Sharlston also played in the Intermediate League.

The season's results were patchy with no silverware won, but with the players available and almost starting a new team from scratch this was only to be expected. The most important point was that they kept going and saw off the threat from an increasing number of association football enthusiasts who had taken the opportunity to try and get a foothold and were providing strong opposition in what has hitherto been known as a rugby league stronghold. The newly inaugurated Sharlston Youth Association Football Club were playing in the Wakefield & District Junior League and Mr J. H. Frew, the West Riding Football Association coach visited the village to coach some 50 boys from the Council and National Schools.

It would have been interesting to have had the thoughts of Mr Dey, the recently retired headmaster of the Council School on this. 'Gaffer' Dey had been at the school since it first opened just after the First World War broke out and before then had been a master at the school when it was at New Sharlston. He was a great supporter of rugby league football and had coached and encouraged most of the boys to take up the game, including Jonty Parkin and Herbert Goodfellow.

The 1946-47 season also will be remembered for severe snow and frost, mainly during February, completely upsetting the fixtures. The season was extended into the middle of the summer.

Don Froggett played for Sharlston around this time, before joining Wakefield Trinity, and playing for England in November 1953 against France. He made 219 appearances for Trinity, scoring 94 tries.

1947-48

Under former players Billy Howcroft as coach and Tubby Wilson as trainer, things improved for Rovers. Consistency in the league - they were in the top four for most of the season - brought them a place in the league championship play-offs and a victory at Glasshoughton by the only try of the match, only to lose 21-6 to Wheldale Colliery in the final at Featherstone.

Twice Rovers topped over 50 points in the league, against Ferry Lane, 59-2, and Wrenthorpe, 79-2. Wheldale Colliery beat them in both league encounters, the KO Cup semi-final - only by a point - and the Championship Final.

Rovers won the Yorkshire Junior Cup for the second time in their history, with victories against Glasshoughton, Thornhill Lees, Wyke, and Boulevard Juniors in the earlier rounds and a resounding semi-final win over Heworth (York), 33-5. East Hunslet Labour Club were Rovers' opponents in the final at Featherstone and there was a good crowd of 3,760 to see the match.

Sharlston 6
East Hunslet LC 0
Yorkshire Junior
Cup Final

Both tries were scored in the first half by Andrews, who, with his centre, Fisher, helped to form a dangerous right wing.

Part of the fixture card for the 1947-48 season

Andrews got his first try after a fine pick up at full speed. East Hunslet threw several good scoring chances away through poor finishing but on the whole the Sharlston defence was too good for them. A record number of teams had entered the cup and this victory was a good achievement by Sharlston.

1948-49

The Sharlston club has always been able to fight back when faced with adversity. Two seasons before they had difficulty raising a team and were threatened with a 'take over' by the football enthusiasts on the village. This season they won three cups, were league champions and retained their hold on the Yorkshire Cup. It was a remarkable comeback.

The Wakefield & District League lost Wheldale Colliery and Glasshoughton, two of the previous season's strongest teams, who had joined the revived Castleford & District League. Streethouse, Stanley Rangers, Eastmoor, Balne Lane, Hartley Bank Colliery, Westgate Rovers, British Jeffrey Diamond, Walton Colliery and Sutcliffe's, formed the league. Jim Fisher was appointed club captain and Billy Howcroft remained as coach.

To win the league title Sharlston defeated Streethouse, who had been top of the league all season, but Sharlston were worthy champions. They had defeated their near neighbours in league and cup on four occasions. In the Final at Featherstone, which Sharlston won 13-4, Isaiah Hale, who filled the breach in an emergency at full-back for Streethouse, was 41 years old.

In the Yorkshire Junior Cup there was only one easy victory for the Rovers in the earlier rounds and in the last four of them there was never more than seven points in any of the matches. Stanley Rangers were beaten 19-6 in the first round, and this was followed with a 29-6 triumph over Hartley Bank Colliery. Queensbury were then beaten 13-6, and Lock Lane 10-4. The quarter-final saw a narrow 9-5 win over Moldgreen, and Hull NDLB were beaten 6-3 in the semi-final. This took Sharlston into the final again, and once again their opponents were East Hunslet Labour Club.

Sharlston Rovers 7 East Hunslet LC 0
Yorkshire Junior Cup Final

Gerald Jackson, Rovers' 17-year-old winger scored a great try, to put Rovers ahead at Leeds. The conversion was added by captain J. Fisher, who also kicked a penalty. Gold medals were presented to members of the team.

The *Wakefield Express* said that "the villagers should feel proud of their team, retaining the right to be called the best amateur rugby league team in Yorkshire."

Streethouse were unbeaten in the league when they met the Rovers in the First Round of the KO Cup Competition but they had already suffered defeat at Sharlston in the First Qualifying Round of the Rugby League Challenge Cup and there was no doubt Sharlston had the measure of them, winning again, this time 8-4. Four bus loads of supporters went to Stanley for the semi-final of this competition and cheered the lads to victory, albeit by a narrow margin of three points. The cup was won against Eastmoor on the Stanley Rangers ground.

Following the defeat of Streethouse in the Rugby League Challenge Cup, Sharlston had a home second round draw against Stanley Rangers but they had to give up ground advantage because the annual feast was being held. This did not halt their progress for they had a 10-3 victory and a third round visit to Mansfield and there the cup run ended.

However, this defeat did not end Sharlston's interest in the Challenge Cup. Denis Chalkley, one of the heroes of the 1946 win over Workington, was in the Halifax team at full-back in the final at Wembley. Denis had played for Halifax for three seasons. He was the youngest player on the field and played a sound game, but could not prevent his team losing 12-0 to Bradford Northern. The *Wakefield Express* said: "The villagers are justly proud of this 22 year old youngster, who joins the select band of Sharlston products achieving rugby league fame."

The Sharlston club and friends organised a match for the benefit of J. Dooler, one of their former players. Halifax's Denis Chalkley and Trinity's Herbert Goodfellow helped the competing teams. A match was also held in aid of Bill Wood.

1949-50

As defending league champions, Sharlston's impressive form of last season continued in 1949-50, as they marched towards another Championship final. There were some notable victories on the way. In a fortnight in March they rattled up 112 points in two matches and earlier in the season their display against Silkstone Row brought a glowing report from the *Wakefield Express* reporter: "The downfall of Silkstone Row was not unexpected and the Altofts players were the first to congratulate the home side on their attractive and inclusive play. Sharlston spent the game collecting no fewer than 45 points in reply to which the visitors had a try and goal to show."

In the final, Streethouse were the opponents as they were last season but there was some added 'needle' this time as Rovers were keen to avenge being unexpectedly knocked out of the Yorkshire Cup at the first round stage by their neighbours. They did so with a 12-7 win at Belle Vue. All the points for Streethouse were scored by a youngster, Frank Mortimer. He had signed for Trinity in 1947 and then allowed to develop with Streethouse Open-age side. He had a distinguished career with Trinity and gained representative honours for Yorkshire and Great Britain.

In the qualifying rounds of the Rugby League Cup Sharlston had a narrow 5-2 win over Heworth (York) in the fifth round at home. Sharlston took a two point lead from a penalty by Jones in the first half, but in the second it was their turn to face the gale. Heworth must have fancied their chances of springing a surprise. However, Bolton, Sharlston's hooker, easily won the battle for possession from the scrums, and by the tactics of the Sharlston side as a whole in keeping the ball 'tight' in the second half, 15 minutes from the end, Jones caught Heworth out by punting forward from a free kick. M. Cardall took the ball on the burst, and 17 year old winger Jackson scored in the corner. A penalty by Heworth made the final score 5-2. The semi-final of the Yorkshire zone had been reached and Sharlston had to visit the tough Castleford outfit, Lock Lane.

Before 1,000 spectators, Sharlston lost 9-2 in the semi-final of the Yorkshire zone of the Challenge Cup qualifying rounds. Sharlston began with the wind, but their only score came from a penalty kick by Green, who also struck the crossbar with a second kick. They had a fair share of the ball from the scrums but Lock Lane's defence was impressive. The visitors were unlucky to lose their loose-forward for most of the first half and though he returned at the interval, they finished with 11 men. Lock Lane also lost Skitt through injury for a considerable time. In the second half, the Lock Lane forwards heeled quickly and as Austerberry was usually up to make the extra man, their back moves were always menacing. The only try came from such a move, Austerberry moved up from full-back to put Spears over. Bond kicked two goals. There was much to be admired in Sharlston's play but they were usually second best, even at full strength. Gone was the magic of the Challenge Cup for another year.

In addition to the League Championship, the Wakefield & District Fotherby Cup was also won. A further honour was that four Sharlston players: Birkett, Bailey, Fisher and Jones, were chosen for the Yorkshire County amateur team.

Left: Ernie Bell, Jim Fisher and Billy Howcroft at the White Horse Inn in 1949, with the three trophies won by the team. Ernie Bell was the landlord of the White Horse Inn. Right: Billy Howcroft (coach) and Eric Allan (captain) with the Yorkshire Cup after the win in the 1947-48 season.

The benefit match for Bill Wood:
Herbert Goodfellow's XIII against Vic Darlison's XIII on 19 December 1948

Vic Darlison and Herbert Goodfellow with Bill Wood

T. Bland, Spencer, H. Murphy, F. Webb, T. Larvin, J. Fisher, Unknown, Unknown, L. Jones, A. Fletcher, Marson, Pollard, E. Hudson, A. Cardall, W. Wood, L. Bratley, D. Chalkley, M. Cardall, E. Batten, E. Luckman, C. Andrews, F. Moore, V. Darlison, Bert Cook, Major, H. Goodfellow.

Four famous Sharlston players who turned professional

Above: Don Froggett – Wakefield Trinity & England
Above right: Len Marson – Wakefield Trinity & England
Below right: Joe Mullaney – Featherstone Rovers & England
Below: Tommy Smales - Barrow, Wigan & Featherstone Rovers
(All photos courtesy Robert Gate)

6. The 1950s - The Yorkshire Cup

1950-51

There was a great deal of activity before the season started. A women's section of the club was formed to raise funds. They met weekly at the Sharlston Hotel, arranged raffles with prizes of a bag of sugar, quarter pound of tea and packet of biscuits. The committee women would take it in turns to provide the prizes. They were good prizes in those days, for there was still food rationing. A dance was organised in St Luke's Hall at the beginning of the season, with about 200 attending.

In the league, Sharlston won the title for the third year in succession, a reward for consistency season after season. There were some interesting moments and a generous gesture by the club. In a fairly even game against Eastmoor at Sharlston, two Sharlston players were sent off, but Rovers held on to win 15-10. In November, Manygates OB inflicted the team's first defeat. However, Sharlston lost only two of 16 league fixtures.

The match against Balne Lane was called off because transport for the team could not be arranged. Half the gate money from the fixture with Nostell Welfare was donated to a fund for sending 12 Sharlston old age pensioners to Blackpool for a holiday.

The play-offs for the title and the final were played in May with only a day between them. Nine of Sharlston's points in the semi-final against Nostell Welfare came from Bailey, a hat-trick of tries in a game when he never put a foot wrong.

The final against Eastmoor was at Belle Vue and at the first time of asking the teams could not be separated, playing out a 10-10 draw. In the replay Sharlston took the title.

Sharlston Rovers 14 Eastmoor 5
Championship Final replay

Sharlston were worthy winners. Eastmoor hammered at their opponents' line for most of the second half, but their finishing was poor. Sharlston led at the break 7-0; but Eastmoor reduced the lead with a try by Crowcroft and a dropped goal by Richardson. Fisher put Sharlston further ahead with a penalty and they ran in another five points in the game's closing minutes. The cup was presented to Fisher, the Sharlston captain, by Mrs Ronnie Rylance.

Sharlston's progress in the Challenge Cup was halted after only one win. They played Stanley in the first qualifying round at home and won easily 24-2. Stanley was thrown on the defensive almost from the start of the game and any hopes they had of holding Rovers quickly receded, as the Sharlston score mounted. Sharlston's try scorers were Fisher with two, Cardall, Maskill, Green and Hobbs. Green kicked three goals.

The cup trail ended when Rovers visited Nostell Welfare in the next round. Nostell scored a try at the start of the match, which was converted and before half-time added a penalty to lead 7-0. Sharlston then rallied with a try by Hobbs and a penalty from Green, reducing the deficit to two points. At this stage Sharlston looked as though they might pull the game round, but Nostell marked well and kept the game close and clinched the game with another try and goal to win 12-5.

The Yorkshire Junior Cup produced some excellent matches and Sharlston's downfall came in the semi-final against Willow Park, a marathon tie that took 240 minutes to settle. In the first round Sharlston travelled to Manygates OB. A cleverly conceived try in the opening minutes put Sharlston ahead. From a scrum almost on the home line,

Sharlston won possession. Mo Cardall drew the opposition before passing to Fisher, who went over unopposed. Then Fisher landed a penalty from short range. Sharlston's forwards created a second try after the break, from Joyce and were worthy 8-0 winners.

Then came a trip to East Hunslet. Again, Sharlston started well, with Rowley crossing the home line in the opening minutes. Alf Cardall converted. Hunslet replied with a penalty, but Mo Cardall restored Sharlston's advantage with a drop-goal. In the second half, Hunslet were penalised and from the penalty Hobbs sprinted along the touchline to score. Sharlston's next try came from Nightingale, who went over between the posts. The home side scored a try, then Fisher and one of the Hunslet players were sent off. Sharlston later lost Nightingale through injury, but managed to hold onto their 13-5 lead.

The third round brought another away trip, to Keighley Albion. With two minutes left, the home side scored a try, which brought them to within one point of Sharlston. Everything depended on the goal kick and as they missed it, Keighley were beaten 7-6. Alf Cardall had given Sharlston the lead early on with a penalty. Then Mo Cardall made a try for Nightingale, converted by Alf Cardall. The home side's scoring was restricted to a single try until the dramatic final minutes.

Rastrick were the visitors to Sharlston for the fourth round, their first visit for 30 years. Sharlston won 19-2 to reach the semi-final in front of the season's biggest gate. The home side hammered at the Rastrick defence for 20 minutes, before Mo Cardall scored a drop goal. Seconds later Green was penalised for off-side and Lythe kicked a goal to put the visitors on even terms.

After the interval, the home side dominated with good open football. From a scrum, Bailey drew the Rastrick defence and passed to Joyce, who scored in the corner. Green failed to convert. Joyce then scored another unconverted try. Cardall was the next Sharlston player to cross the line after a run from the Rastrick '25'. Green again missed the conversion. Then Mo Cardall won the ball, ran diagonally, and passed to Fisher, who scored under the posts. Davies got the last try, which was improved by Alf Cardall.

Then Willow Park came to Sharlston. Twenty three mud coated players - they had been preceded a few minutes earlier by three of their colleagues who had been sent off by the referee - dragged their bodies from Sharlston's pitch after 80 gruelling minutes play which failed to decide whether the home club or Willow Park should be finalists in this competition. This was a real battle, sportingly accepted by both sides until the last 10 minutes when several unsavoury incidents led to the referee dismissing two Sharlston players, Wood and Bridges and one from Willow Park - Major. The game contained far more scrums than usual, due largely to handling mistakes caused by the slippery ball, some effective tackling and very few thrills. For the home supporters, the big moment of the game came in the last minute, when Sharlston levelled the scores at 5-5 to earn a second chance.

For two-thirds of the game they were encamped inside their opponents '25', striving to crack a defence which, according to the *Wakefield Express*, "was as effective as the 'Iron Curtain' itself." Kelly made an overlap for his winger Davies. It was a split second chance for Davies, and the winger hurled himself over the line with three defenders hanging on. Sharlston's other points came from a penalty by Alf Cardall. The replay winners would meet Lock Lane from Castleford in the final.

The replay was at Willow Park. A 6-6 draw resulted and a second replay was fixed for Featherstone Rovers' ground. The replay followed the same pattern as the original meeting with Sharlston doing more attacking than their opponents, but this time Park got an equaliser in the last seconds. All Sharlston's points came from Fisher. His third goal put the Rovers ahead for the first time at 6-4 mid-way through the second half and they looked quite capable of holding on to the advantage until they conceded a penalty on their own '25' in the dying seconds.

Willow Park finally won the second replay. They went into Sharlston territory only three times in the second half. The first J. Major kicked a penalty to restore their one point lead; the second time H. Morgan from Willow Park and Rovers' Oldroyd were sent off for fighting; and on the third time Major failed to send a penalty into touch, Sharlston accepted possession gleefully and almost scored. Willow Park won by a goal and a try, 5 points to two goals, 4 points. This made the aggregate scores after 280 minutes Willow Park 16 Sharlston 15. Sharlston had more of the ball and made better use of it, except once, near half-time, when Willow Park's Lofthouse took a pass, after G. Morgan had broken through, and beat two men in a spirited dash for a try in the corner. Major missed the goal, but at half time they were 3-2 up, Fisher having landed a penalty for Sharlston. He and Major kicked their second half penalties within seconds of each other. Joyce was Sharlston's danger man and he would have had at least one try if Clarke, Willow Park's full-back, had not been in such good form. The teams were:
Sharlston Rovers: Nightingale; Joyce, Kelly, Davies, Moseley; Bailey, Cardall; Oldroyd, Bridges, Rowley, Wood, Simpson, Fisher.
Willow Park: Clarke; Jarvis, Martin, Worrall, Lofthouse; G. Morgan, Nicholls; Reynolds, Goodwin, Major, Eyre, Lockett, H. Morgan.
Referee: Mr E. Hopkins (Leeds)

Sharlston won the Wakefield Fotherby Cup for the third year in succession. They had a hard home game against Nostell Welfare in round one and, though beaten in the scrums, secured a 12-3 win. The semi-final brought Stanley to Sharlston and a feature of the first part of the match was the see-saw scoring. Green went over for the Rovers after five minutes but Cardall missed the goal. Then Stanley got two quick goals but Cardall replied in kind before the visitors secured a drop goal from the half-way line. After the interval Sharlston's supremacy was unchallenged. Fisher got a try which Cardall converted, making the score 12-6. Again Fisher went over but this time Cardall missed the kick. Stanley added two more points before Simpson's last minute try for Sharlston made the score 20-8, which took Rovers into the Final.

Sharlston Rovers 13 Silkstone Rovers 9
Wakefield Fotherby Cup

By beating Silkstone Rovers 13-9 in the final of the Wakefield Challenge Cup competition at Normanton, Sharlston Rovers completed the league and cup double for the third successive season. After Silkstone had opened the scoring with a penalty, Nightingale came up field to make the extra man for Davies to touch down. Fisher failed to convert. Again, Sharlston were penalised and Silkstone held the lead until Kelly intercepted a pass and went over between the posts. This time Fisher converted. Then a misunderstanding in the Sharlston defence let in Silkstone who, with a converted try, led 9-8 at half-time. After half-time it was all Sharlston, with Silkstone desperately defending. Fisher added a penalty for Sharlston and near the end set up a try for Bridges to score. After the game, the Batley player Jack Perry presented the trophy and a clock to each Sharlston player.

Champions clash

Sharlston met Runcorn, winners of the Lancashire and Cheshire League, in a challenge match at Sharlston. Brilliant sunshine drew a large crowd. There were thrills galore and the sides were so evenly matched that it was anyone's game up to the final whistle. The Lancashire team emerged as victors by a narrow margin. Runcorn scored three tries and two goals to tries from Bailey, Mo Cardall and Nightingale and a goal from Fisher for Sharlston, making the half-time score 13-11 to the visitors.

After the break a fourth try came for Runcorn and though Sharlston fought back they only managed a penalty from Fisher. After the game both sides, with about 100 guests attended a presentation tea at Sharlston Hotel. Wakefield League president Mr J. Reyner presided and Mr William Chalkley presented the Wakefield League and Challenge cups and individual trophies to the Sharlston side. Mr A. Holland, the Runcorn secretary, thanked the players and officials of Sharlston Rovers for "a good game and such a friendly welcome". A vote of thanks to the visitors, local tradesmen, and others who had helped to make the tea possible came from by Mr William Howcroft, the club chairman.

The village was still producing young players. Don Fox, Roy Beech and Trevor Somers, went to Castleford Modern School for training by James Crossley, a rugby league coach. All three were prospective members of the Castleford Town boys' team. Don Fox, the son of footballing father Tommy Fox, had been reserve for the Yorkshire boys' side for the past two seasons.

In schools rugby, the Sharlston senior boys' side played Castleford St Joseph's. In the match report, "worthy of mention in the Sharlston side was 'midget' hooker, Tommy Mullaney whose untiring spirit provided inspiration to his team." He later signed for Castleford.

Mr William Dey, the former headmaster of Sharlston Council School, who moved to Bridlington on his retirement, visited some of his former Sharlston acquaintances. Mr Dey was remembered by local sports fans for his work in introducing to first class rugby league game such players as Jonty Parkin, Herbert Goodfellow, the Lingards, Henry Dooler, George Goldie and Charlie Hepworth.

1951-52

No trophies were won this season but there was plenty to talk about. Everything was going well until November when, following a moment of madness, the club was suspended from the Rugby Football League. Despite this suspension, Rovers were still involved in the league play-offs and went on to the final. It was January, after being reformed following suspension, before they suffered their first defeat, against Wakefield Loco, and in March Balne Lane were vanquished 60-7, with Nightingale scoring nine tries in the match, a club record. Wakefield Loco were beaten in the semi-final and a big crowd was expected for the final at Belle Vue, Wakefield, against Eastmoor.

Eastmoor 15 Sharlston 3
Wakefield and District Open-Age League Final

This attractive match drew an appreciative crowd and they were excited throughout the game. Sharlston applied pressure from the start, and after five minutes were rewarded with a try by Richardson who broke through from a scrum on the Eastmoor '25'. Peter Fox failed to add the goal points. Thewlis then landed a penalty for Eastmoor. Play continued in the Sharlston half and 10 minutes later Thewlis gave his side the lead with another penalty, after he had hit the post from a similar position. This was real cup-tie fare with both sides neither giving, nor asking, any quarter. The half-time score was 4-3 to Eastmoor, Fox having been unsuccessful with two shots at goal.

On the resumption Sharlston attacked but were held in their own half by keen tackling. After a sustained attack, Rowell, Eastmoor's winger, scrambled over for a try; the conversion failed. From the ensuing drop out at the half-way line Tilford gained possession and went straight down the field, serving Davies, who had dashed through, with a pass to send the stand-off in at the corner, the conversion again failing. Sharlston never gave up, but tired and from a lobbed pass on the Eastmoor '25' in Sharlston's best attack in the second-half Rowell intercepted and scored the best try of the match. Craven converted, Thewlis previously having hit an upright for the second time. Sharlston hung on, but the score ended 15-3. For Sharlston, Richardson, Fisher and Joyce stood out.

The qualifying rounds of the Challenge Cup started with a home tie against Manygates OB, by no means easy opponents. Sharlston were beaten in the scrums, but won 13-6. They had to visit Silkstone Row in the second qualifying round and a match full of unpleasant second half incidents would, not for the first time, lead to the club being banned by the Rugby Football League.

Four players - two from each side - were sent off following incidents during the match at Altofts. The incidents occurred after an entertaining first half had ended with Silkstone one point ahead.

Both sides allege that the trouble started over a drop-goal awarded to the home side. They had built up their lead to 13-6 when Jack Webb picked up a loose ball on the Sharlston '25' and tried a drop-goal. The Sharlston players said the ball had fallen short of the posts, but referee Mr A. Barraclough, stuck to his decision to award a goal.

Then, alleged a Silkstone official, a number of the Sharlston spectators ran on to the field to call off their players. Several members of the Sharlston side went to the touch-line, but returned when play was re-started. A Sharlston player, it was alleged, attempted to strike the referee, and was sent off. The four players sent off were Mosley and Paver from Sharlston and Webb and Hudson from Silkstone.

A Silkstone official told the *Wakefield Express* that the club were almost certain to appeal against the sending off of Hudson; while Henry Dooler, the Sharlston secretary, said that his club would appeal against the sending off of their two players. Mr Dooler has also sent a written complaint to Mr Reyner, the secretary of the Wakefield League.

Mr Barraclough said he had forwarded a 'bad report' to the RFL disciplinary committee.

Sharlston had won 23-18 and the next round took them to Normanton. There, any hopes of an appearance in the first round ended with an 8-3 defeat.

After the fracas at Altofts, this game at St John's showed a new tone of rivalry between these enemies of many years standing. This was a sporting encounter, for which, obviously, much of the credit belonged to the players.

The atmosphere also came from the referee, Mr R. Gelder, described as "an official of rising status in the Rugby League." The first - and only incident in the game - occurred in the opening minutes, and provoked from Mr Gelder a stern reprimand. Thereafter, the match pursued an unruffled course with Mr Gelder in efficient control.

Normanton won their way to the fourth round. Sharlston were unfortunate to lose a game they won territorially. But, promising as their backs looked when in possession, there were shortcomings which explained their failure to breach the Normanton defence.

Normanton produced the first half's only scoring move. The ball was transferred along their backs until Booth saw his chance. He shot into the open and found Tilford ready to accept his pass to score unchallenged.

Normanton had more possession after the interval, yet had their work cut out to

Sharlston Rovers 1951-52.
Back: J. Clark, M. Haigh, P. Chalkley, F. Simpson, C. Richardson, J. Lapish, A. Oldroyd;
Front: F. Wynn, P. Fox, B. Flowers, J. Fisher (captain), E. Booth, M. Wood, R. Hobbs.

keep their opponents at bay. At last, Rovers' passing forced the extra man and Kelly knocked over the corner flag as he dived in for an equalising try with a defender hanging on. With only 15 minutes left, a replay at Sharlston seemed likely. Normanton, however, staged a powerful rally against tiring opponents playing with a weakened side caused by the withdrawal of Oldroyd with a shoulder injury. Townend just missed with a penalty, but a few minutes later, from a similar position, he got his kick home. And the final nail in Sharlston's coffin was driven home six minutes from time when Hossack picked up a dropped pass on the '25' and the ball was worked out to Colin Northern who scored in the corner.

As it turned out had Sharlston been successful they would not have been allowed to progress any further in the competition.

Club banned from rugby league

The Rugby Football League's disciplinary committee met in Leeds to inquire into the Challenge Cup qualifying round tie between Sharlston Rovers and Silkstone Row on 27 October. They suspended the Sharlston club from taking any further part in rugby league football.

The committee also suspended *sine die* Henry Dooler, the former Sharlston secretary and five Sharlston players: Alf Cardall (club captain), K. Mosley, J. W. 'Bilc' Paver, Keith Bridges and Peter Joyce.

The RFL secretary, Bill Fallowfield stated that in the match concerned two Sharlston players were sent off the field and it was alleged that wrong names were given to the referee.

The committee further ruled that all Sharlston players not concerned in the inquiry were to be released from their registrations so that they could play for other clubs.

However, a new club arose from the ashes of the disciplinary committee's decision. Supporters hoped for rugby league by the New Year following developments from the village's reaction to the suspension.

The Rugby League Disciplinary Committee were sent a letter from Sharlston club officers appealing against the ban on the Rovers. Commenting on the committee's re-action yesterday, in the *Wakefield Express*, Bill Fallowfield, made it clear there was no objection to the club name Sharlston Rovers being used in any re-formation. He said "If the Sharlston people want to have rugby again there is nothing to stop them from forming a suggested committee and letting us have the names. It must be clearly understood however that none of the members coming under the disciplinary action of the Rugby League should be included."

This largely confirms a letter which a Sharlston resident received from Mr Fallowfield following that person's representation against what appeared to be a blank future for rugby at Sharlston. Mr Fallowfield's letter read: "I very much regret that the decision of my committee in any way affects persons other than those intimately connected with the Sharlston club. It was unfortunate that no alternative could be taken in view of the circumstances which arose. If any club is formed in Sharlston on the same ground I do not anticipate there will be any objection from my committee, provided that none of the persons who were suspended *sine die* are allowed to take part in the club. If any officials of the old club become associated with the new one, if it is formed, they should take good care that similar circumstances do not arise in the future as they would undoubtedly lead to serious punishment."

The club was reformed at a meeting attended by Mr J. R. Reyner, the organiser of the Wakefield Rugby League and Mr J. W. Smith, secretary of the County Amateur Committee. E. Shackleton, J. Musgrave, J. L. Berry and W. H. Ward were elected to the new Committee, and took responsibility for launching the club again. They would have the support of a ladies committee of five. There were plans to enlarge the committee in the future. There were hopes of Rovers returning in two weeks with a Wakefield League game against Hemsworth. They were in time to enter the Yorkshire Junior Cup.

Happy return

The re-formed Sharlston rugby league club celebrated their return to the Wakefield League by inflicting a crushing defeat upon visitors Hemsworth on Saturday 29 December 1951. The first part of the game was evenly contested, and at half-time the score stood at 9-7 in Sharlston's favour. On resuming, however, the home side scored at more than twice the rate of their visitors, adding a further 24 points to Hemsworth's 10, to make the result 33-17. Sharlston's try scorers included Kelly who got two, Nightingale, Fox, Wood, Goodfellow and Davies. Their goals came from Fox, with two, and Jones.

In January 1952 application was made to the Rugby Football League for the suspended players to be re-instated but the Committee dealing with the matter decided that they could not reconsider the cases until at least the end of the present season.

Rovers made the most of their 'second life' and looked forward to a good run in the Yorkshire Junior Cup. Hall Green were easily beaten in round one, 36-2, and Silkstone Rovers 31-11 in the following round, when centre Nightingale touched top form and ran in three tries. They then had to travel to Burton Sports and after being two points behind at half-time, quickly made up the leeway and went on to win 11-4. Round four was a close call, a last minute try by Wynn carrying them into the sixth round at the expense of Manygates OB when supporters of both sides had resigned themselves to a replay. Manygates were five points up in two minutes and it looked as though the home team's cup hopes were fading especially when minutes later they lost Nightingale to injury. They fought back and Peter Fox kicked three penalties to give them a one point lead at the interval. After the break Fox landed another penalty, but Manygates replied with a try to which they added the goal points, thus taking the lead for a second time. Joyce then crossed the Old Boys' line for an unimproved try, and a further five points by the visitors and goals by Fox for Sharlston, left the issue at 15-15, until that dramatic winning effort by Wynn.

A 14-7 victory over Heworth in the semi-final gave Sharlston their second Yorkshire Junior Cup final in three seasons. Heworth may have lost more heavily but for an injury to Booth, the Rovers' scrum-half, whose place was eventually taken by full-back Fox, with considerable credit. Rovers got away to a flying start with a penalty by Fisher, which was followed by a Maurice Wood try, which Fisher improved, and a drop goal by Jones. The York side could only reply with a penalty, and their hopes were dashed when Hobbs burst through for a try to give Rovers a 12-2 advantage. Another Fisher goal made the result virtually certain and Heworth's other five points came near the end.

Middleton OB 8 Sharlston Rovers 5
Yorkshire Junior Cup Final

If Sharlston Rovers had made use of three overlaps during the final with Middleton OB at Featherstone, they would have won the Yorkshire Junior Cup. However, in each case the player concerned ignored his unmarked colleagues and was brought down yards from the line. The game opened quietly with Middleton getting possession more than Sharlston, who were without their regular hooker. After 10 minutes Sharlston lost Nightingale with a broken ankle and Middleton looked even more menacing. Rovers' forwards held on and kept the ball tight, but their policy starved their wingers, Wynn and Hobbs of possession. Just before the interval Joyce scored a try to put Rovers ahead, Fox converted. Middleton ran in eight points soon after the interval. Sharlston's outstanding players were Booth at scrum-half and Peter Fox at full-back.

This final concluded a season which at one time looked very bleak indeed and ended with Rovers in two finals but losing both. It should have been three for they had won the right to be in the Wakefield Cup Final with an emphatic 37-7 victory over Wakefield Loco in the semi-final, but this was before they were suspended and kicked out of the cup.

Special mention should be made of the contribution made by Jim Fisher in Sharlston's achievements over the past few seasons. Jim was an inspirational captain and a fierce competitor who didn't like to lose.

Another young Sharlston star, Joe Mullaney made his debut, but for Stanley. In April 1952 Sharlston visited Stanley in a league game and had to loan the home team two players. One of them was Joe Mullaney, who later played for Featherstone Rovers, Yorkshire and England, who had gone on the team bus as a spectator and offered to make the numbers up for the Stanley team. Ironically enough the two players scored all Stanley's points and Rovers lost 11-7. Joe scored one of the tries and this was his baptism in junior open-age football.

In the same month, Sharlston scored 97 points without reply in their two league matches against Hall Green. In the home game, Brian Flowers scored seven tries and kicked a goal in the 53-0 massacre and on Easter Monday, Peter Fox kicked 10 goals when Hall Green were swamped 44-0.

1952-53

After the previous season's troubles, the good news for Sharlston was that the players suspended *sine die* were reinstated and back in action.

It was not a very auspicious start to the season for Sharlston, who lost two of their first three league fixtures. The first setback came, not unexpectedly, at Normanton, always a hard side to beat, but the issue was in doubt right until the end. Sharlston fielded a young side with a nucleus of experienced players and were as good as Normanton in most departments. The defeat was mainly due to defensive errors. After victory at Balne Lane, they then suffered a home defeat at the hands of Eastmoor. It seemed that Rovers were revitalised when they rattled up 44 points against Manygates OB, but then the unbeaten Stanley team visited Back o' t' Wall and claimed what they said was their first victory there in their history

It was a see-saw season. However, Sharlston were pleased to beat a usually boastful Normanton side when they came to Sharlston seeking a double. Not this time!

Sharlston Rovers 20 Normanton 9

That they could always beat Sharlston had been the undisputed boast of Normanton for some years and Rovers had lost consistently to Normanton since 1946. However, this time Normanton received a dose of their own medicine, from a Sharlston side that was on top from mid-way through the first-half.

Normanton were not at full strength, Coyne and Harrington being missing from their ranks. But Rovers also were without several regulars.

Rovers were the faster side and had far more striking power than Normanton. In the scrums, hooker Hague beat Normanton's Hall regularly and Rovers' backs, ably led by Flowers, who was playing his first match since being released from the Services, were first rate. Though he contributed only one try to Sharlston's total, Flowers was the technician behind his side's success and his intelligent running and high speed passing caught Normanton defence out and made scoring chances for his colleagues.

Sharlston's first try came after 10 minutes when Jackson burst through. Fox missed the goal. Minutes later Waite had an easy chance to reduce Normanton's arrears but his penalty hit the cross-bar. From then until the interval, Rovers hammered away at their opponents' line and were rewarded by a second try by Flowers just before half-time. Fox again failed to convert.

After the break, Rovers turned on the pressure again and made the game safe with two tries by Fox, and one apiece from Jackson and Nightingale. Fox also kicked a goal. Rovers eased off and Normanton scored nine points through tries by Marchant, Bentley and Breakwell. The teams were:

Sharlston Rovers: Fox; Jackson, Nightingale, Flowers, Clark; A. Cardall, Mullaney; Fisher, Hague, Simpson, P. Joyce, Maskill, A. Joyce.
Normanton: Golding; Breakwell, Wilkinson, Marchant, Atkinson; McDermott, Goode; Bentley, Hall, Pearson, Speakman, Glassell, Waite.

Stanley, Eastmoor and Wakefield Loco were the top teams in the League. Sharlston did secure a play-off spot, but got no further, being outplayed by Wakefield Loco 18-2. Rovers were by no means at full strength and Nightingale took a grave risk in playing at full-back, as he had not completely recovered from injury.

In the Challenge Cup, Rovers beat Manygates OB 38-0 at home in the first qualifying round, after leading 22-0 at half-time. Then Stanley were vanquished 12-6. Stanley proved tough opponents but the Rovers gave a good account of themselves and fully deserved their victory.

Rovers had another home match in the third qualifying round, when Eastmoor were beaten 16-11. The match could have gone either way. Sharlston were fortunate to maintain their five point lead in the second half, for 15 minutes from the end Eastmoor were pressing within five yards of their line and had the game lasted a few minutes longer they would almost certainly have scored.

Taking quite a time to settle down, Sharlston had to back-pedal by the visitors' vigorous tactics and in quick time they were seven points behind through a penalty by Thewlis and a try by Micklefield, which Thewlis converted. This seemed to stir Sharlston and they fought yard by yard into Eastmoor's territory, where Mullaney burst through for a try. Fox kicked the goal and a few minutes later was on the mark again to put Sharlston level. This did not last long, however, for Thewlis landed a goal to retrieve the lead for Eastmoor. After this Sharlston gained an ascendancy which they maintained until a late Eastmoor bid to save the match. Sharlston's score increased through two goals by Cardall and one by Fox and a try by Bailey. Eastmoor then attacked and after Thewlis had landed a penalty they put Sharlston's line under great pressure. The home side's defence was commendable but in the dying seconds it showed signs of cracking.

The fourth qualifying round saw Rovers at home again. In another hard fought encounter, Hebden Bridge were beaten 14-13.

Rovers were losing throughout the game, but scored a try two minutes from time to clinch victory. Though Hebden Bridge managed to maintain the lead for such a long period, Rovers looked the better side when on the attack. Reason for the half-time deficit of three points was handling mistakes at crucial moments and a cover defence which slipped up several times in its anxiety to keep the home side out. Sharlston three goals, Hebden Bridge three tries was the interval position and in the second half, Rovers attacked repeatedly in an all out effort to assert their obvious superiority. Luck seemed to be against them until two minutes from the end. Chalkley made a fine run, drew the Hebden Bridge defence before passing to Bolton, who touched down. Mullaney with a try, Cardall and Fox two goals each, completed the Rovers' points scorers.

The next round brought Hull NDLB to Sharlston for a 9-9 draw. The game was postponed for a week due to bad weather, and never reached great heights. With 15 minutes left, Sharlston were leading 9-7 and the Dockers lost Hill, who was sent off. Rovers' appearance in the next round seemed certain. However, after Metcalfe made the scores level with a penalty, the Dockers withstood all Sharlston's frantic efforts to score. Fox narrowly failed with two drop-goals; the same player had an unsuccessful shot at goal from well inside his own half; Clark was almost in at the corner on a couple of occasions; but still the defence held. Had either side possessed a reliable kicker they could have won the game with penalties.

Peter Fox was the pick of the Rovers' backs. His fielding of the ball was almost faultless, he linked up intelligently with his backs and he kicked all the important goals. Clark, on the right wing, worked hard and showed an astonishing turn of speed, running strongly and fearlessly despite the slippery surface. Alf Cardall was a tricky scrum-half and Fisher led the forwards well.

Sharlston scored after 10 minutes, when Alf Cardall fell on a loose ball over the Dockers' line. Fox missed the goal. The Hull side reduced the arrears five minutes later, when Metcalfe kicked a penalty, and shortly after they went ahead with a goal from the same man. Then Rawlins breached Sharlston's defence and passed to R. Brigham, who scored too far out for Metcalfe to convert. Alf Cardall, Fisher and Fox had all failed with

A Sharlston team – Tiny's Thirteen – from a Workshops knock out competition at this time. Former Sharlston player Denis Chalkley, then with Hull KR, played as a guest. Back: Les Jones, Jimmy Fisher, Peter Chalkley, Fred Simpson, Tommy Townend, Bill Bullock, Jeff Leake; Front: Mick Joyce, Herbert Mosley, Joe Mullaney, Denis Chalkley, Alf Cardall, Fred Wynn. Mascot: Joe Wynn.

penalty attempts, the last named reduced Sharlston's arrears with a goal just before half-time. The second half was a grim forward struggle and two penalty goals each by Fox for Sharlston and Metcalfe for the visitors, were the only scores.

Hopes of Challenge Cup glory ended when Sharlston lost the replay at Hull 8-7. Hull scored all their points in the first half and although Sharlston rallied they ended just short. After the break Rovers pack achieved better results. With goals by Fox and Fisher and a try by Clark, it looked as though the Rovers might win. Late on they claimed another try, but it was disallowed.

In the Wakefield Cup, Sharlston won their first round tie with Wakefield Loco 11-9 in the last two minutes with a penalty by Fox and were lucky as Loco had a late try disallowed.

In the next round, Sharlston lost 15-14 at Eastmoor. Sharlston made light work of the poor Eastmoor defence and Bridges forced his way over under the posts. Fox landed the goal and followed up with a penalty goal and later dropped a goal. Then Eastmoor fought back, scoring 15 points, leaving Sharlston badly shaken, though they fought back with a try by Joyce, Fox kicking the goal.

Eastmoor also ended Rovers' hopes in the Yorkshire Junior Cup, with a deserved 11-3 win. The match was on a slowly thawing pitch, and never reached great heights. Eastmoor always appeared likely winners. For Sharlston, Clark and Mick Joyce were most impressive in the backs and Bridges and Chalkley were the pick of the forwards. Eastmoor opened the scoring after 10 minutes when Bedford went over for an unimproved try. The visitors drew level shortly after when Clark scored too far out for Fisher to add the goal points. Failure to 'play to the whistle' cost Sharlston the lead, when, with half the team waiting for an offside decision, D. Tilford ran 30 yards almost unopposed to score, which Thewlis could not improve. After the break, Eastmoor went further ahead when a length of the field movement saw Hodgson score under the posts for Craven easily to kick the goal. Sharlston came more into the picture during the last half hour but Eastmoor's sturdy tackling, coupled with their own mistakes, left them a well beaten side.

It was not a good season for Sharlston, but they had players good enough to make the transition to senior rugby and they lost Joe Mullaney to Featherstone Rovers and Barry Chalkley to Hull Kingston Rovers. Peter Fox joined his brother Don at Featherstone. Don had signed for Featherstone after playing for their intermediates side.

1953-54

Before the start of the season the Sharlston Secretary, Mr G. R. Lumb, told the *Wakefield Express*: "The club is likely to have their best side for a year or two. The villagers will be expecting at least that for they have been brought up on the best in junior football and last season's disappointing team caused grave misgivings." Not much of a prophetic statement as it turned out, for the side wasn't any better than that of last season, but this did not make it a poor side, only a disappointing one. They had set high standards at Sharlston which no team can maintain season after season. But, once again, there was no silverware to show, the nearest they got was the Final of the Wakefield Cup, when they lost narrowly.

Rovers ended the league campaign in third place, but did not make the final. There were some good performances; Eastmoor were trounced 34-0 and there were two exciting draws, 11-11 with Manygates and 22-22 with Nostell.

The local paper reported that "The general opinion was that this game was the best ever match at Nostell... all eight tries were the outcome of good open football." Both teams played to the rules, and the referee did not have to issue a single caution. Both captains, Nostell's Heritage and Jim Fisher of Sharlston controlled their teams. Heritage's speed and kicking were always dangerous. Sharlston's Joyce made some very good runs and his tackling could not be faulted. Both teams scored four tries and five goals.

In the Challenge Cup, Rovers lost 5-0 to Trinity Boys in round one, and fared only little better in the Yorkshire Junior Cup, with a shock 20-7 defeat by Leeds Electric in the third round.

Rovers' best success came in the Wakefield Cup. An easy victory against Silkstone was followed by a great struggle at Eastmoor, with a 4-3 victory. A scoring spree followed against Hall Green, 30-12, in the semi-final. This meant a Final encounter with Wakefield Trinity Boys and a chance to gain revenge for the Challenge Cup defeat.

Trinity Boys' Club 10 Sharlston Rovers 8
Wakefield and District Cup final

With the last kick of the game stand-off half, Dilks, landed a penalty from in front of the posts to give victory to Trinity Boys' Club after an exciting match at Belle Vue.

A draw would have been a more fitting result to a game between two well matched teams. At times Trinity Boys' enthusiasm seemed likely to prove decisive but Sharlston showed the better teamwork in the second-half and subjected their opponents' line to severe pressure.

An early penalty from Fisher gave Sharlston a lead which they held until near the interval, when Moore forced his way over and Dilks added the goal. Richardson put Sharlston on level terms in the second-half, but winger Campbell scored a remarkable try for Trinity Boys when, though hemmed in on the touch line, he turned infield and scored in the corner after beating the Sharlston defence.

The scores were level again when Banks crossed for Sharlston, but Fisher missed the kick and it was Dilks's penalty which ended Sharlston's hopes.

The trophy was presented to Lockwood, Trinity Boys' captain, by the Mayor of Wakefield, Councillor F. West, who was introduced by the League organiser, Mr J. R. Reyner.

1954-55

Normanton, who had left the League the previous season were back, with two newcomers, Ryhill & Havercroft and Holmfield Park. However, Manygates OB, Thornes and Nostell all withdrew.

This was Sharlston's worst season since the War. They finished outside the top four, went out of the Challenge Cup and Wakefield Cup at the first stage, and did not enter the Yorkshire Junior Cup. Despite losing the first match to Wakefield Loco, the League champions in successive seasons, Rovers got off to a good start and were not defeated again in the league until December. They then lost three matches in succession. They still had hopes of finishing in the top four up to their last match of the season, against Hall Green. The result would decide which team would get the fourth spot. The home team, Hall Green, won 15-5.

History was made on 15 December 1954 when, by permission of Mr G. Cooling, the Lord of the Manor, Sharlston played a home fixture against Balne Lane on the village green. Although defeated 5-3, it was the first time in the life of Sharlston Rovers that the team fulfilled an official fixture on the village green. The Back' o' t' wall ground was being levelled. The team were not strangers to playing on the green, however, because 'touch and pass' had been played there for many years on Sunday afternoons, with as many as 20-a-side, of all ages.

Rovers had to go to Eastmoor in the first qualifying round of the Challenge Cup and lost 8-6, but successfully appealed against the home side playing an ineligible player, Hodson, and the match was ordered to be replayed.

In the replay Eastmoor registered an emphatic reply to Sharlston's protest and at one period in an excellent game, the home team led by 17-0. Aided by strong wind at times, Eastmoor's attack was clever and prolonged. When the teams turned round at half-time, Eastmoor continued to dominate against the wind. Though Sharlston fought to the end, their nearest chance of retrieving the game came in a period midway through the half when sporadic raids brought three tries and a goal. Eastmoor won 23-11. For Sharlston Clark, with two, and Jim Fisher scored tries. The latter also kicked a goal.

The RFL had sent a Grade 1 referee, Herbert Harrison of Ossett, to control the tie and his firm, but pleasant approach helped both players and fans enjoy the game.

A large crowd contributed to a collection made by the competing clubs' secretaries and the line of cars parked outside the King George V Recreation Ground gave the proceedings almost top grade rugby league prominence.

Having beaten Normanton easily away from home in the league, Sharlston were very confident of victory in the first round of the Wakefield Cup, but were in for a shock.

In a very keenly, but cleanly fought game at St John's, the Sharlston forwards, through the efforts of Goodwin, won more of the ball from the scrums and from a

A day out in the 1950s: Peter Chalkley, Les Jones, Jack Adams, Mick Joyce, Wilf Green, Moss Wood, Joe Mullaney, Walt Maskill, Eddie Jackson, Nobby Clarke, Don Fox, Billy Howcroft, Fred Simpson, Mick Cardall, Sid Ward, Jeff Leake, Ray Bennett, Ted Birkett, Alf Cardall, Les Bailey, Keith Bridges, George Green, Jimmy Conway, Jim Fisher, Barry Chalkley, Ray Lumn.

position near the posts, Downs was penalised and Crump kicked a penalty for Sharlston. Shortly before half-time, after good work by Goode and Milland, Normanton gained a position from which they equalised from a goal by Downs. Sharlston, who were playing their speedy winger Nobby Clark at scrum-half, had failed to use the wind.

Normanton made use of the stiff breeze and when Till was penalised for not playing the ball properly, Bullough kicked a penalty to give them the lead mid-way through the half. Sharlston hooked the ball and Clark quickly passed the ball to Kenny Banks, and ran round him to take a return pass and, after running nearly half the length of the field, scored a fine try to which Crump kicked a goal in-off the post.

Normanton retaliated and from a scrum, Bullough scored for a converted try to give Normanton a 9-7 lead. With 10 minutes to go and their ranks depleted to 11 men through injury to their wingers, Milner and Milland, it looked as though Sharlston, with Clark back on the wing, and Peter Joyce as centre, would win, but when the final whistle came Normanton were on the Sharlston line. Sharlston missed Fisher's play and appeared to lack inspiration.

Rovers were rebuilding, some players having moved on and others retired. In the latter category was Jim Fisher, whose efforts on behalf of the club cannot be praised too much. Once again, players were lost to the professional ranks. Keith Bridges signed for Wakefield Trinity. Winger Nobby Clark signed for Batley and scored a hat-trick of tries against Wakefield Trinity, who had discarded him after trials.

Some junior clubs flourished, others struggled, finding it difficult to recruit. Wakefield

Loco, despite success in the League, were urgently asking for players to join their club. Sharlston must have had problems as well, for they took a breather and did not appear in 1955-56.

In November 1954, Featherstone Rovers' Joe Mullaney was chosen to play for a Northern RL XIII against the Australians at Odsal, but missed the match due to an injury. He had played for Yorkshire twice that season. In September 1955 he played for England against Other Nationalities at Wigan, and became the first player from the village who had played for a Sharlston Rovers open age league team to win a professional international cap.

1956-57

Sharlston returned to action in 1956-57, joining Askern, Stanley, Trinity Rovers, Hall Green, Eastmoor, Pilkington Recs (Doncaster), Wakefield Loco and Balne Lane. Sharlston usually got off to a good start and this season was no exception. The first four matches were won, 58-3 against Askern, 54-2 at Pilkington Recs, 28-4 against Eastmoor and 46-3 at Balne Lane.

When they visited Wakefield Loco, the winning run came to an end with a 26-15 defeat which the Loco repeated a week later with a 20-3 drubbing. Rovers quickly got back to winning ways and finished their league programme in second place, but found Trinity Rovers too good for them in the semi-final play-off. This was the nearest they got to silverware which has now eluded them since 1951.

Following two easy home victories against Balne Lane and Wyke in the Challenge Cup, the Rovers were beaten in the third qualifying round at Stanningley. In the Wakefield Cup, Askern were the first round visitors and were decisively beaten 61-3, but then at Sharlston, in atrocious conditions which resulted in a forward dominated game, Stanley Rangers were the visitors and won 10-4. The tough Lock Lane side were too good for the Rovers in the first round of the Yorkshire Junior Cup.

It was not all a season of disappointment for the Sharlston club for they had in 18-year-old forward Tommy Smales an outstanding junior footballer. In this season with Sharlston, in 21 matches, he piled up 218 points in what was believed to be a record for the Wakefield and District League, beating the 216 points by Jack Taylor, the Trinity Rovers full-back. He gained many medals for his achievements in junior football and represented the County at under-19 level. While at Sharlston, Bradford Northern, Dewsbury and Featherstone Rovers showed interest in signing him, but he surprised everybody by signing for Wigan in 1958. He then had a spell with Barrow, but he was not fulfilling his early promise and it was not until Featherstone came along in 1965 and snapped him up for £750 that he was seen at his best.

Although Sharlston had indicated that they were looking forward to the 1957-58 season in the Wakefield & District Open Age League, they did not fulfil any fixtures and withdrew from the league. It would be a long time before an open age team would be seen again on the famous Back o' t' wall ground.

1958-59

In 1958-59 an under-17 team was formed to operate in the Wakefield & District and also the Dewsbury & Batley District Leagues. The team was supplied with jerseys by the Wakefield & District League and shorts and stockings by the Featherstone Rovers club and, happily, played at Back o' t' wall. The other teams in the league were Crigglestone,

The under-17 Sharlston team. Back: John Speight, Brian Gidman, Walters, Tommy Lackenby, Tommy Lingard, Gilbert Crawshaw, Frank Shepherd, Albert Cardall; Front: Carl Dooler, Ivor Lingard, Mick Brook, Brian Gaskell, Frank Harper. Carl Dooler and Ivor Lingard signed for Featherstone Juniors, and in 1960-61 for Featherstone Rovers. Both had distinguished careers in the professional game.

Trinity Juniors, Crabtrees, Featherstone, Shaw Cross, Alverthorpe, Wheldale, Ossett, Staincliffe and Mirfield. The enthusiasm for the new club was such that a Ladies Committee was formed, led by Mrs Crawshaw, to provide refreshments and hot drinks for the visiting teams.

Sharlston did not make the top four in the league, but they did put in some good performances and none better than that against Alverthorpe, the outstanding team in the league. After losing 5-2 at Sharlston - their first defeat of the season, Alverthorpe queried the ages of certain members of the Sharlston team, and it was discovered that one player was over-age. In view of this Alverthorpe objected to the League Management Committee, who ruled that the fixture be replayed. Rovers were not disgraced when they went to Alverthorpe and lost 17-0 with a weakened team. But there was no doubting Alverthorpe's superiority when they inflicted on Sharlston their first home defeat of the season, 37-0, and the Sharlston committee complimented the team on their fine win.

Unfortunately for Sharlston, half-back Lingard was injured in the early stages of the game, thus depriving the team of a star player.

Sharlston had easy victories in the first two rounds of the County Cup, against Ossett, 31-3 and Huddersfield, 57-2 and they were full of confidence for the third round tie away to Headingley Boys, but were not quite good enough. They did get to the final for the Oldroyd Cup at Crown Flatt, Dewsbury, and, once again, were convincingly beaten, 34-0 by Alverthorpe.

Alverthorpe quickly had Sharlston on the defence with repeated forward attacks which resulted in Hardcastle breaking through to set up Parkinson to score the first try. Lowe failed to convert and again failed to improve a try by Crewe. Alverthorpe kept up the pressure and Edwards scored. This time Lowe succeeded with the goal kick. In almost every scrum Gunn gained possession and his probing runs gave Hardcastle the try of the match. Faultless passing by the Alverthorpe forwards undermined Sharlston's confidence and meant that Alverthorpe kept their undefeated record so far this season.

In November, for rugby league enthusiasts there was a lecture for teenagers on the rugby league code at the Sharlston Hotel. This was given by Laurie Gant, supported by Mr Smith, the secretary of Dewsbury and Batley Amateur League. Also present were local professional stars, Joe Mullaney of Featherstone Rovers, Neil Fox of Wakefield Trinity, Tommy Smales of Wigan, Denis Chalkley and Herbert Goodfellow. Mr Gant described Sharlston as a rich nursery for parent clubs, commented on players past and present and said that Herbert Goodfellow was the finest half-back he had ever seen.

He hoped that one or two of the newly formed team would follow his example or that of the other players mentioned. Mr Smith also spoke after which he held a quiz competition, the prizes for which were souvenir books of the last rugby league British Lions tour. The winners were Carl Dooler, Ivor Lingard, Albert Cardall and Jack Gill.

In January 1959, a film show was presented in St. Luke's Hall, by Bill Fallowfield, the RFL secretary. There was an enthusiastic audience of 200 who saw films on Challenge Cup finals and the last Australian tour. There were also on display international caps, medals and jerseys, which had been won by past and present Sharlston born players. After the show, Bill Fallowfield invited questions to which there was a very good response. A vote of thanks to Mr Fallowfield was moved by Mr. W. Howcroft and seconded by Mr J. Musgrave. Mr R. Bennett, the Sharlston club secretary, thanked everyone who helped to make the event a success.

The next month the club women's section held a dance in St Luke's Hall, with the Greatrex Band in attendance. Henry Dooler was MC. Supper was served and catered for by Mr Bacom, who is a great admirer of the boys team. The women were congratulated on the success of their first effort for the social side of the club.

In March the Women's Supporters Club presented the team with a set of shorts and stockings in the club colours. The presentation of this much-needed equipment was made by Mrs Ward and the young players were grateful for the gift.

For all the enthusiasm shown, the under-17 team only played for this one season.

Two Sharlston teams from the 1960s

Sharlston Rovers 1965-66: Back: Gilbert Crawshaw, Graham Reeves, Dave Betts, Horace Goodman, Doug Davies, Lou Woodfield, Bob Thompson; Front: Tony Bailey, Jimmy Wood, Ritchie Davies, Johnny Bullock, Brian Waller, Billy Wood, Bernard Golby, Johnny Long.

Sharlston Rovers 1966-67: Back: Gilbert Cranshaw, Billy Wood, Doug Davies, David Miller, Tommy Lackenby, Dave Betts, Graham Reeves, Carl O'Neil; Front: Lou Woodfield, Bernard Golby, Brian Waller, Tony Bailey, Trevor Hepworth, Jimmy Wood, Jack Davies.

7. The 1960s - Revival

1960 to 1965

There had been times in Sharlston's long history when the club has taken a breather and missed a season or two, but their absence had now turned into a long sleep with no signs of an awakening.

There was rugby league not very far away at New Sharlston where under-19 and under-17 teams were formed with their headquarters at the new Welfare Ground, with dressing rooms. They had hoped to form an open age team, but it did not happen. They had no connection with the Sharlston Rovers Football Club, but it is interesting to recall their progress.

The under-19s did not fare too well in the League, being anchored at the bottom for most of the season, and lost 13 of their first 14 matches. They had some players of promise for Thompson and Matthews were selected for the Wakefield & District team and Waller and Chapman for the under-17 District team.

Both teams survived into 1961-62 and did improve. The under-17s got to the semi-final of the Wakefield & District Cup, but lost to Wakefield Trinity. This was the last season for both teams; they did not appear again. There was no one to run the club.

In February 1962, the *Yorkshire Evening News* featured Sharlston in their series 'This is your village'. It said that Sharlston Common is famous for rugby league, and was the birthplace of many famous players. Equally well known was the ground on which much of this rugby was played, Back o' t' wall. However, the report went on "Now, alas, the village's proud landmark is no more. The field is still there, waiting for mining subsidence to settle before [a decision is made about its future]. But the wall, once a six foot high edifice stretching for 200 yards along the main road through the village, has been pulled down to a noble 18 inches."

It said that everyone regretted the passing and winding up of Sharlston Rovers. Wilfred Wildman, who was a member of the team that held the record of playing 36 games without defeat said "Everyone knew of Back o' t' wall. It was famous, as famous as the grounds of top rank soccer clubs are to-day. It was used as a 'whippet run' on Sunday mornings, when the miners brought their dogs and raced them against their neighbours. On Friday and Saturday nights it was well-known as the spot where the miners went to settle any difference that might have arisen over a pint or two of ale. Nobody remembers it being built but it was certainly well used. It even came in handy as a shelter from the wind and rain."

The report said that New Sharlston Colliery, with a better ground and facilities attracted more and more of Rovers' players, until four or five years ago the club finally went out of existence and its proud record finished. "Somebody tried to get association football going at Back o' t' wall, but it came to nothing," recalled Mr Wildman. He went on: "This place is really lost without its rugby league club.

Parish Councillor James Wager wanted it to stay as a playing field. "There's talk of the Rural Council putting bungalows on the land", he said. "I shall fight for it to be turned into a proper playing field. There isn't one in the village at the moment. Councillor William Sandham said: "Nothing will be decided about the place until next year, when the subsidence may have settled ... but the Council has to build houses somewhere". For Councillor Sandham, a miner at New Sharlston Colliery, Back o' t' wall held many memories. He learnt his rugby there, later playing for Wakefield Trinity.

While rugby in the village may have been in the doldrums for a period, players from Sharlston were still winning honours. Three players from Sharlston won the Lance Todd Trophy in six years: Neil Fox in 1962, Carl Dooler in 1967 and Don Fox in 1968.

1965-66

At last, a rugby league revival came to Sharlston. In July 1965, an exploratory meeting was held and it was decided to restart activities and to enter an open age team in the Wakefield and District League. Matches were to be played at Back o' t' wall.

Mr Hammond became president, Mr Howcroft chairman, Mr Hoare treasurer and Mr Anthony Dooler from Grime Lane became Secretary. A committee of 18 members was elected. The meeting was unanimous in their determination to make rugby football once more a successful part of village life.

The Wakefield & District League teams were Bentley, Sharlston, Eastmoor, Brook House, Ackworth, Horbury, Stanley, Rossington, Thorpe Boys, Trinity Rovers and New Monckton. Sharlston's players included Keith Bridges, Johnny Bullock (player-coach), Jack Davies, Ritchie Davies, Doug Davies, Horace Goodman, Johnny Long, Jimmy Wood, Graham Reeves, Tony Bailey, Brian Waller, Tommy Lackenby, Dave Miller, Bob Thompson, Dave Betts, Billy Wood, Mick Brook, Gilbert Crawshaw and Bernard Golby.

The season got under way and Bentley were the visitors for the first home match and before a large crowd, Rovers won 26-19, with Betts scoring the first try.

The re-born club got off to a splendid start. With two matches played the team has retained an unbeaten record. Against Eastmoor, Sharlston won 8-0 with tries from Bailey and Brooke, and a goal from Ward.

There is very little information about this season, but the club did make the top four, but failed to turn up at Brook House for the semi-final play-off. Brook House were a top side and had easily beaten Sharlston in the Wakefield Cup Final on Easter Tuesday.

Brook House 22 Sharlston 0
Wakefield & District Cup Final

"Send for Pickles" was a comment at Belle Vue during this clash between Brook House and Sharlston. The dog, which famously found the World Cup in 1966 when it had been stolen, would have been useful for Brook House, as the holders, had mislaid the cup

One was needed for the presentation after the game and it was decided that the League Championship Trophy would be used.

While the game was being played, the League secretary, Harry Consterdine, dashed off to Ackworth, the Championship Trophy holders, to borrow it from them. But he was refused permission to take the trophy until he could establish his identity.

He arrived back at Belle Vue just before the end of the match, but in time for the Wakefield Trinity chairman, Mr Stuart Hadfield, to make the presentation - again to Brook House, who won 22-0.

Afterwards however a further twist was added when it was discovered that the trophy presented was in fact the Challenge Cup. Brook House and Ackworth had apparently each received the other's cup last year and it was the Championship cup which was missing. The Cup was eventually found. It was in the possession of a former Brook House player.

In the Challenge Cup, a first qualifying round victory against Trinity Rovers was followed by a visit to Halifax based team Siddal in round two. In a very unpleasant tie

Sharlston, who lost, had five players sent off. The pitch was lined with police and their dogs. Sharlston finished with eight men and Johnny Bullock had no alternative other than to pull his men from the field. Sharlston were escorted back to the dressing room by the police.

In a further boost to the game at Sharlston, the Wakefield & District League arranged a fixture with the Huddersfield & District League to be played at Sharlston. The hosts had three players in the Wakefield team, Betts, Reeves and Wood. These players retained their places for the match against York & District later in the season. Betts and Reeves played in the County Final against Hull & District.

Glamour came to rugby league in the village when Miss Marlene Lowrie of Weeland Crescent in Sharlston, was chosen as the Sharlston Rugby League Queen at a Dance in St Luke's Hall.

Sharlston also had an under-17 team operating in the Leeds and District League and with much success, carrying off the League Championship trophy.

They played Thorpe in the Leeds and District Championship Final at Buslingthorpe and took home the cup and medals after a great 40-2 victory. Thorpe scored first, but three tries and a drop goal from half-way by Goldie put Sharlston on the winning path and further points were scored by Bassinder, Lingard and Sayer with tries and five goals by Clayton.

In June 1966, it was announced that a team led by Wakefield Trinity's international centre, Neil Fox, would play a side chosen from village boys who have made the grade with professional clubs. The proceeds were to be divided between the Sharlston club and Neil Fox's benefit fund.

There was doubt as to whether the Wakefield & District League would survive. However, the Wakefield Workshops Rugby League competition was a great success.

John Ridge, the competition organiser and secretary of the Wakefield Trinity Supporters Club, said that there was tremendous enthusiasm. Sharlston Hotel entered a team and had a 13-2 first round victory against Parkhill Colliery, but then lost to Nostell Miners Welfare.

It had been a good comeback season for Sharlston and the club looked forward to next season with high hopes.

1966-67

This season there were 11 teams in the league, Horbury and Thorpe Boys had left and West Riding joined. In August, Sharlston and Brook House both made urgent appeals for players to join their clubs for the new season.

Sharlston's season started with four wins out of six and they were in or just outside the top four all season. They secured a top four spot, but it went right to the wire with a must-win match in the final league game. In the penultimate match, Eastmoor visited Sharlston in a crucial game for both clubs and went away with the points, putting Sharlston in fifth place position.

Although both sides were below normal strength, this was a first class exhibition in which the result was in doubt until the final whistle. With a top four place at stake, the game was keenly fought, but usually sporting.

Sharlston took an early lead when Eastmoor were offside and Bernard Golby kicked a penalty. From the restart Sharlston failed to keep the ball in play and J. Hastelow kicked a penalty from the centre spot. No tries came in the first half, and at the break,

Action from a Sharlston match – David Betts and Doug Davies breaking from the scrum. Gilbert Crawshaw is coming round the scrum with Johnny Long ready to tackle.

Eastmoor were 8-4 ahead. All their points were from penalties, Sharlston's second goal was a drop-goal. The second half opened with play swinging from end to end. Sharlston, with the wind behind them, were kicking deep into the Eastmoor half but Johnson made some valuable ground for Eastmoor with good clearing runs.

With a drop-goal and a penalty Sharlston drew level at 8-8. Hastelow put Eastmoor back into the lead with yet another penalty goal. Fletcher, who moved to full-back, gathered a kick and made a very good run in which he beat four Sharlston defenders before sending Magee over for a try. The goal kick failed. After some good passing, Golby scored a try for Sharlston and converted to make the score 13-13. With five minutes left, Hastelow kicked what turned out to be the winning goal.

For Sharlston, Waller was an able leader as captain and was well supported by Golby. In the Eastmoor side, McGowan who moved to loose forward when Fletcher was injured, led the forwards well. Johnson and Magee were the pick of the backs.

Sharlston then had to beat Trinity Rovers to finish fourth. Sharlston coasted home, 25-5, with Graham Reeves, for the second time this season against Trinity Rovers, scoring a hat trick of tries. The reward was a visit to unbeaten Brook House in the semi-final, a match they were not expected to win, but the defeat was kept to a respectable 15 points. They did turn up this time. Brook House had now beaten Sharlston four times in the season.

In the Wakefield Cup, Sharlston reached the final with victories over Rossington and Bentley, the latter 51-0. Jim Wood had returned to the side for the latter match and celebrated his return by kicking nine goals. The Final against Brook House was on Good Friday at Belle Vue. Brook House won the Cup for the seventh successive season, beating Sharlston 10-2.

It was a rough, tough and rather undistinguished match. It was not until the later stages in the game, and then, only after referee Scott had issued a general warning to both teams, that they were able to establish their supremacy.

Brook House had opened well, with good handling that sent both wingmen, Rodwell and Nixon, into action, but Sharlston's tackling put them out of their stride. For long periods the forwards dominated the game.

Baines for Brook House and Dooler for Sharlston landed first half penalties. Davies, Sharlston's captain, was their chief threat. Although Brook House had failed to maintain their early form they always looked the more likely to score. Barraclough broke through and ran 40 yards for their first try. Baines missed the goal.

Sharlston struggled hard to save the game, but Brook House were not to be shaken. In the last minute, Rodwell racing in unopposed for a good try, well converted by Baines. For Sharlston, Davies and Bailey stood out in the backs and Waller and Crawshaw in the pack.

In the Challenge Cup, Sharlston had a bye in the first qualifying round, then followed victories at Keighley Albion and Huddersfield side Moldgreen. In past meetings with the Castleford-based side Lock Lane, Sharlston have usually been second best, and this was so again in the fourth round at Back o' t' wall. Sharlston lost 18-12.

Early goals by Sharlston's Jim Wood gave them a four point lead, but this was soon rubbed out when Lock Lane scored a try which was converted from the half-way mark. At the interval, Lock Lane deserved their 14-6 lead.

Sharlston lost their loose-forward with a broken nose, but fought back to reduce the deficit to 14-10. They should have gone into the lead, if one of three players could have gathered near the line. Instead, Lock Lane scored two goals. Sharlston pressed for the last 10 minutes with only a goal to show for their efforts.

A runaway 63-0 victory came against Boothtown in the first round of the Yorkshire Junior Cup, with five tries from Tony Bailey, three from Reeves, two each by Davies and Betts and one apiece for Miller, Woodfield and Jim Wood. The latter also kicked nine goals. Their cup hopes ended when they were beaten 18-2 by BOCM at Hull in the second round.

Four Sharlston players, Miller, Crawshaw, Billy Wood and Jim Wood, played for the Wakefield and District team in the Inter-town Final against Hull.

One Sharlston player was picked for England, but in the other code. Stuart Clayton, a pupil of Normanton Grammar School, was chosen for the English Schools rugby union team against Wales at Twickenham on 22 March. Stuart, who lived at Weeland Road in Sharlston, was a second-row forward.

Sharlston entered the Blackpool 7s, but after a 16-3 victory over Raistrick, lost 13-5 to Lock Lane.

1967-68

This season had much in common with the last two. Sharlston finished in fourth position in the league and interest in the cup competitions soon faded. The season started well, but as soon as Sharlston came up against the few good teams in the league they were just not up to the task. To make matters worse, after struggling to make the fourth spot, for the second time in three seasons, they took no part in the semi-final matches. However, the league programme produced some bright moments.

Sharlston amassed 59 points against Rossington, with Golby kicking 10 goals from 13 attempts and Childs scoring 4 tries. When Sharlston visited Ackworth, both sides were unbeaten and weakened due to players being on duty with the Wakefield & District team. The home side just triumphed 14-12.

Stand-off Dooler scored three tries and kicked two goals against Kellingley. In a very exciting game at Back o' t' wall, Sharlston scraped home against Eastmoor by the odd point. If Eastmoor had their regular goalkicker the result could have been different as they scored two tries to Sharlston's one. Chalkley backed up a break by Dooler to go over for a try, which Jim Wood converted. He also kicked a penalty goal to give Sharlston a seven point lead. Eastmoor came back strongly before the interval and Sygrove crossed for a try. Just after the break, Jim Wood kicked another goal for Sharlston and Eastmoor replied with a try by Bartle and a goal by B. Lindop.

In the Challenge Cup, Sharlston lost 23-9 at Brook House in the first qualifying round. Sharlston were outclassed. Graham Reeves scored their only try and Bernard Golby kicked three goals.

There was a little more progress in the Junior Cup. In the first round, Ovenden were beaten 14-5. This was a good win against the Halifax League leaders. Graham Chalkley, the Sharlston forward, was their man of the match. The match report said that "He was in at everything and also scored a good try." The other Sharlston points were scored by Jim Wood who scored a try and kicked four goals. But in the next round, Sharlston travelled to Bison's Sports and lost 14-4. Sharlston took an early lead when Jim Wood kicked 2 goals. There was a lot of rough play and Sharlston were reduced to nine men. In the end lack of numbers took its toll and Bison's were too strong. For Sharlston, Doug Davies was sent off, and Crawshaw, Bailey and Jim Wood were all injured.

In the Wakefield Cup Sharlston beat Eastmoor at Back o' t' wall 26-2. The home forwards created their side's victory. Fletcher and Hayward tried all they knew to hold the Eastmoor pack together, but there was no stopping the home six. Sharlston collected 13 points in each half while the only Eastmoor score was an early goal by P. Hobson. Dooler with two, Graham Chalkley, Cardall, Lingard and Jim Wood scored tries for Sharlston, with Wood also kicking four goals.

In the semi-final, Sharlston travelled to Brook House and went out 27-20. This was a rough house affair with the lead changing hands several times. Players from both sides were injured and the match was abandoned before the end with both sets of players fighting with spectators.

On a more positive note, Crawshaw, Graham Reeves and Jim Wood all played for the Wakefield & District team this season.

Once again, Sharlston entered the Blackpool Sevens. The team was: Glyn Dooler, Billy Wood, Graham Chalkley, Jack Davies, Brian Waller, Graham Reeves, Tony Bailey. Subs: Bernard Golby and Jim Wood. Their professional player was Carl Dooler. Sharlston beat Hensingham 16-5, then Ossett Trinity 11-3 before losing to Lock Lane 6-3 in the semi-final.

In February, Norman Bedford, the club secretary, spoke to the *Wakefield Express* about the club. He said that "far from being underdogs the amateurs were the life and blood of rugby league. It amazes me that professionals who started their days as amateurs and have had their time in professional ranks do not come back and give the young amateurs the benefit of their experience for one or two seasons. We at Sharlston would welcome any ex professional even though he did not originate from the village."

He recalled that Tom Bailey, now 85 years old, played rugby in Sharlston 70 years ago. Since that time, he said that the 'production line' had turned out many professionals, among them some of the game's greatest stars.

He confessed that he had never played rugby league, but had played union and had played for the All England Army XV against All Ireland at Newcastle in 1944.

Norman Bedford was not born in Sharlston but had lived there for 16 years and had learnt a lot about rugby league. He also pointed out that the club was known as

Sharlston since it was re-formed three years ago, not Sharlston Rovers.

Apart from the name change, he said that there was no longer a 'nine 'ole' on the field where spectators used to stand and shout their heads off exhorting the Sharlston lads to 'get 'em darn i' nine 'ole and drown 'em'.

Also, the old fashioned iron tank holding about 20 gallons of water and heated by a coal fire had gone. "We have now electrically operated showers of hot water for which thanks are owed largely to Beverley Brothers Brewery who paid the major part of the cost. We have a wonderful set of lads on our books; all of them are a credit to the club" he said.

His main concern was persecution: "I would not like to point towards any particular official but there is one point which I do deplore. In a Yorkshire Cup match we had three players dismissed from the field. Two dismissals I would not dispute but one of them was a shocking decision for which I do not blame the referee but the Yorkshire Rugby League authority for not detailing touch judges for such matches."

He expressed his appreciation of the help given by Neil Fox in organising a team of past and present professionals from the village for an All-Star versus Sharlston match at the end of the season.

1968-69

Brook House and Ackworth had been occupying the top two positions in the league for some time now and there was no doubt about their superiority over the rest of the teams. Ackworth were one of the oldest clubs in Yorkshire, formed in 1875, and playing in the Wakefield & District League in the early Northern Union days, they had been in and out of the game for long spells. This season they reached the first round proper of the Rugby League Challenge Cup. Brook House was the old Wakefield Loco club with a name change. The Loco had surprisingly gone out of the league about the same time as Sharlston and reformed later as Brook House. They had won through to the Challenge Cup first round proper in 1962 and 1966 and the Loco had done this in 1957.

Sharlston suffered from 'fourthitis', again finishing in that position in the league again. With only nine teams this was no great achievement. It meant a visit to Ackworth in the semi-final play-off and an inevitable defeat. There were two new faces this season, Langley and Sadler joining the club.

Ackworth disposed of Sharlston in the Yorkshire Junior Cup and the Wakefield Cup. In the Junior Cup second round, Sharlston lost 13-7 at Back o' t' wall. Ackworth were made to fight all the way at Sharlston. Rovers led 7-6 at the interval, but Ackworth got on top in the second half. Sharlston fought on gamely to the end in arctic conditions, when most of the other games had been called off.

In the Wakefield Cup, Ackworth won 25-6. Until 16 minutes of the second half had gone and Ackworth were awarded a penalty try, Sharlston were well worth their lead from two goals by Jim Wood to a drop-goal by Dunning. Ackworth scored four more tries and four goals. Sharlston replied with a goal by Golby. Maskill and Golby were outstanding for Sharlston.

In the Challenge Cup qualifying competition, a first round victory at Dudley Hill gave Sharlston a home tie against BOCM (Hull), one of the strongest teams in the qualifying rounds. The visitors had a player sent off in the first half and for a time Sharlston had the edge, but BOCM were the better side and won 14-7.

There was still no sign of silverware. To keep finishing fourth was consistent and good enough for some clubs, but not Sharlston. They had the players to do better.

That the club had some good players was shown by the Wakefield & District League's team to play York which included six Sharlston lads of whom two, Glyn Dooler and Graham Chalkley, also played for Yorkshire. Graham Chalkley received the highest honour for an amateur player when he was picked to represent England against France at Bordeaux.

Inter-Town Competition

The Wakefield team beat York 20-3 at York's Clarence Street ground on 22 November. The Sharlston players selected were Glyn Dooler, Graham Chalkley, Jim Wood, Billy Wood, Dave Morris and Bernard Golby.

The visiting forwards were on top, and Chalkley ran on to a pass from Wright to score near the posts. Wood converted. Five minutes into the second half, Dooler picked up a dropped pass by a York defender and ran 30 yards to score. Wood added the goal. A dropped goal by Dooler increased Wakefield's lead. The local paper said that "This was the best performance by a district open-age side for a long time. Bradley, Wood and Spittle were a hard-working front row and Wigley and Chalkley were a strong running second row. Loose forward and captain Arthur Wright was the man with sufficient experience to knit the side into a splendid combination."

The semi-final was at Halifax's Thrum Hall on 8 December. The Wakefield team won 27-12. The same six Sharlston players were again chosen for Wakefield.

After only three minutes, Wakefield won a penalty. From the resulting tap-kick the forwards worked a planned move and Chalkley sent Dooler in near the posts. Jim Wood missed the kick.

Then Dooler intercepted a Halifax pass, found Babbage in support, received the reverse pass and scored under the posts. Wood converted. Dooler completed his hat trick before half-time.

Immediately after the break, Dooler scored his fourth try. The move was started by Bradley who sent Chalkley away on a brilliant sprint. Unfortunately, there was a head-on collision with the Halifax fullback and the Wakefield player had to leave the field with a cut mouth. The loss of Chalkley hit the team and Halifax narrowed the gap with a try and a goal.

For Wakefield, Babbage scored a try but Wood missed the goal. Soon afterwards, Nixon easily beat the Halifax fullback to score in the corner. Halifax struck back and gained a try.

Dooler, with his four tries, was outstanding, but prop Bradley was the man of the match with a truly great performance.

Glyn Dooler and Graham Chalkley were chosen to play for Yorkshire against Cumberland at Hull KR's Craven Park on 2 March.

Chalkley opened the scoring for Yorkshire when he crossed for a try near the posts. This was the outcome of an all Wakefield combination, for Bradley started the move which was carried on by Dooler who passed to his Sharlston colleague. Chalkley scored again in the second half and once again it was a Dooler and Bradley move that led to the try. Yorkshire won 17-3.

1969-70

For many years the Wakefield & District League had struggled to recruit teams and last season only had nine clubs. This season the Open Age Saturday League disbanded and the stronger clubs, Ackworth, Brook House and Eastmoor joined the Leeds & District League but Sharlston opted for the Wakefield & District Sunday League. This comprised mainly of pub, club and works teams.

Sharlston's new opponents were: Jolly Sailor, Bentley, Hemsworth MW, Rossington, Black Horse, Stanley Royd, Kellingley, Ackworth B, Hemsworth YC, Flanshaw Hotel, Duke of York Aces, Kettlethorpe Hotel, Walnut Warriors, West Yorkshire Bus Co., Gate Inn and Sheffield University.

This was the weakest league Sharlston played in for over 60 years; the gap in class was enormous. Some of the matches were merely training sessions with scores of 48-9, 43-9, 96-0, 54-6, 43-5, 64-7, 54-15 and 70-2. Against Hemsworth Youth Club, Frost kicked 19 goals, a club record. Just one league match was lost all season, against Duke of York Aces, but Sharlston took revenge in the Championship Final, beating them 72-0.

There were some new faces this season, Brian Frost, the Brook House stalwart, became player-coach, along with Sykes, Marney and Smales. A local lad, Steve Lingard, was beginning to make his mark in the game. There was one man, hooker Billy Wood, who had been with the club since it revived in 1965, and really came to the fore. His association with the club as player and coach lasted for many years and his value to the club was immeasurable.

The club's training facilities this season were greatly improved with the provision of floodlights which enabled players to put in extra sessions and be fitter.

The Challenge Cup qualifying competition took Sharlston to York-based Southlands in the first round. Sharlston were soon 10 points down, but recovered and with only three points between the teams, 15-12 to Southlands, a brawl spoiled the game. The referee sent off a York prop. Soon after peace had been restored, Vic Loxton levelled the scores at 15-15. In extra time Sharlston moved the ball about better and won with tries by Loxton, John Smales, Steve Lingard and Colin Chapman. Waller kicked four goals. Colin Maskill played well at full-back.

The next round took Sharlston to Hull NDLB, a very strong Dockers side. Sharlston opened the scoring with a penalty by Waller, but Hull soon scored a fine try. Sharlston kept the score to 7-8 at the interval due to a try by Steve Lingard and a goal by Waller. When play resumed, Sharlston started to play as a team and there were impressive breaks by Jack Davies and Graham Chalkley. A good try by Chapman, to which Waller added the goal, put Sharlston ahead, but Hull came back with a try and it was only Waller's kicking that assured Sharlston victory. A brawl broke out a few minutes from time and the referee stopped the game giving Sharlston a well earned 16-13 victory.

Another away draw followed, this time at Brook House. Hopes of a first round proper match vanished with a 14-0 defeat. Sharlston arrived at Barnsley Road with hope, determination and plenty of support but it was not enough to prevent their cup run finishing. All their feverish activity and tackling failed to disturb Brook House. Torrential rain and driving wind made open rugby difficult but Brook House resisted early pressure by the visiting pack and opened out through their wingers. Their quick handling soon beat Sharlston's defence for Nixon to score. Frost missed a penalty for Sharlston, but then Finch increased the lead with a drop-goal. Smales and Davies were prominent for Sharlston, but lack of pace at centre was fatal. Spittle sent Basson in for a great try.

With the wind behind them after the interval, Sharlston tried to pull the game round. But there was no breaking the grip of the home pack. Heeling quickly from a scrum on the Sharlston '25', Brook House moved the ball smartly to Basson, who beat Frost and Waller to score. Although unconverted, this try settled the match. Any lingering doubt was dispelled by Brook House's fourth try.

A trophy at last

When Sharlston defeated Hemsworth MW - the holders - to win the Sunday KO Cup at Belle Vue, it broke a barren spell of 19 years without a trophy. It was the 1950-51 season when Sharlston last tasted a cup win. Their path to the final was by victories over Kellingley, Walnut Warriors, Black Horse and Rossington.

Hemsworth MW 6 Sharlston Rovers 19

It was a really good final, watched by over 1,000 spectators. They got full value for money with both teams giving everything they had. Both teams had new strips for the game and were a credit to amateur rugby league and their clubs.

The game was more even than the score indicates with Hemsworth failing to take their chances and paying dearly for mistakes. Sharlston's scorers were: Jim Wood with two tries and Frost, Davies and Marney with one each. Frost kicked two goals. For Hemsworth, Green kicked three goals. The Stuart Hadfield Trophy for the most outstanding player went to Brian Waller, Sharlston's loose-forward.

There had been no trophies for 19 years, and then Sharlston won two in a season. The double was completed with a runaway 70-2 win over Duke of York Aces in the Championship Final. At the receiving end of this blitz, the Dukes had the crowd's sympathy though they did have the satisfaction of appearing in the final in their first season. Sharlston's Frost won the player-of-the-match award, presented by Mrs Howarth, Councillor J. Howarth's wife. He was the League chairman. Frost and Cardall were the pick of Sharlston's backs, with prop forward Loxton always prominent in the pack. For the losers, full-back Smith played heroically.

The Wakefield amateur rugby league was invited by the *Wakefield Express* to nominate a player-of-the-month. Their first choice was 26 year old Billy Wood, from Horbury Bridge. Billy hails from Streethouse but has played all his rugby for Sharlston.

Often described as 'a rugged hooker', he has had brushes with the game's authorities, but this season was a more disciplined player. He was given the captaincy of the Wakefield Inter-Town Competition side, and impressed enough to win a place in the Yorkshire amateur team against Cumberland.

In the county game he won the scrums 2-1 and did enough in the open play to impress the international selectors present.

Billy was one of the four players from Wakefield amateur rugby league to be chosen for England in the match against France at Salford on 1 March.

He was not the only Sharlston player to win representative honours. Cardall, Chalkley, Chapman, Loxton, Maskill, Morris, Smales, Sykes and Waller were also selected for the Wakefield & District team. Graham Chalkley also played for Yorkshire against Cumberland in January, and for England against France.

Sharlston teams from the 1960s and 1970s

Sharlston Rovers around 1968: Back: B. Golby, V. Loxton, G. Chalkley, B. Waller, D. Betts, J. Childs, R. Davies, G. Sandy; Front: T. Bailey, J. Wood, G. Dooler, G. Crawshaw, J. Cardall, J. Lingard, T. Hepworth; Mascot: G. Cardall

Sharlston Rovers open age 1970-71: Back: J. Long, T. Bailey, B. Golby, V. Loxton, E. Arnold; Middle: D. Parkin, G. Cooper, S. Banks, F. Fox, H. Marney, R. Greatorex, B. Cooper, T. Hepworth; Front: J. Atkinson, G. Dooler, D. Morris, S. Lingard, J. Lingard, W. Wood, H. Greensmith, B. Wood

Sharlston Hotel under-21 1970-71: Back: Tony Bradbury, Mark Williscroft, Stuart Hobbs, Jimmy Crummack, Dave Wassall, Bryn Bennett, Melvyn Jobb, Kevin Bruce, Robin Ward; Front: Clive Speight, Melvin Jowitt, Graham Smith, Johnny Long, Bob Pritchard, Steve Parker, Roger Chalkley, Neil Bennett, Malcolm Beresford

Sharlston Hotel under-21 1971-72, KO Cup winners. Back: Tony Bradbury, Tommy Davies, Jimmy Crummack, Steve Hankins, Trevor Bailey, Roy Holdin, Steve Parker, Melvin Sharp, Bob Pritchard, Garry Silcock, Clive Speight, Martin Hobbs; Front: Graham Smith, John Long, Melvin Jowitt, Mick Whitworth.

Sharlston 1973-74: Captain Billy Wood holds the Sunday League Cup. Dave Betts, John Long, Mick Whitworth, Steve Parker, Sid Whitham, Terry Longley, John Price, Colin Hodgson, Graham Smith, Melvin Jowitt, Stuart Brown, Bernard Barstow, Frank Bull, John Swithenback, Gerald Brown.

Below: A mid-1970s Sharlston team: Back: T. Bailey (trainer), J. Brown, N. Shillitoe, S. Conway, M. Empsall, R. Sykes, S. Smith, D. Betts, T. Chalkley, C. Speight; Front: D. Goodfellow, G. Smith, G. Hankins, W. Wood, J. Long, J. Bridges, S. Whiteley, G. Brown.

104

8. The 1970s - Consolidation

1970-71

Sharlston continued in the Wakefield & District Sunday League, which included the Duke of York Aces, Black Horse, Shaws, Jolly Sailor, Kettlethorpe Hotel, Flanshaw, Malt Shovel, Walnut Warriors, Balne Lane, Lumb's Sports, Jubilee Hotel, Bentley Reserves, Ackworth Reserves and Sanders.

However, the season opened with the club in turmoil. It had no ground or headquarters and was unable to raise a full team for the first match, playing with 11 men and getting walloped 48-6 by the Duke of York Aces. Key players left the club during the season, including Graham Chalkley, who turned professional with Batley, Colin Maskill, Billy Wood, Colin Chapman and B. Frost joined Brook House and M. Sykes went to Malt Shovel. Home fixtures were played at Nostell Miners' Welfare in Crofton, which became the club's headquarters.

What brought all this about? It arose through a difference of opinion between the Licensee of the Sharlston Hotel, Malcolm Jennings, and the players and committee of the Sharlston club. Mr Jennings paid the rent and rates for the rugby field and changing rooms and said he could not tolerate a position where he provided all the facilities and the club took their business and headquarters elsewhere. Mr Jennings had barred four people from the Hotel and the players moved their business to Crofton in protest. Mr Jennings took a firm stand against allowing those barred back into the Hotel and said that he would not be told how to run his business. In an effort to settle the differences Sharlston Parish Council called a meeting of everyone involved. A sub-committee was formed to meet the players and officials, as a result of which five parish councillors and four players were appointed to meet the owners of the field in the hope of settling the dispute and ensuring the future of rugby in the village.

The meeting was successful, and Mr Jennings agreed to the players using the field and the dressing rooms, but said that those barred would not be allowed back into the Hotel. The players refused to accept the conclusions of the negotiations.

Despite all the disruption, Sharlston finished second in the league and for the second successive season were league champions. After losing the two opening matches of the season, they quickly settled down with convincing victories against Flanshaw Hotel by 49-6, Black Horse 50-3 and Balne Lane 45-7. Hemsworth Miners' Welfare - the Tigers - provided stiffer opposition, but two tries from Steve Lingard, Sharlston's best player, saw them through 13-7. Defeat came at the Malt Shovel, the league leaders, but this was only a temporary setback and a succession of victories followed, including revenge over the Duke of York Aces for that opening match drubbing.

There was a surprise defeat at Sanders, which was quickly avenged with a 35-0 victory, and a good win against Hemsworth Miners' Welfare, which carried Sharlston into fourth place.

Sharlston won 9-5, and were inspired by prop-forward Frank Fox, the former Castleford and Hull KR player and Billy Wood. Sharlston led 9-0 at half time, and weathered a second half storm by Hemsworth's forwards. A penalty, drop goal and converted try put Sharlston in command in the first half but after the interval the Tigers came more into the picture and John Green scored a try, which he converted.

In the last home league match of the season (still at Crofton), the opponents were Malt Shovel, who came with an unbeaten record but were completely outplayed and lost

53-6. After 20 minutes it was only 5-4, but then Sharlston turned on a tremendous display which culminated in three tries from Lingard, two each by Morris, Whitaker and Greensmith, and one each for Brian Cooper, Banks, Parkin, Long and Golby.

This win put Sharlston in second place and a home play-off with Kettlethorpe Hotel. Two injuries in the first half handicapped Sharlston, who had to wait until the last quarter to get on top. Steve Lingard was Sharlston's star with a hat-trick of tries

The Malt Shovel, league leaders, must have had an end of season depression for after being comprehensively beaten by Sharlston the week before, could not get the better of Hemsworth Miners' Welfare in the other semi-final.

Sharlston had beaten Hemsworth Miners' Welfare in the two league fixtures but they had both been close scoring games and the Championship Final was expected to be just as close.

Sharlston 16 Hemsworth Miners' Welfare 7
Championship Final at Barnsley Road

Sharlston took the lead after 15 minutes when a drop-goal attempt hit the posts, two Hemsworth players hesitated and Morris took the ball to score near the posts. However, the conversion failed.

Hemsworth fought back and Brian Marston kicked a drop-goal. Just before the break, Sharlston's left-winger Greensmith scored from a well-timed pass from Lingard. Sharlston led 6-2 at the break. Hemsworth reduced the gap when Slaughter dropped a goal, but then had a try disallowed.

This seemed to knock the spirit out of them and Sharlston played their best rugby of the afternoon, scoring tries by Greensmith and Lingard. Golby added the goal for the second try and also kicked a penalty. Hemsworth fought back and B. Marston went over for a try in the corner to complete the scoring.

Greensmith with some good runs and great tackling was Sharlston's player-of-the-match. Lingard, Greatorex and Brian Cooper were outstanding.

The first round of the Yorkshire Cup provided excitement with a first ever win over Brook House by 7-0, only to turn to disappointment when Brook House objected to Sharlston playing Frank Fox, whom they said was ineligible. The League agreed and ordered a replay, this time Brook House gained an unconvincing 10-0 win. Outstanding for Brook House were Maskill and Frost, who had joined them from Sharlston in the early part of the season.

Sharlston reached the semi-final of the knock-out Cup. This meant a visit to Malt Shovel's Horbury Road ground and a large crowd turned up. They were not disappointed with a very close match. Carter, with four penalties and a drop-goal won the match for the home side. For Sharlston the Cooper brothers worked tirelessly. The final score was Malt Shovel 10 Sharlston 7

The Sharlston Hotel under-21 team

With the open age team deserting the village for Crofton, the brewery approached the licensee of the Hotel with a view to him releasing the field to them possibly for building if it was not to be used for rugby. Nothing came of this, but the issue would crop up again.

In October 1970 Malcolm Jennings of the Sharlston Hotel held a meeting of people interested in forming an under-21 team to play at Back o' t' wall. Efforts were made to raise funds and a 20 mile sponsored walk raised £75.

A team was entered in the Wakefield and District Amateur Youth Rugby League with the following teams: Sheffield University, Nottingham University, Eastmoor, Sharlston Hotel, Fitzwilliam and Hemsworth. It is interesting to note the presence of two student teams. Student rugby league started in the late 1960s, and was battling to establish itself in the colleges and universities at this time.

The team was run by a committee of four: Malcolm Jennings, Harry Pickles, Melvyn Jubb and Kevin Bruce. The coaches were Malcolm Jennings and Trevor Bailey.

The team performed well. A first match defeat at Sheffield was followed by victories over Fitzwilliam, Hemsworth and Nottingham. They were so impressive that professional rugby league scouts had watched their matches. After two close results with Hemsworth in the league and both sides being at their strongest for the league semi-final play off, Sharlston's runaway 39-4 victory was a surprise. The match was won by half-time with a 23-2 lead.

Sheffield University were the other finalists at Belle Vue in a match Les Pounder, the Wakefield Trinity chairman described as "one of the finest games of amateur rugby I have seen for many years".

Sheffield University 15 Sharlston Hotel 14
Youth League Championship Final

The Sheffield students became the first university side to enter the honours lists of Wakefield and District Amateur Rugby League. They came from behind to beat Sharlston Hotel 15-14 with a last minute try.

Sharlston scored from their first attack of consequence, Pritchard forcing his way over beside the posts and Williams converting. Hirst cut the deficit with a drop-goal, but the Sharlston pack was on top, and Hobbs forced his way over for their second try. Sheffield's first try came shortly before the break when Ferguson scored.

They got nearer to Sharlston's score with a penalty from Arnold but the game seemed to be going to Sharlston when brothers Neil and Bryn Bennett scored tries, although neither was converted. Sharlston were seven points ahead with only 10 minutes left.

However, Sheffield rallied to score their second try through Hawley and crowned their efforts with a move that sent in winger Lakin to score under the posts. Skipper Arnold converted for a dramatic one-point win.

For Sharlston, full-back Jowett, scrum-half Parker and the Bennett brothers stood out. The Cup and medals were presented by Les Pounder, who complimented the teams on an excellent game.

And so ended a season that started in turmoil and ended in uncertainty. Would the open age team next season return to their rightful home?

1971-2

The Sharlston Rovers open age team who had deserted the village to play at Crofton in 1970-71 collapsed. It had been a disastrous move. In October, Malcolm Tate, a former chairman of Hemsworth Welfare RLFC tried to revive the team and called a meeting at the Sharlston Hotel, but he said there was no interest. Nostell took Sharlston's name and Steve Lingard, Jack Davies, Joe Cardall, Tony Bailey and Glyn Dooler signed for them. Other players moved to other clubs, Colin Maskill to Brook House and Billy Wood to the Malt Shovel.

John Lingard, Eric Arnold, Bernard Golby and Dave Morris all went to Normanton. Later in the season when Don Fox became Batley's 'A' team coach he recruited from local teams and took John Lingard, Dave Morris, Jack Davies, Bernard Golby, Steve Briggs, John Bell, Billy Wood, Steve Lingard and Colin Maskill to Mount Pleasant. The last two went straight into the first team.

Had it not been for the Hotel under-21 team, rugby in the village would have disappeared. However, they were having one or two problems. There were discussions as to whether they should go into the open age Sunday League Second Division as some players were now over age for the under-21 league, and new players were needed. In the end, new players were found and they continued in the Wakefield and District Youth League, coached for the second season by Trevor Bailey. The League consisted of Sheffield Wasps, Sheffield Bees, Fitzwilliam, Sharlston Hotel, Rossington, Bentley and Travellers.

The under-21 team were unbeaten this season and had an easy 37-5 victory against Rossington to lift the knock-out Cup. Pritchard scored four tries and Steve Hankins and Tony Bradbury had outstanding games for Sharlston.

Although the season's records are incomplete the main try-scorers were Steve Parker, Steve Hankins, Melvyn Sharp and Bob Pritchard. Hankins was the leading goalkicker. Johnny Long was a fan of the drop- goal and landed four.

An under-17 team was also operating, but no league tables survive and there is very little information about them. They did lose to Willow Garth Wizards in the play-off final at Belle Vue which was a curtain raiser to the Trinity and Featherstone Rovers match.

Their players included Steve Dooler, Martin Hobbs, Graham Smith, Keith Hartshorne, Howard Firth, Steve Smith, Chris Holland, Tweedy Arnold, Colin Hitchin, Graham Teale and Dunk Fisher.

Earlier in the season, former Featherstone Rovers half-back Ivor Lingard, who was born in Sharlston, but had emigrated to Australia, returned for a holiday. He was playing in Australia for Parramatta. He visited his old school - Sharlston County Primary - where he and so many other players had their baptism in rugby league.

In 1970-71, the Sharlston County School rugby league players won two major trophies - the Wakefield Junior Schools League and the Featherstone Sevens. The local working men's club members decided that the boys deserved some lasting recognition of their achievements. As each trophy is held for one year only, members of Sharlston, Sharlston Villa and New Sharlston WM Clubs joined together to buy each boy an individual trophy. They were presented at the School by Ivor Lingard.

Back o' t' wall

The future of Back o' t' wall was discussed at the annual Parish meeting in Sharlston in May and reported in the *Wakefield Express*. It seemed that the village would be able to keep its football field without the Parish Council having to buy it. "It did look, at one time, as if we were going to lose it", the Council chairman, Councillor N. Hartshorne, told the meeting, "but now we are hoping that we can save it".

Mr G. H. Shiel, the Council Clerk, said the Council wanted to preserve the field because of its historic importance to the village. Sharlston teams had played football there for more than 100 years but there had been fears that the owners, Wilson's Brewery, were planning to sell it for building development.

However, these fears had been partly allayed in discussions Mr Shiel had with the Wakefield Rural District Valuer. He reported that: "Wilson's Brewery have told me that they have no intention at present of selling the land for development purposes, but are thinking of coming to the Council or the football players for a rental."

Councillor R. Reynolds was suspicious. The brewery, he said, had applied for outline planning permission for development. Mr Shiel reiterated that they had said they had no intention of selling. Councillor T. A. Berry commented: "But there's nothing to prevent them from developing the field themselves". He claimed this was their original idea.

Councillor A. Teal was suspicious of verbal assurances. He said: "Can't we get something in writing, making sure they don't back down on this." A parish resident, Mr D. Green, said that the field was of importance to more than footballers: "Small children round here have no area to play in. I would be inclined to treat this as a leisure area. Also, its part of our heritage."

Councillor Berry agreed: "It would be a good thing if it could be retained not only as a rugby field. It is large enough to serve for other things." Councillor Reynolds said that the Council would need some control over the field to keep it in a satisfactory condition. "We have had trouble with the brewery in the past in keeping this land clear" he said, and continued "We get very little cooperation from them."

Mr Shiel pointed out that it was private land and said "If we talk about buying it, then we can talk about this kind of thing."

Councillor Hartshorne said that the point was that the brewery had wanted to use the field as building land. Did the suggestion that they might accept a rent for it, change that? Councillor C. W. Hooley warned that "we should not be lulled into a false sense of security. I think we should see if we can have this declared green belt." Councillor Reynolds thought a written assurance from the Brewery, that no development was envisaged, would "go a long way" towards satisfying the Council. Councillor George Green, a former Sharlston Rovers player, said that "Watneys having taken over Wilson's, would have honoured the commitments of the previous brewery, who said that as long as there was a rugby team in Sharlston, the field would be put to its existing use."

He was surprised at the latest turn of events because when a group of villagers had met the brewery some time ago the talk had been about selling the land. If only the brewery had met Council representatives, and told them there was no intention of developing, all the work already done in preparing a possible bid for the land could have been avoided.

"I can't understand how a concern such as this, which all up and down the country is sponsoring sport, can come to a village and take its sport away from it" he added. Mr D. Green proposed that a letter be sent to the brewery seeking permission to rent the land, with an option to purchase if and when the brewery no longer required it. This was seconded by Mr T. Wager, and agreed unanimously.

1972-73

This season the Hotel team played in the Second Division of the Wakefield & Castleford Sunday Open Age League. This was a big step up from a league of eight teams to 16, but they were up to the task under the excellent coaching of Trevor Bailey together with Billy Wood, who was back as club captain.

The teams in the league were Ackworth, GPO, Redhill, Travellers, Black Horse, Crown Hotel, Lane End Park, Duke of York Aces, Stanley Royd, Walnut Warriors, Sharlston Hotel, Eastmoor Albion, Balne Lane, Doncaster Transport, Bentley and Sheffield University.

Some of the players had a good warm up pre-season when a team was entered in

Sharlston Hotel 7-a-sde team (Photo: *Wakefield Express*)

the Seven-a-Side Sports Spectacular organised by the Trinity Supporters Club at Belle Vue. The temperature was close to 70 degrees.

There was nothing tangible to see for their efforts over the season but Sharlston were always up with the leaders, finishing fourth, and were runners-up in the knock out Cup Final.

A semi-final play-off meeting with league leaders Duke of York was their reward for finishing fourth. They had got the better of Duke in the semi-final of the knock out Cup but on this occasion luck was against them and they went down to a drop-goal in the last few minutes.

Duke took the lead after 10 minutes when centre Molloy broke clear from his own half before passing to Brewin who scored near the posts. He also added the goal. Duke increased their lead when Dyson sent a long pass to Ward, who scored in the corner. The goal kick failed. Sharlston opened their account with a penalty and added to their score soon after with a well taken drop-goal.

From what looked like a knock on, the referee waved play on and Sharlston scored in the corner with the Duke players waiting for the whistle. Just on half-time Sharlston scored a try to lead 10-8 at the interval.

Sharlston increased their lead when Miller was penalised for striking. Duke captain and loose-forward Bridge, was carried off with a broken shoulder and all seemed lost for Duke. But again they came back and Brewin rounded off a fine bout of passing to score in the corner - his 32nd try of the season, which equals the club record. His attempt at goal failed. With only two minutes to go Duke attacked again and scrum-half Cartwright dropped a goal to win the match 13-12.

Sharlston had a confident start in the Yorkshire Cup with a 19-0 win at West Bowling, but Fryston, who were next to top in the higher Leeds League and expected to win, put them out in the next round. After ten minutes, Huddlestone put Fryston ahead with a try near the posts. Wadsworth landed the goal. Sharlston failed to break a strong defence and Fryston added a penalty from Wadsworth and drop-goal by Hardy. In the second half Wadsworth added another penalty before Sharlston got their points from a penalty. To round off Fryston's scoring, Brown scored to give his team a 14-2 win.

In the first round of the Open Cup Sharlston lost 16-9 to Jubilee Hotel, but this augured well for the future for when playing against teams from a higher league they could hold their own.

The most disappointing display of the season was kept for the Sunday Cup Final at Belle Vue against Black Horse when poor Sharlston passing gave away two tries.

Sharlston 8 Black Horse 26

After five minutes, R. Townsend intercepted a pass meant for the Sharlston winger, passed to S. Williamson who beat two tacklers and ran 50 yards to score. B. Phoenix added a fine goal. Sharlston hit back with a drop-goal and Williscroft landed a penalty, making it 5-4.

The next score came when Jackson made a break from a play-the-ball and passed to B. Phoenix, who used his strength to force his way over and also added the goal to make to 10-4 at half-time. Black Horse kept up the pressure and from a scrum 10 yards out B Phoenix crashed over between the posts and added the goal.

The next spell of Sharlston pressure resulted in another drop- goal. Sharlston were pressing again when S. Williamson intercepted and ran 60 yards, to score between the posts. Phoenix's kick hit the crossbar. Then N. Cooper ran through the Sharlston defence to score between the posts. The best try of the match came in the dying minutes with seven players handling in a 60 yard drive before Black Horse winger M. Edwards went over in the corner.

It had been a good campaign and the club had acquitted themselves well in their first season in the open age league. When the season started few would have thought that they would enjoy the success of a top four place and a cup final appearance.

1973-74

Still in Division 2 of the Wakefield and Castleford League, Sharlston had a good season, finishing fourth in the league and winning the Sunday League Cup. Two of their four defeats came at the beginning of the season and it was January before Flanshaw lowered their colours again, as they had done in the first match of the season. There were some close duels in the league, none better than those against Allerton Bywater, which the Hotel lost 14-12 and drew 9-9.

The first match was a rousing encounter providing open rugby, hard forward play and twice frayed tempers. Sharlston began in storming fashion and took an early lead with a goal. Only fine tackling, with Henshaw, Dent, Omeroyd and Wood outstanding, kept them from scoring a try in the first quarter.

Hepworth belted over two long range penalties but Sharlston collected a try and a goal to give them 7-4 interval lead.

Sharlston were on top early in the second half but fine rugby from Allerton produced tries for Matthews and Jackson. A touchline goal by Hepworth gave Allerton a slender lead and they had to defend grimly for the last 10 minutes to ensure that they kept their 14-12 winning margin.

The second match was a hard, entertaining tussle with the lead changing hands three times. A weakened Allerton had to tackle grimly against a much bigger pack. Just before half-time scrum-half Battye scored a brilliant solo try to give Allerton a 7-2 lead.

Sharlston levelled the scores but Dixon landed his third goal to give Allerton the lead. Five minutes from the end, Sharlston landed another drop-goal to make the score 9-9.

The two met again in the League Championship semi-final play off, with Allerton winning 13-4.

Intelligent kicking by Wood kept Sharlston penned in their own half and Cowell broke the deadlock when he burst through after 20 minutes to put Allerton ahead. This lead was maintained until half time with both sides kicking a penalty.

Mid-way through the second half Sharlston's defence was shattered by great passing which enabled Wood to score in the corner. Wood failed with the kick and Sharlston came back into the game with a penalty goal. Henshaw increased Allerton's lead when he scored a fine try. Wood put the seal on their victory when he dropped a goal.

In the Sunday Cup, Sharlston beat Shaw's from Batley 28-7. Sharlston attacked their Division 1 opponents from the beginning and were quickly in front with a penalty by Long. After 20 minutes Stuart Brown increased their lead with a try and after Batley had opened their account with a penalty, Sharlston made the score 9-2 with penalties by Long and Barstow.

The points came quickly for Sharlston on the resumption. There were tries from substitute Mick Whitworth, Gerald Brown and Stuart Brown, all goaled by Long. A penalty and drop-goal by Fisher put the home team in an unassailable position despite a converted Batley try. It was a fine team performance by Division 2 Sharlston, with Barstow and Wood outstanding in the pack and the Browns and Fisher moving well in the backs. Long's place kicking was very impressive.

Sharlston reached the Final by beating the Duke of York 11-4 in the semi-final at Normanton. Sharlston began well with Wood heeling from the first three scrums. After that, however, Duke monopolised the set pieces and had their opponents defending for most of the first half.

After 25 minutes Duke took the lead with a penalty, but Sharlston produced their best play for Barstow to sail through for a try which Long converted. Duke replied with a drop-goal which left them trailing by a single point at the break.

Still lacking possession, Sharlston did well to hold their lead and counter-attacked on occasions. It was stalemate until Sharlston's loose-forward Long scored following excellent handling. Duke's hopes were dashed when Sharlston's left winger rounded the defence for his side's third try. It was a splendid team performance by Sharlston, with open prop Dave Betts, having a good game.

Hemsworth MW were Sharlston's opponents in the final, having beaten Normanton in a thriller on the Brook House ground.

Sharlston 15 Hemsworth MW 9
Sunday Cup Final

Hemsworth, who were fourth in Division I were hot favourites to win this match at Belle Vue, but Sharlston had other ideas. From the kick-off Hemsworth attacked and gained a six point lead from penalties. Sharlston soon hit back and from a set piece, Price burst over the line to score near the posts. Long added the goal. At the break, Hemsworth were 6-5 ahead.

On the resumption Sharlston attacked and in an incident from a scrum Billy Wood, their hooker and captain, was kicked in the face by his opposite number which caused a small crowd invasion onto the pitch. Wood had to leave the field for stitches to a cut eye. Wood returned and Sharlston took a 10-6 lead when Longley scored a try, with Long kicking the goal. Sharlston were now pressing again through Betts, Whitworth and Price and from a play-the-ball Wood sent Long over for a try, Long adding the goal. Hemsworth scored a try in the last few minutes.

Sharlston were defeated by Flanshaw in the first qualifying round of the Challenge Cup and by Shaw's from Batley in the Yorkshire Junior Cup first round.

Player of the season in the Wakefield and Castleford League was Billy Jordan of Hemsworth MW, who has been in the amateur game for more than 20 years. Billy Wood had been nominated from the Sharlston club. Billy had played for Yorkshire against

Lancashire and Cumberland during the season.

The British Amateur Rugby League Association was formed in Huddersfield in 1973, a breakaway from the Rugby Football League. At that time the RFL was controlled by the professional clubs and amateur clubs had no say in their destiny and some were in serious decline. The breakaway was acrimonious and strongly opposed by the professional clubs but within 12 months this was turned round to a unanimous vote of approval.

1974-75

In July 1974 Sharlston played in the Wakefield Amateur Sevens. In the under-16 final they beat Jubilee 'A' 34-5, in the under-18 final Trinity Intermediates were vanquished 23-8, but in the open age tournament, Pointer Panthers beat Sharlston 11-6 in the first round. Sharlston Hotel played in the Division 2 of the Wakefield, Castleford & Doncaster League. It was a tribute to Trevor Bailey's coaching skills that since he took over a bunch of lads in 1970 and turned them into the Sharlston Hotel team, they had made tremendous strides. This season he had a good blend of youth and experience and though the hallmark of sporting success is authenticated by trophies possessed - and Sharlston did not win any this season - it was nevertheless a successful campaign. There are times when a team plays consistently well, but their efforts go unrewarded.

The season opened as it did the previous season with a defeat against Flanshaw, but then followed a run of six victories and a draw, the match with Lane End Park of Castleford in November propelling them to the top of the league, where they stayed until well into the New Year.

Sharlston beat their visitors from Castleford 15-5. They left it late, but did their job thoroughly in the end to lift them into the league leadership. The first half had no scoring, both sides being upset by the strong wind blowing cross-field. Sharlston broke the stalemate two minutes into the second half. Full back Mick Whitworth, linked with good forward play to crash over in the corner under the host of defenders. Park promptly equalised, and did so again after a Barstow penalty had edged the home side 5-3 ahead. In the final 10 minutes Sharlston took advantage of weakening opposition. A try by Stuart Brown, goaled by Barstow was followed near time by a tremendous forward surge which saw Maurice Pell finish over the line for Barstow to add his third goal. J. Fisher, Steve Parker, and Gilbert Crawshaw were always in the thick of things for Sharlston, while Billy Wood won something like 70 per cent of possession.

The week before Sharlston had been to Eastmoor. Their play was described as "the best brand seen at King George V Playing Field this season" and it ended a run of five wins for Eastmoor.

The only blot on the league programme was the match with Ryhill & Havercroft, when with the scores level at 2-2, fighting broke out and the game was abandoned with players and spectators joining in. Ryhill & Havercroft's next fixture was due to be a friendly with Sharlston but there is no record of it taking place.

In January Sharlston avenged the opening match defeat by Flanshaw, with a 9-5 win. This was a testing encounter worthy of two teams battling at the top of the table. A Long penalty put Sharlston ahead and the visitors rallied their defence sufficiently well to bring to naught two strong runs by Flanshaw's Parkin. There was little between the two sides as indicated by the interval scoreline, 4-0, Long having kicked a second penalty. Flanshaw's hopes rose when Walker chipped two points off the deficit with a penalty, but they were surprised with a try for Sharlston by Friend, which Long improved.

Flanshaw, who had finished in second place, were again Sharlston's opponents in the semi-final championship play-off at Normanton. Sharlston had finished third, with wins in 16 of their 22 matches. Flanshaw won through to the final 10-7.

Sharlston made a lively start and Long put them ahead with a penalty. The lead changed hands early in the second half as a result of a great solo try for Flanshaw by Jowett, who ran the length of the field. He soon went in for his second try with Harrison adding the goal points on both occasions. Price set up a Long try for Sharlston, converted by the scorer and there was a tense finish with some excellent tackling from Flanshaw. Price, Betts and Brown impressed for Sharlston.

Having defeated the two Doncaster clubs, Bentley and Hatfield, in the earlier rounds of the Senior Cup, Sharlston's opponents in the semi-final were Brook House, a team they had never beaten. They reached the final with an historic 17-7 win.

Sharlston had problems with the referee and were frequently penalised. From one of these awards, Brook House took the lead but Sharlston then had two penalties, both of which found Johnny Long on target. He also scored the game's first try after full-back Mick Whitworth had burst through the defence.

On the resumption prop Maurice Pell sent in Gerald Brown for Sharlston's second try. Brook House replied with a try, but Stuart Brown sprinted 50 yards for the decisive Sharlston try, converted by Long who also kicked a penalty. This was an excellent display by Sharlston. Their man of the match was Stuart Brown

The other finalists were Normanton, from Division 1, who had got the better of their neighbours over many years and were favourites to do so again.

Normanton 16 Sharlston 10
Wakefield Cup Final

Both sides delighted the large crowd at Belle Vue with a fine display of attacking rugby. Normanton gave away a great weight advantage to the Sharlston pack. Sharlston's tactics were to wear down the Normanton forwards. Normanton enjoyed the better of the opening exchanges and Gray charged over after 10 minutes. The same player narrowly missed with the conversion.

After 20 minutes Gray gathered a loose ball on the half way line and beat three men before passing to Dalgreen on the line. The winger beat the full-back and crossed in the corner. Gray missed the conversion and was unlucky a few minutes later when his penalty hit the post.

On the half hour Normanton extended their lead to 11 points. Callon foxed the Sharlston defence with a dummy, gave the ball to Sharpe, whose pace left the tacklers trailing. Gray kicked the conversion. Sharpe was playing superbly against his former team mates, continually making good breaks to gain valuable ground. Sharlston replaced Pell with Betts at half-time and this change caused problems for the Normanton defence.

Sharpe came close to scoring and from the play-the-ball, Callon tapped the ball forward and scored. Gray missed the kick. With 20 minutes left Normanton extended their lead with Riches and Callon drop-goals in quick succession. Sharlston came into the game as their opponents tired, but two converted tries were not enough to deny Normanton victory.

A week later the two teams met again in the semi-final of the Sunday League Cup. Sharlston first had to survive a second round clash with Lane End Park of Castleford, winning 17-15, after trailing 18-8 at half-time, thanks to Billy Wood, who kept Sharlston on top by winning the scrums two-to-one together with some effective tackling, and man-of-the-match Crawshaw.

This time, Normanton won 11-2 on a sodden Horbury Road pitch. Sharlston kicked off and it was clear that the tackling would be hard. Penalties were awarded to both sides for tackling offences. From one of these Gray gave Normanton the lead with a difficult shot at goal. His side came close to scoring a try when Kirton broke clear only to be caught by the Sharlston cover 10 yards out.

There were numerous petty fouls. Sharlston equalised when Normanton were penalised for offside. Tremendous tackling by Normanton on their own line thwarted Sharlston. The scores were level at half-time.

Normanton regained the lead from a Gray penalty but they suffered a setback when Sharpe was sent off. A few minutes later they went still further ahead through another penalty by Gray. Wheeler created the game's only try for Booth. The conversion by Gray failed but the full-back later kicked a penalty to put Normanton 11-2 ahead with 10 minutes left. Sharlston were also reduced to 12 men when Kirton was fouled as he tried to follow up his own kick through.

Representative honours came the club's way when John Price and John Friend were selected for the Wakefield & District Team.

1975-76

This is not a season to dwell upon for long. A new league was formed: the West Yorkshire League and Sharlston joined the Sunday League Division 1, together with Lane End Park, Jubilee, Pointer Panthers, Hemsworth MW, Flanshaw, Crown and Allerton Bywater. This was a big step up, particularly as it was a young new look Sharlston side, no fewer than 10 of the previous season's team having dropped out. They were also hampered with injuries throughout the season. It proved too much for them. They were anchored at the bottom of the league all season, winning just two games. But there was some consolation in that they were not heavily defeated in any of the league games. Their first victory came in December against Hemsworth MW and there were signs of better things to come, but a winning run never happened.

In the opening round of the BARLA Cup Sharlston conceded 50 points to Dewsbury Celtic. The Yorkshire Sunday Cup was played over two legs and Sharlston won the first round against Bentley on aggregate 38-15. The first leg at Sharlston was their best performance this season in which the backs featured in some wonderful running and handling. Stuart Brown, Frank Bull and Clive Speight were outstanding in the backs and Dave Betts, Billy Wood and Mick Whitworth were a useful unit in the pack. Frank Bull scored the best try with a brilliant 70 yards run. It was the best try seen at Sharlston for a decade or more. In the second round, Sharlston lost to the stronger Pointer Panthers 41-10 on aggregate.

In the Wakefield Sunday Cup first round, Sharlston played the Duke of York. Bradley kicked a penalty for the Duke of York and Sharlston replied with a try and a goal. Duke came back with tries by Dunhill and Bradley and a Bradley goal. For Sharlston, Shillitoe and Bennett scored tries, with one goal converted. The match was settled when Ward scored a try for Duke and Bradley converted.

In the Yorkshire Cup, Sharlston travelled to Huddersfield to play Underbank in the second round and were beaten 10-2. The third round of the Open Cup was reached and Parkhill Primrose were the visitors to Sharlston. An 11-11 draw was followed by Parkhill Primrose winning the replay 13-2.

Sharlston's best cup run came in the West Yorkshire Sunday Cup Competition, when, after beating Bentley and Crown in the first two rounds, they faced Smawthorne Hotel in the semi-final at Normanton. Smawthorne won 30-19.

Three penalties by Roberts was all the Hotel had to show before half-time with Sharlston also landing three. Smawthorne had Appleyard sent off. In the second half, Roberts kicked three more penalties, the second after Sharlston's prop-forward was sent off and from then on they were on top. Edwards scored Smawthorne's first try and a minute later Pickerill added another. Roberts added both goals. With 12 minutes left, Sharlston hit back with two well earned tries. But then a quick break ended with Pickerill darting over and Roberts landing his ninth goal. Smith scored again to send Smawthorne's total to 30. Sharlston then got a lucky try; a defender knocking a pass back into an attacker's hands. The goal completed the scoring.

1976-77

This season was an important testing time for Sharlston. After the previous season's disappointing showing they had to drop back to Division 2, and face Duke of York, Manor, Ryhill & Havercroft, Dewsbury Moor, Redhill, Kippax, White Swan, Bentley, Crown and Travellers.

Trevor Bailey was rebuilding the team and clearly this would not happen overnight. There were some harsh comments from those on the touchline impatient for success, but Trevor was confident that the team would blend and become a good side if they stuck together. But it did not happen this season, finishing eighth in the league, winning seven of their 18 matches and drawing one.

There was no success in the cup competitions. An encouraging start in the first round of the BARLA National Cup when they defeated Greenside (Huddersfield) 11-3, but then an exit at York against Punch Bowl, 25-17. In the Wakefield Sunday Cup, Sharlston lost at Manor 16-8.

In the Wakefield Open Cup, Sharlston lost a dour match 6-5 at Flanshaw. In the West Yorkshire Sunday Cup, Duke of York beat Sharlston 15-2.

1977-78

This was another disappointing season. It was no worse or better than the previous one, in fact the final league positions were identical, seventh - fourth from bottom. It did look at one time when they were in mid-table that they would do better, but a dismal run in April, when they did not win a match and seemed to run out of steam, dashed all hopes of a more respectable position. The team lacked consistency and could not put together a decent run of victories. The team was strengthened by the return of Steve Lingard, formerly of Batley and Dewsbury. Steve Ackroyd, who had played for Yorkshire and Great Britain at under-18 level also joined, but key players also left the club.

Despite the below-par team performances, rugby in the village was booming, with under-10, -12 and -14 sides coached by Billy Wood and John Lingard. The future was looking good.

The one bright feature of the season was in reaching the Wakefield Open Cup Final after some closely fought earlier rounds. In the first round, Sharlston won 15-13 at Stanley Rangers, and then beat Eastmoor 8-7 in the last seconds.

Sharlston raced into a six point lead in the first ten minutes of this eagerly awaited cup game. First, Stuart Brown nipped over the Eastmoor line from a play-the-ball, and then Ackroyd finished off a Lingard chip with a touch down.

Junior and open age teams from the 1970s

Sharlston School 1976-77 – Wakefield under-11 League champions. Back: Harry Heaton, Derek Green; Middle: Shaun Craig, Paul Cunniff, Richard Ward, Simon Poppleton, Dean Pearson, Richard Bulmer, Peter Slater, Darren Moorby; Front: Steven Gorman, Mark Smith, Neil Bailey, Martyn Flanagan, Lyndon Chalkley, David Ward, Carl Ward, Nick Berry.

Sharlston under-12s 1977-78. Standing at back: John Lingard (coach). Back: Johnny Mullaney, Graham Stephenson, Richard Ward, Neil Ward, Paul Lingard, Kevin Gill, Garry Dooler; Middle: Darren Gill, Paul Hampson, Darren Lingard, Paul Wood, Chris Baldwin, Steve Ward, Dave Ward; Front: Mark Smith, Neil Bailey, Shaun Craig, Ian Lingard, Andrew Childs.

Sharlston open age 1977-78: Back: Jerry Brown, Martin Empsall, Steve Dooler, Roy Sykes, Steve Lingard, Jess Hobbs, Trevor Bailey, Glyn Carlton, Don Goodfellow, Graham Goldie; Front: Steve Conway, Billy Wood, Vicky Smith, Steve Ackroyd, Clive Speight, Brian Chambers. Billy Wood presented Vicky Smith with the best supporter award.

In the second half, Williscroft twice saved the Sharlston line as Gott and McGee were set clear. However, Lindop was on hand to finish off with tries from breaks by Carter and Gott and the same player was on hand to land a drop-goal and give the visitors a one point lead.

In a grandstand final 10 minutes both teams gave their all. Then with only seconds to go, Steve Dooler won the tie for Sharlston from what Eastmoor saw as a harshly awarded penalty.

In the semi-final, Sharlston returned to Eastmoor to beat Duke of York 15-12. Sharlston took a 10-0 lead, then Duke fought back, but Sharlston kicked a penalty to lead 12-7 at the interval.

On the resumption, Duke scored a converted try to level the scores. Sharlston scored wide out to clinch the game.

Normanton 15 Sharlston 7
Wakefield Open Cup Final

A crowd of between 700 and 800 at Belle Vue saw Bob Pritchard give Normanton the lead with a try. Steve Lingard soon hit back to level the scores. He scored all of Sharlston's points, adding two goals. However, Normanton were the better side with Brian Booth and Jed Ward both scoring tries and Graham Blakeway kicking three goals.

In the BARLA Yorkshire Cup, Sharlston lost 21-15 to Myson's from Hull in the first round. There was no more joy in the Wakefield Sunday Cup, with a 26-17 defeat to Manor. In the West Yorkshire Sunday Cup, Sharlston beat Jolly Miller 31-0 in the first round, and then drew 10-10 with Jubilee in the second round.

Jubilee had to fight hard to force a replay after having a player sent-off and finding themselves 10-2 down. Hooker Billy Wood scored both Sharlston's tries as Jubilee struggled to find their form. But once they did it was Sharlston who were under pressure as Jubilee scored two tries and kicked the goals.

In the replay, Sharlston lost 7-5. Jubilee gained a late victory when prop Martin Addison landed a penalty. Sharlston scored first, and added the goal. Jubilee replied with a goal, and at half-time, Sharlston led 5-2.

After the break, Jubilee drew level with a try from Steve Fletcher. Then came the late match winning penalty.

On the representative front, Steve Dooler, Martin Empsall, Steve Ackroyd and Stuart Brown were selected for the Wakefield and District team to face Leeds and District at Buslingthorpe Vale.

The secretary of the Junior Section of the Sharlston Amateur Rugby League club was Peter Chalkley. He held the record for a match at Back o' t' wall in the 1950s when he scored 13 goals and 7 tries in a seven-a-side game.

1978-79

At last the tide turned. It was a remarkable transformation from the previous campaign. Sharlston finished as league leaders but did not take further reward as Crown defeated them in the play-offs. With a new-look team Sharlston made a fine start to the season with a hard earned win over a strong Redhill side, with Empsall, Carlton and new scrum-half Hill being outstanding. They were soon tested with a visit from Crown, who were also unbeaten in the league.

Sharlston 14 Crown 10

The big Crown pack drove hard into the Sharlston line from the start but keen defence kept them at bay. Sharlston scored first through a Frank Bull penalty. Another penalty kept pressure on Crown, until good work by John Littlewood and Roy Sykes for Sharlston put Martin Empsall through for the game's first try. Sharlston scored another penalty goal soon afterwards which made the half-time score 11-0.

Both packs maintained their efforts in the second half - neither giving any quarter - with Carlton, Empsall, Littlewood and Sykes outstanding for Sharlston. The deadlock was broken when John Burnage dummied his way over the line for Sharlston from 40 yards. Crown fought back and scored two converted tries. Sharlston's superb tackling held the line against a very strong challenge. Their final victory was deserved and owed much to great team work.

Sharlston won their first three games, going to the top of the league where they stayed all season. Their first defeat came at Dewsbury Moor in December. Then severe weather conditions set in with grounds under two inches of snow and ice and it was March before they got under way again. But they showed no ill effects from the enforced lay-off getting back into winning ways against Magnet and Rossington. Because of the long lay-off many clubs had fallen behind in their league matches and it was impossible to fulfil them all. Sharlston's problems had been made worse because they also enjoyed a successful cup run. It was decided that league matches be played up to the end of April and then decided on a percentage basis, all teams to meet each other at least once before the end of April to make the percentage fairer.

Sharlston were now joint top with Duke of York and Crown and victory against fourth placed Dewsbury Moor would give them the title.

Sharlston 14 Dewsbury Moor 7

This hard earned victory over fellow title chasers Dewsbury Moor made Sharlston the West Yorkshire League Division 2 Champions and also preserved their 100 per cent home record.

In a fast and exciting game before a large crowd, Sharlston started in a determined mood and were given a penalty in the opening minutes after Dewsbury were penalised for offside. John Burnage goaled and put Sharlston ahead.

Dewsbury hit back. But following a period of strong pressure from the visitors, Burnage intercepted a pass, outpaced his pursuers and with a thrilling 75 yard sprint, scored a superb individual try. He added the goal.

Dewsbury then scored two drop-goals and a penalty. But Sharlston hit back. Their forwards won the battle up front and soon increased Sharlston's lead. Sykes and Chambers made storming runs into the Dewsbury half and set up a chance for Empsall to charge for the Dewsbury line scattering the defence. He was held up just short but passed to McMullen, who scored by the posts. Burnage converted, so Sharlston led 12-4.

The second half began with Dewsbury on top. They scored a try in the opening minutes but the conversion was missed. Sharlston replied with a series of clever moves and Maskill combined with Gent and Conway to bring them close to the Dewsbury line. Dewsbury were under a great deal of pressure and when Burnage looked to have outpaced the Dewsbury defence he was flattened by a stiff arm tackle which led to him kicking his fifth goal.

Sharlston met Crown in the top four play-off semi-final. The teams had met twice in the league, each winning the home fixture and this was an eagerly awaited contest.

Crown 12 Sharlston 10

A Sharlston try two minutes from time almost forced the West Yorkshire Division Two top four play-off semi-final into extra time. But the Sharlston goalkicker missed from the touchline to Crown's relief as they had been reduced to 10 men minutes earlier when Eddie Addle was sent off.

Crown went into a 9-2 half-time lead with tries by Addle and two from Phil Harwood. Sharlston hit back with a try then Kevin Townend went over to make it 12-5 before Sharlston kicked a penalty and scored their late try.

Sharlston reached the quarter finals of BARLA Webster's Yorkshire Cup before bowing out to York-based side, Heworth. The match was exciting right to the end and a difficult missed conversion could have earned Sharlston a replay

In the first round, Sharlston beat Ideal Standard from Hull 16-7. The match was a forward battle in midfield with the bigger Hull pack testing the Sharlston six. Despite all Ideal's pressure, they only had a penalty goal to their credit after the first 20 minutes. Sharlston came back after strong running by Sykes, Carlton and Empsall made a try for Chambers. Frank Bull added the conversion.

Empsall then strolled through a gap in the away team's defence to set up Sykes for a try. Further pressure put Stuart Brown across for a try on the stroke of half-time after a fine run by Dooler.

In the second half the Hull side came back strongly but magnificent tackling kept them out, with Smith, Conway and Sykes leading the way. J. Burnage scored after running 40 yards, chipping over the full-back's head and touching down for one of the best tries seen at Sharlston. The conversion was missed. The game was now Sharlston's and although the Hull team scored a converted try, Sharlston advanced into the second round in fine style, with the whole team playing superb rugby.

In the next round, Sharlston beat Bradford side International Harvesters 34-2. Sharlston went ahead with a try by Smith. Frank Bull added the goal. Harvesters replied with a penalty, but Sharlston went further ahead when scrum-half Hill scored a try. F. Bull added the goal and later dropped a goal to make the half-time score 11-2.

Sharlston dominated the second half and scored tries through Stuart Brown and Frank Bull with two each, and one from Steve Smith. Two were goaled by Bull.

Sharlston next beat another Hull side, Corporation Telephones 15-5. They attacked from the start and were unlucky in the early stages when winger Roger Maskill was bundled into touch at the corner. But their defence was soon under pressure as the big Hull pack began to dominate the play.

Corporation scored first from a penalty after Sharlston were caught offside and followed this with a great effort which eventually succeeded in breaking down the home team's defence when their winger scored. But the try was not converted and the teams went in at half-time with the score 5-0 to the Hull side.

Sharlston started the second-half strongly with Dooler, Sykes and Hill leading the attacks - but they could find no way through. The visitors' defence was finally broken with only 20 minutes to go when Steve Dooler passed to Kevin Sharp, who scored a great try.

Frank Bull converted to level the scores, giving Sharlston the inspiration needed to maintain the attack. Corporation fought back, but the deadlock was eventually broken when Graham Goldie scored a superb interception try which Frank Bull converted for Sharlston.

With only minutes remaining Sharlston set up yet another attack with Sharp, Carlton and Empsall breaking down the visitors' defence before passing to Steve Conway who held off two defenders to score in the corner. Frank Bull converted.

The fourth round brought more visitors from Hull to Sharlston, with Reckitts being beaten 23-3. Sharlston opened the scoring after five minutes when Martin Empsall shot through a gap in Reckitts defence and passed to John Burnage who touched down between the posts. He added the goal.

That was the start of a magnificent afternoon for Burnage who scored 17 points as well as continually worrying the opposition with his elusive running. Before half-time, after withstanding a great deal of pressure, Sharlston battled their way into the opposition half and although Carlton, Empsall and Littlewood all went close, two penalties by Burnage brought the first half to a close. Almost immediately after the restart Reckitts scored their only points of the game when they went over in the corner. However, this only spurred Sharlston on and they dominated the rest of the match. Burnage kicked two penalties to increase Sharlston's lead.

In the closing stages Sharlston opened out and played some great football with Steve Dooler scoring a fine individual try and winger Kevin Sharp dashing over in the corner from 20 yards. Both tries were converted by Burnage.

This was an outstanding team performance with the forwards in particular, Littlewood, Empsall, Goldie and Carlton, leading the way to victory and a step nearer to that cup. But it was not to be.

Sharlston 8 Heworth 10

The first half of this Yorkshire Cup fifth round game was dominated by a strong Heworth side with a great fight back by Sharlston in the second half, which added up to a thrilling match. The more experienced York-based side settled quickly and put Sharlston under pressure. After some great defensive work particularly by McCullen, Heworth scored their first try, when their winger crossed in the corner. The goal attempt failed.

Heworth kept up their attacks and Sharlston's line took a terrific pounding before Heworth broke through for a second try which was improved. Sharlston then came back into the game and on the stroke of half-time had a try under the posts disallowed.

In the second half Sharlston won more of the ball and played some superb football. After conceding an early penalty goal they launched an all-out attack on the Heworth line and a three-quarter movement put John Price over for a try. John Burnage added the goal. It was now Heworth's turn to defend and only last ditch tackling kept Sharlston out, until seconds before the final whistle when, after great runs by Price, Hall and Empsall, Stuart Brown scored a try wide out. John Burnage missed the difficult goalkick which would have earned Sharlston a replay.

Sharlston's hopes of winning the cup this year had gone after conceding only five tries in 400 minutes of rugby. Outstanding in this game for Sharlston were McMullen, Wood, Price and Hall.

In the Wakefield Sunday Cup, Sharlston lost in the first round, but the tie was in the balance until the final 10 minutes when Walnut Warriors clinched victory with two tries to win 12-2.

Normanton 'A' from Division 4 continued their giant-killing in the West Yorkshire Sunday League Cup, with Sharlston as the victims, losing 9-8. It was a hard-fought cup tie which produced five good tries and a punch up involving all the players after which John Price of Sharlston and Steve Lingard of Normanton were sent off. The first half was full of incident and chances but the Normanton defence stood firm until Mick Gent put the home side ahead with a try. Normanton drew level after the break from an interception try and a try by W. Smales put them ahead. Sharlston came back however with a try by Kevin Sharp and a penalty by Steve Dooler made it 8-6 to Sharlston. Then, with the minutes ticking away, Grey created a gap for Smith to score the winning try for the visitors. Martin Empsall, Steve Dooler and Glyn Carlton all worked hard for Sharlston.

Two late superb 70 yard tries by Kevin Sharp were the highlights of Sharlston's first round 23-9 win against Eastmoor Select in the Wakefield Open Cup, which set up a gripping encounter with Flanshaw in the second round, which Sharlston won 7-3.

Sharlston attacked from the start but Flanshaw's tackling was equal to the task. This was a fine cup-tie between two evenly matched sides. Flanshaw took the lead when Parkin made a fine break and put the wingman over in the corner. The conversion was missed. Martin Empsall, Glyn Carlton and Roy Sykes led the Sharlston counter-attack, but Flanshaw's defence held firm

After 25 minutes Sharlston notched their first points when Steve Dooler kicked a magnificent touchline penalty. The second half started well with Sharlston reproducing form that took them to the last eight of the Yorkshire Cup. Graham Goldie, John Littlewood and Steve Dooler set up a chance for Roger Maskill who was tackled just short of the line. Brown and Hill combined to unleash Ackroyd on a 35-yard sortie which ended when the home full-back made a good tackle. Then Glyn Carlton went on a thundering run to put Stuart Brown over for a try near the posts. Steve Dooler converted to put Sharlston into the lead for the first time. Flanshaw threw everything at Sharlston but were unable to make any headway.

Sharlston's superb forwards and magnificent tackling had won the game. Outstanding for Sharlston were Roy Sykes, John Littlewood, Glyn Carlton and Martin Empsall.

The Duke of York were Sharlston's opponents in the semi-final. They reached the Final by beating off a stern challenge from Sharlston. Duke went into a 12-point lead, but Sharlston came back with a try and two goals. Duke replied quickly with more points but could never relax when Sharlston countered with two tries and two goals. The final score was Duke of York 20 Sharlston 17.

This was a very good season and the team has played some of the best rugby seen in the village for a long time, particularly in the Yorkshire Cup matches which were all played at home.

In October, the *Wakefield Express* reported that Sharlston Parish Council had discussed providing new sports pitches on the village common. The chairman, Councillor T. Berry, said that they were concerned at the growth of leisure time and were determined that the village should be able to cope with the future demand for sports facilities. It was decided there was little the Council could do to expand existing facilities. They noted that the rugby league club was growing at a startling rate and they have approached the Parish Council to ask if they could help them improve their ground behind the Sharlston Hotel.

But as the field was owned by a Brewery there was little the Council could do. The same applied to the cricket field which was owned by the Church and the Sharlston Colliery Welfare pitch.

The Council decided that the only way it could make a significant contribution was to develop the common land. This land was covered with gorse which caught fire regularly in the summer. The Council hoped to be able to raise enough money to develop it into several new sports pitches and add a lot of beauty to the village at the same time.

But there was a problem in who legally controlled the development of the land. This would involve discussions with West Yorkshire County Council and Mr Maurice Cooling of Old Hall Farm in Sharlston. Councillor Berry denied that the Council's action was prompted by the controversy over sports facilities in Normanton.

1979-80

This season Sharlston were in the West Yorkshire Premier Division Sunday League, along with Normanton, Fryston, Travellers, Walnut Warriors, Jubilee, Pointer Panthers and Hemsworth MW. Having gained promotion to the Premier Division this was the worst season in the long history of the club. Played 14, lost 14. Never before had Sharlston failed to win a league fixture. And they were well and truly bottom, 11 points adrift of Travellers the club one from bottom who won five matches. The Premier Division was a big step up for the team, but this does not entirely account for what was an abysmal season. For one reason or another players moved to other clubs and there was unrest in the dressing room.

There were very few matches to get excited about in the league. Normanton went to Sharlston and tore them apart in the second half in a 29-15 win, after having five tries disallowed. Lingard, Normanton's new signing, who was playing against his old club, had a lively and impressive game.

Sharlston saved some of their best rugby for the BARLA Webster's Yorkshire Cup first round match at Brighouse, coming away with a 23-8 win, only to go out at the next stage to Myson's. In the match at Brighouse, Sharlston fielded a team with seven changes from the one beaten in the quarter-final last season, but they still produced a sterling performance to book a place in the second round.

After beginning to dominate, Sharlston put together a good move through Chambers and Goldie, and Mick Gent touched down in the corner. The goal was missed. Sharlston then had to defend as Brighouse went all out to equalise. After going close on a number of occasions they levelled the scores but also missed the goal.

Sharlston came back into the game with their forwards working their way up the middle of the field and John Price produced a run to take them within a few yards of the Brighouse line before he was tackled, but managed to get the ball away to Chambers who passed to Graham Goldie, who scored a superb try. Roger Maskill's goal made the half-time score 8-3.

In the second half Sharlston's superior fitness began to tell and half-backs McMullen and Chambers, were a handful for the Brighouse defence. A great run from McMullen led to Sharlston's next try - the best of the game. His break took Brighouse by surprise and he raced over for a fine individual try. Roger Maskill added the goal.

Brighouse bounced back, mounting another attack which saw them cross the Sharlston line for the second time. They added the goal to keep them within striking distance of Sharlston's 13-8 lead. This score seemed to spur Sharlston on and they now began to produce some of their best rugby all season. D. Hopkins was having a fine game on his debut and started the move which led to Mick Gent's second try. Maskill landed a great touchline goal.

Sharlston secured their place in the next round in the closing minutes when Don Goodfellow crossed for their fifth try and Maskill added his fourth goal. Outstanding for Sharlston were Goldie, Chambers, Price and Nick Hill.

Hemsworth MW had comfortable first round victories against Sharlston in the West

Yorkshire League Cup and the Wakefield Sunday Cup. Four players were sent off, three from Sharlston in the Wakefield Cup tie.

Sharlston put up a good performance to beat Manor 19-4 in the preliminary round of the Wakefield Open Cup. Sharlston gave away a penalty to give Manor a 2-0 lead. This motivated Sharlston and they attacked. Fine work by Don Goodfellow paved the way for Mick McMullen to cross for a try from 30 yards out. The conversion was missed.

Both sides went all out in an attempt to score a vital try before the half-time whistle. Manor threatened on a number of occasions but Sharlston defended well. A fine run from Jack Tallot took Sharlston into Manor's '25'. From a quick play the ball Jeremy Hobbs darted over to give Sharlston a 6-2 half-time lead.

Manor pulled back to 6-4 early in the second half when Shaw kicked his second penalty. But with halfbacks Hobbs and McMullen dictating play, Sharlston began to take control. Sharlston scored their third try when a 10-man handling move allowed Trevor Kingsbury to cross in the corner. Roger Maskill added the goal to put Sharlston 11-4 up.

Sharlston played some great rugby with forwards Carlton, Endersby and Hill making some strong runs. From one of these, Sharlston increased their lead when Steve Conway went over and Roger Maskill kicked his second goal to put Sharlston 16-4 ahead.

Straight from the restart Sharlston surged back up field, and hooker Graham Goldie popped up to complete the scoring with a try. Jack Tallot, Ian Endersby, G. Hobbs and Glyn Carlton were outstanding for Sharlston.

Walnut Warriors were Sharlston's second round opponents. Walnut grabbed two early tries and later added a penalty. All Sharlston's attempts at scoring were frustrated until five minutes from time when they scored two quick tries. They failed to convert the first and were left in the position of having to convert the second try to level the game. Much to Walnut's relief they were unable to add the goal and Sharlston's chance of saving the match vanished.

This was Trevor Bailey's last season as coach after 10 years and there is no doubt that Sharlston were lucky to get him and keep him for so long. Trevor arrived on the coaching scene in 1970 when the Rovers open age team had gone off to Crofton. A small committee, with Trevor as coach, formed the Sharlston Hotel under-17 team and he had the awesome task of piecing together a new team. In their first season they were in the League Championship Final and the season after unbeaten in the league. After two seasons they joined the open age league. He took them to six cup finals, winning two, and last season they were league leaders and played some superb rugby. He must have been bitterly disappointed with this season's results.

As a coach he was a good tactician and thinker, and brought along many promising players. Sharlston owed him a big thank you. He went on to coach at Wakefield Trinity in the 1980s.

9. The 1980s - Progress and Parramatta

1980-81

Having been relegated from the Premier League, Sharlston were now in Division 1 of the West Yorkshire League. The other teams were Dewsbury Moor, Askern, Bullcroft, Truck Components, King William IV, Duke of York, Flanshaw and Sailors' Home.

Former Featherstone Rovers player Colin Smith took over the coaching duties from Trevor Bailey and was assisted by Billy Wood. They did not get the start they would have wanted. The team was bottom of the table and did not win a match until January, but then won five and drew one of their last eight games. It was a remarkable turnaround.

One good win towards the end of the season was 21-10 over Duke of York, their third in a row. Carlton burst through the Duke defence to put Benny Westwood in for a well taken try, his first for the club since joining them on permit from Featherstone Rovers in the New Year.

Duke reduced the arrears with a penalty. But then Kevin Sharp burst his way over from close range to score a good try to which Ackroyd added the goal. Full-back Colin Maskill extended their lead with a try under the posts after some good work by Hobbs. Ackroyd again converted.

In the second-half, Sharlston went further ahead with a well deserved try by Nigel Leaworthy. Sharlston were helped by an abundant supply of ball from the scrums won by skipper Chip Goldie. Hobbs slipped through two tackles to send Roger Maskill on a run down the wing to score a simple try. Ackroyd converted to complete their scoring.

The winning run was brought to an end by Truck Components, who won 10-0. Sharlston, urged on by their supporters, fought hard in this game but failed to score against high flying Truckers. Sharlston can take credit from their performance against a side which contained several former professionals. A converted try and a penalty gave Truckers a 7-0 half-time lead. In the second session Sharlston, using the narrow pitch to their advantage, dominated for long spells but failed to beat Truckers' excellent defence.

By April they had shot up into fourth place but had to beat King William IV in the last match of the season to qualify for the play-offs, but failed to do so and had to be content with fifth place. It had been a good comeback after a poor start to the season. They had to play their home games on the Council School field because levelling and re-seeding was taking place at Back o' t' wall.

Wheldale, unbeaten and top of Division 2, knocked them out of the West Yorkshire League Cup, 16-9. Their best cup run came in the Sunday Cup when they reached the semi-final stage. A last minute breakaway try clinched the first round tie against Premier Division side Walnut Warriors, followed by victory against Woolpack 'A' from Division 4. Manor from Division 2 were their semi-final opponents, and Sharlston lost 7-5.

In the Open Cup, Hemsworth MW beat Sharlston 37-0, and in the Yorkshire Cup, Sharlston lost 28-2 to Hull-based Ace Amateurs, after receiving a bye in the first round.

1981-82

The club continued in the West Yorkshire League Division 1. Billy Wood was now player-coach and hoped to build on the momentum from the previous season, but his hopes must soon have turned to despair when, after another poor start to the season, the

Teams and presentations from the early 1980s

Sharlston 1980-81: Back: John Gledhill, Glyn Ward, Glyn Carlton, Dave Golding, Trevor Wood, Ian Westwood, Steve Ackroyd, Mick Golding, Jack Tallot, Dave Wood, Colin Smith, Pete Redshaw, John Swithenbank; Front: Roger Maskill, Jess Hobbs, Billy Wood, Graham Goldie, Colin Maskill.

Left: Billy Wood and Colin Smith at the 1980-81 presentations evening.

Below: The Sharlston team at the 1980-81 Hall Green 7s.
Back: D. Goodfellow, T. Wood, B. Mitchell, S. Ackroyd, K. Sharp;
Front:
J. Hobbs, G. Goldie, G. Carlton, R. Maskill.

Sharlston Junior School 1981-82 – winners of the Les Pounder 7s Cup. Back: A. Barker, A. Silcock, A. Dyson, M. Pearson, S. Baylis, C. Pullen; Front: G. Smith, A. Smith, K. Bingham, L. Stroud, D. Harpin.

M. Pearson is Martin Pearson who played for Featherstone Rovers, Halifax and Wakefield Trinity.

Left: John Burnage with Betty Ward at the 1981-82 presentation night.

Below: The Sharlston side in the 1983-84 Flanshaw 7s. Back: Billy Wood (coach), Trevor Wood, Graham Parkinson, Martin Empsall, Glyn Ward; Front: Alan Maskill, Shaun Bullock, John Swithenbank, Steve Tottie. The trophy is the Challenge Cup, won by Featherstone Rovers in a memorable victory over Hull in 1983 at Wembley.

team slumped to a final position of third from bottom, winning just four league games.

There are a couple of league games worth recalling where, with a bit of luck, the results could have gone in Sharlston's favour. One was a 16-14 home defeat against Flanshaw. The visitors lost the lead in injury time only to regain it within a minute to clinch the match. Flanshaw took the lead with a try by Petrauskas, who supported a forward break.

Sharlston closed the gap with a penalty but fell further behind early in the second half when a break by Lockwood ended with Dicken crossing unopposed. Flanshaw relaxed their grip after this try and Sharlston hauled themselves back into contention with a super winger's try. The goal was added. Flanshaw regained the lead with a penalty by Jacques and Dicken consolidated their advantage with a try after taking a good pass from Wakelam. Jacques added the goal. The game looked to be over at 13-7, but a superb individual try by a Sharlston centre to which he added the goal, threw the game wide open once more. Sharlston looked to have won the game with an injury time penalty, but a minute later Flanshaw forwards Palfreyman and Jacques linked up from a tap penalty to send winger Smith over for the match-winning score.

Sharlston also made Flanshaw battle all the way for their 16-0 victory at Flanshaw and the score did not do them justice. The sending off of veteran Billy Wood for dissent did not help their cause.

Another close encounter was a 20-17 home defeat against Magnet. At half-time, the visitors led 5-0. Sharlston rallied to go in front 7-5, but Magnet drew level with a penalty. Magnet scored three more tries and two goals to go 20-7 ahead. Sharlston started a late rally and scored 10 points, but Magnet just held on to win.

When Sharlston went to Magnet for the return fixture it was an ill tempered game and a 20th minute brawl threatened to stop the game. Magnet won 23-3.

There was defeat in the first round in the BARLA Yorkshire Cup by 55-15 at home to Travellers Saints. In the Wakefield Open Cup, Sharlston won 10-3 at Westgate in the first round, but then crashed 19-3 at Oulton.

Sharlston got a bye in the first round of the Wakefield Sunday Cup, and then a visit from Premier Division Globe Truckers in round two. Truckers went through with a hard earned victory over Sharlston, who looked capable at one point of pulling off a surprise victory over Premier Division Truckers. With only four minutes remaining Sharlston led 12-11 but Truckers finished strongly and scored a converted try to clinch their win.

Sharlston led 12-8 at the interval. Truckers attacked strongly in the second-half, but Sharlston monopolised the scrums to stay in contention. Truckers continued to press but the shortage of possession and some last-ditch cover tackling kept them out until 10 minutes from time when Mastin sent Elms galloping over. Sharlston still led by one point but Truckers snatched victory with a try by Elms near enough to the posts for Godfrey to add the goal.

The reward for early round victories against Bullcroft and Sherburn in the West Yorkshire Sunday Cup was a third round tie with Premier Division Jubilee, which resulted in a 16-16 draw. Twice Jubilee built up what appeared to be match-winning leads but they were forced to a replay. Clive Tennant with two, Tony Smith and Billy Bownes scored Jubilee's tries and Tennant added two goals. But their stumbling block was former Normanton Grammar School player John Burnage, who grabbed two tries, kicked three goals and landed a last minute drop-goal. In the replay, Jubilee won 49-0. To save Sharlston from further humiliation, the referee mercifully called a halt to the game with 15 minutes left. Jubilee were too good for their outclassed rivals, and scored 11 tries.

1982-83

After three league matches and a cup tie, all defeats, the future of the club was in doubt. They were desperate for players and if they were unable to sign any more, it was clear that the club would fold. It came as no surprise therefore when the following headline appeared in the *Wakefield Express* in October: "West Yorkshire League Two lose fight".

The report said that two of the three clubs who had been in danger because of a shortage of players have decided to resign from the West Yorkshire League. One was Sharlston, who it was said at one time contemplated switching to play on Saturdays. The other side was Globe Truckers.

1983-84

This time it was only a short break from rugby league for the village. The club came back for the 1983-84 season, but dropped to Division 2 from Division 1. They got off to a cracking start which they kept up throughout the season, always in the top four and eventually fishing third, winning 11 and drawing two of their 18 matches. They could not progress beyond the semi-final play-off against Selby but Billy Wood was well satisfied with the performance of his team this season. The West Yorkshire Sunday League Division 2 included Garforth, Swillington, Mirfield, Sherburn, Normanton 'A', Travellers, Selby, Bentley, Castle and Sharlston.

In the BARLA Yorkshire Cup, Sharlston lost 48-4 at West Hull. In the West Yorkshire Sunday Cup, Sharlston won 22-18 in the first round at Brodsworth, but then lost 28-6 at Redhill. In the Wakefield Open Cup, they lost 14-10 to Flanshaw, after leading 8-0 in the first half. These two local rivals staged a tremendous first round battle with Flanshaw just about deserving to go through after an action packed tussle. Sharlston could have won the game in the last minute when one of their wingers caught a kick, but was tackled by the Flanshaw full-back before he could score.

In the Wakefield Sunday Cup Sharlston beat Hemsworth MW 'A' 21-8, and then beat Ryhill 28-12. But hopes of a cup final appearance were dashed with an 18-9 defeat against Duke of York in the semi-final.

The match attracted a crowd of around 200 and Sharlston were the first side to impress when half-back John Burnage kicked a penalty. However, Sharlston's joy was short lived as Duke hit back with their forwards powering in to set up a try for Gascoigne. Chappell failed at goal.

Sharlston tightened up their defence but Duke centre Craig scored to put his side 8-2 ahead. Duke scored again for a 12-2 lead. This was reduced when Burnage intercepted and raced 60 yards to score, although he could not convert. Chappell added another try for Duke. Sharlston battled on, but could not penetrate Duke's defence and had to be content with a John Burnage penalty to pull back to 16-9 down at the interval. Duke held out comfortably in the second half, and consolidated their win with another penalty.

Under-17s

Sharlston had an under-17s team this season, but it was really Sharlston in name only, for the players were drawn from Wakefield, Featherstone, Normanton and Castleford and also included some Wakefield Trinity Colts players.

Coached by Trevor Bailey, they were a formidable side, only beaten once in the season and winning several pieces of silverware in sparkling style. Wakefield Trinity were so impressed with what Trevor had achieved that they axed their respected Colts coach, Alan Box, and asked him to take over.

The icing on the cake was an invitation to tour Australia for three officials and 21 players. But before the tour could go ahead there was the mammoth task of raising £20,000 which was achieved through very much hard work, sponsorship and fund raising events.

Behind the invitation from the Balmain Junior League was 41 year old civil servant Duncan Farrer, who spent nearly a month 'down under' the previous year meeting old friends and looking at the area's phenomenal youth set-up. One of the officials suggested that Duncan should arrange for a British junior side to go over. When the offer was later confirmed in writing, he looked for a suitable side. A Wakefield team declined to go because of the expense involved, but when he approached Sharlston coach Trevor Bailey, he jumped at the chance. The team spent two weeks in Balmain and seven days on the coast in Cronulla and lived with Australian families.

Trevor Bailey was delighted the way his young side took on - and often beat - the cream of Australian youth rugby. Manager Duncan Farrer was delighted with both on and off the field aspects of the trip. "We were made welcome wherever we went and really the Australians could not have done any more to ensure the success of the tour" he commented. On the field, Sharlston's youngsters stunned the Australians with their determined displays which produced a tour record of four wins and two defeats in six matches. The defeats came against Penrith and St Patrick's, and victories against Reinhardt Wanderers, Cronulla, Parramatta and Balmain. Problems with Australian referees, a different size and shaped ball and pre-match parties were all overcome by the Sharlston tourists. The Parramatta result stunned the Australians because Sharlston's opponents had won a staggering 75 games on the trot before they came up against the determined Yorkshire youngsters. Barbecues, sightseeing trips and dinners which included up to seven courses were just three of the ways in which the Australians made sure the lads from the local mining village enjoyed the trip of a lifetime.

Duncan Farrer recalled that on the evening before the clash with Penrith, Sharlston were well entertained, the events arranged by Wakefield Trinity prop Brad Waugh. "Unfortunately, this lasted until the early hours of the morning of the match" he explained. "It's hardly surprising that we lost," he added. The tourists met many top Australian players, trained with the New Zealand All Blacks on Sydney Cricket ground and returned with many souvenirs, stories and memories.

One sad event in January 1984 was the death at the age of 58 of George Green. He scored nine points in the Challenge Cup victory over Workington in 1946, and then turned professional with Halifax. He was also president of the Sharlston branch of the NUM for many years, and was a member of the Wakefield Rural Council, District Council and Sharlston Parish Council.

At the end of the season, the Parish Council finally bought Back o' t' wall from Beverley Brothers Ltd and Mecca Leisure Ltd for £10,000. Described in the sale document as "a plot of land fronting to Weeland Road, Sharlston", this secured it for rugby league for the foreseeable future. The purchase meant that the Council could invest in the ground. In 1990, the ground was renamed the G.H. Green Memorial Playing Fields in memory of George Green. The plaque was unveiled by his widow Doreen, Councillor Norman Hartstone, Bill O'Brien MP and Parish Council Clerk Geoff Smith.

George Green

Above left: The memorial plaque. Above right: The modern changing rooms.
(Bottom two photos: Peter Lush)

Memories from 1983-84

Sharlston 1983-84: Back: Glyn Ward, Harold Ward, Trevor Wood, Brian Chambers, Graham Goldie, Steve Tottie, Bernard Barstow, Billy Mitchell, Alan Maskill, Mark Caswell, Jess Hobbs, Graham Parkinson, Billy Wood; Front: Don Goodfellow, John Mullaney, Shaun Bullock, Nigel Leaworthy Peter Harrison, Martill Empsall, John Burnage, Keith Empsall.

20-year-old Lynn Sidebottom was Sharlston's 1983-84 Rugby Queen. She won the beauty contest at the Sharlston Hotel in October 1983. The judges included Featherstone Rovers coach Alan Agar, Councillor Norman Hartstone and Mrs Wendy Hayes, the first winner of the competition in 1971. Her first duty was to kick off the next home game on 9 October. (Photo: *Wakefield Express*)

Teams from the mid-1980s

Left: Wakefield 7s 1984-85: Sharlston: Back: Johnny Mullaney, Nigel Leaworthy, Ritchie Davies, Pete Harrison, Billy Mitchell; Front: John Swithenbank, Alan Maskill, Steve Tottie, Don Goodfellow.

Below: Sharlston school under-10s – winners of the Wakefield Schools under-10s trophy. Sharlston beat Sandal Middle School 8-0 at Belle Vue to win the trophy for the first time.

Back: Tony Strutt, Alan Wilkinson, Lee Garside, Darren Dooler, Edward Roberts, Mr Ward, Richard Broadbent, Gary Danvers, Andrew Skidmore, Scott Herbert, Russ Barlow; Front: David Spacey, Paul Fowler, Lee Chalkley, Lee Evans, Steven Mullaney, Alan Nash, Steve Goodwin, Paul Nichols, Kevin Ward.

Wakefield Park 7s 1985: Sharlston: Back: Melvin Brook, Roger Maskill, Billy Wood, Billy Mitchell, Alan Maskill, Graham Goldie, John Littlewood, Pete Harrison, Graham Parkinson, Kevin Sharp, Trevor Bailey, Dave Sykes; Front: Paul Hampson, Alan Chalkley, Martin Empsall, John Burnage, Ritchie Davies, Shaun Bullock, Glyn Ward.

1984-85

After winning promotion from Division 2, this was another good season for Sharlston, who finished in second place. This was despite the miners' strike which lasted for most of the season. The West Yorkshire Sunday League Division 1 included Normanton, Sharlston, Barnsley, Duke of York, Flanshaw, Walnut Warriors, Jubilee 'A', Swillington and Oddfellows.

Sharlston clocked a record score of 93-16 against Walnut Warriors. Having disposed of Jubilee 'A' in the semi-final play-off, they saved one of their least convincing performances of the season for the final against Duke of York when, with numerical advantage, they should have done better.

Duke of York 14 Sharlston 4
League Championship Final

Duke rounded off a tremendous season on a high note when they produced a power packed finish to clinch a deserved victory in this hard fought Division One play-off final against local rivals Sharlston. However, their win was tarnished by the sending off of two players, Chappell and Cooper.

Chappell was dismissed in the first half after an off-the-ball incident and when Cooper received his marching orders for a head high tackle after the interval Duke were reduced to 11 men. At half time, Duke were leading 8-0, despite the efforts of Wood and Burnage. In the second half, gradually Sharlston eased their way out of trouble with Burnage playing well and Swithenbank almost wriggled over, but he fell to a great tackle from his opposite number Jones.

Duke then suffered a hammer blow to their victory hopes when Cooper was given his marching orders but Sharlston - despite enjoying a two player advantage - made little impression. Play became very scrappy and Sharlston lost the services of Swithenbank - the third player to be dismissed - and a Bradley penalty put Duke further ahead. A well-taken try from Wood kept Sharlston's hopes alive but in the last 10 minutes Duke finally produced the vital score as Gascoigne went on his own from acting half-back to score.

In West Yorkshire Sunday Cup, Sharlston drew 12-12 with Upton, and then lost the replay 28-4. In the Wakefield Sunday Cup, they got a bye in the first round, beat Walnut Warriors 56-12, but then lost in the semi-final to Duke of York 16-6.

In front of a big crowd, impressive Duke marched confidently into the final. They proved too strong for a brave, battling Sharlston, but it took a late touchdown from strong running centre Craig to put the issue beyond doubt

In the Sunday Open cup, Sharlston won 8-6 at Normanton, then beat Eastmoor 14-9, but lost in the semi-final to Hemsworth MW.

A new contest was for the Billy Wood Trophy. Sharlston lost 28-20 to Streethouse-based Station Hotel. They produced a tremendous giant killing performance to beat local rivals Sharlston. First division Sharlston started the clash as hot favourites but they were shocked by the determination and skill of their fifth division opponents who fully deserved their victory after staging a terrific second half recovery.

Sharlston led 10-8 at the break after tries from Gill and Leaworthy and a goal from Bullock. Hughes and Stenson crossed for Station. And it was Station who enjoyed the best of an action packed second half with Bateman, Smith and Dawson all crossing for vital tries. Hunter with three and Goodwin tagged on goals.

Sharlston never stopped battling with Tottie and Chambers grabbing touch downs and Bullock adding a goal, but Station fully deserved their win. After the match the trophies were presented by Featherstone Rovers coach Alan Agar.

It was good to see a team from Sharlston's close neighbours Streethouse back in the game after a gap of 30 years. Back in the early 1950s Streethouse Red Rose boasted some of the top amateur talent in this area. But they were snapped up by professional clubs and the Streethouse name disappeared from the amateur ranks.

Players like Frank and Albert Mortimer were signed by Wakefield Trinity. Frank played for Great Britain at full-back against the Australians at Odsal in 1956. Streethouse team mates Wilf Adams and John Bullock also signed for Wakefield while Rowland Berry was snapped up by Castleford.

But after a gap of 30 years the Streethouse banner was resurrected by publican Brian Boulton, the landlord of the Station pub, where the new team was based. He suggested the formation of an amateur rugby team and because of the miners' strike he had 38 signatures within two days. Club secretary Pete Hodgson, who was also a miner explained: "It was the miners' dispute that led to the formation of the team. The lads had nothing else to do so they decided to form a team. They all buckled down and have been pretty successful."

1985-86

Sharlston had been promoted to the West Yorkshire Premier League, to face Cutsyke, Shaws, Duke of York, Normanton, Pointer Panthers and Jubilee 'A'. But once again, the club finished bottom of the league.

It was a repeat of 1979-80, when Sharlston gained promotion to the Premier League and finished bottom of the table. It was expecting too much of them to go from Division 2 to the Premier League in successive seasons but whereas in 1979-80 they failed to win a match, this season they did win four of their 13 matches, but they were never able to put two good results together.

They got off to a good start with a victory against Normanton in a close battle, 20-18. The most satisfying of their four victories was against old foes Duke of York. Duke had overwhelmed Sharlston at home, 30-1, but a fortnight later at Sharlston they were beaten in a thriller 12-11. The long awaited game between the two rivals proved to be every bit as exciting as pre-match predictions and Duke could well have won the spoils in an electrifying finale.

Their hopes suffered a blow when Sharlston's half-back John Burnage sprinted 75 yards for a great interception try to seemingly put the home side in an invincible position. However, with just two minutes left, Duke came storming back and Craig plunged over in the corner. Everything hinged on Chappel's touchline goalkick, but to Duke's dismay - and Sharlston's delight - the ball shaved the upright as the home side celebrated a marvellous victory.

In the West Yorkshire Sunday Cup, Sharlston won 24-18 at Garforth, beat Peacock 18-0, won 10-8 at Spenborough before losing 16-0 at Earlsheaton in the fourth round.

Once again, Duke of York knocked out Sharlston in the Wakefield Sunday Cup semi-final. A first round bye was followed by a 12-3 win at Peacock, before Duke won the semi-final 9-5.

In the Wakefield Sunday Open Cup, Sharlston beat Horse & Jockey (Horbury) 34-12, then drew 12-12 with Manor before losing the replay 13-5. The impressive Manor team produced a devastating first half performance to brush aside Sharlston and power into the semi-finals of the Open Cup. Manor, inspired by man-of-the-match Tony Robinson, scored all their points in the first half and established a commanding lead of 13-1 at the interval. Although Sharlston battled hard to pull back, Manor's rock solid defence won the day.

On the representative front, John Swithenbank, Trevor Wood, Graham Parkinson and Shaun Bullock were selected for the Wakefield & District team.

Sharlston Schoolboys play at Wembley

On the 3 May 1986 Steven Mullaney and Paul Fowler of Sharlston Junior School played in the under-11 Schoolboy curtain raiser before the Challenge Cup Final at Wembley Stadium between Wakefield under-11s and St Helens under-11s.

The emotion and pride of a victory at Wembley was summed up by the pictures seen on television throughout the country as the Wakefield scrum-half Steven Mullaney walked away from scoring a superb solo try with tears welling in his eyes.

The *Wakefield Express* reported that "Mullaney cut inside from the left touch line and danced his way passed three tacklers to score a fine try" and "with three minutes to go Fowler was put clear on his wing and raced 30 yards round the St Helens cover to slip in for a fine try."

1986-87

Sharlston continued in the West Yorkshire League Premier Division, competing with Shaws, Cutsyke, Normanton, Jubilee 'A', Bradford Woolpack, Mirfield, Duke of York and Swillington. Billy Wood continued as coach.

Sharlston made a good start with successive victories against Shaws, Bradford Woolpack and Swillington and by March they were top of the table. Then they lost their last five matches, rapidly moved downwards and out of the top four. Contrast this with the Normanton club who, at one time when Sharlston were flying high at the top of the table, were propping it up but went on to win the play-off trophy. Normanton's victory at Back o' t' wall in April was the start of Sharlston's depression.

Sharlston 4 Normanton 10

Normanton had the first chance only for Finch's kick to hit the post. Two penalties from Sharlston saw the home side go into the break 4-0 ahead. However Normanton found their rhythm after the interval and some hard forward running especially from Tonks and Mears wore down the home defence.

Slater put the sides level with a Normanton try and once into their stride, Normanton began to dominate the game. A Finch penalty followed and despite fierce resistance from Sharlston's Swithenbank, Bullock and Mullaney, Finch put Tonks in for another try to make it 10-4 to the visitors. Although the game was not a classic, both teams tried to play entertaining rugby in difficult conditions and it was a credit to their determination.

In the Open Cup, Eastmoor Select and Normanton 'A' were dispatched before Hemsworth overcame Sharlston 28-8 in the semi-final. The Yorkshire League side weathered the early onslaught from Sharlston and stepped up a gear in the second half to win in convincing fashion.

In the West Yorkshire League Cup, Sharlston beat Peacock, Ferrybridge Magnet and Brotherton before narrowly losing 10-8 to Streethouse in the fourth round.

Once again Sharlston could not beat Duke of York in the Wakefield Sunday Cup. But at least this time Sharlston had the compensation of a final appearance, after beating Westgate Common, Normanton 'A' and then Streethouse 28-16 in the semi-final.

Duke of York won the trophy for the fourth successive year. Their experience showed, but Sharlston stand-off John Burnage, who along with centre Richard Davies, was the pick of their side will be ruing missed opportunities as Duke gave away penalty after penalty in the first half

Burnage watched three early penalty attempts pull wide and even had the misfortune of a drop goal attempt coming off a post while at the other end Gascoigne gave Duke a one-nil lead in the 13th minute.

Duke scored a try after 20 minutes. Mick Robinson added an impressive touchline goal. Burnage countered for Sharlston with two penalties, but Duke came back and hooker Mark Roberts crossed in the corner from a Harkin pass.

Burnage again cut the lead with a penalty before half-time but just five minutes into the second period Harkin freed Gascoigne to cross and put Duke nine points in front.

For 20 minutes after that try Sharlston camped in the Duke '25' but could not produce the guile to beat a resolute Duke rearguard.

The pressure seemed to tell on Sharlston more than Duke and with Benioni and Stokes running the ball out well, Duke controlled the last 10 minutes and a late Stokes drop goal concluded the scoring.

Better facilities

In December, the issue of the facilities for Sharlston's players was raised at the local Parish Council meeting. The *Wakefield Express* reported that after years of stripping in the damp cellars of a local pub before matches, Sharlston's players and supporters had asked the Parish Council to support them in a project to build concrete changing rooms.

The club have done their homework and estimate they could build a block measuring 32 feet by 10 feet at their Weeland Road ground for a little over £1,000. Connecting in electricity and water supplies and other fittings would push the price up, but the members were prepared to put in some hard work and fund raising and submitted a rough plan to a council meeting in December.

Club secretary Mrs June Redshaw feels they deserve some success off the pitch after four years of changing in the cellars of the Sharlston Hotel.

At the meeting Councillor Trevor Berry said the idea was a good one in principle and added that the council had £3,000 in their deposit account if a contribution to the cost of building was felt to be appropriate.

Councillor Norman Hartshorne also backed the scheme, commenting: "It is our land, they need the facilities and we may well have to help out with some cash if it can't be found elsewhere." However, Councillor Bill Hooley said he hoped Wakefield District Council would help out with any outside funding, outlining that "It is not the parish council's job alone to pay".

The council agreed to Councillor Hooley's suggestion that the chairman of the Wakefield Council Leisure Service Committee, Councillor Chris Heinitz, be invited to a special meeting between parish and rugby club officials in Sharlston on Monday

Memories from 1986-87

Sharlston 1986-87: Back: Alan Maskill, Jeff Exley, Ritchie Davies, John Hoyle, Johnny Mullaney, John Padgett, Don Goodfellow, Paul Wood; Front: Nigel Leaworthy, Tim Kaye, Pete Harrison, Roger Maskill, Nigel Southern, Chris Shepherd, Tony Dews.

Lads versus Lassies – A fund raising event.

8 December. It was felt that he might be able to provide useful advice and information on how best to approach the project.

The new facilities would provide much needed showers, officials' room and small shop as well as room to change according to Mrs Redshaw. "At the moment, most visiting teams get changed on their bus and such basic items as cups of tea have to be provided by thermos flasks" she said. Everyone agreed that this project could give a great boost to the club off the field while their teams were winning on it.

Presentation Night

The club held a presentation night at the end of the season. The winners of the various trophies and awards were:

The Granville Allen Memorial Trophy: Chris Shepherd
Player of the Year: John Swithenbank
Young Player of the Year: Nigel Southern
Most improved player: Chris Shepherd
Leading Try Scorer: Nigel Leaworthy

Most Man of the Match Awards: John Swithenbank & Shaun Bullock (shared)
Clubman of the Year: Harold Ward
Most Appearances: Paul Wood
Leading Points Scorer: John Burnage
Billy Wood Trophy: Pete Harrison

The Granville Allen Memorial Trophy was in memory of one of the club's longest standing and most loyal supporters. Mr Allen died in September 1986, aged 76. He lived in Weeland Drive, Sharlston, and ran a hairdressers' shop opposite the rugby club's pitch for many years. He had followed the club's fortunes for decades and was himself presented with a trophy last season to mark his years of loyal support. "He thought that was great and I hope this new trophy will be enjoyed as much" said Mrs Pat Sidebottom, Mr Allen's daughter.

Trevor Bailey presents Nigel Southern with the Young Player of the Year Trophy

1987-88

The start of the season was overshadowed by the death of young Steven Mullaney. He tragically died after a road accident outside his school in September 1987.

Steven was regarded as one of Yorkshire's most promising rugby league players and his skills were seen by millions last year when he captained the Wakefield under-11s team in a televised curtain raiser to the Rugby League Challenge Cup Final scoring a brilliant try and capturing the hearts of the Wembley crowd and television audience.

Steven's rugby league talents were first spotted at Sharlston Junior School and the Travellers Saints club based in Featherstone. He captained both teams and received three player-of-the-year awards from the two sides. In 1986-87 he also played for Yorkshire at Headingley in a curtain raiser to the senior Roses rugby league match.

Mr R. Cribbes, the headmaster of Crofton High School, where Steven was a pupil, captaining the first year rugby league team, said the school was very shocked at the news of Steven's death. In a tribute to the young sportsman he said "In his captaincy of the first year team Steven was a brilliant tactician, could turn a game himself with one play and showed a maturity which was exceptional for his age".

Steven's parents, Mr and Mrs Terry Mullaney, donated his heart in the hope of saving another child's life and also gave permission for other organs to be taken for transplants. Steven's father, a director of the Featherstone Rovers Rugby League club, told the *Wakefield Express*: "We had no hesitation about donating Steven's organs. He had done so much in his short life, he was a lovely boy and his death is such a tragic waste. But if it can save the life of another child it won't be a total waste."

The trophy that the under-11 teams play for before the Challenge Cup Final was named in memory of Steven.

The club were again playing in the West Yorkshire Premier League. Things moved fast for the club during the close season, with Kenny Endersby replacing the long serving Billy Wood as player coach and plans were afoot for the building of a set of changing rooms at Back o' t' wall.

Former coach of Agbrigg side, Duke of York, Kenny was also a Wakefield Trinity regular in the mid 1970s and could play in the pack as either prop or loose-forward. Despite giving 21 years service to the club, Billy Wood was determined to remain active at Sharlston and he was planning to work closely with the new coach during the season as club president.

Sharlston had two victories in pre-season friendlies. They swamped Walton MW 42-10, but then had a testing time against the Manor club from Wakefield, eventually coming out on top 10-8.

Streethouse were the leading side in the League all season and their encounters with Sharlston were closely fought and not without incident. The two sides met five times in league and cup and Streethouse just edged it with three victories. The league match at Sharlston was not completed after Pontefract referee Paul Crashley was taken to hospital after an alleged incident involving a Streethouse player, who was sent off. The League investigated the alleged attack and suspended Streethouse's Neil Goodwin until September 2000. He was entitled to appeal to BARLA.

In late May the teams met in the semi-final play-off, Streethouse having finished in top spot and Sharlston fourth, and though Sharlston won 18-12, it was decided that the final would not be played.

In the West Yorkshire League Cup, Sharlston had three easy wins against Hoyland,

94-4, at Mirfield 36-6 and at home to Houghton Greyhound 32-16. The fourth round brought old opponents Normanton to Back o' t' wall.

The big Sharlston pack pounded Normanton down the hill for the first 40 minutes, but in spite of their constant pressure, the first half was scoreless. Normanton made a dream start to the second half, with Nicky Smart scoring. With only five minutes left Sharlston second-row Steve Tottie forced his way over for a try. The game was played in a traditionally competitive spirit and things boiled over on occasions. Both teams had a man sent off.

In the replay, Sharlston knocked out the cup holders 29-18 to reach the semi-final. John Burnage put the visitors ahead with an early penalty but Normanton hit back as Graham dropped on a loose ball over the line and Slater converted to make it 6-2.

Burnage kicked a second penalty but Graham replied for Normanton to make it 8-4. But then Steve Tottie crossed for an unconverted try. Burnage then found room to put Sharlston ahead with a try he converted and at the break Sharlston led 14-8. They extended this lead within two minutes of the restart when Paul Douglas was allowed to score on the last tackle, despite being apparently surrounded by Normanton defenders.

Normanton rallied with a try by Ward in the corner. Bad tackling allowed Sharlston to hit back through a Nigel Southern, try, 22-12, but Normanton again reduced the deficit. From the kick-off Westwood scored, with his try converted by Graham.

With just four points in it Normanton had a slender chance to hang on to the trophy but excellent kicking by Burnage repeatedly relieved the pressure for Sharlston.

He was on target with the conversion as John Swithenbank crossed for Sharlston's last try, then added a 40 yard drop-goal to make the final score 29-18. Sharlston deserved to win and the biggest crowd of the season at St John's Terrace were treated to a worthy cup-tie. Sharlston reached the final by beating an ill-disciplined Jubilee side in the semi-final. In a typical cup-tie Jubilee were repeatedly offside and gave away two kickable penalties and three for foul play. John Burnage kicked the home side into a 2-0 lead after the first offside decision. He then made it 4-0 with a repeat of the same offence. The Featherstone-based outfit came back to take the lead with a converted try, but before the break Burnage landed another penalty, this time for an off-the-ball incident, to level the match.

Sharlston found new life in the second half and Pete Harrison looked certain to score with an 80 yard break. He handed off two men only to be tackled just short but as the ball was moved away another penalty for foul play allowed Burnage his fourth goal of the game. Sharlston held on for 12 tackles on their own line as Jubilee pressed to regain the lead, but then as the home side broke away indiscipline proved to let the visitors down once more. They again gave away a penalty in a kickable position. Burnage was expected to kick but he caught the defence napping with a quick tap penalty and winger Ian Frost scored in the corner. Jubilee pressed for the last 10 minutes but Sharlston were home. Their opponents at Post Office Road in the Final would be neighbours Streethouse who overcame Shaws of Batley 13-6 in their semi-final.

Sharlston 22 Streethouse 37
West Yorkshire Cup

Streethouse were always too good for Sharlston and only two late tries gave the scoreline an air of respectability. The two sides had different styles of play with Sharlston relying on strength in the pack and Streethouse using their speedy backs.

Sharlston had second-row John Swithenbank sent off after some dangerous footwork early on. By then Streethouse were already 11-2 up and on top. Sharlston were 9-0 adrift before they touched the ball. John Burnage kicked a penalty for Sharlston, who could only come up with a second Burnage penalty and Streethouse had a deserved 22-4 half-time lead.

They struck immediately in the second half through prop Neil Pritchard but Sharlston reduced the deficit when they touched down first in a scramble over the Streethouse line. Burnage added the goal before Streethouse scored another try. Wood added his second try after going alone from the play-the-ball with a Chance Leake conversion making it 36-10.

Wood hit a third drop-goal but then Streethouse lost concentration to allow Sharlston 12 late points, John Mullaney crossed for a try and then second row Steve Tottie crashed over. Burnage added both conversions to complete scoring.

For Sharlston, Stuart Bailey put in a quality display at full-back before being stretchered off after a crunching tackle. Burnage kicked superbly throughout but his side lacked pace in attack.

There was some compensation for Sharlston in the Sunday Cup. Burnage kicked them to a narrow quarter-final win over Streethouse and they then overcame Wrenthorpe in the semi-final to go on to meet Normanton in the final at Belle Vue the week after the West Yorkshire Cup defeat.

Sharlston 16 Normanton 8
Wakefield Sunday Cup Final

Sharlston were determined not to let a second trophy slip inside a week. Stuart Bailey was solid at full-back and John Burnage played well at stand-off. In the pack Steve Tottie never stopped working and John Swithenbank showed an excellent combination of strength, skill and pace.

Only a piece of individual brilliance by Burnage separated the sides at the break- He took the ball from a scrum and raced 50 yards to touch down. Immediately on the restart Steve Tottie pinched the ball in a tackle and scored before the Normanton defence could react. Burnage added the conversion.

Normanton narrowed the score to 10-2 with a Mark Graham penalty but then Stuart Bailey was the last man in a move across the field for Sharlston's third try. Burnage hit a superb touchline conversion. A Nicky Smart try in the last five minutes, converted by Graham, restored some Normanton pride. The teams were:
Normanton: Mark Westwood, Jed Ward, Andrew Parks, Shaun Hudson, Glen Howitt, Mark Graham, Nicky Smart, Neil Mears, Martin Slater. Alan Worrall, Mick Tilford, Ian Watts, Wayne Westwood, Graham Walker, Tony Chapman.
Sharlston: Stuart Bailey, Peter Harrison, Richard Davies, John Mullaney, Ian Frost, John Burnage. Shaun Bullock, Tim Robinson, Nigel Southern, Steve Tottie, Nigel Leaworthy, John Swithenbank. Ken Endersby, Richard Craven, Roger Maskill.

In the Open Cup, Sharlston lost at home to Manor 15-14.

The end of season presentation night had a new award, the George Green trophy donated by Mrs Doreen Green in memory of George, a former Sharlston and Halifax player and local councillor. He scored nine points against Workington Town in the famous cup win in 1946. Stuart Bailey was the first winner. The other trophies and awards went to:

Chairman's award: Stuart Bailey
Granville Allen Award: Steve Tottie
Man of the match award: Paul Douglas, John Burnage & Steve Tottie
Most appearances: Roger Maskill
Billy Wood Trophy: Roger Maskill
Leading try scorer: Steve Tottie, John Burnage
Clubman of the year: Pete Redshaw
Most improved player: Stuart Bailey
Players, player of the year: Paul Douglas
Player of the year: John Burnage

1988-89

Once again, Sharlston competed in the West Yorkshire Sunday Premier League. Billy Wood showed his dedication by returning as coach to the Premier side in his 24th season at the club. Bernard Bastow was in charge of the newly formed Sharlston 'A' team, who were in Division 5.

The first team squad was:

Mark Reeves: Utility player in his first season, very fast player with an excellent side-step.
Steve Taylor: Winger aged 18, six feet four inches tall and weighing 11 and a half stone, one of the biggest wingers on the local scene, a good try scorer and fine prospect for the future.
Paul Wood: Centre or second-row, 100 per cent grafter and clubman, robust player with a fine turn of speed.
John Mullaney: Centre, played for Sharlston for the last five years, fine defensive player.
Roger Maskill: Utility player in his 12th season at the club, former captain, also represented the Wakefield & District in 1986. A good ball handler and sound in defence.
John Burnage: Stand-off, firm favourite with Sharlston supporters; in his 11th season. Very classy player and astute goal-kicker.
Shaun Bullock: Scrum-half, a very nippy player round the base of the scrum; in his sixth season at the club.
Terry Mullaney: Prop in his second season, another excellent prospect for the future.
Nigel Southern: Hooker, a stocky player and another favourite with the Sharlston crowd.
Kevin Wood: Hooker, aggressive player who always gives 100%; aged 19 has a fine future in the game.
Paul Douglas: Prop, robust forward who is always looking for work; travels from Leeds to play for the side.
Stuart Bailey: Full-back or second-row, former Doncaster and Huddersfield professional, strong runner and tackler.
Nigel Morris: Second row, first season with the club; travelled from Leeds to play, strong runner who backs up well.
Nigel Leaworthy: Loose-forward, eight years with the club, strong runner, leading try scorer for the last two seasons.
Pete Richardson: Utility player, first season at Sharlston; strong tackler with exceptional pace.
Alan Maskill: Full-back or prop, a very robust player who gives 100 per cent work rate, loved to join the attack when playing full-back.
Darren Lingard: Utility player, joined Sharlston this season from Streethouse; won a West Yorkshire cup medal with Streethouse last season against Sharlston; a very fast and strong player.
Micky Robinson: Hooker, first season; a very good cover tackler; 18 years old.

There was optimism carried over from the previous season, but apart from winning the Sunday Cup, this season will be remembered as one of the worst in the club's history. The campaign opened with a draw, one of four during the season, and it was December before they notched up their first victory and the end of the season before the next one came. Streethouse, now coached by Trevor Bailey, were the leading side with Sharlston propping up the table all season and finishing last.

Some relief was found in the Sunday Cup. In the first round, holders Sharlston won 16-6 at Duke of York. Duke went 6-0 up. Sharlston hit back with centre Cawthraw scoring under the posts and Ward added a penalty to the conversion to give them an 8-6 half-time lead. Burnage kicked on to score, Ward converted then added another penalty to give the holders a 16-6 cushion. In the second round, Normanton 'A' were beaten 12-0. and in the semi-final Sharlston beat Kettlethorpe Poachers 30-0.

Sharlston's opponents in the Final were Walton Miners Welfare from Division Two, who had only been formed two seasons ago. Their coach was Steve Hankins, a former Featherstone Rovers player and the Walton side also included former Sharlston players Ian Frost and John Swithenbank.

Sharlston 18 Walton MW 10
Wakefield Sunday Cup Final

Sharlston retained the Brian Wray Sunday Cup on Easter Monday. A 30 yard Burnage drop-goal gave Sharlston the lead but Walton hit back with a try from centre Peter Storey. Burnage chipped ahead to regather the ball for Sharlston's first try and just before the break he added a conversion as Reeves intercepted to score from 30 yards. That gave the holders an 11-4 lead and Burnage stretched this with a penalty on the restart. Bailey came into the line to add another Sharlston try and put them 17-4 up, but Walton's Ian Oldroyd beat five men to score. John Sharp converted to narrow the score to 17-10 but a Ward drop-goal gave Sharlston their eight point winning margin. The game marked the 50th anniversary of the Sunday Cup and the 10th year of sponsorship by Brian Wray.

The Open Cup produced an easy 30-2 win against Sharlston 'A', but then Sharlston were comfortably beaten by Hemsworth MW in the next round. Any hopes of a shock Sharlston win finished when they lost their captain who was dismissed for kicking.

Normanton 'A" 20 Sharlston 16
West Yorkshire League Cup Semi-Final

Third Division Normanton drew a 600 strong crowd at St John's rugby pitch when they faced premier division Sharlston in the semi-final of the West Yorkshire Cup.

Things didn't look too good for Normanton in the first 25 minutes when handling errors put Sharlston into a 12-0 lead. Sharlston's John Burnage was on target with three penalty attempts and full-back Roger Maskill stormed in for an excellent try, converted by Burnage, Normanton kept up the fight though and after settling down looked the better side. Four good long range penalties from David Walker put them back into the game, with the half-time score 12-8.

In the first 10 minutes after the interval, Normanton let themselves down by allowing Sharlston's Burnage in again to take two simple penalties, giving them a 16-8 cushion.

Normanton started to show signs of good team work and excellent handling to Geoff

Day led to a 12 yard wingman's try. A Dave Walker penalty made it 14-16 and the home side were back in the game. Eight minutes from time when they were looking fitter than the Sharlston squad, hooker Larry Carter touched down for a vital try, converted by Walker, to give the Normanton team victory.

Nines end in chaos

The Walton MW nine-a-side rugby league competition ended on a sour note. The final between Sharlston and Streethouse was abandoned after only four minutes with players from both sides brawling on the pitch.

Trouble started when two players - one from each side - were sent-off, allegedly for fighting, shortly after Sharlston had taken a 4-0 lead thanks to a 60 yard try by Burnage. As they were leaving the field the two allegedly began fighting again and a number of other players joined in. The referee had no alternative but to call a halt to the match. The Walton club secretary, Alan Reynolds, said: "This was a setback for such a fine competition with a bumper crowd of more that 700 being disappointed. It was a disgrace by two great teams who earlier had showed they could play rugby, but decided to settle some old scores instead."

Streethouse and Sharlston were both disqualified from the competition. The trophy and prize money were awarded to Hemsworth MW, who had beaten Westgate Common in a thrilling game for third and fourth position. Earlier in the day Streethouse and Sharlston had overcome Hemsworth 26-14 and Westgate 16-14 respectively.

The 'A' team

The 'A' team's opponents in Division 5 were: Knottingley 'A', Kettlethorpe, Prince of Wales, Askern 'A', Thorne Colliery 'A', Ferrybridge Greyhound, Fox Inn, Armthorpe Ploughman, Sheffield & Kimberworth, Bentley GC 'A', Rotherham 'A', and Woodman Inn. The kit for the season was sponsored by Wayne Chalkley of Featherstone based Kirby Vacuums. They had a good season, just being edged out of the top four into fifth place, winning 14 and drawing two of their 24 league fixtures and playing crowd pleasing rugby. They passed 50 points twice, against Rotherham 'A' 58-10 and Sheffield & Kimberworth 52-6. Players who received man-of-the-match awards included Paul Hampson, Brent Chalkley, Richard Bulmer and their captain Roy Sykes.

In the West Yorkshire Cup preliminary round they faced Division One side Duke of York going down 32-20, after trailing 24-6 at the interval.

The 1988-89 Sharlston Junior team that won the Les Pounder Trophy. Back: Michael Easterby, Steve Geenhalgh, Wayne Luckman, Stewart Ward; Middle: Ajaz Saghir, Garry Endersby, Andrew Baines, Front: Rob Howell, Craig Lingard, Steve Dooler, Neil Ripley. Steve Dooler and Craig Lingard were both selected for the Yorkshire under-11 side. They received special trophies from Mr Maurice Knapper, the chairman of the Sharlston School governors to mark their selection for the county side.

1989-90

There were worrying signs at the beginning of the season with Sharlston advertising in the *Wakefield Express* for players for most positions. This was not a good sign for a team in the Premier Division, but they had lost key players and were without a coach until Bob Spurr, who had played for Castleford and Featherstone, was appointed. It soon became clear following heavy defeats against Streethouse and Fryston Crown that they were out of their depth in the Premier Division and were allowed to drop to Division One. Their opponents there were Dodworth, Duke of York, Bentley, Travellers 'A', Normanton 'A', Earlsheaton Rangers, Manor, Chequerfield Rangers, Crofton and Wrenthorpe.

They didn't find things any easier at first and it was November before they registered their first victory against previously unbeaten Crofton, 17-4. Sharlston opened the scoring with a Pete Richardson try and a penalty from David Ward 10 minutes later. With only minutes of the first half left Ward coolly dropped a goal to give the home side a 7-0 lead. Sharlston were 11 points clear after 15 minutes of the restart through a Darren Pearson try, then the visitors scored their try. The home side hit back with an individual try by Ward who beat three men and raced 25 yards to score. He also added the goal.

This form was not maintained, but they kicked off the New Year with a 36-26 victory over Dodworth and a flurry of victories at the end of the season, doing the double over Crofton, who were in the top four, and a 12-0 win at Duke of York, always described as bitter rivals, saw them finish in seventh position.

Chequerfield defeated Sharlston 41-8 in the first round of the Yorkshire Cup, Wrenthorpe knocked them out 23-13 in the same round of the Open Cup and Ackworth finished Sharlston's interest in the Sunday Cup in round two.

In January 1990 Billy Wood was named as the Wakefield & District ARL team manager. He had complete responsibility for the Wakefield and District open-age side in the inter-town competition and in any other friendly games. There had been a feeling for some years that Wakefield's potential to produce a top class open age amateur side has not been realised and Billy's appointment was part of an effort to correct the situation.

It was good for Sharlston to see Neil Fox MBE, the game's world record points scorer, enter the Rugby League Hall of Fame. He joined another Sharlston-born player, Jonty Parkin, among the all-time greats, and received a medal struck by the Queen's jewellers.

Before the season started the Rugby Football League had granted a testimonial season to Sharlston assistant coach Phil Johnson after a distinguished 20-year professional career. The first of his benefit events was a combined team from Sharlston and Prince of Wales (Pontefract) ARFC against the professional players from Huddersfield.

Phil began his professional career when he was 16 years old in 1969 at Castleford where he stayed for 13 years and by the end of this season will be one of only a handful of players who have played rugby league in three different decades. He then moved on to Featherstone where he was a leading squad member in a team that eventually won the 1983 Challenge Cup at Wembley, beating favourites Hull, 14-12, before he moved on to Bramley and then to present club Huddersfield. At 36, he was still going strong with his playing duties at Huddersfield where he was also assistant coach, as well as running the Sharlston Hotel, where he was the landlord.

The Sharlston ARLFC committee welcomed the Parish Council's decision to erect railings on the Weeland Road side of the ground. They felt that this improvement added status to both the club and the village.

10. The 1990s - The Rovers return

1990-91

This season the club got its full name back after an absence of 20 years. In 1970, the open age team, Sharlston Rovers, moved their headquarters to Crofton and a season later ceased to exist. A Sharlston Hotel team was formed, played at Back o' t' wall and after a couple of seasons dropped 'Hotel' and were known as Sharlston. Since 1902 the team had been known as Sharlston Rovers or The Rovers and supporters and players were pleased to see the old name back again.

This was the only good news about the season though. It was disappointing with the team finishing sixth in a 10 team league. Rovers' opponents in the West Yorkshire Premier Division consisted of Walton MW, Wrenthorpe, Moorends, Bentley, Crofton, Walnut Warriors, Travellers 'A', Fryston Crown and Jubilee 'A'. Bob Spurr continued as coach.

Once again, like so many times before, the league programme opened disastrously. Sharlston lost their first five matches and it was October before they registered their first victory at Wrenthorpe, who had taken the points at Sharlston in the first match of the season. In the meantime Walton MW, assisted by former Sharlston players John Swithenbank and Steve Hankins, Fryston Crown and Bentley had inflicted heavy defeats on them. The final league position was much better than appeared likely at one time due to a flourish before Christmas which brought three successive victories and was ended by a home defeat to Crofton.

Ackworth knocked them out in the preliminary round of the Sunday Cup and Westgate Redoubt, with an avalanche of points, 42-10, in the second round of the Open Cup. Their best performance was in the West Yorkshire Cup.

Rovers started with an easy 46-12 victory against Skellow Grange in the preliminary round in which the visitors were never able to cope with the strong running of man-of-the-match Lingard and accurate kicking by Ward, who kicked seven conversions. The first round was a home tie against Hanging Heaton and Rovers scraped through 30-28. Swillington were out-gunned and outclassed in the second round. Sharlston led 26-0 at half-time and won 48-6, man-of-the match Richard Hall grabbing a fine hat trick of tries. Fryston Crown's intimidatory tactics failed to stop Sharlston surging into the final, notching 12 points in each half as Bailey, Mullaney and Hird hit top form and skipper Ward kicked six goals.

The other finalists were Bentley, the bottom team in the league. As Sharlston had comfortably defeated them a few weeks before the final, victory at Post Office Road was confidently expected.

Sharlston 12 Bentley 21
West Yorkshire Sunday Cup Final

Ace goalkicking from former professional David Noble thwarted Sharlston's bid to land the West Yorkshire Sunday Cup. The former Doncaster player landed three drop-goals and three conversions that were ultimately decisive.

Sharlston showed only glimpses of the form that had taken them to the final. Their play was littered with handling errors and they trailed 14-6 at half-time with prop forward Aidey Hird's touch down one of their few successes.

Terry Mullaney's try and Ward's penalty reduced the deficit to two points in the second half, but Sharlston neglected penalty chances and were punished when Bentley clinched the cup with a further drop-goal and a converted try. Sharlston's best players were John Mullaney, Ian Lingard, Nigel Southern and Jeff Exley.

Nigel Southern was Sharlston's Player of the Year.

1991-92

A close season switch from the West Yorkshire League to Division Six of the Saturday Yorkshire League seemed to work wonders for Rovers' confidence. Their opponents in the new league were Clowne, Drighlington, Westgate 'A', Eastmoor Select 'A', Outwood Victoria, Garforth, York Acorn 'A', Redhill 'A' and Black Dog. Bob Spurr continued as coach for the new season.

Rovers looked promising in pre-season wins against Jesmond and Emley Moor and they swept aside Clowne, 30-12, with ease in their opening league game. Sharlston and Outwood Victoria were never out of the top two places this season. The teams met three times and only two points separated them on each occasion as they vied for top spot. Unfortunately, Sharlston were the losers at home in March when they needed a draw or a win to finish top and had to settle for runners-up. They got off to a bad start in the match when they lost prop Tim Kaye with a broken collar bone and Pete Richardson with an injured knee.

Sharlston completed their away fixtures with a 100 per cent record when they defeated Westgate Redoubt 'A' in fine style with their most impressive win of the season, 72-3. They were 22-0 ahead after less than 20 minutes play and in the second half really went to town. Centre Pete Richardson grabbed three tries and was man-of-the-match. Skipper Dave Ward landed 10 conversions.

The top four semi-final play-off against Redhill 'A' was an evenly fought contest. Sharlston went down to an unfamiliar Redhill 'A' side which contained a number of different players from when the teams met in the league. They fought back from being 12-2 behind to go 13-12 in front through six penalties and a drop-goal from skipper Dave Ward's immaculate kicking.

However, they conceded a late try when a high kick was fumbled and a Redhill player dropped on the ball over the Sharlston line. The conversion and a penalty in front of the posts completed the scoring and Sharlston's season. Man-of-the-match was hard working loose-forward Peter Bean, closely followed by scrum-half Ian Lingard and skipper Dave Ward playing out of position at hooker in the absence of Nigel Southern.

In the White Rose Trophy a 19-12 away defeat at the hands of East Leeds 'A' put Sharlston out at the first hurdle. They fared no better in the Open Cup, going down to Duke of York 22-18.

After a bye in the first round of the Yorkshire Cup they got their revenge on Duke of York in the second round, despite having a man sent off. Playing with 12 men seemed to strengthen their resolve in the second half and there were impressive displays from man-of-the-match Tony Palmer, Bean and Ian Lingard. Rovers were comprehensively beaten 32-0 at Stelrad in round three. They had to go to Normanton in the City Plasterers Cup and were crushed in a one-sided game, 50-6. After 15 minutes a Sharlston player was sent-off for tripping and kicking a Normanton player.

Presentation night

Wakefield Trinity player Andy Wilson was the star attraction at the club's presentation night. He presented the following awards:

Billy Wood trophy: Alan Benyon	Young Player: Peter Bean
Most tries scored: Peter Richardson	Coach's Prize: Alan Benyon
Man of the Matches: Peter Bean	Player of the Year: David Ward.
Most Improved Player: Tony Palmer	Chairman's Prize: Peter Southern
Players' Player: David Ward	Club person's Prize: June Redshaw.

A trophy donated by Mrs Jill Shepherd in memory of her late husband Chris, who played for the club, was awarded to Alan Benyon. A plaque was also presented to coach Bob Spurr who retired as the Rovers coach after three seasons. His wife was presented with a bouquet. Other bouquets went to the ladies who lend a hand to the club and special thanks were given to Ken Endicott for his donation at the start of the season.

Chris Shepherd

The club were shocked in January when Chris Shepherd was tragically killed by a hydraulic digger while working in a roadside trench. An all-round rugby player, he was a valuable member of Sharlston Rovers who would turn out whatever the weather and play his hardest for the team he loved. Always helping others, he once had his head shaved for a local charity - earning himself the nickname 'Walt' which stuck with him for many years. Mrs Shepherd said: "He was devoted to me and the children and loved his rugby - he really lived life to the full. There were hundreds of people at his funeral and flowers from rugby clubs he'd never even played with."

1992-93

Sharlston Rovers now faced a new challenge in the West Yorkshire Saturday League Division 5. Their opponents were Outwood Victoria, who had also been promoted, Wetherby, Lock Lane 'A', Thornhill Rangers, Batley Boys, Bramley Social, Dewsbury Shamrocks and Shaw Cross Wasps. Dave Taylor took over as coach.

Rovers and Outwood Victoria continued where they left off last season in Division 6, and were runaway leaders in Division 5. The only league encounters worthy of note were the games between the two sides which produced fine games, Sharlston won at Outwood, 14-10, and Outwood put in a solid attacking performance to win 18-12 at Sharlston.

Sharlston's first league defeat of the season came in December at Bramley Social, a team they had completely outclassed a fortnight earlier, 40-2. Sharlston were again league runners-up to Outwood Victoria but were the victors against them in the play-off final at Walton, having defeated Bramley Social in the semi-final.

Sharlston Rovers 15 Outwood Victoria 8
Division Five Championship Final

In the first half, Sharlston soaked up early Outwood pressure with solid defending. When Rovers scored, Taylor broke a tackle to pass to Nigel Southern who touched down. David Ward added the goal to see them 6-0 up at half-time. After the break Rovers continued to attack. Outwood scored their second try against the run of play for an 8-6 lead.

Skipper David Ward led by example and inspired his team with a fine kicking game. He pinned Outwood back with some kicks deep into their half. A well taken drop-goal by stand-off Peter Bean was the final nail in Outwood's coffin. Outstanding for Rovers was skipper and man-of-the-match David Ward, a try and three goals, with Ian Lingard, Pete Richardson and Paul Wood all running him close.

Following a comfortable 22-1 victory at Crofton in the first round of the Open Cup when a fine team performance impressed the home supporters, Sharlston had to visit Normanton and were not discredited in losing 28-14. They were 12-8 down at half-time and it was not until mid-way through the second half that the home side secured victory.

In the Plasterers Saturday Cup, Sharlston reached the semi-final. They lost 34-12 to Westgate, but could be proud of their effort. Fielding a much weakened side, Sharlston were soon playing catch-up rugby, as they went behind 16-0 in as many minutes against the current premier division leaders.

Westgate must have thought they were going to have a field day, but Sharlston captain and stand-in hooker David Ward, had other ideas. After sustained pressure he scored a try under the posts and added the conversion to reduce the arrears to 16-6. Some fierce attacking rugby from Sharlston had their opponents on the rack although they could not add to their score before half-time. In the second-half Westgate came out much more determined and almost immediately increased their score.

Only some strong defending by Sharlston prevented a much bigger score. David Ward increased Sharlston's score as he cleverly kicked through and pounced on the ball to score his second try. He added the conversion. Sharlston's man-of-the-match, John Mullaney had an outstanding game and was well supported by player-coach Dave Taylor and strong prop Adrian Hird. Fine performances came from stand-off Peter Bean who showed clever footwork to make yards for Sharlston and scrum-half Ian Lingard produced a mammoth effort in defence.

Eleven man Sharlston Rovers came back from the dead to earn a dramatic win in the BARLA National Cup first round when they beat Cockermouth 32-18. The odds were heavily stacked against Rovers when they took a weakened side to face the Cumbrian Cup finalists, had two men sent off in the first 25 minutes and turned round to face the slope in the second half already trailing 18-4.

Amazingly they not only snatched victory in the final 40 minutes - they scored 28 points to nil in the second half. "They were up to their ankles in sludge, but it was a fantastic performance. Coach David Taylor must have given them some half-time pep talk," commented a club official. Loose-forward Johnny Mullaney inspired the comeback and try scorers were centres Paul Wood and Peter Richardson, scrum-half David Ward, prop Adrian Hird and second-rows Peter Bean and Nigel Southern. Ward adding four goals. The man-of-the-match award went to Johnny Mullaney. But the second round brought an anti-climax. Rovers travelled to Walney Central and narrowly lost 10-6.

Two easy victories against Maltby, 56-2, and fourth division Cross Gates, 22-8, in the White Rose Trophy, earned Rovers a home tie against division three Manor.

Sharlston edged in front early on with a penalty. Manor, however, quickly settled down and levelled before a well-drilled move created a try for Carl Fallas, converted by Craig Riley. The home side failed to turn first half pressure into points while Manor had a try disallowed before going further ahead with a Riley drop-goal followed by a couple of penalties. A Sharlston try either side of a fourth Riley penalty conversion put the home side back in the reckoning, but a drop-goal, try and conversion for Riley put the result just beyond the home side's reach.

Nigel Southern was Sharlston's Player of the Year.

1993-4

Rovers were promoted higher than expected, from division five to three, but then the players were asked if they would consider going into the First Division. It was a big jump from fifth to first, but a challenge they readily accepted. Their opponents were Kippax, Walnut Warriors, Middleton, York West Bank, Stanley Rangers OB, Mirfield, Prince of Wales and Dewsbury Norths. Dave Taylor continued as coach.

Pre-season friendlies saw Sharlston beat Upton, Eastmoor and Ryhill with victory over Upton being perhaps the most significant. With Upton from the Premier Division fielding a strong side, Sharlston overcame a first half deficit to dominate the second half and run out convincing winners.

The season began properly with a home clash on the 4 September with the West Yorkshire Fire Service (Division Three) and the Rovers ran out convincing winners, 52-8, with Ian Lingard, Peter Richardson and Nigel Kirton all impressing. The next game was a tough trip to Hull to the Premier side Bransholme in the first Round of the Yorkshire Cup

In a tight match Sharlston not only matched their opponents' aggression, but also played skilfully to run out winners 16-10. Ian Lingard was outstanding with Adrian Hird and Peter Bean close behind.

In the league, Mirfield came to Back o' t' wall for the first match in the First Division. Rovers' players and supporters were wondering how the team would fare. No worries - Sharlston completely dominated throughout and ran out easy winners 48-6. Skipper David Ward led by example; Darren Lingard and Nigel Southern had good games and Alan Reidford weighed in with a hat-trick of tries.

The second round of the Yorkshire Cup saw Thornhill Rangers from the fifth division visit Sharlston. This proved to be a measure of how much Rovers had improved as a team because the same side held Rovers to a 14-14 draw at Thornhill, which probably cost Sharlston the Fifth Division championship the previous season. However, the 64-8 scoreline told its own story and showed that the team's training had paid off.

A visit to Middleton brought Sharlston back down to earth as Rovers lost 21-12, although not disgraced this set the standard of how Rovers had to play not only with skill, but as Middleton showed, plenty of aggression.

Illingworth from the First Division in the Pennine League were Rovers' next opponents in the Yorkshire Cup Third Round. The journey to Halifax proved to be a major disappointment as Rovers were beaten 22-18, but felt that the home side were more than fortunate to go into the next round of the competition. The City Plasterers Cup saw Sharlston defeat first Stanley Rangers Old Boys then only to lose a thriller at Westgate Redoubt 11-10 with a drop-goal in the final minutes sealing Sharlston's fate.

Sharlston also went out of the Senior Cup losing 22-10 at Upton, who avenged their pre-season friendly defeat. Rovers bounced back in tremendous style beating the 'mighty' Walnut Warriors in convincing fashion 19-8. With prop Adrian Hird in tremendous form and Stuart Bailey and Dave Taylor also taking on the Walnut pack this was a victory to savour. Kippax were unfortunate enough to be Rovers' next opponents. With confidence sky high they were well beaten 30-16. Nigel Kirton and Nigel Southern were Kippax's chief tormentors. Sharlston then had a couple of easy away wins beating Prince of Wales 42-0 and then travelled to York to tame a fiery West Bank side 30-8.

In January the BARLA Cup started and after a first round walk over against Batley Old Boys, Wigan St Cuthberts were Rovers second round opponents. Sharlston were trailing 16-12 at half-time, but came out firing on all cylinders in the second half to seal a tremendous 31-16 victory. Adrian Hird was an outstanding man-of-the-match.

Teams from the early 1990s

Sharlston Rovers 1990-91: Back: Bob Spurr (coach); Roger Maskill, Stuart Bailey, Richard Hall, Alan Benyon, Paul Hampson, Ian Frost, Tommy Mullaney, Adrian Hird, Brian Lockey; Front: Andy Knapper, Jeff Exley, Ian Lingard, Dave Ward, Pete Richardson, Nigel Southern, Paul Wood.

Sharlston Rovers 1992: Back: Dave Crummack, Ian Moverley, Tim Kaye, Dickie Ashcroft, Adrian Hird, Nigel Southern, Tony Palmer, Neil Cooke, Tommy Mullaney, Alan Reidford, Jeff Exley, Dave Taylor (coach); Front: Alan Ainsworth, Alan Benyon, Ian Lingard, Pete Bean, Pete Richardson, Paul Wood, Joe Stanley.

Sharlston Rovers 1992-93: Back: June Redshaw, Pete Redshaw, Andy Wincup, Dave Crummack, Ian Moverley, Tony Palmer, Stuart Bailey, Nigel Southern, Tommy Mullaney, Dave Taylor (coach), Adrian Hird, Tim Kaye, Dave Ainsworth, Hughie Barr, Mick Ward, Pete Southern, Billy Wood; Front: Dave Evans, Paul Wood, Alan Reidford, Ian Lingard, Dave Ward, Pete Richardson, Alan Benyon, Pete Bean, Gary Endersby.

Teams and action from the mid 1990s

Sharlston Rovers 1993-94: Back: Pete Bean, Darren Lingard, Nigel Kirton, Adrian Hird, Dave Taylor (coach), Tommy Mullaney, Stuart Bailey, Tim Kaye, Mick Ward, Kevin Wood; Front: Kev Dawson, Jason Clough, Pete Richardson, Ian Lingard, Pete Downham (sponsor), Dave Ward, Alan Benyon, Tony Palmer, Alan Reidford.

Action from a 1994 Sharlston match.
(Photo: *Wakefield Express*)

Matches were now harder, as Sharlston were in higher company. The visit of Dewsbury Norths was a tense affair with Rovers sneaking home 28-26.

The BARLA Cup third round saw Sharlston drawn at Conference Division One side Leigh Miners. This was one of the biggest tests that Sharlston had faced in recent years. The final score of 19-6 was not really a true reflection of the game, as with only 12 minutes remaining Rovers were trailing 8-6 and had been putting the Leigh defence under tremendous pressure. A pass went astray and that bounced fortuitously for the Leigh winger to race the length of the field to score, and they scored again in the game's dying seconds. Sharlston did their reputation a power of good with a tremendous performance. Stuart Bailey and Kevin Dawson were outstanding, but it was again prop forward Adrian Hird who was arguably the best player on the field. Former professional Great Britain and Leigh player John Woods said after the game "I wish we had him at this club".

The following week Rovers were back in local cup competition, seeing off a determined challenge from Ryhill, 32-14, with the referee abandoning the match in the closing minutes after he was assaulted by a Ryhill supporter.

It was back to league action the following week with a short trip across town to local rivals Stanley Rangers Old Boys. Rovers again ran out 26-10 winners with Kevin Dawson taking the man-of-the match award, but the game was soured by an ugly incident when Peter Bean was hit from behind resulting in his jaw being broken in two places. He missed the rest of the season which was a massive blow to the team's chances of winning the championship. Next came another short trip to Walnut and although confidence was high with two victories over them already this season this was potentially the decider for the league title. After a close first half, Walnut began to gain the upper hand and were leading 16-6. Sharlston fought back to 16-12 and were beginning to take control, but were dealt a severe blow as they lost playmaker Kevin Dawson, centre Andy Kirmond and Nigel Southern all in quick succession with injuries. This had a massive bearing on the game and Walnut ran out winners 24-12.

The following week saw Sharlston up against their old enemies Outwood Victoria in the Wakefield Saturday Cup semi-final. Things began well for Sharlston as they dominated the first half leading 18-10 at half-time, but Outwood would not give up and they fought their way back into the game and ran out eventual winners by 21-18. Peter Richardson was outstanding for Sharlston.

A week later saw Sharlston complete the double over York West Bank 26-15 with Stuart Bailey, Alan Reidford and Ian Lingard all impressing.

Then Rovers faced Westgate Redoubt in the N. B. Hough Construction Open Cup semi-final on 2 April at Thornes House School. Rovers were decimated by injuries, produced a brilliant team effort, but lost 11-10. Sharlston took an early lead through a Stuart Bailey penalty. Westgate replied with a try, but another Bailey penalty made the half-time score 4-4. Westgate went ahead with a converted try, and after having a try disallowed, Dave Taylor scored for Sharlston under the posts. Bailey converted, but a drop-goal won the game for Westgate. Hird, Taylor, Lingard and Bailey all played well for Sharlston.

Victory at Kippax kept Sharlston in touch with leaders Walnut and Middleton. This was a hard fought victory but with Ian Lingard: Jason Clough and Stuart Bailey running the show Rovers ran out 28-18 winners. Then Rovers lost 24-22 at Dewsbury Norths. This was a disappointing result, and finally ended Sharlston's championship hopes. Sharlston were leading 22-10 at half-time, but Norths came back strongly in the second half to snatch victory in the last few minutes. Nigel Southern and Johnny Mullaney had tremendous games. Then came the final league match of the season and the visit of Middleton to Back o' t' wall.

Sharlston needed to win to finish second and gain automatic promotion to the Senior Division and make sure that they would have a home tie in the top-four play-offs. They produced a brilliant performance to destroy Middleton 46-20 with every player playing his part in this tremendous display. The referee had a difficult decision making his choice for the man-of-the-match award, but he finally chose second-rower Richard Hall whose long range try was one of the best seen at Sharlston for a long time, running him close was every other player in the team.

The top four play-offs

Middleton must have arrived at Sharlston for this top four semi-final clash wondering how they could stop Rovers. The first half ended with Sharlston leading 20-9, and the game looked to be going the same way as the previous encounter a fortnight earlier. But in the second half Rovers lacked the same fire and determination as they had shown in the first half and Middleton grew in confidence as they came back into the match. They levelled the score at 26-26 to set up a frantic final few minutes. Both sides had their chances with Stuart Bailey crossing the line twice, but was unable to ground the ball. Player-coach Dave Taylor had a try disallowed for a double movement, but Middleton took the game with a try in the dying seconds.

Everyone at the club were disappointed at the way the season ended, but there were more good things than bad to come out of this season. Rovers achieved promotion, more than anyone could ever have hoped for.

Supporters

Player David Ainsworth reflected on the support for the players in his diary of the season: "One of the things that has been a pleasure in this campaign is the tremendous support we have received both home and away. In fact on many occasions we have had more supporters at away matches than the team we were playing have had. So it goes without saying that when you travel to bigger clubs such as Leigh Miners etc, your support helps to lift the team and that reflects in the team's performance. So the players and committee would like to take this opportunity to thank everyone for their support during the 1993-94 season."

Rovers' Player of the Year was Andy Kirmond.

1994-95

In August Sharlston won the Walton Nine-A-Side competition. They overcame tough opposition to win the qualifying rounds, drawing 6-6 with Eastmoor, then beating Ackworth 12-4.

This left a tough final match with senior division side Upton. In a close game Sharlston had match winners in Pete Richardson and Jason Clough who tormented Upton throughout. Sharlston won 6-0.

In the semi-final, Sharlston beat Walnut 14-0. In the Final, they beat Manor 28-17. Rovers gave a thrilling display to beat a young, but spirited Manor side. Peter Richardson and Stuart Bailey had outstanding games, but man-of-the-match Ian Lingard shone with strong running.

Sharlston had been promoted for three consecutive seasons and now faced the toughest test in their recent history. Could they take the pressure of the Senior Division? Their opponents in the Yorkshire Senior League were Walnut Warriors, Dewsbury Moor, Featherstone Miners Welfare, BRK (Burwell-Reid-Kinghorn), Middleton, Stanley, Shaws and Glasshoughton. Dave Taylor continued as coach.

The season opened at home with a slim triumph over Walnut Warriors, 22-20, with Ian Lingard, Stuart Bailey and Adrian Hird outstanding. The following week Rovers travelled to Dewsbury Moor with a much weakened team, missing several key players due to holiday and injuries. But they showed tremendous spirit and determination to compete at the highest level. With the scores level at 10-10 with six minutes to go a well-worked move from Dewsbury saw their full-back score a converted try. Rovers finished the match with 12 men as the outstanding Ian Lingard was sent off for tripping.

Sharlston were still recovering from the loss of several players to a re-formed Streethouse, when they met Featherstone Miners Welfare in a lively match which ended 14-14. Stand-off Johnny Mullaney and his cousin Tommy in the second-row and hooker Nigel Southern all scored tries, but Dave Ward only kicked one goal from five attempts.

There was a break from the league programme for the second round of the Yorkshire Cup, Rovers having had a bye in the first round. Sharlston progressed to the next round with a comprehensive victory, 38-14, over Kingston Communications from the First Division of the Humberside League. Dave Taylor took the man-of-the-match award, but he was closely run by Seb Easton and Ian Lingard with Peter Richardson and Steve Watson also in impressive form.

It was back to league action at Middleton and in a game that did no credit to anyone Sharlston looked like the walking wounded after a fierce clash. Rovers' 32-16 defeat meant little in the cauldron created by an ugly atmosphere that included abuse of the referee by some elements in the crowd. Rovers' casualty list was horrendous. They lost Nigel Southern with a rib injury, David Ward with a broken nose, Stuart Bailey from an eye injury and Peter Richardson with concussion due to foul play. Richardson had to be taken to hospital. Alan Reidford also limped off with a leg injury. Middleton had three men sent off, but still won. The Sharlston coach believed that "the referee just couldn't handle the intimidation he got from Middleton players and supporters."

A week after losing at Middleton, Sharlston were dragged into another battle on the pitch. Their third round Yorkshire Cup match against Moldgreen was abandoned by the referee in the 53rd minute after fighting broke out between the players. The brawl occurred following a late tackle on Alan Maskill, a Sharlston substitute, who was on a run when he was taken out by a Moldgreen forward who had just returned from the sin bin. The referee failed to regain control and had to call a halt. "We didn't expect Moldgreen, who are a Conference League team to mix it", commented a Sharlston spokesman. He said the cup-tie had been a good one up to the brawl, with both sides fired up. Moldgreen had an 11-2 lead at half-time, but Sharlston came back with a try by loose-forward Nigel Southern and two Dave Ward goals. Former Featherstone star Tommy Smales was at the match and picked out the performances of centre Andy Palmer, Alan Benyon and prop Stuart Bailey. There was no let up for Rovers as Queens were the visitors in the Senior Cup and chalked up 50 points in their demolition of Sharlston.

"Simply the best game of the season" was how the Sharlston coach described Sharlston's defeat of Walnut Warriors, 40-12. Man-of-the-match was shared between Easton, Kirmond and Ward. BRK came to Sharlston as table toppers and just piped them to the post 23-22.

Rovers and Crofton combined to produce an entertaining first round tie in the

Wakefield (Guilfoyle) Open Cup before a large and vociferous crowd. The referee helped by standing no nonsense and sin binned two players from each side. Crofton led with a converted try. Sharlston winger Jason Clough replied and Dave Ward duly converted, before man-of-the-match Stuart Bailey touched down and Ward's goal made it 12-6 at half-time. Sharlston player-coach 'Spud' Taylor then went in and it was all over at 24-6 when Andy Kirmond chipped over and won the race to the line.

Two defeats and a draw in the league followed. With Sharlston leading Shaws 20-0 and playing superb rugby the game should have been won in the first half but slack tackling, bad handling and complacency let Shaws back into the game, to win 32-20. At Stanningley, a 30-18 loss, the game was much closer than the score suggests.

Rovers drew with Featherstone Miners Welfare in a repeat of the encounter between the two sides earlier in the season, which also ended with a 14-14 draw. It was end-to-end stuff with plenty of excitement in both attack and defence with Stuart Bailey and Jason Clough, with two, scoring tries, and Dave Watson adding a goal. Scrum-half Ian Lingard was outstanding.

To get into the first round proper of the BARLA Cup, Rovers had to overcome Wyke from Division Two of the Pennine League, who were unbeaten in seven games prior to Sharlston's visit. Sharlston came safely through 10-4, and did not let Wyke score a try.

Then Richmond from the Fourth Division were heavily defeated 56-0 in the first round with Andy Kirmond scoring 4 tries.

Although their league record was only moderate, Sharlston pulled off a superb 13-8 victory at high-flying second placed BRK. Nigel Southern switched to scrum-half, showing how versatile he was. Stuart Bailey and Paul Wood played well, and the team welcomed back Tony Palmer after his knee operation. Stuart Bailey deservedly got the man-of-the-match award with nine of Sharlston's 13 points.

In the next round of the Open Cup, Rovers won 38-10 at Stanley Rangers in atrocious conditions.

A home league defeat to Middleton, 24-10, was a major disappointment. Although trailing 16-6 at the break and going further behind when they were caught offside, the introduction of substitutes Dave Ward and Ian Lingard lifted Rovers as the latter scored a try. Tempers flared and Sharlston lost both Richard Hall and Andy Palmer in quick succession for holding down. The man-of-the-match deservedly went to Andy Palmer, who was outstanding in attack and defence.

Rovers put in a gutsy performance before being beaten 13-9 in the BARLA Cup third round by Conference League side York Acorn. The home side scored two of the best tries ever seen at Sharlston with Peter Bean and Steve Watson involved in both of them. Andy Kirmond went over for the first and then Kevin Wood finished off the second.

A short trip to Castleford for a vital league game with bottom of the league Glasshoughton saw Sharlston needing points to climb out of the relegation zone. They came away with two points with a 27-22 win.

It was back to cup football with semi- and quarter-final ties against Stanley Rangers Old Boys and Normanton respectfully.

Rovers reached their first final for a long time as they overcame a strong challenge from Rangers in the Saturday Cup semi-final. Stanley led 10-6 at half-time, but shortly after the break Sharlston brought on Adrian Hird. He had an immediate impact and inspired the team. Rovers began to dominate and full-back Peter Richardson kicked through and touched down. Adrian Hird made big gains through the defence and from near the line Nigel Southern kicked through and touched down. Stuart Bailey added the goal for a 16-10 victory.

A week later near neighbours and Premier Division side Normanton were the visitors in the quarter-final of the Open Cup. In atrocious conditions both sides defied the weather to provide a thrilling cup-tie. Sharlston led 4-0 at the interval with two penalties. After the break Sharlston went further in front with another Ward penalty.

But Normanton fought back and cut the deficit with a penalty. Then after four quick passes, Jason Blockley sprinted over for the first try of the game, but the conversion was missed - leaving the scores level.

Sharlston regained the lead with another penalty which turned out to be the match-winning kick. Man-of-the-match for Sharlston was Nigel Southern.

A fortnight later it was the Open Cup (Guilfoyle) semi-final against formidable Westgate Redoubt at the Thornes House School ground. There have been some titanic battles between these two sides and a keenly fought game was expected. Last season when the two teams met at the same stage of the competition Sharlston nearly caused a major shock and just went down, 11-10.

Sharlston won and ended Westgate Redoubt's long winning run in the Open Cup. Westgate had maintained a vice-like grip on the trophy, winning 32 successive matches in the competition stretching back to 1989. But Sharlston's 17-10 victory meant that a new name will go on the cup for the first time in seven seasons. Sharlston went ahead 4-0 early on and were never behind though Westgate levelled at 10-10 on half-time. Hooker Nigel Southern was Sharlston's hero, scoring two tries, while centre Steve Watson added another and Stuart Bailey kicked two goals and a drop-goal.

Needing to score twice, Westgate tempers frayed and they had a player sent off for throwing a punch at Seb Easton.

There were two defeats and a victory in the closing league matches, but Sharlston were now clear of the relegation zone and assured of their place in the Senior Division for next season. There were now two finals to round-off the season.

Sharlston Rovers 12 Eastmoor Select 21
Wakefield City Plasterers Open Cup Final

Eastmoor lifted the Wakefield Open Cup at Belle Vue thanks to a remarkable display against Sharlston Rovers. They won despite relying on the second teamers who had carried them to the final.

Sharlston went in front through a penalty by loose-forward Dave Ward. He followed this with a further penalty and a try to put Sharlston 8-0 ahead.

Eastmoor's defence held and second row Wayne Jones set up Dave Brown for a try five minutes from the interval. Lee Southward added the conversion, then kicked a penalty to square the game on half-time. A Southward penalty put Eastmoor in front, then centre Chris McDermott sent in winger Ian Simmons for a try. A drop-goal by stand-off Southward put Eastmoor 15-8 up, but Sharlston were not finished and a second Ward touchdown set up a nail-biting finale. Southward sealed Eastmoor's victory with a try and conversion.

Westgate Redoubt 20 Sharlston Rovers 8
Wakefield & District Saturday Cup Final

Westgate Redoubt were well on the way to lifting the Wakefield & District Saturday Cup Final trophy when referee Malcolm Whiteley abandoned the match as scenes of violence erupted on, and then off, the pitch.

Sharlston had taken an early lead when Richard Hall took several defenders with him when he crossed for a try. Stuart Moran then opened Redoubt's account with a penalty and they took the lead when they opened up the Sharlston defence and left Stuart Price to dive between the posts. Moran converted. Sharlston then rallied and from a scrum in a deep position moved the ball up field quickly for centre Steve Watson to go over and level the scores. Redoubt hit back with a flowing move that ended with centre Jeremy Rodgers going over in the corner to establish a 12-8 half-time lead.

On the restart Moran punished Sharlston for foul play with a well-struck penalty. The same player looked to have put the Final beyond Sharlston's reach when he went on a glorious 75-yard touchline run, but fumbled the ball over the Sharlston line. However, he soon kicked another penalty. At this point Redoubt looked in full control. They continued to pile on the pressure, Sharlston's defence began to tire and Redoubt took advantage when the ball was swept wide for Andy Rodgers to put Matthew Bramold over. Moran kicked a superb touchline goal.

Sadly the restart prompted the skirmish which led to the referee issuing marching orders and that in turn led to the off-field trouble that was followed by the abandonment.

The Wakefield & District ARL disciplinary committee fined Westgate Redoubt and Sharlston Rovers equal amounts in punishment for their part in the abandoned match.

The committee considered replaying the final and inviting the beaten semi-finalists to contest the final. However, it was agreed not to present a trophy at all. Both teams were fined £180.

Sharlston's Player of the Year was Peter Richardson

1995-96

Stuart Bailey was appointed coach. He replaced David Taylor who was clearly not happy with the way he had been treated. He had taken the team from fifth division to senior division in three seasons. He had suffered a serious back injury while playing for Sharlston last season but was told by the committee not to worry about his post and that Stuart Bailey was helping out with training.

The team continued in the Yorkshire League Senior Division and faced Dewsbury Moor, Walnut Warriors, Roundhill, BRK, Kippax, Middleton, Glasshoughton and Featherstone Amateurs.

There is very little recorded for this season but it was a successful campaign, finishing third in the league. This was followed by a play-off semi-final victory, 22-12, over Featherstone Amateurs, who had hammered Sharlston 53-14 in the opening game of the season. Table toppers Dewsbury Moor were the other finalists, the match being played at Owl Lane, Dewsbury.

Sharlston Rovers 22 Dewsbury Moor 38
Yorkshire League Senior Division play-offs Final

Sharlston never quite hit top form in this match, but still came within a whisker of glory at Owl Lane. Rovers began sluggishly and soon found themselves trailing 4-0 to an early Moor touchdown. But despite their slow start a converted try out of the blue from centre Peter Richardson put Sharlston two points in front.

Even that failed to spark Rovers from their lethargy and Moor took full advantage to go in at the break 12-6 ahead.

Sharlston's problems increased 10 minutes before half-time when influential scrum-half Ian Lingard was taken off with injury. Despite the reshuffle his departure prompted, an interval telling-off seemed to kick Rovers into life.

They recovered from Moor's sizzling point scoring start to the second period to pull back to 24-12 down with another Richardson try. When David Ward kicked two penalties soon afterwards to make it 24-16, Sharlston looked on course for a winning revival. But when Ward was sent off it was all Dewsbury.

Cup competitions

In the BARLA Cup, an easy 32-1 win over Trafford in the first round was followed by a 25-19 defeat, after a dogged display against Clayton from Bradford.

The visitors ran into an early lead before a try, from Benyon, hauled Rovers back into the match, and when Clough's touchdown was followed by a Sharp drop-goal to give the hosts a 9-7 interval lead they seemed to be on their way.

But Clayton swung into action after the break and although Southern scored the best try of the game for Sharlston, it was not enough to see them home.

In the Saturday Plasterers' Cup, Sharlston beat Upton 'A' 60-6, and then Crigglestone 20-6. This produced a semi-final with Normanton, who won 26-10.

Normanton's sizzling first half booked their place in the final. They blasted into the lead with their first attack when Hampshire scored to give his side a lead they never lost. The hosts added to their total soon after when Riddell scored. Although Sharlston battled hard to gain a foothold in the match, Normanton's power pushed them back. Determined tackling from man of the match Brennan, Gunn and Slater helped set up a string of chances for Normanton. They were 20-0 up at the break.

Normanton began the second half as they had ended the first - on top. Wright scored and Riddell converted to make it 26-0. Sharlston got their name on the score sheet soon after with a penalty try for Brewerton, but there was no way back.

The best cup run came in the Open (Guilfoyle) Competition where Rovers reached the final. Bailey inspired Sharlston to a second round victory over Stanley Rangers Old Boys, scoring all their 15 points in a game dominated by defences.

Three Rovers first half tries gave them the edge over Walnut Warriors in the semi-final and with two conversions they led 16-8 at the break. Walnut hit back after the interval, but with penalties going against them at regular intervals they were unable to get back into the game. Sharlston lost the Final at Belle Vue 26-10 to Upton.

Rovers were eliminated at the preliminary stage of the Senior Cup by Knottingley. In the Yorkshire Cup, they reached round three before losing to Hull Dockers.

Tony Palmer was the club's Player of the Year.

1996-97

The season opened with the annual Wakefield & District ARL seven- a-side tournament in the Clarence Park arena. The teams produced a feast of rugby to delight the crowd.

Surprise finalists were Stanley Rangers whose squad had an average age of just 20 and who played in the lowest division of all who took part. In the final Sharlston hammered Stanley 20-0. Sharlston's Peter Bean was the player of the tournament.

Once again Sharlston played in the Yorkshire League Senior Division, along with Kippax, Westgate Redoubt. Cross Gates, Walnut Warriors, Glasshoughton, Bradley Arms,

Two teams from the mid-1990s

The 1995-96 Sharlston Junior & Infants School team that won the Yorkshire & Humberside Cup, beating Alderman Logan School 16-12 in the final, with three tries from Gareth Davies and goals from Karl Dawson and Chris Hill. Back: Adam Goldie, James Howell, Luke Stringer, Chris Hill, Danny Hannah, Sonny Pearson, Daniel Kirmond, Douglas Murdock, Mr Rumgay; Front: Nichola Shepherd, Jamie Hobbs, Jodie Lingard, Gareth Davies, Karl Dawson, Daniel Grimshaw.
(Photo: *Wakefield Express*).

Sharlston Rovers 1996-97: Back: Mick Taylor, Chris Berry, Tony Palmer, Russ Barlow, Neil Longstaff, Tommy Mullaney, Stuart Bailey (Coach), Adrian Hird, Craig Cooper, Mick Wilkinson; Front: Gordon Long, Jason Clough, Pete Richardson, Johnny Mullaney, Stuart Glentworth (sponsor), Ian Lingard, Alan Benyon, Jeff Exley, Johnny Brewerton; Mascots: Joshua and Kaine Glentworth.
(Photo: *Wakefield Express*)

The victorious Wakefield 7s squad: Back: Dave Ward, Gordon Long, Jason Clough, Johnny Brewerton, Garry Cross, Stuart Bailey, Russ Barlow, Andy Kirmond, Mick Wilkinson; Front: Pete Bean, Alan Benyon, Tony Palmer, Pete Richardson, Jeff Exley, Ian Moverley. (Photo: *Wakefield Express*)

Knottingley Rockware and Chequerfield. The coaches were Stuart Bailey, Andy Kirmond and Gordon Long.

Rovers' league results were not good enough to get them into the top four, and they ended their campaign on a downbeat, finishing in fifth position. They also lacked discipline at times; against Knottingley Rockware they had a player sent off after the very first tackle, lost the match and valuable league points. He was not the only player to be sent off during the season. But on the bright side, whereas a few seasons ago they found the step up to higher leagues too tough, they could now compete with the big boys and looked to the future with confidence.

In the cup competitions, Sharlston went out in the first round of the Senior Cup and the Guilfoyle Cup at the hands of Brass Moulders of Leeds 34-8, and Normanton 'A', 23-20, respectively.

Fifth Division Clifton Moor, travelling from York were always going to have an uphill struggle in the first round of the BARLA Cup as Sharlston took the lead early on with a try from winger Martin. Clifton were then dealt a blow which effectively ended any chance they had when their number eight had to be carried off, leaving them with 12 men for the rest of the game. Rovers led 18-0 at half-time and second half tries by Benyon, Palmer, Clough and the popular figure of Hall sealed a comfortable 38-0 win. The man-of-the-match was Nigel Southern.

Rovers' progress was halted in round two at Featherstone Amateurs' Mill Pond ground with a 30-24 defeat. Rovers came within a whisker of an upset. They looked dead and buried when Featherstone led 30-8 on the hour with their third try in a seven minute spell. But that was the signal for Sharlston to click into gear with Ian Lingard leading their revival.

They racked up two tries and a Bailey conversion in quick succession to make it 30-18. Then they nabbed a penalty try with Bailey again kicking the goal. And in the very last minute they were agonisingly held up just a foot short of the line as they went in search of the match-levelling points. Richard Hall was Rovers' man-of-the-match.

The first round Builders Supply Cup clash between neighbours Sharlston and Crofton was eagerly awaited and lived up to its billing as a battle royal.

Clean breaks were few and scoring opportunities rarer and it was no surprise the half-time whistle went without any score. The deadlock was finally broken by Crofton with a penalty from Tottie, which spurred Rovers forward with renewed purpose. A try finally came 15 minutes from the end; the resilient Crofton defence was broken by Rovers' captain Tony Palmer with Stuart Bailey converting for a 6-2 win. It showed the strength and commitment of the Rovers squad that they won this match after two difficult games in the previous six days.

In the semi-final, Sharlston faced Stanley Rovers. Castleford prop and Stanley coach

Dean Sampson delivered the right messages to his charges at half-time to turn a 22-8 deficit into a 26-22 victory.

After a solid start by both sides Stanley conceded a penalty converted by Dave Ward. But Sharlston conceded two tries in three minutes to give the home side an 8-2 lead; Sam Harkin went over for Stanley on both occasions. These tries shocked Sharlston into life and Stuart Bailey went in for a try converted by Ward to level the scores. Jason Clough, who had an outstanding game for Sharlston, ran in two more tries to leave Sharlston in the driving seat at half-time.

Any thoughts of a landslide victory, however, were quickly erased by Stanley who started the second half with renewed vigour. Two tries in quick succession, both converted, brought Stanley to within four points of Sharlston's total.

Sharlston tried desperately hard to break through Stanley's defence but to no avail. Man-of-the-match Ian Lingard played tirelessly, while forwards Tony Palmer and Richard Hall made great ground gains. But Stanley were not going to be denied a place in the final. A late converted try sealed Sharlston's fate in a 24-22 defeat.

Sharlston produced a fine display in the third round of the Yorkshire Cup but it was not enough to deny Park Amateurs a place in the next round. The Halifax side put the first points on the board with an excellent try and conversion. But this served only to spark Rovers into action and after a series of attacks Palmer grabbed a try, converted by Fowler.

Sharlston's second half was plagued by injuries, the most serious being a knock on the head for Terry Mullaney, who was taken to hospital as a precaution. Stuart Bailey, also showing fine form, was forced into the blood bin but returned later and Nigel Southern was knocked out in a tackle.

Park Amateurs edged in front with a drop-goal, which looked good enough to settle the outcome as Sharlston struggled to re-organise their injury ravaged defence. Two late tries by Park sealed the match. Tony Palmer was Sharlston's man-of-the-match.

Sharlston reached the City Plasterers Cup final at the expense of a woeful Eastmoor side. Eastmoor included eight second-team members but Sharlston were also lacking three key players. Rovers put on a superb show to win 25-0 at Eastmoor. The Eastmoor club issued an apology to their fans for their disappointing show. Crofton had battled through to the final at the expense of the two Stanley sides, Ranger and Rovers, and had to survive a gritty semi-final draw against Westgate Redoubt before eventually winning the replay. Crofton were in the final for the first time in their history.

Sharlston Rovers 10 Crofton 13
City Plasterers' Cup

Courageous Crofton defied the odds at Belle Vue to win the cup for the first time in their history. Sharlston Rovers were tackled out of the game by their division two village neighbours. Former Rovers coach Trevor Bailey planned the game to near perfection.

Having one player, centre Andy Bannister, sent off for what appeared to be the illegal use of the forearm and Dave Brown sin binned nearing the final quarter couldn't have helped his plans, but his remaining players responded magnificently.

But the sending off and the following sin binning very nearly proved the turning point of the game. Rovers sprang suddenly into overdrive and cut a 12-0 half-time deficit with a try within minutes of the sending off. Crofton worked for position and put over a drop-goal which meant Sharlston had to score at least twice at 13-4 down.

Sharlston's extra players started to tell. Rovers released the ball well in the tackle and made more ground that at any other time in the game, but Crofton's defence worked wonders until a second Sharlston try, this time converted, cut the gap to just three points, with minutes left. Rovers fought to the end, but their fight-back was beaten by the clock.

Sharlston were one of the four Wakefield teams in the Hall and Co. mid-week Floodlit Competition, with prize money of £500. The teams were in groups with Sharlston in group 3. The matches were played at Post Office Road.

A defeat at the hands of Westgate Redoubt, 26-22, but victories against Knottingley Rockware, 26-19, and Upton, 10-8, when inspirational man-of-the-match Ian Lingard was stretchered off, got them into the final tie to meet Chequerfield.

Sharlston Rovers 16 Chequerfield 27
Hall and Co Floodlit Plate final

These two sides both played a style of rugby that would grace any of the top amateur competitions. Chequerfield went ahead with two penalties in the third and sixth minutes, both by Senior.

After 10 minutes Sharlston hit back and levelled with a super try by Ian Lingard. But this was Rovers' only score in the first half, with Chequerfield dominating. Sharlston had to work overtime to try and contain the Pontefract side.

A drop-goal from Senior on 20 minutes restored Chequerfield's lead. Chequerfield scored a try on the half-hour and again five minutes before half-time, both converted by the outstanding Senior. Two minutes before the break another try made it 21-4 to Chequerfield. Sharlston started the second half with renewed vigour. A try by Nigel Southern, converted by Stuart Bailey, restored their morale. But Chequerfield replied with yet another try, scored and converted by Senior. The score, however, sparked fresh life from Sharlston and Bailey burst through from 20 yards for a try which he converted that cut the gap to 27-16. Andy Palmer and Stuart Bailey were just pipped for man of the match honours by Ian Lingard.

Compensation came when Sharlston Rovers won the Walton Nines tournament with two tries in the last minute of the final. They had a tough tournament with a 13-12 success over Upton before meeting fellow finalists, Featherstone, who had hammered Upton 28-10.

Featherstone managed a try against Sharlston who also had their noses in front before securing the silverware with the last minute blitz. Ian Lingard was Sharlston's man of the match in the final.

Awards

Numerous outstanding performers were honoured at the end of season presentation night. An evening of trophies, handshakes and Tetley Bitter took place at the Sharlston Hotel. Among the season's stars were Ian Lingard and Nigel Southern, who picked up two awards each.

Ian was voted player of the year, alongside a trophy for picking up most man-of-the-match nominations during the season. Nigel collected the coveted players' player of the year and coaches' player of the year awards. The other awards were:

Most Tries: Jason Clough
Young Player of the Year: Russ Barlow
Most Improved Player: Steven Hall
Club Person of the Year: Malcolm Richardson
Chairman's Trophy: Tony Palmer

Sharlston Rovers Juniors also held a presentation night to honour some of the young players. Bradford Bulls forward Brian McDermott presented trophies to the winners in front of a packed house at the Sharlston Hotel. Every youngster received a trophy for completing the season with several extra awards going to the outstanding players in each age category. The following awards were presented:

Most Improved Players: D. Long (under-8s), J. Gardner (under-9s), I. M. Illingworth (under 11s).
Best Trainer: M. Ward (under-8s), M. Hague (under-9s), S. Haslam (under-11s).
Coach's Players: D. Long & C. Stevens (under-8s), B. Richardson & R. Scott (under-9s), M. Lynes & G. Arnold (under-11s).
Men of Steel: S. Jones (under-8s), M. Andrews (under-9s), J. Beaumont (under-11s).
Most Outstanding Player: M. Padgett (under-8s), S. Brealey (under-9s), G. Arnold (under-11s).
Players' Player: C. Stevens (under-8s), B. Richardson (under-9s), L. Stringer (under-11s).
Supporters' Player: C. Stevens (under-8s), S. Brealey (under-9s), M. Lynes (under-11s).

1997-98

Tony 'Tosh' Wright took over as coach and presided over a big improvement in Sharlston's league position, finishing in second place to Middleton and gaining promotion to the Premier Division.

Their opponents in the Yorkshire Saturday League Senior Division were Middleton, Cross Gates, Ackworth, Glasshoughton, Featherstone MW, Brotherton and Kippax.

Rovers' best results were against Brotherton, 38-4, with one spectator describing it as the best display he'd seen for a long time, thrashing Cross Gates 66-6, a nail biting 16-14 win against Middleton, when Sharlston notched a penalty with time ticking away.

Sharlston did the double over Kippax, Brotherton, Cross Gates, and Glasshoughton, but could not get the better of Ackworth, who were the only top four team they failed to beat.

In the semi-final play-off with Featherstone MW, the Welfare looked on course for victory early in the second period when they led 12-4, but Sharlston responded with Jonathan Mullaney's second try and Stuart Bailey's goal. Sharlston secured a hard-earned win 15 minutes from time when Tony Palmer crossed and Bailey added the goal.

Sharlston Rovers 16 Middleton 28
Yorkshire Saturday League Senior Division Play-off Final

Rovers nosed in front at Post Office Road with a Stuart Bailey penalty, but the first try went to Middleton in the 25th minute and more pressure produced a second.

Rovers replied on half-time with a brilliant try by Rich Davies, converted by Bailey to square matters.

Under pressure Sharlston conceded a third converted try on 48 minutes and a converted try two minutes later all but settled the match. But Sharlston did not collapse and in the 65th minute Andy Palmer scored with Bailey converting.

At 20-14 Sharlston were still in contention. Just when it looked as if Sharlston might have enough in reserve to win, Middleton scored the killer try.

In the cup competitions, Westgate Redoubt edged a thrilling City Plasterers Cup first round tie at Sharlston, 28-26, with man-of-the-match Stuart Moran scoring all their points. With Westgate leading 26-20, Sharlston were not finished and with five minutes left broke through to score a try and a goal. Westgate survived a few nervy moments close to their line before Moran sealed victory with a last gasp penalty.

Rovers bowed out of the BARLA Cup in the first round to Featherstone MW, 14-8. Welfare produced the break-through in the 38th minute, a try by Allan Hobson, converted by Mark Reeves to turn around with a six point lead.

The second half started with neither side giving an inch, but a drop-goal from player-coach Reeves edged Featherstone further ahead. Stuart Bailey pulled back two points with a penalty, but Rovers were not producing their best rugby. A brilliant try by Ian Lingard lifted the side. Bailey's conversion gave Sharlston a one point lead.

The game was set for a grand finale. Featherstone took advantage of Sharlston's errors and Dawson put the visitors in front again with a well-taken try. At 12-8 down there was still enough time on the clock for Sharlston to steal the tie but a penalty by the visitors in the dying minutes swung the result Featherstone's way.

Jonathan Mullaney was Sharlston's man-of-the-match and he was pressed all the way by impressive Ian Lingard.

Rovers turned the form book on its head in a second round Yorkshire Cup thriller when they knocked out premier division side Stanningley. After 10 minutes, David Ward put Rovers in front with a well struck penalty.

Twenty minutes were up before the spectators were treated to another score. Rovers broke the deadlock with a brilliant try by full-back Craig Lingard. Ward missed the kick.

Stanningley recovered and levelled with a converted try. But two minutes before the break Andy Palmer sent pulses racing with a second try for Rovers, this time goaled by Ward for a 12-6 half-time lead.

Rovers were under the cosh at the start of the second half. Stanningley levelled for the second time with their second converted try. And a penalty gave the home side the lead for the first time while a try scored five minutes later for a six point cushion seemed enough for the win.

But Rovers were not finished. Substitute Stuart Bailey barged over by the posts to give Ward an easy conversion. With the scores again all square Sharlston made their superior fitness and defensive capabilities tell. Stanningley conceded a penalty five minutes from the end of normal time and Ward kept a cool head under pressure to score and give Sharlston a 20-18 advantage.

A comfortable 18-0 victory against Mirfield followed in the third round. The next tie was at Queens and brought the end of the cup run. Under strength, missing three regular first teamers, Rovers produced a brave display and gave 100 per cent, with their forwards matching the Queens pack. Richard Hall spearheaded their efforts, with hooker Martin Brown also showing well. The difference between the two sides though came in the threequarters, where Queens had former Dewsbury man Bailey and former Wakefield player Andy Wilson.

Rich Davies did well to keep Wilson in check for most of the game, but Bailey was in imperious mood throughout. He was at the heart of some early scoring as Queens raced into a 14 point lead by the 25th minute mark courtesy of two penalties, two tries and a conversion. Although Terry Mullaney eventually got Rovers on to the scoresheet with a try, two more touchdowns and a goal gave the hosts a 24-4 lead at half-time

Queens carried on after the restart, running in an unconverted try in the fifth minute. Rovers were still in the hunt but they could just not turn their build-up play into chances. And that cost them on the hour when a try and a goal sealed it for Queens. Still Sharlston did not lie down, though, and even though the home side nabbed a breakaway effort, Rovers ended with a Brown touchdown and Stuart Bailey goal.

Sharlston had to win a replay against Upton before they entered the second round of the Senior Cup. Trailing 14-6, Upton looked beaten, but fought back and with time running out scored an unconverted try to earn a 16-16 draw. Sharlston won the replay comfortably, but then almost came unstuck against First Division Batley Boys, but hung on for a 19-16 win. Rovers who trailed 9-6 at the break, recovered with tries from John Dickens, Andy Palmer and Stuart Bailey, who also landed a drop-goal, to lead by nine points with just four minutes remaining

The Boys came close to mounting an astonishing recovery, fighting back with two tries in the last three minutes from Steve Hornby, who had scored his side's first half touchdown. Darren Hinchliffe however was unable to add either of the difficult kicks.

In a scrappy third round tie against Westgate Redoubt, Sharlston dominated the first 15 minutes, but could not score, missing two kickable penalties. Rovers were only trailing by two points going into the last 20 minutes, but then Westgate scored again. Matty Smart pounced on Wright's high kick to score under the posts. This time Moran made no mistake with the conversion. Evergreen Andy Wright dropped a goal and Wayne Bentley dived in behind the posts for the match settling try, again converted by Moran, who added a penalty a minute before full-time.

Sharlston blasted into the second round of the Guilfoyle Open Cup at the expense of Normanton Knights, 38-6. Full-back Craig Lingard took centre stage and scored a hat-trick of tries. The quarter-final with Crofton at Back o' t' wall lived up to all expectations - a fiercely fought contest. It was a superb match, which kept the crowd of 300 to 400 on their toes for the whole 80 minutes.

After only three minutes Crofton's Chris Wright intercepted a wild pass and raced 80 yards to score, which Tottie converted. The next quarter saw end-to-end rugby before Sharlston broke through and Jason Clough touched down. Ward failed to convert. Five minutes later Craig Lingard raced from halfway to score a try, which Ward converted.

Crofton started the second half in determined mood and Lovelock scored a fine try which Tottie goaled to put his side ahead again. Ten minutes later Rich Davies scored to close the gap. But Chris Wright popped up again to score another try for Crofton which Tottie goaled. In the 70th minute, Craig Lingard got into action again to level the scores, but Bailey missed the kick.

With both teams feeling the pressure the last 10 minutes produced thrilling action until Sharlston powered home with a great touchline run and try by Jason Clough A superb goal was added by Wright. Martin Brown was Sharlston's man-of-the-match.

A hard earned semi-final victory over Upton secured a place in the final. After heavy Upton pressure Miers kicked a drop-goal in the 11th minute, but Sharlston responded a minute later when a superb 40-yard break by Richard Hall produced a try. Stuart Bailey was unable to convert but shortly afterwards landed a penalty. Upton countered with a try, which Miers converted, to sneak ahead but after that Rovers' Ian Lingard scored a brilliant try which Bailey converted. A Bailey penalty two minutes later put Rovers further ahead. On the stroke of half-time Richard Hall produced a great run from 60 yards out to score. The second half started like the first but this time Wright landed a drop-goal. However, Upton were not finished and Bolton went over for a try which Miers converted. Rovers regained the initiative and a fine handling move involving Bailey, Andy Palmer and Ian Lingard ended with Jason Clough scoring. Wright was unable to convert.

Upton refused to give in and were rewarded with a try, but Miers was unable to convert. Sharlston had the last word with a penalty by Bailey. Richard Hall was Sharlston's man-of-the-match and there were also impressive performances from Ian Lingard, Andy Palmer, Stuart Bailey and Tony Palmer.

Stanley Rangers 30 Sharlston Rovers 8
Guilfoyle Open Cup Final

Stanley Rangers won this one-side final at Belle Vue. Rovers rallied and scored a couple of second half tries through winger Jason Clough in the 62nd and 75th minutes. Sharlston looked more dangerous when down to 12 men following Craig Lingard's 52nd minute sending off. Rovers scored their first try when down to 11 men as Darren Lingard was sin-binned for holding down, outflanking Stanley's defence.

But the final belonged to Stanley Rangers. Mark Colbeck's try from a tap penalty five minutes into the second half for their fourth try, converted by Craig Riley, effectively settled the outcome.

After Anthony Marsh scored in the 56th minute, again converted by Riley, there was no way back for Sharlston at 30-0.

It looked all over at half-time with Rangers in command at 18-0 ahead. But Rovers arrested the slide in the last 15 minutes of the first period to give themselves hope of saving the match. Clough was bundled into touch by the corner flag off Rovers' best attack of the half.

Floodlit Competition

An under-strength Sharlston outfit slipped to a comprehensive defeat in the Featherstone Rovers Floodlit Competition - but not before giving Featherstone Lions an early scare. Rovers cruised into a 12 point lead against the Conference League Division 2 leaders in the first 15 minutes of this Group 2 clash. Sharlston's try scorers during this spell were centre Jason Clough and man-of-the-match Craig Lingard, who also kicked two goals. But from then on Featherstone stepped up a gear and racked up 32 points without reply to sweep Rovers aside.

Sharlston Rovers presented Nigel Southern with an engraved tankard and a cheque for £100 to mark his enforced retirement from the amateur game after 13 years with the club. He broke his fingers when he played at Huddersfield and he was advised by doctors that further damage would result in amputation. He felt he had to stop playing.

There was good news from the local Parish Council after it gave approval to build a new pavilion and changing rooms at Back o' t' wall at an estimated cost of £40,000.

The youngsters of the Sharlston Eagles had under-7, -8, -9 and -10 teams. They were trying to secure more sponsors to allow their coaches to build on this year's successful campaign and strengthen the club for the future.

During the season there was a cash boost for the youngsters. They got their own pitch in the village after a local benefactor chipped in with more than £1,000. John Padgett paid for topsoil to be laid on land next to Sharlston Rovers' ground for the young players to use. His donation covered the cost of levelling the pitch, and it was then seeded and would be ready for use in the summer. Mr Padgett said he was interested in the development of youth rugby in the village: "I would like my children to play for Sharlston Rovers and this is an investment in their future - plus a good step forward for the village."

Awards

Special guests, Steve Dooler and Ben Smallman of Featherstone Rovers, handed out the awards at the recent Sharlston Rovers presentation night. The winners were:

Most man of the match wins: Ian Lingard
Most Tries: Craig Lingard
Player of the Year: Tony Palmer
Young Player of the Year: Neil Ripley
Clubman of the Year: Mick Wilkinson
Players' Player: Martin Brown
Most Improved Player: Andy (Geordie) Martin
Blake Long Trophy for Coach's Player of the Year: Martin Brown
Chairman's Trophy: Stuart Bailey
Billy Wood Man of Steel Award: Richard Hall
Laura Davies Memorial Trophy: Craig Lingard
Chris Shepherd Memorial Trophy: Richard Davies

1998-99

The club were originally in the Yorkshire Saturday League Premier Division, but decided to drop down to the Senior Division to face Good Companions, Crofton, Methley, Brookhouse, Ossett Trinity, Batley Boys, Upton, Batley Victoria, Pudsey and Dewsbury Celtic. Dave Jones took over as coach.

The high hopes which prevailed at the end of last season after promotion was gained to the Premier Division were soon dispelled at the start of the season. Several players left the club either to join other sides or retired. There was also a massive injury crisis. One player had a dislocated pelvis, another a broken jaw and there were many other niggly injuries like broken fingers, shoulder problems and ligament damage.

Rovers turned up at Featherstone MW with only 11 men for the first Premier match and did not take the field. They stepped down from the Premier Division to the Senior Division because the team wasn't big enough or had sufficient experience to compete in the higher league.

They still suffered a string of heavy defeats, the worst 96-0 against Batley Boys, and not unsurprisingly finished bottom of the league. The club also failed to fulfil all their fixtures. There were rumours that the club had folded, but Sharlston Rovers never give up without a fight.

Jason Clough

The club's problems were added to when Jason Clough died at the age of just 26 at the beginning of November after a road accident just outside Sharlston Hotel. A popular member of the Sharlston club for many years, Jason was a threequarter who scored some great tries. But above all he never had a bad word to say about anyone and that everyone liked him was obvious at his funeral when well over 600 attended.

Trish Casey, the landlady of the Sharlston Hotel, was one of the organisers and instrumental in setting up a trust fund to remember Jason and help provide for his son.

A match was arranged between Sharlston and Streethouse and raised the magnificent sum of £1,700, bringing the fund to around £4,500. The famous Fox brothers attended and took part in what was a really good day.

There were quick exits from cup competitions. In the Yorkshire Cup, Hastings from Humberside beat Sharlston 6-2 in the second round. In the City Plasterers Cup first round Westgate Redoubt 'A' beat Sharlston 54-0 after Rovers had turned up with only 12 men. There was a first round exit as well in the Senior Cup, 30-16 at Pudsey.

In the Guilfoyle Open Cup Upton beat Sharlston 39-12 in the preliminary round.

The end of season awards went to:

Most man-of-the-match wins: Tony Palmer
Most Tries: Peter Richardson
Coach's Blake Long Trophy: Tony Palmer
Clubman of the Year: David Jones
Player of the Year: Peter Richardson
Young Player of the Year: Rob Howell
Most Improved Player: Andy Martin
Chairman's Trophy: Peter Richardson
Players' Player (Jason Clough): Peter Richardson
Laura Davies Trophy: Paul Wood
Chris Shepherd Trophy: Tommy Mullaney

Sharlston Rovers 1998: Back: Mick Wilkinson, Tommy Mullaney, Garry Cross, Stephen Hall, Russ Barlow, Rob Radcliffe, Ian Goodfellow, Paul Wood, Mick Taylor; Front: Dave Jones (coach), Pete Richardson, Jason Clough, Shaun Bullock, Tony Palmer, Kevin Wood, Jeff Exley, Andy Martin, Lyndon Chalkley; Mascot: Thomas Harrison.

Sharlston Rovers 1999-2000: back: Mick Wilkinson, Peter Richardson, Rob Radcliffe, Mark Reeves, Garry Cross, Stuart Bailey, Ian Goodfellow, Russ Barlow, John Mullaney, Mick Taylor; Front: Stan Smith, Tony Palmer, Dave Smith, Andy Martin, Ian Bragger (coach), Ian Lingard, Shaun Bullock, Dave Brown, Scott Haig, Andy Palmer.

The Jason Clough Memorial match

Above left: Don, Neil and Peter Fox with the Streethouse and Sharlston captains.
Above right: The Streethouse team: Back: Brian Leake, Dean Pearson, Sam Hughes, Paul Bonson, Terry Leake, Garry Shillabeer, Craig Orm, Andy Kirmond, Ian Harrison; Middle: Nigel Kirton, Terry Smith, Paul Stewson, Wes Neilson, Colin Shillabeer; Front: Lee Gibbins, John Hunter, Dave Wright, Ian Neilson, Kev Sadler, Kev Dawson, Darren Slater, Darren Lingard.
Below: The Sharlston team with the junior players.

Former Sharlston players at the game: Back: Jack Davies, Doug Davies, Graham Chalkley, Malcolm Beresford, Trevor Hepworth, Graham Reeves, Glyn Dooler; Middle: John Lingard, Graham Sandy, Tommy Lingard, Vic Loxton, Terry Hewitt, Dave Miller; Front: Geoff Brown, Johnny Bullock, Billy Wood, Steve Lingard, Brian Waller, Phil Winship, Tommy Lackenby.

1999-2000

Ian Bragger took over as coach to take the club into the new millennium. Rovers were allowed to stay in the Yorkshire Saturday League Senior Division.

After finishing bottom of the league last season the Rovers should have been relegated, but they were now back on course and had assembled a good squad of players and the League allowed them to maintain their status in the Senior Division.

There was a successful league campaign, with the team being in the top two all season and finally finishing second.

They were up for it before the season started, going to Pennine League side Rotherham in a friendly and giving a solid display to win 34-18, the result of hard training under new coach Ian Bragger.

Victories in their first three league engagements, against Wetherby, 52-20, when Mark Reeves stole the show with a hat-trick of tries and 8 goals, Brotherton 36-26 and Ossett Trinity 20-8 before the first defeat of the season came at Pudsey, the eventual league winners.

With 100 per cent records at stake for both sides, Pudsey and Sharlston opted for a safety first approach. The final score was 19-18 to the home side.

Ian Lingard was penalised at a play-the-ball on 20 minutes. Wayne Shearer put Pudsey in front and then Martin Wood dropped a vital one pointer.

Mark Reeves punished a Pudsey infringement on 30 minutes to cut the deficit to one point. Reeves was impeded as he kicked through, but the referee must have been unsighted. Unperturbed, Sharlston pushed forward and Reeves coasted in under the posts. He then converted.

And Reeves then attempted a penalty from the half-way line after Pudsey's re-start had gone out of play on the full, but missed and Sharlston had to settle for an 8-3 advantage at half-time. Shearer cut the gap with a penalty on 48 minutes. Andy Martin was held up over the Pudsey line while Wood made a clean high ball take to touch down at the other end. Shearer converted to give Pudsey the lead.

Tommy Mullaney forced his way over, but Dave Ward's conversion was ruled out by the referee. Sharlston were now on top and on 68 minutes scored their best try of the season. Reeves picked the ball up in his own half, put Booth through the gap and Brown followed up to return the ball to Reeves, who in turn drew the cover and fed Stan Smith for the full-back to touch down. Reeves converted for an 18-11 lead.

But on 73 minutes Martin was penalised for ball stealing and Shearer reduced the arrears. And with time running out Steve Marvell evaded the cover to touch down and Shearer's conversion clinched it for Pudsey.

Sharlston avenged this defeat later in the season, 29-10 - Pudsey's only defeat - and lost only one more league match all season, 15-13 at Batley Victoria. These two sides met again in the play-off semi-final and as Sharlston had a winning margin of 20 points over Batley in January, were confident of victory.

Rovers looked the stronger outfit in the first half and after taking a two point lead scored the try of the match on 23 minutes. Reeves took the ball up to the half-way, chipped the defence and centre Lee Trigg re-gathered and fed Stuart Bailey who passed to Darren Lingard to score behind the posts. Reeves converted.

Reeves missed a good chance to improve the lead but then Rovers gained an extra edge when the opposition scrum-half was sin-binned. Reeves added a penalty for a 12-2 lead at half-time.

The introduction of Neil Kelly for Batley turned the game on its head in the second half. On 44 minutes Harrison crossed and converted to make it 12-8. Batley were now on top and levelled in the 51st minute when winger Phil Waring got to a kick ahead of the Sharlston defence. On 70 minutes John Stainburn added a vital drop-goal. Dave Brown and Jackson were stopped short. Pete Richardson was stretchered off after a high tackle, but Reeves missed the penalty. Deep in injury time Ian Goodfellow just failed to take a try-scoring pass. So the result was Sharlston Rovers 12 Batley Victoria 13.

In the cup competitions an eight-minute blitz early in the second half swept Crigglestone All Blacks to a 32-18 victory against Sharlston in the first round of the City Plasterers Cup. Sharlston started favourites, but were unable to match their hosts' enthusiasm and finishing. New signing Gary Shillabeer, formerly with Huddersfield Giants, bagged two tries for Sharlston, with Mark Reeves taking the other points from a try and goals.

After an fine second round Yorkshire Cup win against Undercliffe from Bradford, with Reeves contributing a hat-trick of tries, Rovers were no match for Elland in round three, going down 64-4.

Sharlston cruised into the second round of the BARLA Cup against Knottingley Rockware, 59-14. It was one-way traffic from the outset; coach Ian Bragger opened the scoring in the third minute. Rovers went out of the competition in disappointing fashion at Bamber Bridge, 14-4. The opening minutes were even but a break over 60 yards by centre Gary Shillabeer put Sharlston on attack. Pete Richardson crossed the whitewash, but the referee ruled out the try.

Rovers seemed to be on top and Dave Brown was stopped short on 34 minutes. Dave Jones was then sent off for retaliation. The half ended scoreless with Rovers a man down. A long high ball caught Richardson on the shoulder and Bamber opened the scoring off the rebound. A melee followed the upshot of which was a 10 minute sin-binning for Sharlston's Andy Palmer that left the side down to 11 men. Sharlston hit back and Stuart Bailey went over to reduce the arrears to 6-4, but within minutes Sharlston had conceded a penalty and Bamber were 8-4 up.

Stan Smith forced his way over but for the second time Rovers had the try ruled out. Frustration led to a 10 minute stint in the sin- bin for Bailey and in his absence Bamber scored the match-securing try and a penalty - a frustrating score that led to another sin-binning, this time for Tommy Mullaney. Shillabeer was Sharlston's man-of-the-match.

Sharlston's re-emergence as one of the district's top teams was underlined by a tremendous derby triumph over neighbours Ackworth in the opening round of the Senior Cup, 44-12, with man-of-the-match Stan Smith scoring four tries.

There was a huge crowd for the second round at Sharlston for the visit of current Premier Division leaders and Yorkshire Cup holders Townville. Rovers went on the offensive from the outset. Good defence forced errors from the Townville players. From one, Sharlston took the scrum and, on the last tackle, Mark Reeves passed to Tony Palmer for the opening try in the corner. Two holding down offences in quick succession cost Dave Brown a spell in the sin-bin and Townville used the extra man to cross for a converted try. Wayne Appleby added a drop-goal to edge Townville further ahead.

Rovers took the initiative on Brown's return. Andy Booth took players over the line with him and Stuart Bailey converted for an 11-7 lead at half-time. Stout defending by the home side denied Townville early in the second half, but on 51 minutes they touched down to level the scores.

Reeves tried a drop-goal and improvised with a cheeky chip and regather, but Stan Smith was unable to take the scoring pass. On 64 minutes Reeves did manage a drop goal for a 12-11 lead. But Townville's Dean Yelland scored a decisive try to regain the

Sharlston celebrate winning the Guilfoyle Cup – but without the Cup. It was not presented due to the match being abandoned.

lead after which the visitors stepped up the late-game pace and secured their place in the next round with a final match clinching try. Andy Palmer was Sharlston's man-of-the-match in a 19-12 defeat.

Sharlston had a relatively easy passage to the final of the Guilfoyle Open Cup with wins over Ryhill 18-0, Brookhouse 36-12 and Eastmoor Dragons 46-16 in the semi-final. Sharlston's opponents in the final were Westgate Redoubt and the match was played at Dewsbury's Ram Stadium.

However, the final had to be abandoned. The referee called a halt to proceedings just before half-time after the game erupted into violence. Two players from Westgate Redoubt had already been sin-binned and when a third was sent-off the referee was seen to be manhandled by Westgate players, which resulted in the immediate abandonment. The match was stopped with Sharlston Rovers leading 14-2.

Kev Dickens had nosed Westgate in front after a couple of minutes, but Mark Reeves scored with a penalty and on nine minutes Dave Brown broke the try deadlock. Reeves converted for an 8-2 lead.

Reeves added a second penalty awarded for a high tackle, and just after the half-hour Andy Martin scored Sharlston's second try, to put them in the driving seat 14-2. No trophies or medals were presented on the night. It was a sad end to a much improved season. There was a history of rough play between these two sides. In 1994-95 the Saturday Cup Final had to be abandoned when violence broke out.

11. Into the new Millennium

2000-2001

The new millennium was to be the start of a wave of success for the club. Fast-forwarding to 2006 and the conclusion of this history, this period from 2000 to 2006 will be regarded as among the best in the club's history, with a team capable of beating the top teams in the amateur game and some professional outfits as well.

This season the club was in the Yorkshire League Premier Division, facing East Hull, Stanley Rangers, Queens, Bilton Sullys (Hull), Pudsey, Hunslet Warriors, Dewsbury Celtic, Norland Sharks and Townville.

Ian Bragger had done a good job as player-coach, but resigned due to work commitments. The committee swooped and appointed Dean Blankley and Gordon Long as joint coaches, both former Bramley players and they introduced a professional attitude to the club. They brought in Gary Whittaker from Dudley Hill, Mick Harrison from Featherstone Rovers, Dave Lee from Dewsbury Rams and James Lowe from Normanton Knights and looked to have a good squad.

The team warmed up for the coming season with a fine 58-10 friendly win at Halifax side, Boothtown Terriers, Stan Smith leading the way with five tries.

In the league, inspired by man-of-the-match Mark Reeves with two tries and four goals, Rovers had a dream start to the campaign, beating Hull-based side Bilton Sullys in a very competitive encounter 20-14.

They started well at home to East Hull, but were ultimately second best in an exciting match. Rovers led 13-2 at half time, but had to reshuffle after Reeves and Richardson suffered injuries and in the second half Hull gained the ascendancy, winning 22-13.

Dean Blankley scored a hat trick of tries at Norland Sharks, but Rovers had to wait until five minutes from time of an enthralling clash before they scored the points that left them victorious.

A forceful first half was decisive for Rovers after a second half comeback by Stanley Rangers almost saw them snatch a draw. Rovers were 18-4 up at the interval, but could only add another four in the second half. As Stanley closed in the pace and tempo grew faster and tempers began to fray, with Scholey flattening Blankley off the ball and receiving a yellow card. Soon after this Brown and Scholey received their marching orders after a clash. With Ripley off injured and Brown sent off, Rovers were under pressure but hung on for a 22-16 victory.

A series of silly penalties and spilled possession left Rovers trailing 10-2 at East Hull but they bounced back to take the points on Humberside. The scores were level five minutes from time until Dave Brown scored the match-winning try, scooping the ball off the ground and brushing players aside for the score.

Two errors cost Sharlston victory at home to Townville in a tough clash. Five minutes from half-time Sharlston were ahead 6-4, Long was sin binned and Rovers were caught offside. Townville levelled the scores with the penalty.

Dave Lee, in Long's absence, had a penalty chance to restore Sharlston's lead on half-time, but missed. Rovers tackled their hearts out in the third quarter, but on the hour Townville crossed for the decisive try. Sharlston elected to run the ball out of trouble instead of kicking and one pass too many gifted possession to Townville who scored a converted try. Tempers flared briefly resulting in the visiting scrum-half going to the sin-bin and Sharlston's Lee being sent-off. The result was a 12-6 home defeat.

A fortnight later at Townville, Sharlston played good rugby, but lapses in concentration meant that they returned from the match with nothing in terms of points. Sharlston scored six tries to Townville's five, but still lost by three points, 31-28.

Rovers put on a stunning show at previously unbeaten Hunslet Warriors and left the title race wide open with an 8-6 victory. They are now only four points adrift of leaders Townville and one point behind fourth placed Hunslet Warriors.

Against Norland, Sharlston started the stronger of the two sides but a second half surge by Norland gained them a point. Trailing 12-4 at the break, Norland looked more confident in the second half and on 50 minutes got back into the game when winger Kevin Short raced 80 metres for a try. Hussey converted. Four minutes later and now looking the stronger side, Norland went ahead when Lee Hutchins touched down, Hussey again adding the goal. But in injury time Sharlston salvaged a point when Mark Reeves forced his way over for the equalising try. The conversion was missed

Sharlston's first half dominance laid the base for their 42-18 triumph over mid-table rivals Queens. Rovers raced into a 30-0 lead after 30 minutes and had three tries disallowed.

A sizzling first half display against Stanley Rangers, with a 52-10 win put Rovers in with a chance of the Premier Division title. They remained five points behind the leaders Townville, but had four games in hand.

A tremendous team performance against Dewsbury Celtic maintained the pressure on the teams at the top. Leading 20-0 at half-time, Rovers had dominated from the start and did not allow the visitors a chance, running out winners 32-4.

A strong first half performance at Bilton Sullys kept Rovers in the title hunt. Leading 28-8 at half time with tries from Whitaker with two, Smith, Reeves and Brown and four goals from Reeves, Sharlston only scored four points in the second half with a Dave Brown try. Sullys replied with three tries to give the score some respectability.

Rovers put in a towering performance against Pudsey with a 66-26 victory to go top of the Division. Rovers scored 11 tries and took advantage of fellow title chasers Hunslet Warriors losing at Norland. The match between Rovers and Hunslet at Back o' t' wall could decide who would be the champions. Hunslet were level on points with Rovers, but had played one game less.

Sharlston then won 22-10 at Pudsey to set up the confrontation with Hunslet Warriors.

But the title was not to be for Rovers. They were just pipped for Championship title in a game that was a credit to the Premier Division. Hunslet settled quickly and applied early pressure to force a drop-out, then a penalty, which they kicked for a 2-0 lead. Rovers gained in confidence and on 13 minutes Mark Reeves levelled with a penalty. Moments later they were in front. Dean Blankley and Reeves exchanged passes for the latter to touch down. Martin Rowse dropped a goal for the visitors. Reeves then chipped through for Peter Richardson to score, but the referee instead awarded a penalty for obstruction on Reeves, which he converted.

Sharlston extended their lead with a penalty on 47 minutes. The Warriors spun the ball about at every opportunity and on 53 minutes were rewarded with a try, converted by Dean Creasser. Rovers defended desperately and despite tiring in the heat managed to keep the Warriors out until Rowse levelled with a drop- goal in the 65th minute. Five minutes later he nosed the visitors- ahead while Sharlston had a couple of tilts at the line in the closing minutes. Hunslet finally sealed the match with a converted try in the fourth minute of stoppage time.

The team's final record was 12 wins and a draw from 16 matches. In the end of season play-offs, Sharlston reached the final through a tough 26-15 home win over Townville. Mark Reeves scored a try and four goals for Rovers who were seeking their third trophy of the season. There were also tries from Dean Blankley, Graham Fisher and Dave Brown. Gordon Long also landed a conversion. In the final Sharlston would meet with champions Hunslet Warriors who beat Pudsey 28-16 in their semi-final.

Sharlston Rovers 12 Hunslet Warriors 26
Premier Division Top Four final

After a magnificent season this final against champions Hunslet Warriors was one match too many for Sharlston. Rovers, winners of the Brian McDermott Memorial City Plasterers Cup and the Guilfoyle Plant Cup, had their eyes on a remarkable treble.

They started the game as though they really believed they could achieve this. It took only five minutes for them to assert their authority. Hunslet, under pressure conceded penalties and Rovers worked their way into a threatening position.

Strong drives by Tony Palmer, Dave Lee and Gordon Long drew in the Hunslet defence and Graham Fisher scored the opening try.

Rovers continued to dominate and after 15 minutes increased their lead. Dean Blankley shook off Hunslet defenders to score a fine try. Dave Lee converted for a 10-0 lead. However, in the 20th minute, influential Gordon Long caught a Hunslet boot in the tackle and had to leave the field. His departure was a blow for Sharlston and they suffered another a few minutes later when Blankley was forced to leave the field with an injury. The loss of two key players at such a crucial time handed the initiative to Hunslet and they took advantage to score a converted try in the 30th minute. Rovers were now under increasing pressure and two Hunslet penalties levelled the scores at 10-10.

A Dave Lee penalty gave the Rovers some respite and the lead once again, but Hunslet looked more impressive at the start of the second half. They quickly added a converted try to lead 16-12. Rovers had a player sin-binned and conceded another penalty which stretched Hunslet's lead to 18-12.

Dave Brown went close for Rovers but back came Hunslet with a try and penalty to put the match beyond Rovers' reach. Dave Brown and Duncan Jackson tackled their hearts out for Rovers before another penalty crowned Hunslet's victory.

Cup competitions

There was a first round exit from the Senior Cup when a last gasp injury time try robbed the Rovers of a hard earned victory over Townville. Deep in stoppage time all the Rovers had to do was hold the ball, but Booth spilled possession on the last tackle. Hardy threw out a long pass and Robert Dow looped around the defence for the match-winning try. Townville won 16-13.

Rovers put up a tremendous effort at Farnsworth to overcome good Widnes-based opponents in the second round of the BARLA National Cup. The game was decided with a last gasp penalty try. Sharlston's fitness told in the later stages, as did good prompting from both Long and Dean Blankley. Smith put in a series of strong runs and Brown and Ripley forced Farnsworth on the back foot. Blankley then knocked players away as he headed for the line, but had the ball knocked from his grasp illegally according to the referee, who awarded a penalty try, converted by Long for victory. Rovers had to hold on to their one point advantage through eight minutes of stoppage time.

Rover's flirtation with the National Cup ended in round three, but not before they gave Castleford Panthers a real fright. The Panthers got into their stride quickly and were on the scoreboard after only four minutes through a try from Pete Thornton, who went on to score a hat trick.

Turning round with an eight point deficit, Rovers threw everything at Castleford in the second half and on 50 minutes got a well earned try. Prop Andy Booth broke down the middle and second-row Neil Ripley backed up superbly to score. Bailey converted. Panthers rallied six minutes later, for Thornton to complete his hat-trick. Benn added a drop-goal and a penalty within five minutes of each other to seemingly put the tie beyond doubt heading into the last 10 minutes. Rovers' Dean Blankley dribbled over for a try, converted by Bailey. But Sharlston ran out of time.

In the Yorkshire Cup, a first round bye was followed by a 27-23 victory at Pudsey. Rovers grabbed a late winner in extra time. With five minutes remaining Bailey made a break before passing to Pete Richardson, who put Dave Lee over. Rovers' man-of-the-match was Stan Smith. In the third round, Rovers beat Clayton 32-6, with Neil Ripley winning man-of-the-Match. Then followed a trip to Hull, and a 24-12 triumph over Charleston Knights. Stan Smith again was man-of-the-match. In the quarter-final, Rovers faced another Hull-based team, East Hull at home and won 32-18. Stan Smith won his third man-of-the-match award.

But in the semi-final, Lindley Swifts ended Sharlston's hopes of a final with a narrow 7-6 victory. The small Swifts' ground stifled Rovers' natural exuberance with the ball. Sharlston kicked off with the slope and breeze advantage and tore into Lindley. Andy Booth was involved in early crunching tackles that forced possession from Swifts. But the combination of a greasy ball and nerves ended with Sharlston losing possession. Then, aided by a penalty, Lindley stormed up field to force another penalty, but their kick went wide. On 20 minutes Mark Reeves had a chance to score with a penalty, but his kick was off target. Moments later, however, Rovers scored. Drives by Ward, Blankley and Richardson took Sharlston to 20 metres out where Reeves dummied over to score, but was unable to add the goal.

Lindley hit straight back and forced Rovers to defend 18 tackles. Reeves again failed to convert after succumbing to a head high challenge. Booth tried a drop-goal seconds before the break, but missed and Rovers maintained their 4-0 lead. Ten minutes into the re-start home prop Antony Simpson found a gap to level. Shane Whittaker's conversion put Lindley ahead for the first time. Sharlston mounted a comeback with Long and Blankley trying to create openings. On 55 minutes the pressure forced a penalty and Gordon Long kicked the goal to level the scores.

The home full-back, Whittaker, moved upfield and in the 65th minute dropped the decisive one pointer. Dave Ward tried one in reply for Rovers - but the wind blew it back. Sharlston had the last attack of the game from a penalty that took them to within drop- goal distance, but credit must go to Lindley for their defence. Andy Palmer with 22 tackles in the second half was Sharlston's man-of-the-match.

Sharlston kept their hold on the Guilfoyle Cup with a 29-6 victory over Upton. The road to the final was not a hard one, a 24-10 win at Ackworth in the preliminary round, played in atrocious weather conditions and a walk over against Crigglestone All Blacks in round one. A visit to Stanley in the semi-final followed.

With a 22-14 lead on 65 minutes they were too far ahead when Blankley raced through and grubber kicked for Andy Booth to touch down by the upright. Reeves added the extras. On 72 minutes Rovers completed the scoring when Reeves kicked a penalty.

Sharlston Rovers 29 Upton 6
Guilfoyle Plant Ltd Cup Final

Holders Sharlston clinched the game in the last 15 minutes to retain the Guilfoyle Plant Ltd Cup at the Lionheart Stadium, Featherstone at the expense of Upton. Man-of-the-match Mark Reeves opened the scoring with a 35 yard penalty after 10 minutes.

Gordon Long crossed in the corner after Sharlston had spurned two chances. Then after 30 minutes Reeves chipped forward, regathered and touched down for a self-converted try to lead 12-0.

Upton hit back and Steve Froggatt scored two minutes later. Mark Walsh added a penalty conversion for a 12-6 Sharlston lead at half-time.

Upton piled on the pressure after the break, but Rovers weathered the storm and after Reeves had missed a drop-goal attempt he scored his second try, which he also converted.

Reeves kicked a drop-goal just before the hour to make it 19-6. Upton rallied before the final 20 minutes when Sharlston pulled away with a stunning try by Gary Whittaker and a final try by Dave Lee from a Reeves kick. Reeves kicked the final conversion.

City Plasterers Cup

Sharlston returned home victorious after a thrilling encounter with Stanley Rangers in the first round. Leading 12-0 just after half-time, Rovers looked to be cruising and when the home scrum-half was sent-off for dissent things looked bleak for Stanley. But when Rovers hooker Jackson was despatched to the sin bin, Stanley hit back. Eight minutes from time hooker Scholey scored and with only three minutes left on the clock Rangers created space for Wright to score. Rovers held on through five minutes stoppage time.

Last season Crigglestone All Blacks knocked Sharlston out of this competition in the first round. This season the two met in the semi-final and it was a very different result as Rovers crushed the All Blacks 42-0, after a 22-0 half-time lead. Brown and Tony Palmer put in mammoth tackling stints for Rovers while Johnny Mullaney caught the eye in the second half, but all three were eclipsed by a match winning performance from Gary Whittaker.

The other finalists were Upton and Sharlston were hoping to complete a double over the Pontefract team having already defeated them in the Guilfoyle Cup.

Sharlston Rovers 34 Upton 8

Upton started the game at Belle Vue well and took the lead on two minutes with a Stuart McCone penalty. But Rovers found their rhythm after 10 minutes when a planned move saw Mark Reeves go over. They increased their lead after 18 minutes when Stan Smith broke from inside the Rovers half, fed Pete Richardson, who sent Andy Martin in for a converted try. Rovers then took control and began to force Upton back. A drive up to the 20 metre line saw Dean Blankley slip through Upton's ranks for a goaled try which made it 16-2. Sharlston were now in top gear and Blankley turned try provider by feeding Mark Reeves, who chipped through for Gary Whittaker to score in the corner.

Rovers started the second half in blistering form with a Mark Reeves try. He converted. His long pass found Whittaker who fed Graham Fisher, who beat off three tacklers to score. Rovers had a try disallowed, and then Upton's substitute Dave Froggatt scored a fine try. Man-of-the-match Mark Reeves had the final say with a penalty.

Supporters

Above: Former players Dave Betts, John Long, Gordon Long and Ritchie Davies, now regular supporters of the team.

Left: Doug Greaves – a wonderful supporter of the club, generous with sponsorship of shirts and match balls, and helpful in many other ways.

Below: Behind the scenes on match days – Wendy Taylor, June Redshaw, Mary Davies and Jill Shepherd in the cabin before the new tea rooms were built.

Sharlston's cup wins in 2000-2001

Left: The Guilfoyle Cup winning team.

Below: The Brian McDermott Memorial City Plasterers Cup winning team (Both photos: *Wakefield Express*)

Man-of-the-match Mark Reeves and captain Stan Smith celebrate after the 29-6 Guilfoyle Cup win over Upton. (Photo: *Wakefield Express*)

2001-02

To start the season, in July Sharlston won the Wakefield 7s at Crigglestone in a final that was abandoned after an alleged assault on a touch judge. Rovers were beating Stanley Rangers 22-0 when there was an alleged incident between a touch judge and a spectator. The game was abandoned late in the second half by the referee and after consultation with both sides it was decided to let the result stand. Sharlston's route to the final included victories over Crofton Cougars and Horbury Hornets.

There were high hopes for the new season in the Yorkshire League Premier Division. Coaches, Gordon Long and Dean Blankley introduced more new players in Matt Foster and Jason Ramshaw from the Keighley club, together with Steve Froggatt and Simon Raybould. It was a good season, but also a frustrating one. Rovers were just pipped for the Championship title again and there was the disappointment of two semi-final cup defeats, both inflicted by Westgate Redoubt, in one week.

One of the highlights of the season was Rovers' appearance in the prestigious Yorkshire Cup Final, last won by the club in 1948-49. Their end of season heavy schedule finally caught up with them and injuries to key players forced them to field depleted sides in crucial games. The team deserved better rewards for their efforts.

In the League, Sharlston started their campaign with a stylish 32-16 win against Norland Sharks. It took a strong second half performance to secure the spoils at Stanley Rangers. Trailing 9-2 after 30 minutes, Rangers continued to press but on half-time Rovers stole in for a stunning try. Chris McDermott put in the ball-dislodging big hit; Johnny Mullaney picked up and fed Steve Froggatt for the try. Sharlston's Ian Lingard was a handful for the home side. At 17-13 Stanley still had a chance, but a quick take from a play-the-ball saw Froggatt power over with three defenders on him for the decisive try. With five minutes left, Long chipped over for full-back Pete Richardson to make the game safe.

Rovers lost their 100 percent league record to a rejuvenated East Hull side coached by Bradford Bulls star Lee Radford, although the 17 point winning margin flattered the home side, who had turned round 15-6 in front.

A week later Rovers snatched an injury time draw at home to title challengers Batley Victoria. Batley shook Rovers with two early tries in the second half to go 14-10 up. Sharlston battled on, but it took until the last 10 minutes to get on top. With the game well into injury time Sharlston attacked again and this time it paid off with Richardson scoring in the corner, but the conversion missed.

Four-try Matt Foster led the Rovers to a comfortable 38-19 victory at Queens, the first coming after only five minutes. Rovers fought back from 12-0 down at Stanningley to pinch the win and stay on track for the Championship.

Rovers returned to league action after a six week break due to cup commitments, but were pipped at home to Dewsbury Celtic despite a good start. The visitors were ahead five minutes from half-time, but the introduction of Reeves was effective as he latched on to a long pass from Jackson to score from 60 yards. Long missed the conversion to leave the score at 10-10 at half-time. The second half was tight and the deadlock was broken after 25 minutes when Dewsbury added a drop goal. Rovers were dealt a further blow after losing their hooker Jackson with a suspected fractured cheekbone. But they continued to press through Palmer and Leake. Celtic scored a converted try to establish a 17-10 lead with just eight minutes left. Rovers then threw everything at the visitors. Harrison broke through and fed Richardson who linked with his skipper, Smith, to score out wide, but Long missed a difficult kick. This was the final score of the game.

March was a busy time for Rovers with six victories from six matches. Stanley Rangers were edged out 14-12 in a close derby encounter at Sharlston. Rovers came from behind twice to beat Leeds outfit Queens at Sharlston. A depleted side moved into fourth place with a fine win at relegation threatened Hull side Bilton Sullys. Rovers were boosted by the return of hooker Duncan Jackson.

Rovers kept the pressure on their rivals in the Premier Division title race with a hard fought win over Pudsey. The man-of-the- match award went to Gordon Long for a near faultless display.

Easy victories against Batley Victoria, 36-10, and Bilton Sullys, 46-10, saw Rovers three points behind leaders East Hull with two games in hand. A cancelled game against Stanningley due to snow was followed by a 26-12 win at Norland Sharks and a midweek win at Dewsbury Celtic kept Rovers' title hopes alive, but they had to work hard for the points. Rovers produced a sound performance at Pudsey in the season's last away game. A new half-back pairing of Ripley and Leake looked impressive. They were top of the table and faced long time leaders East Hull in a winner takes all match.

However, Rovers suffered their first defeat since the Yorkshire Cup final on New Year's Eve when they lost at home 34-10 in front of a large crowd and missed out on the league title. The heavy end of season schedule caught up with them and they never quite got into their stride. They didn't concede the title easily but the visitors absorbed their pressure and were able to reply with points. It was a disappointing end to the league campaign, but they hoped to bounce back in the semi-final play-off game against Queens. The final league record was 13 wins and a draw from 17 matches.

Sharlston Rovers 6 Queens 26
Championship semi-final play-off.

Sharlston put in a brave performance against Queens, but it wasn't enough to take them through to the final. Rovers started well, making inroads thanks to Martin and Carter, with Fisher and Davies leading a formidable defence. But it was the visitors who broke the deadlock after five minutes when a break from a scrum left the home side wrong footed. This spurred Rovers into their best spell of the game as Richardson responded with some classy breaks and Raybould and Long prompted the forwards who responded well. Martin went close after a blockbusting run and Carter was difficult to contain.

Queens then scored a converted try in the 20th minute following a kick through, but this didn't deter the makeshift home side who almost responded through Fisher and then Martin. The Leeds side extended their lead with a penalty before the introduction of Palmer changed the game and his kicking forced the visitors back. But right on half-time, Rovers fell further behind when Queens scored to take an 18-0 lead. Sharlston continued to battle after the break and were rewarded when Smith, Raybould and Fisher forced the visitors to scramble the ball for a drop out.

Then Long broke from a scrum deep in the visitors' half and jinxed his way over for a try which he converted.

Rovers almost added to this when Smith was held up over the line, but shortly afterwards Queens intercepted the ball deep in their own half and broke to score out wide. The Leeds side wrapped up the victory with their final try on 65 minutes. Rovers battled gamely on and both Davies and Richardson went close before the end. The Motorcity man-of-the-match award was shared by Fisher and Martin but all the players deserve credit for their commitment and effort.

The Yorkshire Cup

Sharlston met Elland in the Yorkshire Cup Final at Headingley on New Year's Eve. It was exactly 50 years since they last played in the final of this prestigious competition. Then they lost to Middleton Old Boys.

Rovers had reached the fifth round of the competition without a struggle. They dispatched Lindley Swifts in the quarter-finals. Their semi-final opponents whose home was the famous Fartown ground were the Huddersfield outfit St Joseph's, whose history goes back to 1906-07 and were coached by father and son team Marcus and Peter Southwell.

Sharlston won the match 14-8, but they never quite hit top gear. They were almost back to full strength and entered the game full of confidence. The home side opened the scoring with a drop- goal after four minutes. Rovers hit back and Long's pass to Tony Palmer almost led to a score, but the big forward was stopped just short. Again they almost registered a try after Blankley's kick through was nearly finished off by the wingman Fisher before Long kicked a penalty to put Sharlston on the scoresheet.

Pressure from Richardson was supported by Martin and then Smith and Jackson made some telling breaks, but the visitors could not turn this into points. Blankley had the ball ripped from his grasp for what would have been a good try on 15 minutes.

Strong defence by Leake and Harrison kept the hosts at bay as they were restricted to a single penalty goal in the 22nd minute. The game became increasingly frantic with Rovers' Booth just stopped short of the line. St Joseph's were also making breaks.

On the half-hour Rovers were rewarded for their persistence following a clever kick by Palmer. The home side kicked the ball dead. From the drop-out Rovers attacked with Booth and Harrison going close before Smith gave Long a pass for him to score the opening try. He converted to take Rovers into the half-time break 8-3 up.

Sharlston started the second period in great form and were denied three try-scoring chances by the home defence. Blankley was causing problems for the home side and his breaks were well supported by Booth and Ripley.

Both teams lost a player in the 50th minute following a brief altercation. Rovers again went close, but it was St Joseph's who hit back with a period of pressure resulting in an unconverted try and a drop-goal to level the scores at 8-8.

Full-back Richardson scored what was the decisive score on 73 minutes when he reacted quickly to a pinpoint kick by Blankley. For the last few minutes the visitors endured an onslaught from the Huddersfield side. A covering tackle from Smith with two minutes left clinched Rovers' win. There were impressive performances from Jackson, Leake, Smith and man-of-the-match Long. However, Rovers could not repeat this success in the final.

Sharlston Rovers 6 Elland 17
Tetley's Yorkshire Cup Final

Rovers dominated much of the game, but lost 17-6 in front of a 2,071 crowd at Headingley. Player-coach Dean Blankley told the Yorkshire Evening Post's Peter Smith that the team were "absolutely gutted" to miss out on the prestigious trophy. He vowed "We have got to lift ourselves and have a good go in the Yorkshire League - and I fancy a good run in the National Cup. We are going to use this as a learning curve. We will bounce back, we are too good not to. We didn't take our chances. Elland hung in there and took theirs. They defended well, but in the first half, apart from their try, we were

The 2001-2002 Yorkshire Cup run

Above: The Sharlston team that played St Joseph's in the semi-final at Fartown: Back: Mick Wilkinson, Chris McDermott, Richard Pajor, Dean Blankley (coach), Neil Ripley, Stuart Bailey, Mick Harrison, Andy Booth, Gordon Long (coach), Graham Fisher, Andy Palmer, John Lingard (sponsor), Pete Redshaw; Front: Andy Martin, Pete Richardson, Chance Leake, Duncan Jackson, Dave Brown, Stan Smith, Craig Cooper, Tony Palmer, Adam Thaler.

The Sharlston players being introduced before the Cup Final.

battering their line. It was the same in the second half, but we lacked a few ideas at times."

The match was deadlocked until the 66th minute, when Elland's 11 point rally finished Sharlston's challenge. Sharlston were on top for the opening period, conceded a breakaway try and then dominated the rest of the first half, and pulled level with a wonderful individual try from Dean Blankley.

In the second half Sharlston missed three penalties before Elland clinched the match. Elland's success was clinched by substitute Adam Oldroyd who kicked a drop-goal and scored their third try. His mother, Mary, wife of BARLA chairman, Maurice Oldroyd, died suddenly less than two months before the game.

Sharlston Rovers: Richardson, Fisher, Ripley, Smith, Martin, Long, Blankley, Harrison, Jackson, T. Palmer, A. Palmer, Leake, Brown.
Substitutes: Reeves, McDermott, Booth, Cooper.
Elland: Moore, Redford, Manning, Coulter, Fairbank, Malik, Bailey, M. Shickell, Ainley, A. Shickell, Midgeley, Hood, Shackleton.
Substitutes: Oldroyd, Butterworth, Simpson, Bowker.

Sharlston welcomed back two long term absentees, Lee and Whittaker, for their home first round tie against Pennine Premier League Birkenshaw in the National BARLA Cup and had a 36-12 win. Whittaker crowned his comeback with four tries.

They had to fight hard to gain a 14-4 victory at Chequerfield in round two, though they started well, scored after four minutes and never lost the lead. The man-of-the-match was Raybould who worked tirelessly in both defence and attack.

An impressive crowd witnessed a marvellous rugby league spectacle between Sharlston and the Conference League side Featherstone Lions in round three. Lions settled quickly while Rovers required time to get to grips with the faster pace of their opponents. Featherstone took the lead on 14 minutes, Jon Agar drawing two defenders and slipping a great pass to Chris Morgan for the touchdown. Scott Limb converted.

Rovers, however, settled after the score and it was now the Lions turn to defend. Good running by McDermott, Harrison and Kelly gave Sharlston space and on 25 minutes Dean Blankley stole the ball in the tackle just outside the opposition 20 metre area and passed for Dave Lee to put Gary Whittaker over in the corner.

Sharlston were now troubling their near neighbours' defence, while hard tackling denied the Lions room. As half-time approached Rovers' Peter Richardson scored in the corner, too far out for Gordon Long to convert. He made up for these misses with a well struck penalty in first half stoppage time to give Rovers a 10-6 advantage.

Against the slope and elements Rovers might have been forgiven for falling on to the back foot, but, after denying Lions an early score in the corner through expert cover tackling, the home side made all the early running. Rovers were camped in opposition territory but decisive events occurred between the 65th and 70th minutes. Blankley made a superb break, but a magnificent cover tackle held him on his back over the line. Rovers were looking for the killer try and threw out a pass which was intercepted by winger Dave Raybould who ran 90 metres for the score. Limb converted. Rovers attacked, but it was the visitors who got the final score - deep into stoppage time - when Limb forced his way over.

Sharlston bowed out of the Challenge Cup at the first round stage when they visited Conference high fliers Woolston Rovers, but not without a fight. Despite missing several key players through injury, Rovers entered this cup tie with confidence. But Woolston caught them cold in the third minute when a clever kick through led to the opening converted score.

Woolston increased their lead to eight points on five minutes with a penalty for offside. Sharlston overcame this early setback and made good progress with some fine enterprising rugby.

Andy Palmer's strong run following a neat offload by Tony Palmer left the Woolston defenders trailing in his wake and only a desperate last-ditch tackle by the home full-back could stop him close to the line. But from a quick play-the-ball Stan Smith darted over for a deserved try, converted by Long on 12 minutes.

Flying winger Martin was stopped short of the line before Long slotted home a drop-goal to reduce the deficit to just one point on 34 minutes. Brown scattered would be tacklers in a storming run and at this stage Sharlston had the home side worried. With Rovers camped in the home side's half a score was always possible, but it came at the wrong end as the Woolston winger broke through from deep and this led to a fine converted try just seconds from half-time.

Woolston started the second half as they had the first, kicking through to score with only three minutes gone. Good work from Carter and Brown took Rovers close before Long fed Booth, who crashed over for an excellent score. Bailey, Harrison and both Palmers made good breaks and with man-of-the-match Blankley running the show it was hard to tell which was the Conference team.

Woolston increased their lead with a fourth converted try against the run of play on 65 minutes. Rovers hit back and Lingard's speed was causing endless problems for the home defence. After 73 minutes Blankley's exact kick to the corner saw full-back Richardson score. Long's touch line conversion just missed. Rovers kept the pressure on, but were unable to find a way through the home defence. Brown, Booth and Martin all had chances but Woolston kicked a penalty to win 28-15.

In the Senior Cup, despite a battling performance with key players missing a tricky tie at East Hull was always a challenge and Rovers were unable to progress beyond the second round, going down 22-14.

Westgate Redoubt completed a semi-final double over Sharlston with victories in the City Plasterers Cup and the Guilfoyle Cup.

Westgate Redoubt 17 Sharlston 4
City Plasterers Cup Semi-Final

The first 20 minutes were tight with Moran's missed penalty the closest either side came to breaking the deadlock. An Andy Wright drop-goal gave Westgate a slender 1-0 lead. Sharlston had the chance to snatch the advantage but, with the line open, the last pass was put down. Rovers upped their game and the hosts withstood 10 minutes of pressure before gradually working their way upfield thanks to fine work from Malcolm, Smith and Hepworth. The ball reached stand-off Jamie Beckett and he battled his way over despite the attention of three defenders. Moran missed the kick, but Westgate went in at half-time 5-0 up.

After the break Sharlston's bad kick-off gave the home side a penalty and Andy Wright scored to open up a 7-0 lead. Westgate continued to put the pressure on their illustrious hosts and were rewarded when, from a scrum, Beckett's penetrating run uncovered Moran who rounded the winger to score in the corner. Wright converted with a superb kick from the touchline, 13-0. But Sharlston weren't done and took advantage of their hosts' only lapse of the game when stand-off Raybould burst through to score an unconverted try. The stage was now set for a great finish but Westgate ended hopes of a Sharlston revival when, despite being down to 11 men, they scored another try.

Sharlston Rovers 11 Westgate Redoubt 13
Guilfoyle Plant Cup Semi-Final

Westgate pressed their hosts from the kick-off and went close on several occasions but after 10 minutes of play all the visitors had to show was a Stu Moran drop-goal. Sharlston hit straight back when their hooker found a gap to score and the conversion gave Rovers a 6-1 lead after 15 minutes.

Westgate responded with some attractive rugby through Hepworth, Hirst and Wright and they were rewarded when Wright's pass found Gary Smith who forced his way over from five yards. Moran missed the kick but his side had edged into the lead 7-6.

The see-saw battle continued as the home side made good ground and the ball then reached player-coach Gordon Long whose pass sent prop Bailey in for a fine try. The extras were added to give Sharlston a 10-7 half-time advantage. After the break they increased their lead with a towering drop-goal and the hosts could have stretched away further when Long broke clear but his pass to winger Fisher was put down with the line begging.

Westgate battled their way back and piled on the pressure in the last 15 minutes. Hepworth went over but his effort was ruled out for obstruction and then Smith went close and Andy Wright was held up over the line. But eventually they broke through when Matt Hudson's thundering run drove him forward and he fed Wright who romped over with just two minutes remaining. The scores were tied at 11-11 but Moran's conversion kicked Westgate into the Final.

Rovers and Streethouse played for the Jason Clough Memorial Trophy. All proceeds went to the Simon Tuffs Appeal. Simon had received a bad injury on holiday

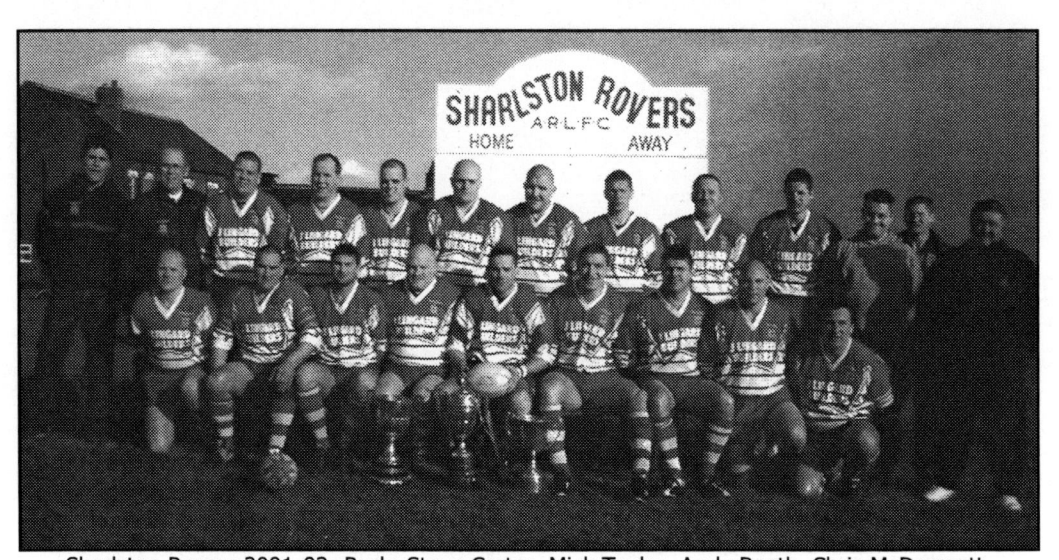

Sharlston Rovers 2001-02: Back: Steve Carter, Mick Taylor, Andy Booth, Chris McDermott, Neil Ripley, Lee Kelly (snr), Mick Harrison, Graham Fisher, Craig Cooper, Garry Whittaker, Richard Pajor, Ritchie Davies, John Lingard; Front: Pete Richardson, Tony Palmer, Simon Raybould, Andy Martin, Stan Smith, Chance Leake, Dean Blankley (coach), Dave Lee, Gordon Long (coach).

2002-03

Dean Blankley, who had been sharing the coaching duties with Gordon Long, called it a day and left the club early in the season to concentrate on his building business. Dean joined the club from the Dudley Hill amateur club but had played professionally with Bramley and Castleford. He had a wealth of experience in the game and the club had benefited from it.

A notable newcomer to the club was Martyn Wood, a classy player who had played professionally with Halifax, Sheffield Eagles, Keighley and Hull KR. He was a Challenge Cup winner with Sheffield Eagles in 1998. Martyn was to play a major part in Rovers' success.

This season began with high hopes and enthusiastic support and several league matches in the Yorkshire League Premier Division are worth recalling.

Rovers gave a majestic display and dethroned Queens 25-6, with Carl Sayer faultless in attack and defence and taking the man-of-the-match award. They went to Stanley and battled back from 10 points down to take the spoils.

In the New Year, Sharlston's fine form continued with victory against Batley Victoria as they stretched their lead at the top of the table. East Hull came to Sharlston and although they got off to a flying start, when Martyn Wood produced a fine pass to put Gareth Davies in, Rovers' lead was short lived as East Hull hit back and took the points with a comfortable 36-14 win. The high penalty count and the sin binning of Dave Lee did not help the Sharlston cause. The Humbersiders did the double over Rovers, having brought to an end their fine run of victories with a 16-8 defeat at East Hull in February. Rovers were then third in the table, behind East Hull and Queens.

Rovers travelled to Queens knowing they would face a hard, physical encounter, so they took the game to the hosts. It paid off as the home team were put on the back foot and after five minutes were penalised. Martyn Wood put Sharlston in front. On 10 minutes Queens cut the gap with a drop-goal and then caught the visitors napping as straight from the kick-off the Queens centre raced away and scored a converted try. Queens kept up the pressure and soon after scored again for a 13-2 lead. At this stage Rovers rang the changes and regained control. A good Stan Smith break down the middle put Queens in disarray and from a neat Gordon Long kick Neil Shoesmith beat the defence to score. Queens were rocking and good running from Carl Sayer, Jamie Cox and Neil Shoesmith put them on the back foot, creating the chance for Shaun Taylor to set up Long to score.

Rovers came out for the second half one point adrift and again made inroads into the Leeds side's defence. However, a cross-field kick fell kindly to Queens and their winger raced away to score. Sharlston battled on through Dave Brown and Cox, but Queens were in the ascendancy, scored a converted try and followed it up with another. Rovers never gave up and in injury time Gordon Long's kick was pounced on by Taylor to score his second try, converted by Long. The final result was a 29-19 win for Queens. Rovers made amends for this defeat with a play-off semi-final win at Queens and booked a place in the final.

Queens 10 Sharlston Rovers 18
Premiership semi-final play-off

Rovers controlled the game from the start with good kicking from Martyn Wood forcing Queens back. Lee Lingard, Gareth Davies and Shaun Taylor hounding the Queens defence. There was also good driving forward from Jamie Cox, Neil Shoesmith and Dave Brown. The first score came on 15 minutes when Shoesmith handed off tacklers to score. Martyn Wood added the goal. Rovers continued in charge and another try came when Wood made a break from inside his own half feeding Lingard who sent Stan Smith over, Wood added the goal. He added a penalty shortly afterwards. At the start of the second half Sharlston came under pressure and Queens reduced the lead with two penalties.

Soon after they got a try after an error from Rovers and after adding the goal the match was very close. Queens eventually started giving away penalties which were converted by Wood to leave the score at 10-18 in Rovers favour. Sharlston lost the Final 6-0 to East Hull.

In the cup competitions, a late Elland try knocked visiting Sharlston out of the Challenge Cup at the first stage in a thrilling encounter. Sharlston started stronger but a succession of early penalties provided Elland with a lifeline. On 10 minutes, the Rovers were punished for ball stealing and the home side went ahead with a penalty. Sharlston, prompted by Martyn Wood and Gordon Long, hit back and Stan Smith and Neil Shoesmith were held just short of the line. But they were unable to turn pressure into points and in the 25th minute Elland capitalised on lost possession and gained a footing in the 20 metre area. Their prop evaded several tackles to cross the line for a try which was converted to put them 8-0 up.

With time running out in the first half, Gordon Long kicked a penalty, then in the dying seconds his kick caught Elland out and Keith Brook pounced to make it 8-6. Long's successful conversion squared matters at the break, 8-8.

Rovers started the second period well as Wood put a drop-goal attempt narrowly wide and Long went close with a penalty attempt. With just 10 minutes left Elland broke down the middle to score the crucial try that condemned Sharlston to defeat.

Any hopes Sharlston had of another good run in the Yorkshire Cup and reaching the final for a second successive season were soon ended by a home defeat to Odsal Sedburgh, 20-22. In a dramatic final 10 minutes the visitors scored the winning try and the Rovers had a score disallowed. Odsal had taken the lead in the seventh minute with a converted try but Shaun Taylor responded with a try out wide that Hill just failed to convert. The visitors made it 12-4 with another converted try but Sharlston didn't give up. Dean Blankley then scored under the posts, and converted. But by the break Odsal added a penalty and a drop-goal for a 15-10 lead.

Twelve minutes into the second period, they added another penalty before Sharlston hit their opponents with a double try blast. Classy Martyn Wood scored first, converted by Dave Lee and then man-of-the-match, Andy Martin, went over and although Lee failed to add the extras, Rovers were 20-17 in front. But Odsal fought back and in the 71st minute were rewarded with a try and then, despite Sharlston's efforts, added a drop-goal. In the dying moments Rovers thought they had snatched it but their try was disallowed for a forward pass.

The BARLA National Cup competition brought Conference First Division Hunslet Warriors to Sharlston and the game soon settled into a battle of defences with gaps hard to find. All the scoring came in the second-half and Sharlston's win was sealed in injury time when Long's chip was clipped over the line by Peter Richardson for centre Keith Brook to score, Long adding a touchline conversion for a 14-4 win.

Another Conference side Normanton Knights, provided the opposition at Sharlston in round two and took a 10-0 lead at the interval. The Knights kicked off the second half into a swift wind and the high ball bounced kindly for Rovers full-back Lee Lingard to collect. He deceived the onrushing defenders, broke the line and sprinted downfield to score a great try under the posts, converted by Gordon Long. From the kick-off the ball was blown back towards halfway with the referee awarding a penalty to Sharlston. The home side took full advantage to attack and second rower Neil Shoesmith scored. The conversion was missed and the scores remained level until Long's drop-goal edged Rovers in front. Sharlston consolidated their lead on 65 minutes when winger Andy Martin scored and then made the game safe three minutes later as Lingard burst through to score in the corner for a 19-10 victory.

Rovers had to overcome stiff opposition to reach the fourth round when they visited Queens. Sharlston were dealt a serious blow on the half hour when Lee Lingard chased a chip through and had his progress prematurely halted by the Queens number eight who clashed off the ball with the Sharlston player and was sent off for violent conduct.

Unfortunately Lingard was unable to continue although his side was given some consolation when Gordon Long kicked the resultant penalty. The dismissal had an adverse effect on Sharlston who lost impetus as Queens took the game to the visitors and levelled matters with a penalty before the break.

Queens took the lead in the 47th minute from a penalty and were still ahead with 25 minutes left when Sharlston introduced Martyn Wood and Chance Leake. Wood's distribution and Leake's expansive running punched holes in the Queens defence and Rovers took control. In the 61st minute Leake burst through and Dwaine Byrne put Tony Palmer through to score with Long converting. Queens adding a penalty to make it 8-6 but Sharlston had the final word when Wood sent Gareth Davies on a run from his own 20 metre line. Davies followed it up with a quick play-the-ball to crash over and, with Long adding the goal, a 14-6 victory was secured for Rovers.

Rovers entertained National Conference League Premier Division Oulton Raiders in the fourth round and had an easy passage to the fifth round leading 18-2 at half time and 30-2 at the final whistle.

The run ended in the fifth round, with a 20-16 defeat at home to National Conference Premier Division Skirlaugh. Rovers almost made the semi-final, but Skirlaugh staged a remarkable comeback from 16 points down with 15 minutes left. Sharlston had got off to a dream start when from their first set of six man-of-the-match Gareth Davies raced 75 yards to score under the posts. Gordon Long converted. Skirlaugh missed an easy penalty on 30 minutes. Sharlston then scored from a Long penalty. Soon after he kicked another for offside to give Rovers a 10-0 half-time lead.

The second half started with a Skirlaugh onslaught, but Rovers defended well with full-back Lee Lingard defending well. They weathered the storm and attacked again. A Martyn Wood and Long combination saw the latter held up five yards out. Skirlaugh were caught offside at the play-the-ball but Long narrowly missed the goal. From the drop-out Skirlaugh conceded possession to Neil Shoesmith who made a forceful run. Wood and Long combined with Wood scoring, converted by Long.

Sharlston were 16 points up with 15 minutes to go, but from the kick-off Skirlaugh regrouped and attacked the Rovers line and on the last tackle they scored a converted try to start their comeback. Then a deep kick put Rovers under pressure, they took the ball to halfway but the clearance was charged down and Skirlaugh scored in the corner. With five minutes left the visitors scored near the posts, but missed the conversion before Rovers were penalised from the kick-off and this time Skirlaugh made no mistake.

They converted two more penalties, the second in the fourth minute of added time to end Sharlston's cup dream in incredible fashion and move through to the last four.

In the City Plasterers Cup Rovers reached the final, beating Ryhill Hammers 18-0, then winning 32-6 at Normanton Knights. Rovers then beat Westgate Redoubt in the semi-final 18-10. They met Upton in the final at the Featherstone Rovers ground.

Sharlston Rovers 52 Upton 12
City Plasterers Cup Final

Gareth Davies scored a sensational double hat-trick as Rovers clinched the Brian McDermott Memorial City Plasterers Cup. Davies was named man-of-the-match though he was run close by team mate Martyn Wood who pulled all the strings for Rovers

Sharlston didn't have things all their own way. Davies opened with a hat-trick of tries for Rovers, but none were converted and Upton hit back to trail just 16-12 at half-time. Keith Brook had scored Sharlston's fourth try of the first half.

Sharlston took control after the break then really went to town when Upton's Mark Walsh was sent off for retaliation. Stan Smith, Gordon Long and Andy Booth added three more tries for Sharlston before Davies took the team's try total to 10 with his second hat-trick of the game. Wood added the conversion points.

Westgate Redoubt put Sharlston out of the Open Cup in the semi-final with Stuart Moran bagging all their points in a 10-0 win.

Rovers lost in the Senior Cup at the hands of Stanley Rangers, 32-16, in round one but only after extra time. The scores were level, 16-16, nearing normal time and Sharlston had a chance to reach the second round with a conversion. But they missed the kick, extra time loomed and Stanley took control

Gareth Davies walked off with a hat-trick of trophies at Sharlston Rovers annual presentation night. Also receiving awards from guest of honour Andy Kelly, the Featherstone Rovers coach were Stan Smith, Lee Kelly, Peter Richardson, Jamie Cox, Michael Haigh, Keith Brook, Richard Pajor, Lee Lingard, Craig Cooper, Andy Palmer, Chris Hill, Shaun Taylor, Russ Barlow, Dave Brown, Tony Palmer, Andy Booth, John Brewerton, Neil Shoesmith, and Danny Grimshaw.

The newly formed 'A' team, under player-coach Johnny Brewerton, joined the Yorkshire League Division One. They finished in the bottom half of the table. At times they fielded young and inexperienced sides and suffered heavy defeats, but ended the season in fine style with a victory over Brookhouse.

One triumph for the 'A' team was in the Mark Lindop Memorial Trophy when they beat the first team. The 'A' team conquered their elite side 16-6 in the final of the seven-a-side Wakefield and District Amateur Rugby League tournament at Sharlston.

The 'A' team beat Westgate Redoubt 22-14 and Crigglestone All Blacks 22-18 on their route to the final. The Rovers first team overcame Kinsley and Ryhill Raiders 12-8 in a great qualifier and arch rivals Stanley Rangers 16-10 in the semi-final. Dave Lee, of Sharlston Rovers 'A', was voted player of the tournament.

Jimmy Gittins

In October 2002, Jimmy Gittins, on his debut for the Rovers against Drighlington, sustained a horrific neck injury in a tackle which left him totally paralysed. A fund was set up to raise money for his rehabilitation and there was a magnificent response resulting in a cheque for £19,500 being presented to him. Doctors at Pinderfields Hospital, Wakefield, told Jimmy he would never walk again but after eight months of determined work the 28-year-old from Outwood thrilled doctors and friends alike by walking unaided at the spinal injuries unit.

Billy Wood

Recognition of Billy Wood's long service to the club came when he received a certificate from the Wakefield & District Amateur Rugby League in recognition of his long service to the game. He had played for the club, been captain, and served behind the scenes in many different roles. It was a well deserved award to a loyal and valued club man.

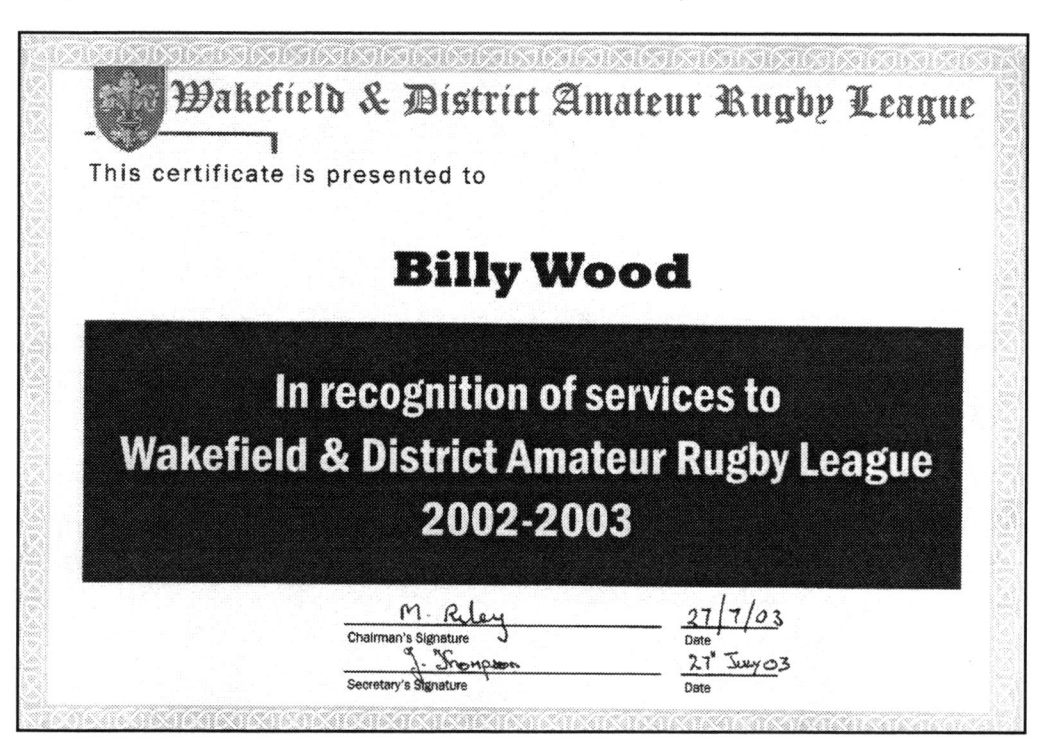

Above: The certificate presented to Billy Wood.

Left: Billy wearing his England cap and holding a French shirt

Right: Clearing the snow so that the team could train before the Yorkshire Cup Final in 2001

Graham Chalkley presenting a cheque for £19,500 to Jimmy Gittins. Back: Dave Lee, Neil Shoesmith, Jamie Cox, Martyn Wood, Chance Leake, Keith Brook, Graham Fisher, Gordon Long (coach), Andy Booth, Phil Golec, Stan Smith; Front: Lee Lingard, Gareth Davies, Danny Grimshaw, Graham Chalkley, Andy Martin, Jimmy Gittins, Dave Brown, Tony Palmer. (Photo: *Wakefield Express*)

Over Forties versus Under Forties

Above: Over forties: Back: Mick Wilkinson, Ken Harris, Gordon Long, Stuart Bailey, Richard Taylor, Johnny Brewerton, Graham Fisher, Nigel Southern, Ian Moverley, Don Goodfellow, Mick Ward; Front: Tommy Mullaney (referee) Dave Ward, Pete Richardson, Ian Lingard, Shaun Wilkinson, Stan Smith. Tony Palmer, Andy Martin.

Below: Under forties: Martin Nunns, Will Easterby, Garry Cross, Shaun Taylor, Russ Barlow, Lee Kelly (Jnr), Gareth Davies, Chris Hill, Steve Hall, Dwain Byrne, Phil Golec, Mick Haigh, James Brickwood, Dave Smith, Rob Radcliffe, Scott Haigh, Simon Hall, Tommy Mullaney (referee)

Teams from the 2002-03 season

Sharlston Rovers celebrate winning the City Plasterers Cup
Back: Mick Taylor, Mick Wilkinson, Lee Kelly (Jnr), Jamie Cox, Keith Brook, Neil Shoesmith,
Tony Palmer, Shaun Taylor, Richard Sharp, Dwaine Burn, Graham Fisher, Pete Redshaw;
Front: Martyn Wood, Gordon Long (coach), Lee Lingard, Dave Brown,
Gareth Davies, Andy Booth, Stan Smith, Andy Martin. (Photo: *Wakefield Express*)

Sharlston Rovers 'A'
Back: Gareth Davies, Mick Haigh, Jamie Cox, Johnny Brewerton (player-coach), Stan Smith,
Andy Booth, Richard Pajor Will Easterby, Carl Wormald, Garry Cross, Andy Palmer;
Front from left: Andy Martin, Ian Lingard, Pete Richardson, Lee Kelly (Jnr), Richard Sharp,
Chris Hobbs, Vanessa Jukes.

2003-04

Under coach Martyn Wood, this was probably Sharlston's best ever season. He was assisted by Chance Leake and Gordon Long, both former professional players. All three enjoyed their early years at Streethouse and were now back together at Sharlston and putting back into the game the years of experience they had acquired between them. Seven trophies, unbeaten in the league, a magnificent Challenge Cup victory and robbed of a place in the Yorkshire Cup Final by a goal that Sharlston's players and supporters believe did not go between the posts

In the Yorkshire League Premier Division they passed the 40 points mark nine times. The only close matches were wins at Batley Victoria, 28-22, and Cutsyke, 32-24. They were worthy champions

After finishing top of the league, Sharlston ran Stanningley ragged in the play-off semi-final, scoring 16 times with Lee Lingard converting 10 along with a try for himself. Rovers' opponents in the final were Queens. It was the second time these two met in a final this season.

Sharlston Rovers 31 Queens 4
Championship Final

Stan Smith opened the scoring on four minutes with a try converted by Lee Lingard. This was followed by a large fracas which was not unexpected between these two sides. When things eventually calmed down both sides started playing rugby. Sharlston were too strong for Queens who really struggled to break Rovers' defensive line.

Martyn Wood then scored with Lingard adding the goal as he did when Gareth Davies scored just after 30 minutes. Wood then dropped a goal on half-time after a period of Sharlston pressure.

After the break Davies and Andy Booth both went over with Lingard converting. Queens scored a try before the end, but never troubled Sharlston. Man-of-the-match was Lee Bettinson, backed up by Lee Kelly and Lingard in a fine team performance.

The Challenge Cup

Every team playing in the game's famous old tournament sets off with a cup dream and for an amateur team playing against professional opposition there is always a chance of causing an upset. Sharlston Rovers did this in 1946 against Workington Town and have appeared in the first (now third) round of the competition on two other occasions, 1935 and 1939. It is still a great achievement when an amateur club beats a professional side.

Rovers' cup journey started with a preliminary round tie at Stanley Rangers and with a 37-18 win Rovers went through to the first round, but had to overcome a monumental effort by Stanley to get there. The lead changed hands several times and despite the efforts of both sides to score the winner, including Wood's drop-goal attempt which hit the post, the score after 80 minutes was 18-all. Extra time caught up with Stanley and Rovers took advantage to run in three tries, all converted, and a Wood drop-goal.

Widnes St Maries, coached by former Great Britain international Bobbie Goulding, were the opposition in the first round. The result was a convincing win for Rovers. It took them 20 minutes to break down the Widnes defence with winger Dale Ferris finishing off a move. After Widnes had a player sent off for swearing at the referee, Sharlston went further ahead when Danny Grimshaw scored from a 25 yard run and Lee

Lingard converted. Before the break Andy Booth passed to Stan Smith, who went over, Lingard converted to leave the score 16-0.

In the second half, Sharlston carried on where they left off and with Martyn Wood leading the way. Five minutes into the second half Keith Brook went over to leave Widnes well in arrears. The game became scrappy towards the end with Rovers having two players sent off and Widnes seeing another dismissed. The home side did get a consolation try.

The second round brought Oldham St Anne's, from three divisions higher than Rovers in the Arriva Trains Conference Premier Division, to Sharlston. The tie lived up to expectations and was a great advert for amateur rugby league. Both teams knew that victory would give them a chance of a lucrative tie against a National League side. The deadlock was broken on 15 minutes when Oldham were penalised and Lee Lingard kicked the goal. Oldham levelled with a penalty, and although Lingard kicked his second penalty, St Anne's ended the half on top as Jackman scored a try, converted by Tyrell.

Danny Grimshaw then scored a try for Rovers, but Lingard missed the kick. Oldham's Jackman dropped a goal to put them ahead, but the introduction of Gordon Long caused the visitors problems and he crossed for the winning try, which was improved by Lingard. The final 10 minutes felt more like 30 for the home side and their fans in a 300 plus crowd but despite St Anne's pressure they held on for a famous victory.

And so Sharlston marched on into round three when the professional teams from National Leagues One and Two joined the competition. The draw was eagerly awaited.

On hearing they had drawn Dewsbury Rams, Martyn Wood said: "After a long career as a professional player I can gage what is needed to win matches and we are not far off. I think we can take them very close and I believe a lot of these players could do a job in a professional side anyway. But it is very difficult for an amateur side to beat a pro side as you would expect. Sharlston have some excellent players particularly in the younger ranks such as Danny Grimshaw, Gareth Davies and Lee Lingard. The level of fitness in the amateur game is much more apparent with players starting strong and then fading but this Sharlston team has a different attitude and are not playing for financial gain, so we will see".

The rules said that the match had to be at a professional club's ground. Featherstone Rovers was chosen because it is near Sharlston's fan base and there are good ties between the clubs.

Another Challenge Cup sensation

The *Yorkshire Evening Post* said that Rovers "overturned the odds in scintillating style with a stirring 30-28 success at Lionheart Stadium." The report said that "Poor Dewsbury were the sacrificial Rams as Sharlston combined inventive attack with determined defence - all backed by a magnificent never-say-die spirit." The crowd was 2,027, the second highest of the third round, and almost 500 more than saw Featherstone's own match against Castleford Lock Lane. Dewsbury led by eight points at one time during the first half, but for much of the match were outplayed. Martyn Wood's experience showed as he created four of Rovers' five tries.

The report recognised the quality of Rovers display: "A couple of costly errors under early bombs apart, Sharlston's ball control was excellent and they kept their discipline far better than their professional rivals, who lacked ideas and seemed shocked by the quality and ferocity of Rovers' play. Veteran substitute Gordon Long produced a splendid all-action display, hooker Lee Bettinson was superb and props Andy Booth and Lee Kelly were towers of strength but Sharlston were a team of heroes."

Rovers scored first after 109 seconds when winger Dale Ferris touched down from Bettinson's kick. Thaler replied for the Rams with a penalty after 14 minutes and two tries in three minutes at the end of the first quarter put them in control. John Waddle and Craig Miles touched down. Thaler kicked one goal.

But Rovers turned the game around with three tries in the final 10 minutes of the first half. First, Wood put Stan Smith in. Then his kick created a try for Danny Grimshaw. Finally Chance Leake scored from Wood's pass. Lee Lingard converted twice to give Rovers a 20-12 lead at the break. He then kicked another penalty before McHugh replied for Dewsbury. Thaler reduced the deficit with a penalty, before Wood's kick deflected to Neil Shoesmith who scored Rovers' fifth try. Lingard converted. Billy Kershaw scored to give Dewsbury hope, but Lingard landed another penalty to make the game safe. Thaler's last minute try, which he converted, was not enough to save them.

Wood told the *Yorkshire Evening Post* that he was "proud" of his team: "Dewsbury threw everything at us, but we can play football and we can dig in when we have to," he said. "Going in eight points ahead up the hill helped, but you have still got to defend it. It was important we scored again in the second half because that meant they had to score twice. We knew they'd cross the line because professional sides should score against amateurs, but it was a case of how many we could keep them to. To score five tries is a great effort, but I wasn't surprised. This is massive for the club and the village and they deserve a big draw against a Super League club in the next round."

Rams coach Andy Fisher recognised Wood's role, and admitted that his team could not counter the former cup winner.

Sharlston Rovers: Shaun Taylor, Lee Lingard, Gareth Davies, Keith Brook, Dale Ferris, Martyn Wood, Danny Grimshaw, Andy Booth. Lee Bettinson, Lee Kelly, Chance Leake, James Ward, Stan Smith.
Substitutes: Gordon Long, Dale Potter, Neil Shoesmith, Carl Sayer.
Dewsbury Rams: Chris Hall, Craig Miles, Wayne McHugh, Ian Kirke, Jon Waddle, Mick Senior, Adam Thaler, Paul Hicks, Darren Robinson, Andy Fisher, Kevin Crouthers, Billy Kershaw, Tim Spears.
Substitutes: Chris Redfearn, Anthony Thewliss, Paul Smith, Ryan Hardy.

Oldham 24 Sharlston Rovers 4

In the fourth round, Sharlston travelled to National League Division One Oldham and lost 24-4. The match was previewed in *The Times* by Christopher Irvine, who interviewed Peter Fox and Graham Chalkley who outlined the history of the club. The prize for the winners of the fourth round tie was a home match with Super League Warrington Wolves. Although Sharlston lost, they gave a courageous display in front of 1,301 fans.

Sharlston's plans were wrecked by an injury in the first minute to full-back Shaun Taylor. He was replaced after eight minutes by Gordon Long, with Stan Smith switching to full-back. Oldham took an early lead from two penalties. Then a penalty from Lee Lingard made the score 4-2 to the National League 1 side. Davies came close to scoring from a Wood kick, then Lingard kicked another penalty to make the score 4-4. On the half hour Rovers' second-row James Ward was sin binned, and Ian Marsh scored a try to put Oldham ahead 8-4 at the break.

Three minutes into the second half, Roden scored for Oldham with Svabic converting. Rovers than lost Lee Kelly with a cut face, and fell further behind when Svabic kicked his third penalty. Marsh and Johnson added further tries, but Sharlston kept their professional opponents at bay for much of the second half, with Chance Leake having an

outstanding game, although Lee Bettinson was man-of-the-match.
Oldham: Gavin Dodd, Will Cowell, James Bunyan, Jon Goddard, Nick Johnson, Simon Svabic, Ian Watson, Steve Molloy, Keith Brennan, Dane Morgan, Lee Doran, Iain Marsh, Lee Marsh.
Subs: Gareth Barber, Neil Roden, Martin McLoughlin, Paul Southern.
Sharlston Rovers: Shaun Taylor, Lee Lingard, Gareth Davies, Keith Brook, Andy Martin, Martyn Wood, Danny Grimshaw, Carl Sayer, Lee Bettinson, Andy Booth, Chance Leake, James Ward, Stan Smith.
Subs: Gordon Long, James Cox, Dale Potter, Lee Kelly.

Yorkshire Cup

In the Yorkshire Cup, Rovers brushed aside Brandsholm 48-13, Cutsyke 34-0 and Drighlington 28-12 - all away from home - in the early rounds of the Yorkshire Cup and had to travel again, to Elland, in the semi-final.

Elland 10 Sharlston Rovers 9
Yorkshire Cup semi-final

Sharlston believed that they were robbed of a place in the Yorkshire Cup Final after Elland were awarded a late penalty to win the tie 10-9. Their players and supporters felt that the kick did not go through the sticks, but the touch judges gave it and the referee could not overrule his assistants. The decision sparked fury among Rovers players' and followers with the club saying the final decision should have been left to the referee.

Elland went ahead on seven minutes before Rovers came back with a try from Gareth Davies. Elland replied after 30 minutes with an unconverted try. Gordon Long put Sharlston ahead again with an unconverted try. The second half was controlled by Rovers but Elland kicked two drop-goals to level the score. After more Sharlston pressure, Martyn Wood dropped a goal to once again give them the lead. Then came the penalty that sealed their fate.

Once again after a good run in the BARLA Cup, it was Conference premier side Skirlaugh who ended Sharlston's hopes, as they did in the same round last season, by just four points.

Sharlston Rovers retained the Brian McDermott Memorial City Plasterers Cup when they defeated Stanley Rangers 36-22. It was a very tight game which looked to be going to Stanley Rangers until the last 20 minutes. Rovers made it a cup double by winning the Unison President's Cup.

Sharlston Rovers 28 Westgate Redoubt 6
Unison President's Cup

Rovers completed a Wakefield and District ARL cup double with this victory. A strong first half performance by the Yorkshire League champions was the difference between the two sides and although Westgate improved after the break they had too much to do.

Sharlston took the lead through Lee Lingard's try which he also converted, but Redoubt hit back to level through Gary Smith with Wayne Hurst adding the goal. Lingard scored again and also added the goal to restore Rovers' lead. From then they never looked back. James Ward's try was converted by Lingard and then a successful penalty by the winger put Sharlston 20-6 in front at half-time.

After the break Redoubt regrouped but despite creating a number of chances were

Sharlston Rovers 30 Dewsbury Rams 28

Third Round Rugby League Challenge Cup 2004

Sharlston Rovers		Dewsbury Rams	
1	S. Taylor	1	Richard Thaler
2	L. Lingard	2	Wayne McHugh
3	G. Davis	3	Steave Beard
4	K. Brook	4	Ian Kirke
5	D. Ferris	5	John Waddle
6	M. Wood	6	Mick Senior
7	D. Grimshaw	7	Chris Redfern
8	A. Booth	8	Paul Hicks
9	L. Bettinson	9	Adam Thaler
10	L. Kelly	10	Anthony Thewliss
11	C. Leake	11	Billy Kershaw
12	J. Ward	12	Tim Spears
13	S. Smith	13	Kevin Crouthers
14	G. Long	14	Darren Robinson
15	J. Cox	15	Mark Hawksley
16	C. Sayer	16	Ian Booth
17	N. Shoesmith	17	Ryan Hardy

Squad Members
D. Potter
A. Martin
A. Palmer

Squad Members
Graham Law
Danny Burne

Match Officials
R. Connolly   M. Hawkes   M. Beadle
P. Carr   I. S. Muir

Above left: The teams from the match programme (courtesy Sharlston Rovers ARLFC)
Above right: The Sharlston front row get ready for a scrum (Photo: Sig Kasatkin)

Above: Martyn Wood.
Right: Gareth Davies charges forward.
(Photos: Sig Kasatkin)

Memories from 2003-04

OLDHAM		V	SHARLSTON ROVERS
Gavin Dodd	1		Richard Taylor
Will Cowell	2		Lee Lingard
James Bunyan	3		Gareth Davis
Jon Goddard	4		Keith Brook
Nick Johnson	5		Dale Potter
Simon Svabic	6		Martyn Wood
Ian Watson	7		Danny Grimshaw
Steve Molloy	8		Andy Booth
Keith Brennan	9		Lee Bettinson
Dane Morgan	10		Lee Kelly
Lee Doran	11		Chance Leake
Iain Marsh	12		James Ward
Lee Marsh	13		Stan Smith
Gareth Barber	14		Gordon Long
Neil Roden	15		Jamie Cox
Paul Southern	16		Carl Sayer
Martin McLoughlin	17		Neil Shoesmith

Match Officials:
REFEREE: J Leahy
TOUCH JUDGES: S Taylor & G Hodgson
RESERVE REFEREE: Geoff Berry

Left: The teamsheet from the programme for the Challenge Cup match at Oldham. (Courtesy: Oldham RLFC)

Middle: The first team, smartly attired, with four trophies: Back: Carl Sayer, Dave Lee, Jamie Cox, Lee Kelly (senior), James Ward, Dale Ferris, Stan Smith, Andy Booth, Dale Potter Lee Lingard, Ian Moverley; Front: Neil Shoesmith, Andy Martin, Gareth Davies, Martyn Wood (coach), Gordon Long, Chance Leake (coach), Lee Bettinson, Danny Grimshaw, Shaun Taylor.

Bottom: The 'A' team: Back: Mick Ward (vice-chairman), Chris McDonald, Richard Sharp, Simon Hall, Carl Wormald, Chris Hill, Lee Kelly (junior), Richard Pajor, Will Easterby, Simon Revell, Mick Wilkinson, John Brewerton 9coach; Front: Tony Palmer, Paul Kelly, Scott Haigh, Peter Richardson, Dave Townend, Chris Heyward, Dave Smith, Phil Golec.

unable to breach Rovers' defence. Sharlston increased their lead with late tries by substitutes Dave Lee and Andy Booth.

In the Senior Cup, Rovers collected over 100 points in their first three matches and there was no let up in the Final when Queens were defeated 34-26.

Sharlston had seven players: Andy Martin, Gareth Davies, Chris Hill, Andy Booth, Lee Kelly (jnr), Phil Golec and Lee Maskill in the Wakefield and District side for the inaugural Stuart Brown Trophy match. They beat Halifax District at Siddal 24-16. Davies was Wakefield's player of the match.

Sharlston Rovers won the Men's Team Performance of the Year Award at an event organised by the Yorkshire Weekly Newspaper Group in conjunction with Wakefield Metropolitan District Council. And finally, Rovers also won the Mick Lindop Memorial Sevens.

2004-05

Pressure of work forced Rovers' best ever coach, Martyn Wood, to stand down. He had just steered Sharlston to their most successful season ever, winning seven trophies

Martyn's last game in charge was against Elland in the third round of the Yorkshire Cup in October, a trophy which eluded him during his successful reign. Once again Sharlston missed out on this trophy as Elland knocked them out again.

Jon Agar was appointed player-coach alongside Gordon Long. Jon switched from Conference League Division One side Featherstone Lions after spending five years with that club.

Sharlston were concerned about the lack of competition in the league. There were only seven teams in the Yorkshire League Premier Division and Sharlston were well above the standard of the league. The first match of the season was an 80-0 win over Hunslet OB, followed by a 36-10 victory at Stanley and the club wanted stronger opposition. They applied to join the Pennine League, which had benefited from clubs leaving the Yorkshire League.

However, it was another highly successful season for Rovers, continuing their success since the new millennium. They retained all the cups they won in 2003-04 and just lost by a point in the first 'Champion of Champions' final against Halton Simms Cross at Blackpool. Once again Sharlston were League champions and Championship play-off winners.

Sharlston Rovers 62 Queens 10
Championship play-off Final

Sharlston had played a cup final two days before this match, and their supporters were afraid it would be a bridge too far for their team. They expected a physical challenge from Queens. But despite Rovers missing players through injury they set about the match. Dale Potter went over after just three minutes with Jon Agar converting, but Queens hit back to level the scores. Gordon Long scored to restore Rovers' lead with Agar adding the goal. Lee Maskill then crossed for the first of his hat-trick, with Agar on target with the kick. A defensive error led to Queens scoring an unconverted try, but a great solo run saw Maskill score before the break with Agar converting.

Rovers came out in a determined mood after the break with four quick tries. Danny Grimshaw scored twice, with Martin and Gareth Davies adding one apiece. Agar, Lee Kelly (jnr) and Davies then added tries with Maskill bagging a conversion to seal the win.

The Challenge Cup

Rovers had to travel to Warrington Wizards in the first round of the Challenge Cup and came from behind before progressing into the second round. They were not helped by the sending off of Lee Kelly early in the second half. Sharlston were trailing five minutes into the second half when he was sent off and it looked as though they would not regain their composure, but the introduction of Gordon Long saw the game turn in Sharlston's favour for a 22-16 win.

The second round saw an exhilarating game at Sharlston with Oulton Raiders. At one point Sharlston led 14-6, but Oulton hit back with a converted try and a penalty to level the scores going into the break Ten minutes after the restart Raiders bagged a drop-goal to move in front but Gordon Long came on for Sharlston and changed the game. He linked up with Lingard in attack and the latter went over and converted to edge Sharlston ahead. Keith Brook made a try from nothing and Long put over another drop-goal. Supporters' man-of-the-match Lee Bettinson scored Sharlston's final try and Lingard converted. Oulton still had time for another converted try, but it was too late. The official man-of-the-match was Carl Sayer.

The draw for the third round meant that Rovers would meet Oldham, who ended their cup hopes last season. The team prepared for another giant-killing effort. This time they had the advantage of playing at Featherstone, the club's other 'home' ground. Played on a Friday night, only 852 fans were present.

Sharlston Rovers 14 Oldham 46

Former Wigan and Great Britain star Simon Haughton ensured there would be no repeat of last season's giant killing feat by Sharlston in the third round of the Powergen Challenge Cup by scoring four tries.

Facing a National League 1 side, Rovers stuck to their task and took the lead when Lee Lingard kicked a penalty following a high tackle by the visitors. But once Simon Roberts had put the visitors on the board after 12 minutes, Oldham took control with Simon Svabic the architect of their downfall.

He had a hand in Haughton's 20 minute first half hat-trick as he sent the forward over after 17 minutes and repeated this on 22 and 37 minutes. In between Rovers showed they could attack when Jamie Cox claimed a 27th minute touchdown following good work by Gareth Davies.

Rovers reduced the gap to four points early in the second half as second row James Ward gathered a loose Oldham pass to score, with Lingard adding the goal. But then the visitors scored three tries in seven minutes to end Sharlston's cup dream.

Martin Elswood, Gareth Barber and substitute Andy Gorey claimed touchdowns for

3rd Round Rugby League Challenge Cup 2005

#	Sharlston Rovers	#	Oldham
1	Lee Lingard	1	G. Dodd
2	Jamie Cox	2	W. Cowell
3	Gareth Davis	3	D. Munro
4	Keith Brook	4	A. Wilkinson
5	Lee Maskill	5	N. Johnson
6	Jon Agar	6	C. Mataora
7	Danny Grimshaw	7	M. Turner
8	Carl Sayer	8	D. Nanyn
9	Lee Bettinson	9	G. Barber
10	Andy Booth	10	P Norman
11	Dale Potter	11	S. Haughton
12	James Ward	12	T. Glassic
13	Adam Thaler	13	S. Svabic
14	Gordon Long	14	J. Hough
15	Stan Smith	15	D. Wilson
16	David Lee	16	M. Roberts
17	Tony Palmer	17	C. Farnmond

Squad Members: Stuart Bailey, Lewis Swithenbank, Lee Kelly Snr, Martin Wood, Lee Kelly Jnr

Squad Members: R. Bibey, M. Elswood, J. Goddard, A. Gorey, J. Kirkland, A. Sharples

Mascot: Mathew Poppleton

The teams from the match programme (courtesy Sharlston Rovers ARLFC)

the Roughyeds. Rovers stuck to their task but with Svabic in control the visitors added three more tries through full-back Gavin Dodd, winger Will Cowell. Finally Simon Haughton claimed his fourth try with Svabic again involved.

Lingard kicked three goals for Sharlston with Svabic landing two and Turner one for the visitors.

Sharlston Rovers: Lee Lingard, Jamie Cox, Gareth Davies, Keith Brook, Lee Maskill, Jon Agar, Danny Grimshaw, Carl Sayer, Lee Bettinson, Andy Booth, Dale Potter, James Ward, Adam Thaler.
Substitutes: Gordon Long, Stan Smith, David Lee, Stuart Bailey.

Oldham: Gavin Dodd, Will Cowell, Damian Munro, Gareth Barber, Nick Johnson, Simon Svabic, Marty Turner, Paul Norman, John Hough, Dana Wilson, Simon Haughton, Martin Elswood, Mark Roberts.
Substitutes: Carlos Mataora, Tere Glassie, James Kirkland, Andy Gorey.

Yorkshire Cup

Any hopes of getting to the final of the Yorkshire Cup were finally dispelled when they were knocked out by Elland, the holders, for the second year running and three times in four years. But unlike last year, when Sharlston believed they were robbed of victory in the semi-final, the result was not in doubt.

With Sharlston again leading the Yorkshire League and Elland the top of the Pennine League the game had the makings of a classic and lived up to the pre-match expectations.

Rovers broke the deadlock with Grimshaw latching on to a pass from Thaler and beating four defenders to score. Lee Lingard added the conversion. Elland hit back with a try through Shickle converted by Bishop to level the scores at half-time and the same player gave the visitors the lead for the first tine when he kicked a penalty 10 minutes into the second half.

But Rovers hit back with a try from Davies, but this time Lingard missed the goal. Rovers gave away another penalty which allowed the visitors to draw level. The home side then edged in front with a penalty. The home side fought to protect their lead with Smith, Ward, Bettinson and Long to the fore.

But Elland edged 16-12 ahead with a try 10 minutes from time by Shackleton, improved by Bishop and despite Sharlston throwing everything at the visitors they could not find a way through.

Sharlston took on Skirlaugh for the third time in three years in the quarter-final of the National BARLA Cup and it was third time unlucky for Rovers. To reach this stage Rovers had comfortable wins until the last round when they went to West Bowling and produced a stunning fightback, scoring 12 points in the last five minutes, leaving both supporters and the Bowling players stunned.

Skirlaugh snatched a 29-22 victory at Sharlston Rovers thanks to a drop-goal and converted try in the last three minutes of this pulsating tie. The game had two starkly contrasting halves, with Skirlaugh dominating the first and Sharlston the second. The visitors raced ahead with a Phil Crane try and four Mark Hewitt goals before Danny Grimshaw finally put Lee Kelly into a gap to score. But Hewitt responded by getting Phil Thacker over for a second Skirlaugh try and with Hewitt adding his fifth goal it looked all over as the Hull-based side led 18-4 at the break.

But then Sharlston player-coach Gordon Long entered the fray and after putting Grimshaw in for a Lee Lingard goaled try he scored a try of his own, before working with Lingard to get centre Gareth Davies in for a fourth home try. Lingard added his third goal to put Sharlston 22-18 ahead after 55 minutes. Then Skirlaugh hit back as Sean Wildbore crossed. But Hewitt missed the goal with the scores locked at 22-22.

In the 77th minute Hewitt kicked a drop-goal for the lead, then Crane scored the match-winning try in the fourth minute of injury time. Hewitt converted and it was the end for the only non-Conference side in the last eight.

Sharlston retained the Senior Cup but were battered and bruised on the way particularly from a fiery quarter-final tie at Queens when two players ended up in hospital. Youngster Chris Hill suffered a broken jaw and James Ward swelling to his cheekbone.

Other Sharlston players felt they were targeted in a tough match. But the Rovers pulled off a fine win. Moorends were their opponents in the Final at Featherstone Rovers' Lionheart Stadium.

Sharlston Rovers 26 Moorends 20
Senior Cup Final.

Rovers opened up with three quick tries; one from Danny Grimshaw and two from Gareth Davies. Agar's conversion gave them a good start. With 14 points on the board they looked to be heading for an easy win, but Moorends hit back with two converted tries to be within two points at the break.

For 15 minutes after the break both teams were stretched to the limit with some outstanding defence on display. Agar broke the deadlock with a converted try before Moorends hit back with an unconverted try. Two match saving tackles from Lee Maskill kept the opposition at bay. Davies completed his hat-trick, with a conversion by Agar, opening up a 26-16 gap. Moorends hit back with a try in the last minute.

Rovers retained their hold on the Brian McDermott Memorial City Plasterers Cup and the Unison President's Cup with easy victories in both finals. Both matches were at Wakefield Trinity Wildcats' Atlantic Solutions Stadium.

Sharlston Rovers 42 Stanley Rangers 8
Unison President's Final

Stanley were still well in touch at the break with the score 10-8. Rangers' points came from a penalty and a converted try but that was to be the end of their scoring. Sharlston's first half points came through tries from Adam Thaler and man-of-the-match Gordon Long, with Lee Lingard kicking a conversion.

In the second half Sharlston dominated the game running in 32 unanswered points. Long got his second try before Lee Maskill and Andy Booth both crossed. Lingard converted all three. Lee Kelly (jnr) was the next to go over as Rovers took control. Lingard was once again on target. Lingard went over for a try of his own and Gareth Davies concluded the scoring for Rovers to lift the trophy.

Sharlston Rovers 42 Westgate Redoubt 10
Brian McDermott Memorial City Plasterers Cup

A strong first half performance saw Sharlston score 26 points without reply and the game was over as a contest before Redoubt scored two late consolation tries. Richard Sharp with two, Gareth Davies, Andy Booth, Dave Lee, Lee Maskill, Danny Grimshaw and Jamie Cox got the Rovers tries with loose forward Adam Thaler kicking five goals.

Prop Lee Kelly (snr) was man-of-the-match and took the inaugural Jack Thompson trophy. It was presented in recognition of his work over 25 years as secretary of the Wakefield and District ARL. He had recently retired due to ill health

Sharlston Rovers 12 Halton Simms Cross 13
Champion of Champions

For the first time ever a Champion of Champions final, between Sharlston Rovers and Halton Simms Cross was staged before the BARLA National Cup Final at Blackpool.

Halton took advantage of Sharlston's mistakes to kick three penalty goals for a six point advantage. Sharlston took the game to Halton, but could not score despite all their pressure. A drop-goal by Halton just before the break saw them carry a 7-0 lead.

After 20 minutes of the second half Rovers were rewarded with a try through Gareth Davies who beat five players on his way to the line, Jon Agar added the goal. With Sharlston on the attack, things were looking good but a high kick found its way to a Halton player and he went over for a converted try.

Sharlston were not finished and Agar scored and Gordon Long converted, but time ran out to the relief of the Halton players.

Sharlston's leading scorers over the season were Lee Lingard with 256 points, 17 tries 94 goals, from 22 matches; and Gareth Davies with 176 from 31 matches, all from 44 tries.

York 9s - Fairfax Cup

Sharlston took part in the prestigious York 9s, a weekend of international rugby and they progressed to the semi-finals, but lost to East Hull, the eventual cup winners.

The 'A' team

The second team had come a long way in the three seasons since its formation, with a good blend of youth and experience and played in the Yorkshire League Division Three. The side was well led by evergreen captain Pete Richardson with support from Tony Palmer and Stuart Bailey. It included some real veterans like Bill Mitchell, Stefan Golec and player-coach John Brewerton

They won through to the Alliance Cup Final at Featherstone against Milford Marlins, but lost 21-12. The best performance of the season came when they went to Oulton Raiders and saw off the league leaders 34-12.

Pete and June Redshaw

This dedicated couple first joined the club back in 1973, probably the worst time in the club's history when there had been a serious fall out, there was no open age team and the future of the club was in doubt. The club was penniless and times were very hard indeed. The team had only one strip which June washed for £2 a week and she also repaired the shirts.

Ever since they have been involved with the club there has always been a team playing. Pete used to book the buses for away matches and on one occasion when the club had no money he even paid for the buses himself so that the club could have a presentation night at the end of the season.

They have been presented with trophies over the years, including Clubman and

The Champion of Champions match at Blackpool

Back: Carl Wormald, Tony Palmer, Jon Agar (coach), Dale Potter, Lee Kelly (senior), Adam Thaler, Andy Booth, Phil Golec, Danny Grimshaw, Ian Moverley, Charlie Robinson (Unison Sponsor); Front: Dave Lee, Andy Martin, Gareth Davies, Lee Maskill, Lee Bettinson (captain), Gordon Long (player-coach), Keith Brook, Lee Kelly (junior), Stan Smith. (Photo: Alpha Photography)

Pete Redshaw

Above: Pete Redshaw with Prince Michael of Kent and Sir Bobby Charlton. (Photo: Courtesy Queens Club, Kensington & Torch Award).

Right: Pete and June Redshaw

Clubwoman of the Year. Pete has also been chairman, president and club delegate. June has been secretary, treasurer, laundry woman, and carried out many other duties. They both recall having countless happy hours at the club they love although there have been some turbulent times

At the time of writing, Pete is 66 and still working very hard, as is June. They realise the club is now a big concern and it takes a lot of work to keep it going. They have been involved with the club now for over 30 years, performing duties which are an essential part of the smooth running of any rugby club. It is a truly magnificent show of loyalty for which the club will be forever grateful.

Their work was recognised when Pete was presented with the Torch Trophy for his voluntary work for sport by Prince Michael of Kent and Bobby Charlton in a ceremony at the Queen's Club in Kensington. He was nominated for the award by the RFL's executive chairman Richard Lewis, and was one of 20 people in Great Britain to receive the award. He said that it was his proudest moment in sport – before this it had been when Sharlston beat Dewsbury in the Challenge Cup.

2005-06: The Yorkshire Cup at last

Rovers' first season in the Pennine League was a huge success despite missing out on the league title, which was within their grasp right up to the last few games of the season. Their opponents were Brighouse Rangers, Clayton, Drighlington, Elland, Illingworth, Keighley Albion, Keighley Town, Queensbury, Siddal 'A' and Westgate Redoubt. Jon Agar and Gordon Long continued as coaches.

A horrendous pile up of fixtures caused by successful runs in the National and Yorkshire Cup competitions – playing a staggering seven games in 13 days - ultimately cost them the title which was retained by Drighlington. Phil Hodgson wrote in *League Weekly:* "Drighlington have retained the Pennine League's championship. The Leeds side made certain of top spot with a 36-10 victory over Sharlston Rovers. The match presented an intriguing contrast of ring-rustiness and exhaustion. Drighlington had been without a game for three weeks while Sharlston had been so active that rumours were circulating in Wakefield that their players were sleeping in their jockstraps and boots. In the event a heavy schedule - not least the need to play extra time in their President's Cup Final success only two days earlier - told on Rovers."

Rovers suffered only four defeats in their 20 league matches; at home to Queensbury and away to Drighlington, Elland and Keighley Albion. At Keighley in the last match of the season, they arrived with only 12 players, but coach Gordon Long managed to field a full side from players who had travelled to watch.

The highlight of the season was the winning of the Yorkshire Cup. Of all the club's achievements in its long history and the many trophies won, their chief aim above all else at the start of every season is to win the Yorkshire Cup and after an absence of 57 years they proudly lifted the trophy. The Pennine League's President's Cup and the Yorkshire League's President's Cup completed the season's silverware.

The Yorkshire Cup

Sharlston had byes in the first and second rounds. They romped through to round four with a 52-8 win at Eastmount (Hull) though they had a wake up call in the third minute, going behind to a try. After that Sharlston were in control, with Lee Kelly scoring a hat-trick of tries, two coming in the first half, and by half-time they held a comfortable 36-4 lead. There was heavy rain throughout the second half with the pace slowing considerably but Eastmount never recovered and Rovers added a further 16 points.

Round four was a much stiffer task, with a visit from Leeds outfit Queens. The two sides had played out some bruising encounters in the past. Jason Scott scored a fine hat-trick of tries as under-strength Rovers booked their place in the last eight after extra time. After 20 minutes of end-to-end football, Sharlston centre Gareth Davies broke the deadlock, with Liam Jarvis adding the goal. But on the half hour Queens rallied with Wright scoring and Damborough kicking the goal to level the scores. The scoreline remained the same going into the second half, with Rovers making the crucial breakthrough five minutes into the second half. Keith Brook was rewarded for his efforts with a try in the corner, with Long missing the goal.

Rovers exerted more pressure on Queens, with Scott bagging his first try, the conversion attempt again missed. Five minutes later, on-song Scott went over for his second try, with the kick off target once more. At 18-6 up Sharlston looked to be cruising but Queens had other ideas and hit back in the 70th minute when Brown went over, with Damborough adding the goal. It was a nail biting time for Rovers' fans and their worries increased with five minutes left when Morton crashed over - and Damborough again converted to level the scores ahead of full-time. The first 10 minutes of extra time saw no change in the score as several players began to suffer from cramp.

With five minutes left, a drop-goal from Robinson looked to have clinched the game for Queens, but they reckoned without the fighting spirit of Rovers and with two minutes to go, Scott claimed his hat-trick try with a superb effort. Ice-cool Jarvis kept his nerve to land a crucial goal.

Hull side Embassy came to Sharlston in the Quarter Final and were hammered 56-0, Jason Scott, Richard Aka, Jon Agar and Ryan Sykes, each got two tries and there was one apiece from Adam Thaler, Danny Grimshaw and Jon Kirk.

Rovers kept their discipline superbly to book their place in the final after triumphing in a tough semi-final encounter at Castleford against Cutsyke. Rovers' pack leader Lee Kelly suffered a suspected fractured cheekbone and went to hospital. Adam Thaler put Rovers ahead after 10 minutes with a penalty. Ten minutes later, Cutsyke replied with a converted try to lead 6-2, but this sparked Rovers into life with Grimshaw scoring five minutes later, with Thaler converting. A Thaler penalty on 30 minutes extended the visitors' lead to 10-6, only for Cutsyke to hit back before the break with an unconverted try to level the scores. Rovers showed plenty of determination after the break, with the impressive Grimshaw putting them ever closer to the final when he scored, with Jarvis adding the goal. With five minutes left, Dale Potter scored, with Jarvis adding the goal to seal the win. Player-of-the-match was Booth who replaced the injured Kelly. Queensbury awaited Rovers in the Final.

Coach Gordon Long, who was bitterly disappointed at having to settle for being runners-up against Elland four years ago, said: "It's a trophy that has eluded us and we have to put that right. We had a meeting at the start of the season when we targeted the Yorkshire Cup as our main goal and, in all honesty, I can't see us failing to achieve that. We're working hard towards that aim and we'll be training right up to Boxing Day, after which we'll relax by going bowling and for a meal. It is hard on the players having to play at Christmas but there is total commitment in the squad. Everybody, to a man, is determined to win and we're leaving no stone unturned in our bid."

Sharlston had won 22-8 at Queensbury recently in the GMB Union BARLA National Cup and Long commented: "It was more comfortable than the scoreline suggests. Fitness told and I think that will again be a factor. My main problem is who to leave out of the 17. That's very hard and I'm giving everybody a chance to stake a claim, probably right up until the last training session. Loose forward Adam Thaler is on the verge of a full recovery from his knee injury. I'm going to give him another week to prove his fitness, that's the least he deserves. We'll put him through his paces on Thursday and make a decision from there."

"We owe the village a victory in the final. The place is buzzing and it will be empty on the day. I'm quietly confident that we'll give them something to celebrate."

Sharlston Rovers 21 Queensbury 18
Tetley's Yorkshire Cup Final

The teams for this encounter at Dewsbury were:
Sharlston Rovers: Lewis; Sykes, Davies, Maskill; S. Smith, Agar; Grimshaw, Booth, Bettinson, Kelly, Potter, Lockwood, Thaler.
Subs: Long, Kirk, Brook, Cox.
Tries: Davies (2), Maskill; Goals: Agar (4); drop-goal: Long
Queensbury: Eyles; K. Smith; Hobson, Stead, Brearcliffe, Wainwright; C. Smith, Wilkinson, Galtress, Senior, Frelbach, Craft, Calvert.
Subs: Hill, Feather, England, Bruce.
Tries: Brearcliffe (2), Hobson; Goals: Calvert (3).

A 2,500 crowd saw the match, which was played in warm sunshine after snow close to the kick off had threatened a postponement.

Queensbury built up an early 8-2 lead, through a penalty and a converted try. A Jon Agar penalty kept Sharlston in the game. Queensbury then had a try disallowed. Agar then set up two tries for Gareth Davies, and converted both to give Sharlston a 14-8 half-time lead.

Queensbury had a second try disallowed, and Sharlston hit back with a long range try from Lee Maskill. Agar's conversion put Sharlston 12 points ahead. Hobson scored for Queensbury, and although Calvert missed the conversion, he scored a penalty to bring the Bradford-based side to within six points of Sharlston. Gordon Long won the match for Sharlston with a drop-goal a minute from time. Queensbury scored again in injury time, but the conversion was missed, leaving Sharlston winners by three points.

In *League Weekly*, Phil Hodgson said that "In the eyes of many neutral observers, Queensbury had been the better side." Man-of-the-match Jon Agar told Hodgson: "We made mistakes but we stayed positive and I thought our defence in the second half was tremendous. If any of us did make an error we dug in as a team, nobody panicked. That's probably what won us the game in the end. We expected a hard game and Queensbury certainly didn't disappoint us."

Agar missed some of the post-match celebrations. He fractured a cheekbone 10 minutes from the end of the match and spent three hours at Dewsbury Hospital before returning to the club's post-match party.

He said: "I left the lads to party while I spent three hours at Dewsbury Hospital on my own. I called back at the pub afterwards and the celebrations were well under way by then. It is a big monkey off our back to finally win the final - we lost it in 2001 and have been favourites every year since then but haven't managed to make it to the final."
At the start of the season, Agar had told Hodgson in *League Weekly*: "We are definitely going to target the Yorkshire Cup" and was vindicated with this win.

The Yorkshire Cup Final
Photos by Alan Grimshaw

Presentation at the start of the match

Left: Charging forward

Below: Sharlston on the attack.

Lee Maskill's try for Sharlston

Ready for a tackle

Sharlston score in the corner.

A forward battle.

The ball comes out of a scrum.

Celebrating an historic victory!

Sharlston Rovers 2005-06. The picture was taken at the Sharlston Hotel before the Yorkshire Cup Final. (Photo: Sig Kasatkin)

The leading scorers this season were Gareth Davies with 39 tries and Liam Jarvis kicked 58 goals. Danny Grimshaw won the man-of-the-match award on six occasions.

Jon Agar was troubled with injuries this season. He received facial injuries in the Yorkshire Cup Final and a bad knee injury in the match against Illingworth in April, which has probably finished his playing career.

Mention should be made of the contribution to the club's recent success made by player-coach and former Bramley player Gordon Long. Gordon was appointed joint-coach with Dean Blankley, another former Bramley player, in 2000-01, and they were responsible for introducing a more professional approach, which transformed the club. His attitude on-and-off the field has been exemplary and he is highly respected by the players and a good role model for the younger ones. He is a good ball player and is capable of turning threatening defeat into victory. He truly has become one of the shining lights of the Sharlston club.

Sharlston's hopes of a good run in the Powergen Challenge Cup were dashed with a preliminary first round defeat against National Conference League side Saddleworth Rangers, but it was only settled after extra time, 28-22.

In the GMB National Cup second round they visited Queensbury and were still smarting from a home defeat by the Bradford team three weeks earlier and gained revenge, 22-8, in superb style. The verdict was narrower against Kells at Whitehaven in round three when Rovers held on for a thrilling 21-20 victory. Sharlston went through to round four and a home tie against Widnes St Maries.

Rovers were too strong for the Conference Division 2 title contenders and centre Gareth Davies registered a hat trick of tries in a 26-14 victory. Sharlston became one of the last two non-Conference sides to make the last 16 and the draw took them to Halifax based Conference Division 2 side Ovenden. The home team took a commanding 26-4 interval lead, but Rovers put up a gutsy second half performance. Playing down the slope, Rovers - with a mountain to climb - hit back and they made the perfect start with a try by Grimshaw, which he converted. Firmly on top, Sharlston pushed on, but on a rare visit into the visitors' half Ovenden dropped a goal, which only prompted Rovers to further efforts. In reply, man-of-the-match Grimshaw went over and tagged on the goal himself to make it 27-22. The last 10 minutes saw Rovers attack the line, but just failed to seal the comeback with a further try, with six players all held up short of the line.

Yorkshire League premier side Stanley Rangers inflicted a shock 35-24 defeat on the Rovers in the second round of the Brian McDermott Memorial City Plasterers Cup thanks to a stunning second half display. Sharlston held an 18-8 interval lead after controlling the first half, but in the second half it was Stanley calling the tune, not letting Sharlston see the ball in a dynamic showing which delighted their supporters.

Dodworth and Clayton were outclassed in rounds one and two of the Pennine President's Cup, conceding 80 and 50 points respectively and Rovers had to visit Brighouse Rangers, newly promoted from division one, in the quarter-final. They were given a real scare and had to fight hard for a place in the last four. After 18 minutes Brighouse had built up an 11 points lead but on the half-hour, Ben Lewis scored a converted try for Rovers. On the stroke of half-time they went ahead when James Lockwood was rewarded with a try, converted by Potter, to give them a 12-11 interval lead. Rovers defence held firm as Brighouse started the second half as they did the first and Danny Grimshaw scored a key converted try for Rovers, but Brighouse hit back immediately as Luxton went over for Williams to convert and set up a close finish. A fumble on the restart gave Sharlston possession on the 10-metre line and Bettinson forced his way over for a try with Lee Maskill converting.

Sharlston then faced Queensbury in the semi-final. This was the fifth clash between the two sides, Rovers coming out on top on four occasions. This was another one-sided affair. Queensbury were never in contention. Rovers were ahead 16-0 at half-time and strolled to a 24-0 victory. Jon Agar made his first appearance since the injury he received in the Yorkshire Cup Final at Christmas.

Sharlston Rovers 28 Dudley Hill 22
Pennine League President's Cup Final

A crucial try from Liam Jarvis - against his former club - ensured more cup glory for Sharlston after a thrilling match at Dewsbury.

The Dewsbury stadium was turning into a real 'home from home' for Rovers, who claimed silverware there for the second time in the space of four months, following on from their Yorkshire Cup success over Queensbury at Christmas.

Anxious to put on a show for their supporters after the disappointment of relegation, the Bradford based side put in a game display, which belied their league position, but Sharlston - in the midst of a strength sapping schedule of games - had enough in the tank to see off their gritty rivals, despite a scare or two.

Hill were level pegging with their illustrious rivals at 10-10 at the interval and 16-16 at the end of normal time, but the experience and class of Rovers told in the end.

Left to curse his luck for Hill was stand-out player Evans, who incredibly scored four tries only to still finish up on the losing side.

Rovers were never behind in normal time but, having led 16-0 in the early stages, looked in danger of slipping to defeat when Hill levelled matters four minutes from time with Evans' hat trick score, Gawthorpe adding his second goal.

It was left to former Dudley Hill ace Liam Jarvis to swing the issue, with the half-back nipping over within three minutes of the restart and adding the extras.

Keith Brook stretched Sharlston's lead with his second try of the game, Danny

Grimshaw landing his second goal, with Evans' fourth touchdown, again goaled by Gawthorpe, coming too late to affect the outcome.

Earlier impressive loose-forward Johnny Kirk had bagged an early brace for Sharlston, Lee Maskill landing a conversion.

Outstanding stand-off Grimshaw collected the man-of-the-match award, with second-rower James Lockwood also in blistering form.

The only downside of the victory was an injury sustained by try hero Jarvis, carried off with a knee injury before the end and he is set to miss the rest of the season.

Rovers' chairman, Mick Taylor, whose side's crowded recent programme has seen them fit in 10 games in the final month of the season, commented: "The Yorkshire Cup was the big one for us this season, but it's fantastic to get our hands on another trophy and there was plenty of celebrating on Monday night."

Due to the fixture congestion the final for the Unison President's Cup was played very late in the season – 25 May - but Rovers claimed a hat trick of trophies for the season with a 42-10 win over Stanley Rangers at Crofton's Cougar Park. Stanley scored first but Sharlston soon hit back with a Gareth Davies try, the first of a try treble. The scores were level 10-10 at the interval but the Rovers showed their class and skill in the second half to run up 32 points without reply, despite Dave Lee being dismissed only minutes into the half. Lee Maskill also scored a hat-trick, Sharlston running in eight tries in total.

The 'A' team also had a successful season. They lifted the Yorkshire CMS Division 3 title with a thrilling and well-deserved success against Nevision Leap, 29-20, in the top four play-off final at Normanton. With both sides scoring four tries, kicking was the difference. Sharlston's Chris Hill kicked six goals and a drop-goal. It was an impressive performance by a young Rovers side.

As a marvellous season ends the Sharlston Rovers story is now up-to-date. The past has been and gone, but it has left behind a host of memories of a great little village rugby league club.

For me it has been a long and enjoyable journey down memory lane, and I have done my best to recall the matches, players and all those who have made Sharlston Rovers a name to be proud of. Very few established facts and records about the club exist, so this book has been based on newspaper reports of events when they took place, and although every care has been taken to ensure accuracy, there was so much to cover that it would be too much to hope that there are no mistakes.

As to the future, the club is as healthy as it has ever been and a new season is just about to start. There will be many challenges ahead, but having regard to the great traditions of the past these will be met and the Rovers will still be playing rugby league at Back o' t' wall into the next century.

Appendix 1. Professional players from Sharlston

Sharlston is famed for its production of rugby league players and below is a list of some of those who went on to play for professional clubs. Most, but not all, played for Rovers. This is as complete a list as possible, apologies to anyone that has been left out. It does show that this little village has produced some of the greatest players in the game.

Colin Andrews, Wakefield Trinity
Frank Astbury, York & Hull KR
Astbury, Castleford
Charlie Baddeley, York
Stuart Bailey, Doncaster
Bernard Bastow, Halifax
John Bastow, Hunslet
John Bell, Batley
Bryn Bennett, Wakefield Trinity
John Berry, Castleford
Rowland Berry, Castleford
John William Betteridge, York
Joe Bingham, Bramley
James Blower, Dewsbury
Walter Booth, Halifax
Keith Bridges, Wakefield Trinity & Castleford
Steve Briggs, Batley
Joe Broadbent, Wakefield Trinity
Jack Bruce, Dewsbury & Hull
Tommy Bruce, Hull
George Bruce, Dewsbury & Wakefield Trinity
John Bullock, Wakefield Trinity & Dewsbury
John Burnage, Leeds
Percy Butcher, Featherstone Rovers
Tommy Cahill, Wakefield Trinity
Barry Chalkley, Hull KR
Denis Chalkley, Halifax, Wakefield Trinity & Hull KR
Graham Chalkley, Batley & Dewsbury, England amateur international
Jim Chalkley, Wakefield Trinity
William Chalkley, Batley
Colin Chapman, Featherstone
Nobby Clarke, Batley
Billy Conway, Wakefield
Ronnie Cowey, Dewsbury
H. Crummack, Featherstone Rovers
Jack Davies, Dewsbury & Batley
Gareth Davies, Featherstone Rovers
Tommy Davis, Huddersfield
J. Derry, Dewsbury
Carl Dooler, Featherstone Rovers, Hull KR, Yorkshire, 1966 Great Britain tourist to Australia & New Zealand, Lance Todd Trophy Winner 1967

Harry Dooler Featherstone Rovers & Wakefield Trinity
Henry Dooler, Batley
Jack Dooler, Wakefield Trinity
L. Dooler, Wakefield Trinity
Steve Dooler, Featherstone Rovers
Lewis Downs, Doncaster
A. Earnshaw, Wakefield Trinity
Jack Evans, Dewsbury
England, Castleford
Jim Fisher, York
Matty Foster, Keighley
Donald Fox, Featherstone Rovers & Wakefield Trinity, Yorkshire, Great Britain, 1962 Tourist to Australia & New Zealand, Lance Todd Trophy Winner 1968
Neil Fox, Wakefield Trinity, Bradford Northern, Hull KR, York, Bramley, Huddersfield, Yorkshire, England, Great Britain, 1962 tourist to Australia & New Zealand, Lance Todd Trophy Winner 1962, World Record rugby league points scorer, 6,220, Rugby League Hall of Fame.
Peter Fox, Featherstone Rovers, Batley, Hull KR, Wakefield Trinity. Yorkshire, England & Great Britain coach
Tommy Fox, Featherstone Rovers
Don Froggett, Wakefield Trinity, Yorkshire & England
Brian Frost, Doncaster
Jack Garitty, Dewsbury
Charlie Gaskill, Batley
Fred Gidman, Hull KR
Bernard Golby, Batley
George Goldie, Featherstone Rovers, Leeds & Batley
Fred Goodfellow, Holbeck, Hull, Dewsbury, Yorkshire (RU), Yorkshire (RL)
Herbert Goodfellow, Wakefield Trinity, Oldham, Yorkshire, England
George Green, Halifax
Gladstone Green, Wakefield Trinity
Howard Greensmith, Batley
Danny Grimshaw, Doncaster
Richard Hall, Featherstone
Paul Hampson, Wakefield Trinity
Steve Hankin, Dewsbury, Featherstone Rovers, Yorkshire
Fred Harrison, Leeds

John Harrison, Leeds
J. Harrop, Wakefield Trinity
Harold Henderson, Wakefield Trinity
Pep Hepworth, Featherstone Rovers
John Holland, Dewsbury
William Howcroft, Wakefield Trinity
Albert Howell, Leeds
'Porky' Hudson, Keighley
Willie Hughes, Featherstone Rovers
Melvin Jowitt, York
Lee Kelly (Snr), Dewsbury
Andy Kirmond, Scarborough Pirates
Albert Leake, Featherstone Rovers
J. Lee, Wakefield Trinity
Benny Lingard, Batley & Featherstone Rovers
Craig Lingard, Batley
Frank Lingard, Wakefield Trinity, Leeds & Bramley
Glyn Lingard, Doncaster
Ivor Lingard, Featherstone Rovers & Parramatta
John Lingard, Batley
Lee Lingard, York
Steve Lingard, Batley
J. E. Lister, Featherstone Rovers
James Lockwood, Featherstone Rovers
Cliff Lumb, Wakefield Trinity
Mick Lumb, Wakefield & Dewsbury
F. Marshall, York
Len Marson, Wakefield Trinity, Hunslet, Yorkshire, England
Colin Maskill, Batley
I. Morris, Wakefield Trinity
Dave Morris, Batley
Tommy Mullaney, Castleford
Joe Mullaney, Featherstone Rovers, Yorkshire, England
Musgrave, Wakefield Trinity
Frank Newitt, Dewsbury
Joe Nicholson, Hull KR
Luke Nixon, York
Percy Owen, Wakefield Trinity
Jonty Parkin, Wakefield Trinity & Hull KR, Yorkshire, England, Great Britain, 1920 tourist to Australia & New Zealand, 1924 tourist to Australia & New Zealand (captain), 1928 tourist to Australia & New Zealand (captain) Rugby League Hall of Fame
Piper, Wakefield Trinity
John Pollitt, Castleford & Featherstone Rovers
Martin Pearson, Featherstone Rovers Halifax, Wakefield Trinity
Cliff Ramsden, Dewsbury
Mark Reeves, Doncaster
Norman Reeves, Featherstone Rovers
Walter Reeves, Featherstone Rovers
Albert Roscoe, Wakefield Trinity
Fred Stott, Featherstone Rovers
John William Stott, Featherstone Rovers
Percy Silcock, Dewsbury
Horace Sandon, Wakefield Trinity
Carl Sayer, Dewsbury
Steve Sayer, Featherstone
Tommy Scamans, Leeds
William Shaw, Wakefield Trinity
Gary Shillabeer, Featherstone Rovers & Batley
Tommy Smales, Featherstone Rovers, Wigan & Barrow
Colin Smith, Featherstone Rovers
Harry Smith Featherstone Rovers
Nigel Southern, Huddersfield
Chris Stringer, Wakefield Trinity
A. Taylor, Hull KR
Taylor, Featherstone Rovers
Vaughan Thomas, Featherstone Rovers & Bradford Northern
Steve Tottie, Huddersfield
Ward, Featherstone Rovers
Harold Ward, Dewsbury
James Ward, York
L. Westwood, Wakefield Trinity
Phil Winship, Wakefield Trinity
Wood, Batley & Bramley
Wood, Holbeck
Billy Wood, Batley, England amateur international

Appendix 2. Club Honours

Rugby Union
1895-96	Wakefield & District League	Champions
1896-97	Wakefield & District League	Champions
1897-98	Barnsley Beckett League	Champions

Northern Union
1901-02	Wakefield Wellington Cup	Runners Up
1905-06	Charlesworth Cup	Runners Up
1906-07	Dewsbury, Wakefield & District League	Champions
	Intermediates - J B Cooke Shield	Winners
1912-13	Intermediates - J B Cooke Shield	Runners Up
1913-14	Junior Championship League	Runners Up
1916-17	Intermediate Challenge Cup	Runners Up
1917-18	Intermediates - J B Cooke Shield	Runners Up
	Intermediates - Cup Competition	Runners Up
1919-20	Wakefield & District Junior Final	Runners Up
	Intermediates - Wakefield & District League	Runners Up
1920-21	Leeds & District Cup	Winners
	Leeds & District Championship	Runners Up
1921-22	Intermediates - Wakefield & District League Cup	Runners Up
	Intermediates - J B Cooke Shield	Runners Up

Rugby Football League
1922-23	Intermediates - Fotherby Cup	Runners Up
	Intermediates - Wakefield & District League	Runners Up
1923-24	Yorkshire Junior Cup	Winners
	Dewsbury, Wakefield & District Cup	Winners
1924-25	Dewsbury, Wakefield & District League	Champions
	Castleford & District Cup	Winners
1927-28	Dewsbury, Wakefield & District Cup	Winners
	Dewsbury, Wakefield & District League	Champions
1928-29	Wakefield & District Cup	Runners Up
	Wakefield & District League	Runners Up
1930-31	Yorkshire Junior Cup	Runners Up
	Wakefield & District League	Champions
1931-32	Wakefield & District Cup	Runners Up
	Intermediates - Wakefield & District League	Champions
	Intermediates - Fotherby Cup	Winners
1932-33	Intermediates - Wakefield & District League	Champions
	Intermediates - Wakefield & District Cup	Winners
	Intermediates - Yorkshire County Cup	Winners
	Intermediates - Fotherby Cup	Winners
1934-35	Wakefield & District League	Champions
1935-36	Intermediates - Fotherby Cup	Winners
	Intermediates - Wakefield & District League	Champions
	Intermediates - Yorkshire District Cup	Runners Up
	Intermediates - Wakefield & District Cup	Winners
1936-37	Intermediates - Fotherby Cup	Winners
	Intermediates - Wakefield & District League	Runners Up
1937-38	Intermediates - Fotherby Cup	Runners Up
1938-39	Leeds & District Cup	Runners Up

	Yorkshire Junior Cup	Runners Up
1945-46	Intermediates - Fotherby Cup	Winners
1947-48	Yorkshire Junior Cup	Winners
	Wakefield & District League	Runners Up
1948-49	Yorkshire Junior Cup	Winners
	Wakefield & District Cup	Winners
	Wakefield & District League	Champions
1949-50	Wakefield & District League	Champions
	Wakefield & District Cup	Winners
1950-51	Wakefield & District League	Champions
	Wakefield & District Cup	Winners
1951-52	Yorkshire Junior Cup	Runners Up
	Wakefield & District League	Runners Up
1953-54	Wakefield & District Cup	Runners Up
1954-55 to 1964-65 No Open Age team		
1958-59	Oldroyd Challenge Cup (under-17s)	Runners Up
1965-66	Wakefield & District Cup	Runners Up
	Open Cup (under-17s) –	
	Leeds & District League	Champions
1966-67	Wakefield & District Cup	Runners Up
1969-70	Wakefield Sunday League	Champions
	Wakefield Sunday Cup	Winners
1970-71	Wakefield Sunday League	Champions
	Youth Cup (under-21s)	Runners Up
1971-72	KO Cup (under-21s)	Winners
1972-73	Wakefield Sunday Cup	Runners Up
1973-74	Wakefield Sunday Cup	Winners
1974-75	Wakefield Open Cup	Runners Up
1977-78	Wakefield Open Cup	Runners Up
1978-79	Wakefield League	Champions
1980-81	Hall Green 7s	Runners Up
1984-85	West Yorkshire League Division One	Runners Up
1986-87	West Yorkshire Wakefield Sunday	
	Cup (Premier Division)	Runners Up
1987-88	Sunday West Yorkshire Premier Division Cup	Runners Up
	Wakefield Sunday Cup	Winners
	West Yorkshire Premier League	Runners Up
1988-89	West Yorkshire Premier Division Sunday Cup	Winners
1990-91	West Yorkshire Premier Division Sunday Cup	Runners Up
1992-93	West Yorkshire Division Five	Champions
1994-95	Yorkshire Senior League,	
	Wakefield Open Cup	Runners Up
	Wakefield & District Saturday Cup	Runners Up
	Walton 9s	Winners
1995-96	Guilfoyle Plant Open Cup	Runners Up
	Yorkshire League Senior Division	Runners Up
	Walton 9s	Winners
	Wakefield 7s	Winners
1996-97	City Plasterers Cup	Runners Up
	Hall & Co Floodlit Plate	Runners Up
	Walton 9s	Winners
1997-98	Yorkshire Senior Division	Runners Up
	Guilfoyle Open Cup	Runners Up
1999-2000	Guilfoyle Open Cup	Winners

2000-01	Guilfoyle Open Cup	Winners
	Brian McDermott Memorial City Plasterers Cup	Winners
	Yorkshire Premier League	Runners Up
	Wakefield 7s	Winners
2001-02	Yorkshire Cup	Runners Up
	Wakefield 7s	Winners
	Wakefield Express Team Trophy Award	Winners
2002-03	Brian McDermott Memorial City Plasterers Cup	Winners
	Yorkshire Premier Division	Runners Up
2003-04	Yorkshire Premier Division	Champions
	Yorkshire Senior Cup	Winners
	Unison President's Cup	Winners
	Brian McDermott Memorial City Plasterers Cup	Winners
	Wakefield 7s	Winners
	Wakefield Express Team Trophy Award	Winners
2004-05	Yorkshire Premier Division	Champions
	Yorkshire Senior Cup	Winners
	Unison President's Cup	Winners
	Brian McDermott Memorial City Plasterers Cup	Winners
	Champion of Champions	Runners Up
	'A' team - CMS Yorkshire League Division 3 Cup Final	Runners Up
2005-06	Yorkshire Cup	Winners
	Pennine League President's Cup	Winners
	Unison President's Cup	Winners
	'A' team - CMS Yorkshire League Division 3	Winners

Rugby league books from London League Publications

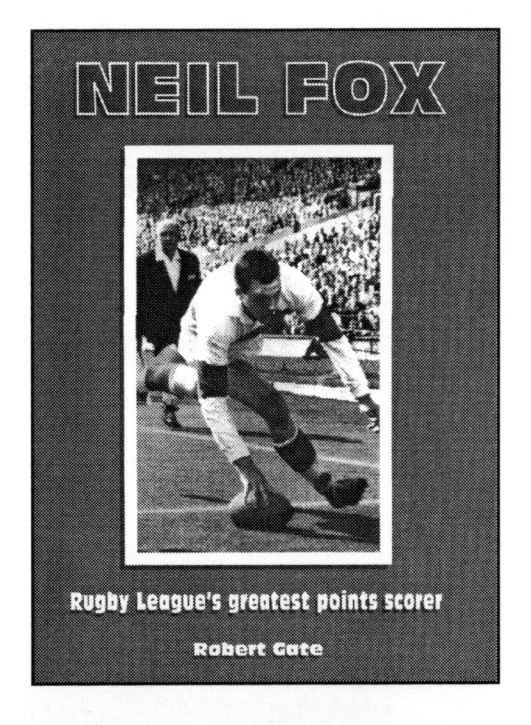

Neil Fox by Robert Gate: £18.95   *Play to Win* by Maurice Bamford: £12.95
Rugby's Berlin Wall: £11.95   *We'll Support You Evermore* by David Kuzio £11.95

Available from www.llpshop.co.uk (credit card orders) or PO Box 10441, London E14 8WR (Cheques to London League Publications Ltd) or from bookshops.